Photoshop® Elements 3 QuickSteps

CAROLE MATTHEWS
DOUG SAHLIN

McGraw-Hill/Osborne
New York Chicago San Francisco
Lisbon London Madrid Mexico City
Milan New Delhi San Juan
Seoul Singapore Sydney Toronto

McGraw-Hill/Osborne
2100 Powell Street, 10th Floor
Emeryville, California 94608
U.S.A.

To arrange bulk purchase discounts for sales promotions, premiums, or fund-raisers, please contact **McGraw-Hill**/Osborne at the above address. For information on translations or book distributors outside the U.S.A., please see the International Contact Information page immediately following the index of this book.

This book was composed with Adobe® InDesign®.

PHOTOSHOP® ELEMENTS 3 QUICKSTEPS

1234567890 WCK WCK 0198765

ISBN 0-07-225859-4

VICE PRESIDENT, GROUP PUBLISHER / Phillip Ruppel

VICE PRESIDENT, PUBLISHER / Jeffrey Krames

ACQUISITIONS EDITOR / Roger Stewart

ACQUISITIONS COORDINATOR / Agatha Kim

SERIES CREATORS & EDITORS / Martin and Carole Matthews

TECHNICAL EDITORS / Carole Matthews and Doug Sahlin

COPY EDITOR / Lisa McCoy

PROOFREADER / Karyle Kramer, Harriet O'Neal, and Edward McKillop

INDEXER / Valerie Perry

LAYOUT ARTIST / Laura Canby

ILLUSTRATORS / Kathleen Edwards, Pattie Lee, Bruce Hopkins, and Laura Canby

SERIES DESIGN / Bailey Cunningham

COVER DESIGN / Pattie Lee

To my son, Michael, whose image fills the pages of this book, along with those in my heart.

Carole Matthews

Dedicated to the memory of Dr. Winston O'Boogie, a wise and gentle man who helped make the world a better place with his music.

Doug Sahlin

About the Authors

Carole Matthews:

Carole Boggs Matthews has more than 30 years of computing experience. She has authored or co-authored over 60 books, including *PhotoShop CS QuickSteps, eBay QuickSteps, Microsoft Office PowerPoint 2003 QuickSteps*, and *FrontPage 2003: The Complete Reference*. Prior to her writing career, she co-founded and operated a computer business, developing tools to help others use computers in their businesses. A long-time Photoshop Elements user, Carole now applies that experience and many years of writing to *Photoshop Elements 3 QuickSteps*, bringing both business and computer knowledge to the book. Carole lives in Washington State with her husband Marty, son Michael, two cats, and the family dog.

Doug Sahlin:

Doug Sahlin is an author, photographer, and videographer who lives in Lakeland, Florida, with his stalwart companion, Niki the Cat. He is the author of 15 books on computer applications, including the popular, *How to Do Everything with Adobe Acrobat 6.0*. He is an avid photographer and the author of *Digital Photography QuickSteps*. Doug has written and co-authored books on digital video, and is a co-author of *Photoshop CS QuickSteps*. Doug's images have been published in books and displayed on Web sites. His clients include professional models, personalities, and businesses who need images to promote their products or themselves.

Contents at a Glance

1 2 3 4 5 6 7 8 9 10

Acknowledgments

Although this book has only two names on the cover, it was really produced by a fantastic team of truly talented people. This team, the QuickSteps backbone, continues to produce a really great book in an incredibly short time. They did this by putting in endless hours, working selflessly with each other, and applying a great amount of skill.

Laura Canby, layout artist and prepress expert, continues to contribute quality and professionalism to her work. She is an artist, with an ability to make the book shine. Thanks, Laura!

Lisa McCoy, copy editor, has skillfully guided our poor attempts at writing, making it readable and accurate—and it is done with a winning attitude. Thanks, Lisa!

Karyle Kramer, Harriet O'Neal, and Edward McKillop, proofreaders, have done a great job of catching errors that no one else caught. They were our final quality control. Thanks, Karyle, Harriet, and Edward.

Valerie Perry, indexer, and our newest contributor, patiently waited for all the pages, delivered at the last minute, to create a wonderful and comprehensive index. Well done, and thanks, Valerie.

Roger Stewart, Editorial Director at Osborne, always stood behind us throughout the production process—keeping the faith in us. Thanks, Roger!

...and to the many Photoshop Elements users and businesses we contacted while writing this book who shared their experiences, suggestions, listings data, and other materials. Thanks to all for helping make this a better book!

Contents

1

2

5

6

Introduction

QuickSteps books are recipe books for computer users. They answer the question "How do I…?" by providing a quick set of steps to accomplish the most common tasks with a particular program. The sets of steps are the central focus of the book. Sidebar QuickSteps provide information on how to do quickly many small functions or tasks that are in support of the primary functions. Sidebar QuickFacts supply information that you need to know about a subject. Notes, Tips, and Cautions augment the steps, but they are presented in a separate column to not interrupt the flow. Brief introductions are present, but there is minimal narrative otherwise. Many illustrations and figures, a number with callouts, are also included where they support the steps.

QuickSteps books are organized by function and the tasks needed to perform those functions. Each function is a chapter. Each task, or "How To," contains the steps needed for its accomplishment along with the relevant Notes, Tips, Cautions, and screenshots. Tasks are easy to find through:

- The Table of Contents, which lists the functional areas (chapters) and tasks in the order they are presented
- A How To list of tasks on the opening page of each chapter
- The index, which provides an alphabetical list of the terms that are used to describe the functions and tasks
- Color-coded tabs for each chapter or functional area with an index to the tabs in the Contents at a Glance

Conventions Used in this Book

Photoshop Elements 3 QuickSteps uses several conventions designed to make the book easier for you to follow. Conventions used include:

- An icon in the Table of Contents and in the How To list in each chapter references a QuickSteps or a QuickFacts sidebar in a chapter.
- **Bold type** is used for words or objects on the screen that you are to do something with, like click **Save As**, open **File**, and click **Close**.
- *Italic type* is used for a word or phrase that is being defined or otherwise deserves special emphasis.
- Underlined type is used for text that you are to type from the keyboard.
- SMALL CAPITAL LETTERS are used for keys on the keyboard, such as **ENTER** and **SHIFT**.
- When you are expected to enter a command, you are told to press the key(s). If you are to enter text or numbers, you are told to type them.

How to...

- *Explore the Product Overview*
- *Browse the Organizer*
- *Explore the Quick Fix Workspace*
- *Explore the Standard Edit Workspace*
- *Using the Shortcuts Bar*
- *Using the Menu Bar*
- *Review Palettes*
- *Using Undo and Redo*
- *Using Help*
- *Using Rulers and Grids*
- *Using the Palette Bin*
- *Set General Preferences*
- *Change File Preferences*
- *Change Cursor Displays*
- *Change Plug-Ins and Scratch Disks*
- *Change Memory and Cache Usage*
- *Set Preset Manager Options*

Chapter 1
Stepping into Photoshop Elements

Photoshop Elements is an incredibly powerful tool for editing and enhancing your images. With it, you can download digital images and then organize the photos on your computer; use keywords, tags, and collections to identify them; repair or correct imperfections; enhance photos with drawing and painting tools, filters, color, and lighting changes; create composites, panoramas, slide shows; and more.

This book explains how to use all facets of Photoshop Elements in step-by-step segments. You will learn how to find your way around Photoshop Elements, how to organize your photo albums, how to enhance your photos, and how to create ways of presenting them.

In this chapter you will learn about the primary components of Photoshop Elements: how to use menus, toolbars, shortcuts, and Help; and to perform basic tasks.

1

2

3

4

5

6

7

8

9

10

TIP

The Welcome screen can be changed to display the Organizer or Editor components. Click the **Start Up In** down arrow, and select the component you would like to see when you start Photoshop Elements.

Welcome to Photoshop Elements

Navigating in Photoshop Elements is quite simple. When you first start Photoshop Elements, you will see the Welcome screen displayed in Figure 1-1. It contains seven possibilities. As you pass the pointer over Product Overview, View And Organize Photos, Quickly Fix Photos, Edit And Enhance Photos, Make Photo Creations, and Start From Scratch, you will see a description of the task you can accomplish with that part of the program. The following sections review the main functions offered.

Figure 1-1: The initial Welcome screen provides buttons that you can click to select the function you want to perform.

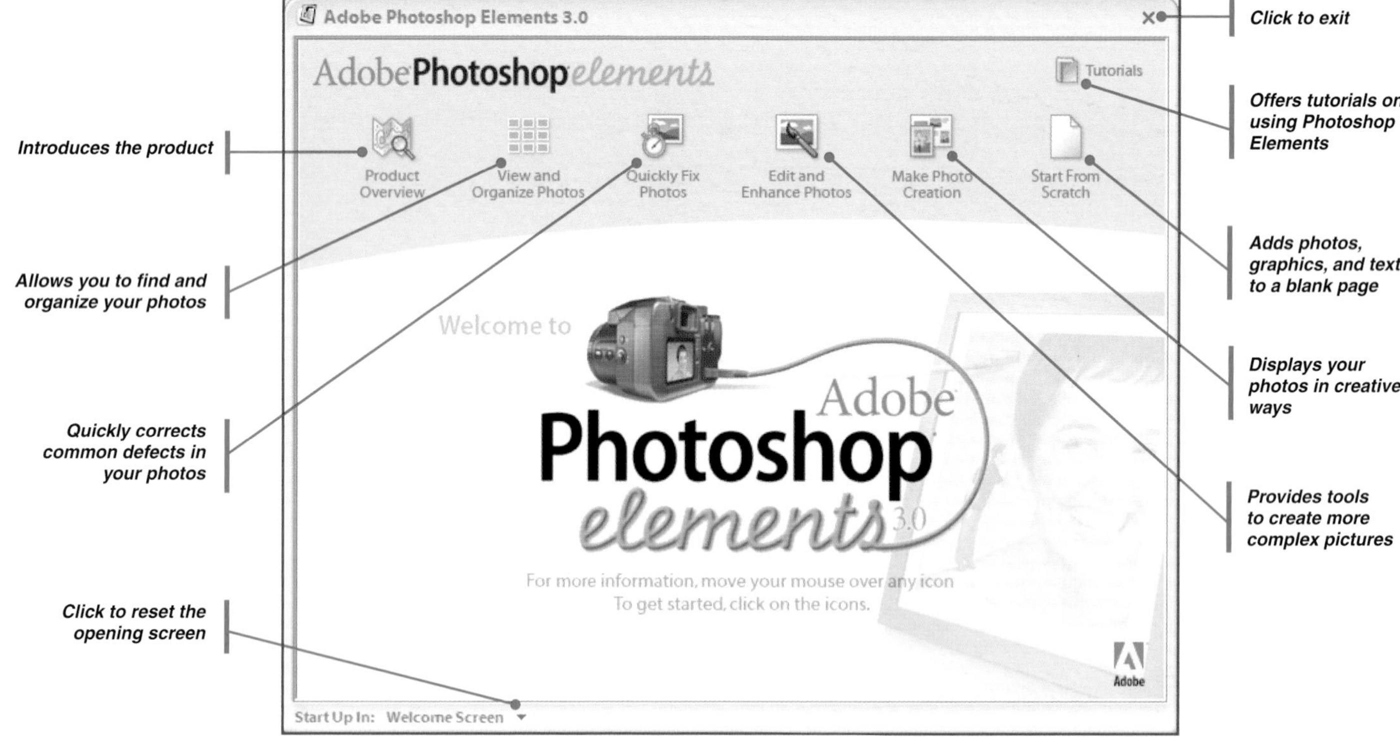

Explore the Product Overview

The Product Overview provides a quick look at the primary functions of Photoshop Elements.

Click **Product Overview**. The screen in Figure 1-2 appears. You have two options for viewing additional information:

- Click **Product Overview** to see additional information about Photoshop Elements.
- Click **Upgrading From A Previous Version Of Photoshop Elements** to see the differences available in this release of Photoshop Elements as compared to a previous version.

Figure 1-2: The Product Overview lets you see the main functions, as well as upgrading information from a previous version.

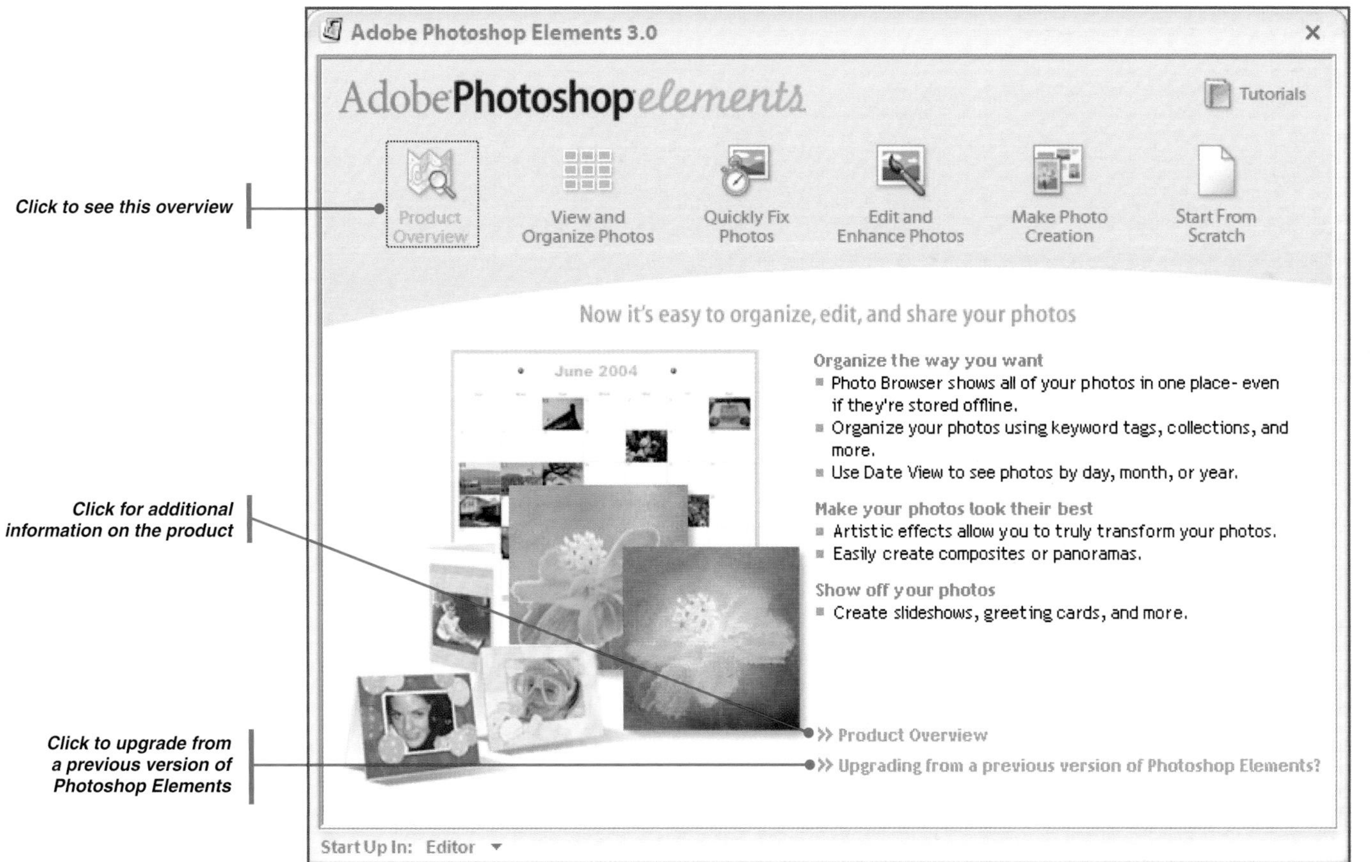

TIP

If you select an image in the Organizer, you can then click Quick Fix or Standard Edit to see the image in those modes.

Browse the Organizer

The Organizer, described in Chapter 2, is used to view, catalog, and manage your library of photos and pictures.

1. Click **View And Organize Photos**. The screen shown in Figure 1-3 is displayed.
2. Choose from the following options:
   - Click **Collections** to create a collection or to see current collections.

Figure 1-3: The Organizer workspace allows you to find and manage photos.

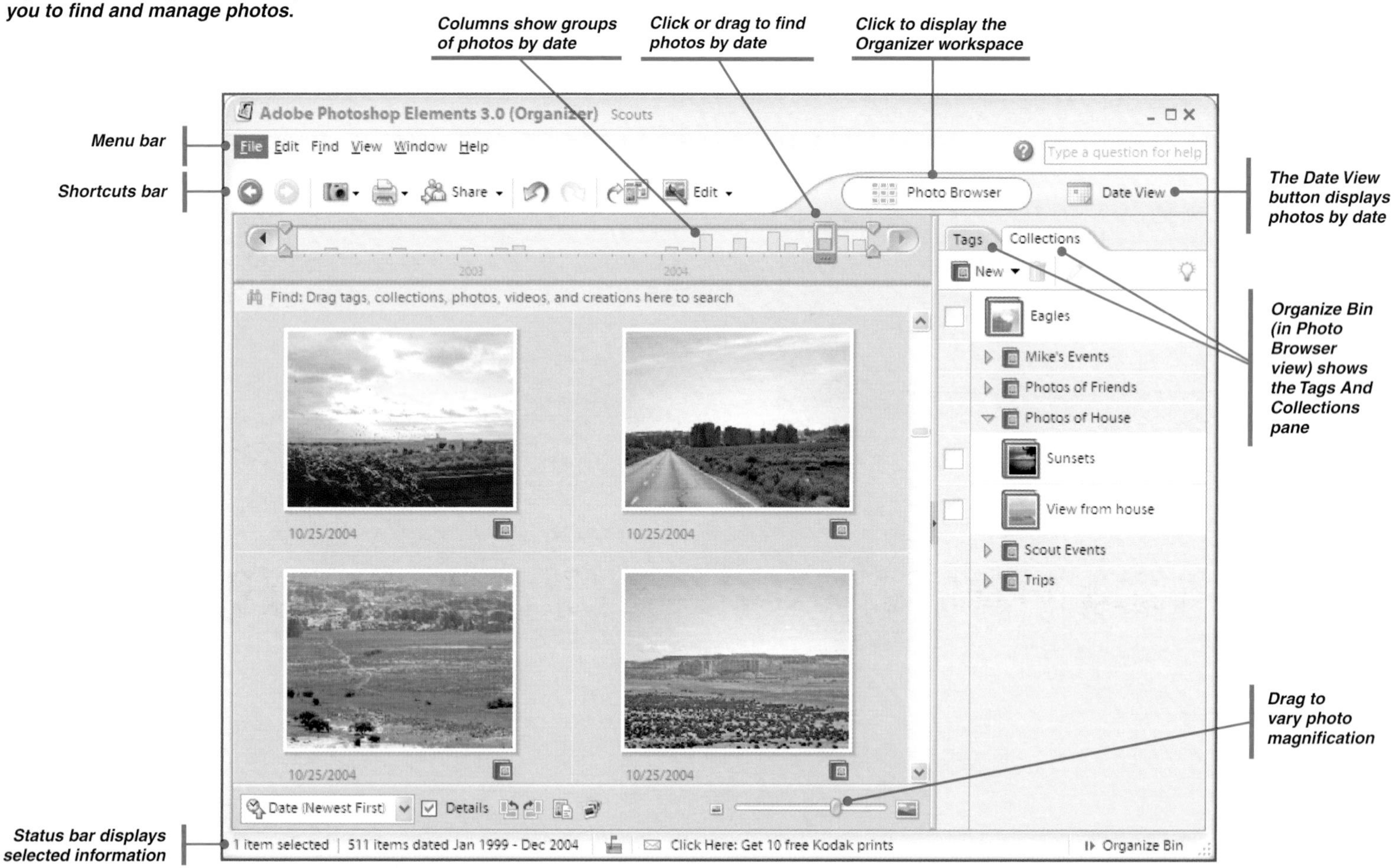

Columns show groups of photos by date

Click or drag to find photos by date

Click to display the Organizer workspace

Menu bar

Shortcuts bar

The Date View button displays photos by date

Organize Bin (in Photo Browser view) shows the Tags And Collections pane

Drag to vary photo magnification

Status bar displays selected information

NOTE

Photoshop Elements gets its date information from your camera's EXIF (Exchangeable Image File format—a standard for storing information in image files) data when you download the images, when you scan the images into your computer, when you download the images from a digital camera, or from dates you enter.

NOTE

To return to the Welcome screen from the Editor, click **Window** and then click **Welcome**.

- Click **Tags** to see a list of the categories of tags. Click the right arrow to see the details of the category. Click **New** to create a new tag.

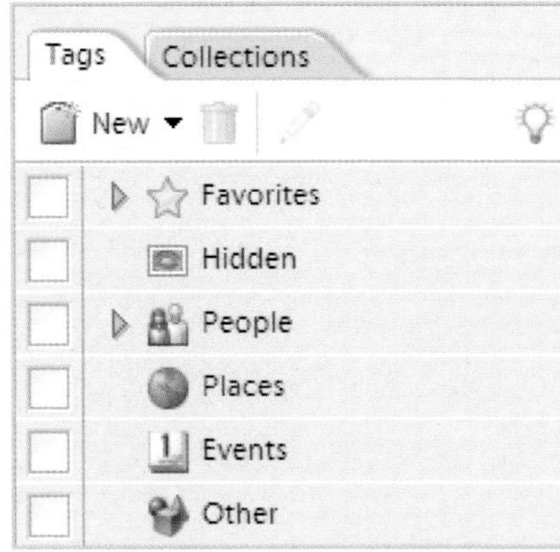

- Drag the slider or click a date to see photos in a range by date.
- Click **Date View** to see all the photos for a given date.
- Click **Photo Browser** to see all photos.
- Drag the **size** slider to enlarge or diminish the size of the thumbnail.

- Click the **Photo Browser Arrangement** down arrow to establish how the photos will be viewed: by newest or oldest first, by folder, or by input batch.

Explore the Quick Fix Workspace

The Quick Fix workspace, shown in Figure 1-4, presents options for quickly and easily editing a photo. Chapter 5 covers the Quick Fix workspace in more detail. Quick Fix offers tools for automatically fixing common problems, such as color cast, images that are improperly exposed, images that lack contrast, and so on.

Figure 1-4: The Quick Fix workspace is used to make common corrections to photos.

Toolbar with Quick Fix tools: Zoom, Grab, Crop, Red Eye Removal

Option bar displays options for the selected tool

Menu bar

Shortcut menu displays commands as shortcut buttons

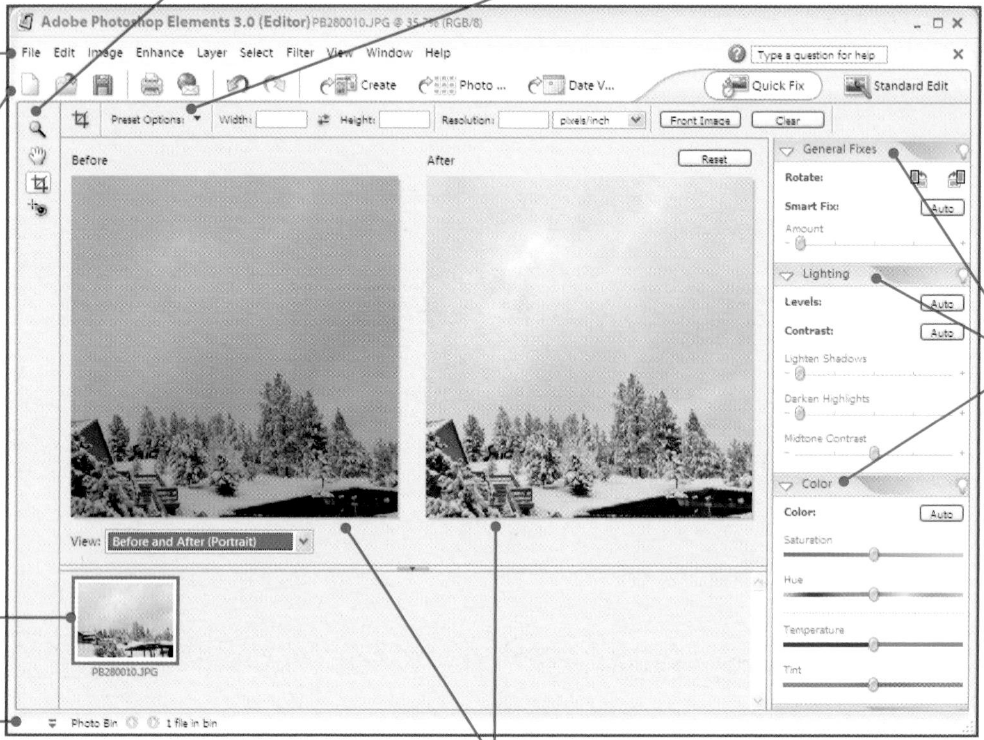

Quick Fix palettes

Photo Bin

Status bar

Workspace containing photo

TIP

You can also get to the Standard Edit workspace from the Organizer or Quick Fix workspace by clicking the **Standard Edit** button.

1. From the Welcome screen, click **Quickly Fix Photos**. The Quick Fix workspace is displayed.
2. Choose from the following options:
   - Open a photo from the File menu by clicking **File** and then clicking **Open**. Or, open a blank page by clicking **File**, clicking **New**, and clicking **Blank File**.
   - To quickly correct defects in a photo, click the **Enhance** menu and select an option.
   - Click a tool in the Quick Fix toolbar to zoom in, grab, and move an image; crop an image; or remove red eye.

TIP

Move your pointer over a tool, icon, or button to see what it does. The name—and often the function—of the tool is displayed.

- Click the **View** down arrow in the photo work area, and select how you want to see an image: before and after in portrait orientation (as shown in Figure 1-4); only the "after" image; only the "before" image; or before and after in landscape orientation.
- Use the palettes to control some of the quick fixes, as described in Chapter 5.

Explore the Standard Edit Workspace

The Standard Editor is covered in most of the chapters in this book. Figure 1-5 shows the Standard Edit workspace. The Standard Editor, also just called the Editor in this book, offers more comprehensive ways to work with images.

From the Welcome page, click **Edit And Enhance Photos**. The screen shown in Figure 1-5 is displayed.

Figure 1-5: The Standard Edit workspace is where you make more comprehensive editing changes to your photo.

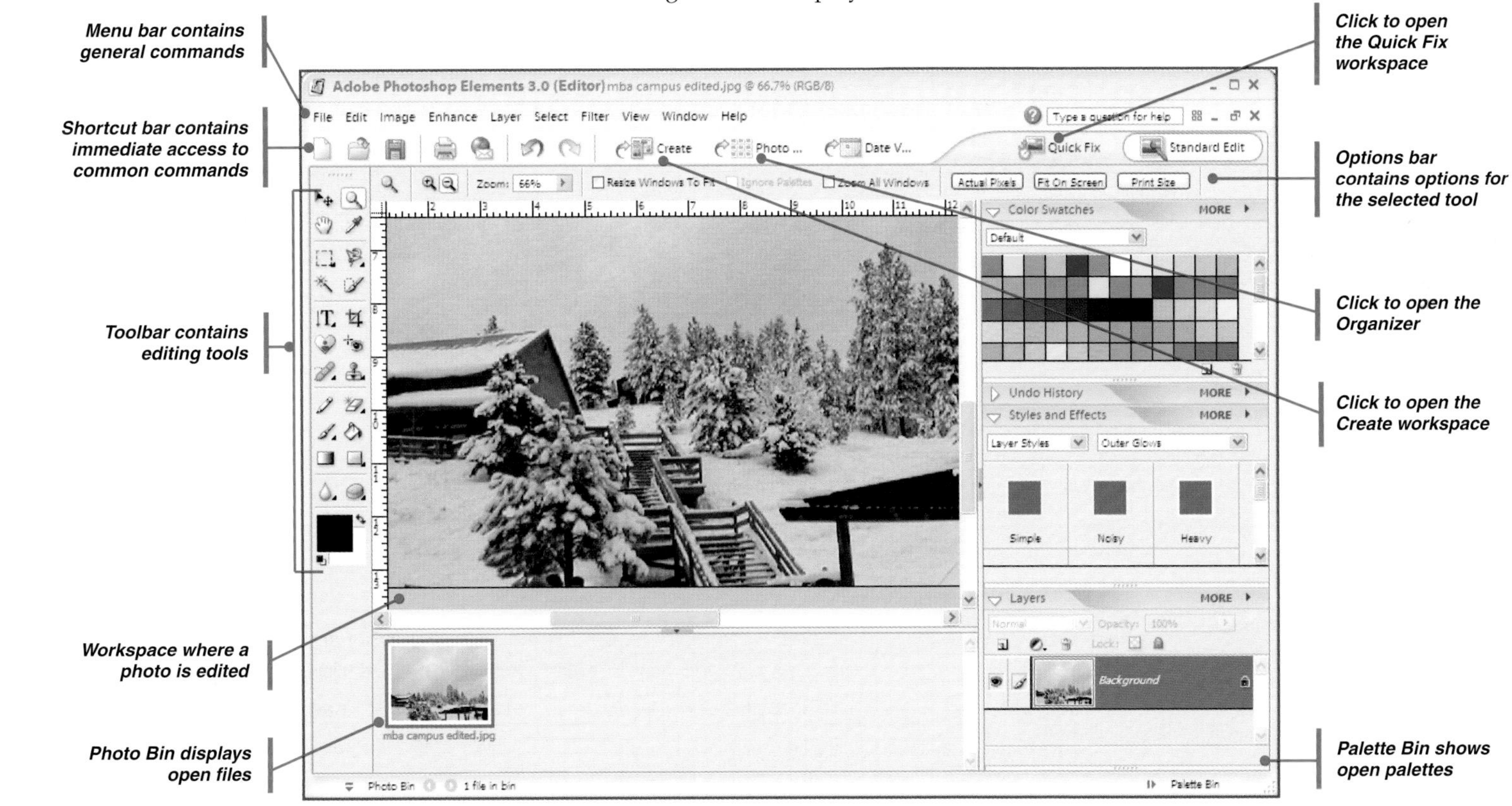

1 2 3 4 5 6 7 8 9 10

USING THE SHORTCUTS BAR

The Shortcuts bar displays commonly used commands, as shown in Figure 1-6. The commands are also available on the menus, but you have quicker access to them from here. You can see the names of the commands by hovering your pointer over the icons.

OPEN A FILE

To open an image file from the Standard Edit workspace:

1. Click **File** and then click **Open.** The Open dialog box appears.
2. Click the **Look In** down arrow, and find the folder containing the image file.
3. Click the file name so that it appears in the File Name text box.
4. Click **Open** to display the file in Photoshop Elements.

Figure 1-6: The Shortcuts bar contains commonly used commands.

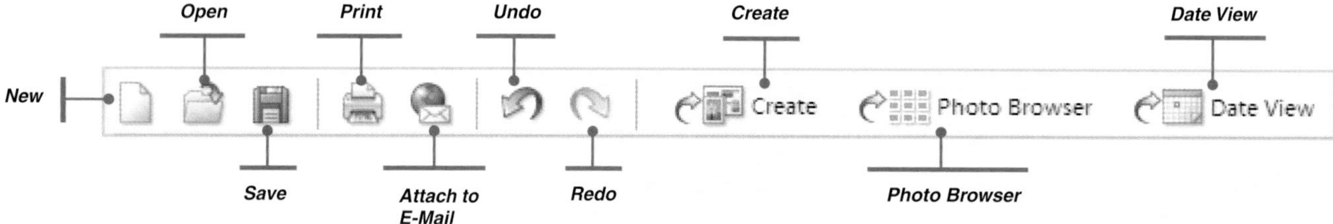

TIP

You can click **My Recent Documents** to display a list of the ten most recently opened files. Click **Desktop** to find a file that may be stored on the desktop. Click **My Documents** or **My Computer** to browse for your folder or file name. Click **My Network** to find a file on your network.

TIP

To learn how to save your edited images, see Chapter 10.

INVESTIGATE THE TOOLBOX

The toolbox contains tools used to edit, select, paint, draw, add text, and move images. To use a tool, you select it by clicking it, set options in the Options bar, and then use it. For some of the tools (Marquee, Lasso, Stamp, Blur, and Sponge), there are multiple tool choices available in the category of tools—for example, within the Lasso tools, you can choose a Lasso tool, Magnetic Lasso tool, or a Polygonal Lasso tool; if there is a triangle located to the right of the toolbox icon, click that and select a tool from the menu that appears.

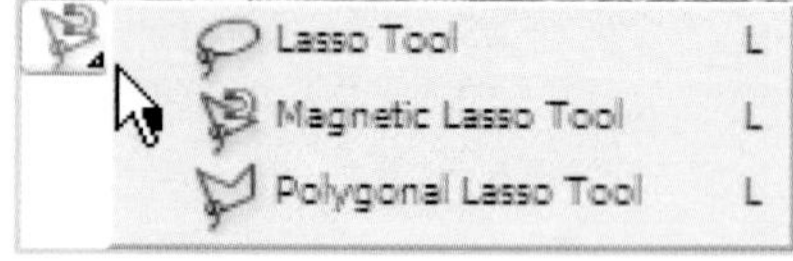

QUICKFACTS

USING THE MENU BAR

The menu bar consists of groups of drop-down menus containing commands used in most of the workspaces in Photoshop Elements. The menu groups and commands change depending on the workspace you're currently using. For instance, the Select menu found in Standard Edit mode is unavailable in the Photo Browser. The Standard Edit menu bar contains the following menus (among others):

- The **File** menu provides commands for opening, finding, saving, printing, batch-processing, and importing files.
- The **Edit** menu provides commands used to edit an image, such as cut, paste, undo, and delete; to change a fill layer; to define brush or pattern options; and to set options regarding color and product preferences.
- The **Image** menu provides commands to manipulate the selected image by rotating it, skewing it, distorting it, or dragging it into perspective. You can also use the free-transform command, crop the image, resize the image or the canvas, divide a scanned group of photos into separate images, or set the color mode.
- The **Enhance** menu provides quick-fix options for correcting errors on a photo. Auto Smart Fix corrects for lighting and color; Auto Levels changes the balance between light and dark—the contrast of an image (color may be affected); Auto Contrast changes the light and dark balances without affecting color; and Auto Color Correction changes tone and hues. Adjust commands are used to manually adjust for color, lighting, and dark and light. Chapters 5 and 6 explain these commands in more detail.
- The **Layer** menu, available only in Standard Edit mode, provides commands for working with image layers. You can create and delete layers; duplicate layers; create fill or adjustment layers; change style or layer content; and arrange, group, merge, or simplify layers. See Chapter 4 for more detail.

Continued...

Each tool also has a keyboard key associated with it (this is known as a shortcut key). When you type that key, the tool is selected. If the tool is in a group, such as the Lasso tools, pressing the key will toggle between the various tools in the group. You can also press the SHIFT key and the corresponding shortcut key to toggle between the tools in a group. Figure 1-7 shows the tools available in Photoshop Elements, as well as the related shortcut keys.

Figure 1-7: The toolbar contains tools that you use to edit your image.

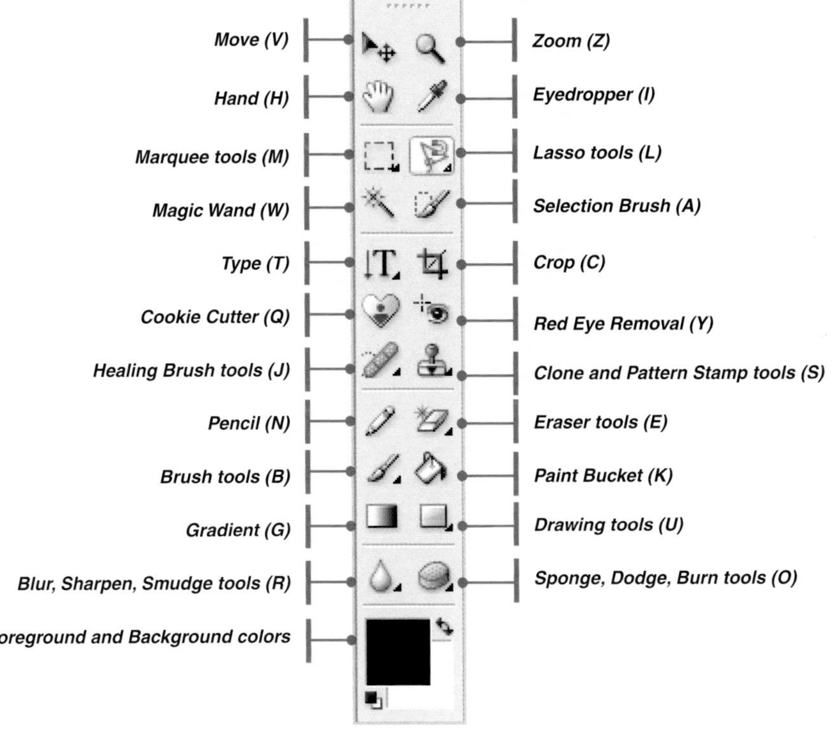

1 2 3 4 5 6 7 8 9 10

USING THE MENU BAR *(Continued)*

- The **Select** menu offers ways to manipulate or enhance selections. You can deselect or reselect a selection; create the inverse of a selection; feather the edges; modify selection borders; smooth, expand, or contract a selection; grow a selection; or select similar components in an image. You can also save and restore commonly used selections. Chapter 3 covers selections in more detail.
- The **Filter** menu provides various filters to use with an image to create special effects. Chapters 5 and 7 discuss filters in more detail.
- The **View** menu provides commands to alter the view of the image on the screen, such as zoom in, zoom out, place rulers or grids on the screen, and others.
- The **Window** menu contains commands to display palettes in the Palette Bin. These commands are unavailable in Quick Fix mode. You can also arrange the image windows, load the File Browser, or display the Welcome screen.

USE THE OPTIONS BAR

The Options bar, located beneath the Shortcuts bar, changes to reflect the currently selected tool. The options for each tool are discussed in the specific chapters of this book (see the Table of Contents or the index). For instance, the options for selection tools are explained in Chapter 3. An example using the Options bar as it relates to the Magic Wand tool is shown here.

Tolerance: 50 ☑ Anti-aliased ☐ Contiguous ☐ Use All Layers

To use the Options bar:

1. Select a tool by clicking it in the toolbox or by typing the relevant keyboard key.
2. Set the options in the Options bar as needed.

Explore Palettes

Palettes, located on the right side of the Photoshop Elements Standard Edit window in the Palette Bin, are designed to help you work with your images. They contain special effects tools, history and layer information, and other important elements you'll use in editing. You can display them as needed in a variety of ways. You can display the whole palette or just the title bar. You can remove the palette from the window if you don't use it often. You can float it onto the workspace for easier access, or use it within the Palette Bin.

Review Palettes

Photoshop Elements contains seven palettes that can be placed in the Palette Bin. To open a palette in the Palette Bin, click the right-pointing arrow on the upper-left corner of the palette. The arrow will point downwards, and the palette will open. To close the palette, click the down arrow.

TIP

You can return to the default settings for a tool by clicking **Reset Tool**; click **Reset All Tools** to return to the default settings for all tools.

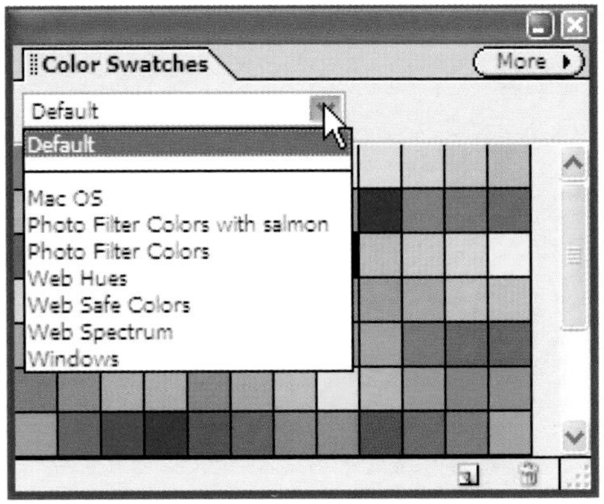

QUICKSTEPS

USING UNDO AND REDO

You can undo, or reverse, most changes you make to an image in Photoshop Elements. If you undo an action by mistake, you can redo it:

- Click **Edit** and then click **Undo *Task*** to reverse the last action. (The last command will be attached to the Undo command so you know precisely what you are undoing.) You can also press **CTRL+Z**.
- Click **Edit** and then click **Redo** to repeat the step you've just undone. You can also press **CTRL+Y**.

USE THE COLOR SWATCHES PALETTE

The Color Swatches palette is used to assign color to the foreground or background color of an image. If it is not already in the Palette Bin, click **Window** and click **Color Swatches** to display it. Click the down arrow to see the menu of color libraries. Click a color to select it for one of the tools or to reset the foreground or background colors. Chapter 6 explains how to use the Color Swatches palette in more detail.

USE THE HISTOGRAM PALETTE

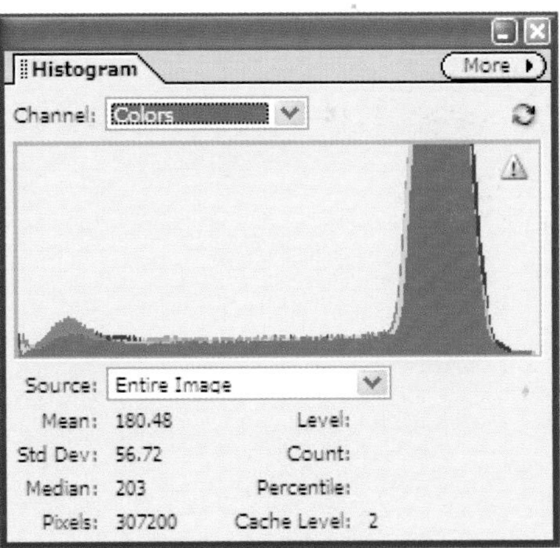

A *histogram* is a series of bars read from left to right over a range of values spanning from 0 to 255. The illustration shows the distribution of pixels in an image from light to dark. On the left end are the darkest values (0 is the darkest value in the image), and on the right are the lightest (255 is the lightest value in the image). You can see the distribution of pixels in the image for the selected color or quality. For instance, if you are looking at the Red channel, you can see how the intensity, or lightness and darkness, of the color red is distributed in the photo. You can also tell whether light and dark are balanced in a picture. If the Histogram palette is not already in the Palette Bin, click **Window** and click **Histogram** to display it.

QUICKSTEPS

USING HELP

Photoshop Elements has many ways in which you can obtain help. You can use the Help file and type a subject or query in the Search field; or you can search for your topic in the contents, index, or glossary. In addition, Photoshop Elements has embedded help throughout the product.

USE HELP

To use the Help file:

1. Click **Help** and then click **Photoshop Elements Help**. The Help dialog box appears, as shown in Figure 1-8. You can also click the **question mark** icon in the upper-right corner of the workspace to display this dialog box.
2. Choose from among the following options:
   - To find out how to do a task, click the **Contents** tab and click the **How To** right arrow. Click the next level of topics, and continue clicking through the levels until you find what you need.
   - To find a task by topic, click the **Contents** tab and click the **Help Topics** right arrow. Search for the topic you need, and click it to display instructions.
   - To search for the topic alphabetically, click the **Index** tab. Click the right arrow next to the letter you want. Topics beginning with that letter are then displayed.
   - To search for your topic, type keywords in the field located at the top of the Adobe Help window, and click **Search**. Adobe Help displays a list of topics matching your keywords.

To use the Histogram palette:

1. If your image contains layers, select the source of the histogram by clicking the **Source** down arrow and clicking **Entire Image**, **Selected Layer**, or **Adjustment Composite** (a composite of several adjustment layers and the layers beneath it). If your image contains no layers, the Source menu will be unavailable.
2. Click the **Channel** down arrow, and click one of the following options:
   - **RGB** displays the pixel distribution of a composite of red, green, and blue colors.
   - **Red** displays the distribution of pixels in the red color channel in the image.
   - **Green** displays the distribution of pixels in the green color channel in the image.
   - **Blue** displays the distribution of pixels in the blue color channel in the image.
   - **Luminosity** displays the distribution of luminosity, or intensity, in the image.
   - **Colors** displays pixel distributions of all colors, including red, green, and blue channels, as well as cyan, magenta, and yellow where individual channels (red, green, and blue) overlap. Grayscale distributions are displayed where the three color channels overlap.
3. Click the **Cached Data Warning** icon to recalculate the histogram data. The numbers are recalculated as follows:
   - **Mean** averages the intensity.
   - **Standard Deviation** measures the variance of intensity.
   - **Median** indicates the middle value in the range of intensity.
   - **Pixels** indicates the number of pixels used in the calculations.
   - **Levels** indicates the level of intensity beneath the cursor.
   - **Count** displays the number of pixels matching the intensity level beneath the cursor.
   - **Percentile** shows the percentage of pixels equal to and below the level beneath the cursor.
   - **Cache Level** displays the setting for the image cache. If Use Cache For Histograms In Levels is selected in the Preferences dialog box, histograms display quickly but are less accurate. If unselected, histograms display more accurately but take more time to appear.
4. Click the **Close** button to remove the palette from the window (as opposed to closing the palette and still having it remain visible).

TIP

In the Info palette, you can click the arrow next to the eyedropper icon to choose a different color model, and then click the arrow next to the plus sign (indicating cursor coordinates) to change the unit of measure.

USE THE HOW TO PALETTE

The How To palette contains aids to help you quickly find out how to perform simple tasks. To use the How To palette:

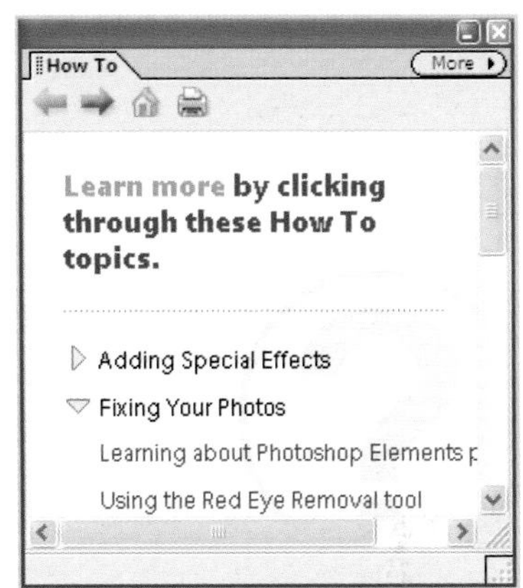

1. Click **Window** and click **How To**. The How To palette is displayed.
2. Find a topic pertaining to your question. Click the right arrow beside the topic to see a list of contents displayed.
3. Click the topic name. The procedure is displayed in the same window.

Figure 1-8: Adobe Help presents several ways for you to access help, including a table of contents, an index, and a glossary.

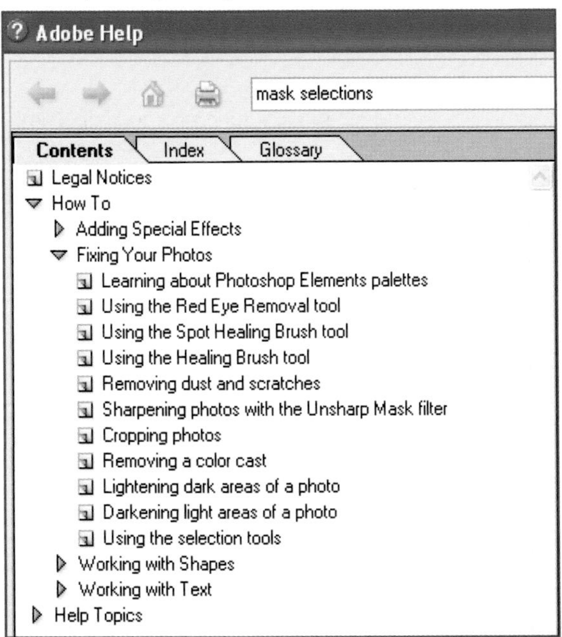

USE THE INFO PALETTE

The Info palette provides instant information about the area beneath the pointer. As you move the pointer over the image, the Info palette changes to reflect the new values. If the Info palette is not already displayed in the workspace, click **Window** and click **Info**. The following list contains some of the values displayed—they will differ depending on the tool being used:

- Numeric definitions for the selected color modes, such as RGB, red, green, blue, or indexed color
- X and Y coordinates of the pointer
- Height and width of a selection
- Status, which can be set by clicking the right arrow at the bottom right of the dialog box; choices are document size, profile, dimensions, scratch size, efficiency, timing, or the current tool being used

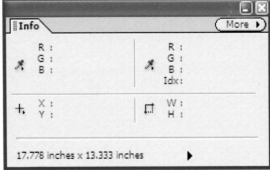

QUICKSTEPS

USING RULERS AND GRIDS

You can display vertical and horizontal rulers in the workspace, which enables you to determine an exact position when creating a selection. Use grids to accurately align and position the various components of an image.

USE RULERS

- To display rulers, click **View** and then click **Rulers**. Rulers are displayed along the top and left side of the workspace.
- To set preferences for rulers, click **Edit**, click **Preferences**, and click **Units & Rulers**. Click the **Ruler** down arrow, and choose to display the ruler measurements in pixels, inches (the default), centimeters, millimeters, points, picas, or percent.

USE GRIDS

To display a grid on the image:

Click **View** and click **Grid**. A grid is imposed on the image.

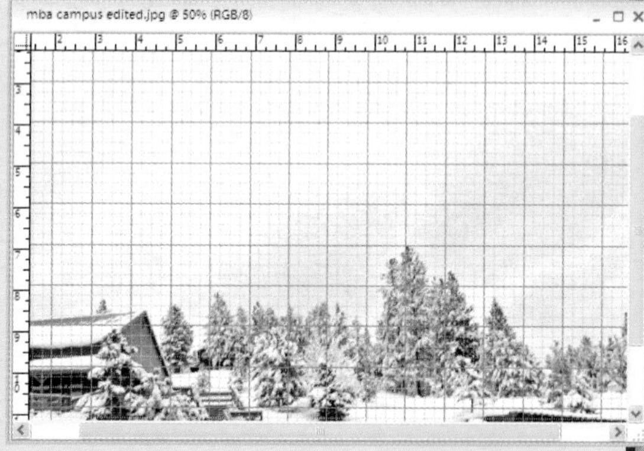

To set preferences for a grid:

1. Click **Edit**, click **Preferences**, and click **Grid**.
2. Click the **Color** down arrow, and choose a color.

Continued...

USE THE LAYERS PALETTE

The Layers palette contains information about the layers of an image and provides commands to manipulate them. If the Layers palette is not already in the Palette Bin, click **Window** and click **Layers**. The palette lists the layers in order from the bottom background layer (the beginning image) to the top layer. To work with a layer, click it to select it. A menu provides a variety of blending modes used to create special effects, and there is an Opacity drop-down list used to control the transparency of the effects. The buttons on top of the palette provide tools for creating, deleting, or locking layers. The icons on the individual layers provide data about the characteristics they contain. See Chapter 4 for additional information on layers.

USE THE NAVIGATOR PALETTE

The Navigator palette is used to vary the magnification of the image and to move from place to place within it. If the Navigator palette is not already in the Palette Bin, click **Window** and click **Navigator**. The view box (outlined in red) represents the area of the image being displayed in the workspace; you can only drag the view box when it is smaller than the image in the Navigator palette (by using the Zoom tool to zoom into a portion of the image).

To vary the magnification:

Type a percentage by which to magnify an image in the text box.

–Or–

Click the **Zoom Out** icon to decrease the magnification; click the **Zoom In** icon to increase it.

–Or–

Drag the slider to the left to decrease the magnification; drag it to the right to increase it.

USING RULERS AND GRIDS

(Continued)

3. Click the **Style** down arrow, and choose between lines, dashed lines, and dots.
4. Type a value in the **Gridline Every** text box to set how frequently grid lines will appear.
5. Click the down arrow to the right, and choose the unit of measurement.
6. Type a value in the **Subdivisions** text box to establish how many sections each grid square is subdivided into. Four is the default number.
7. Click **OK** to save your changes.

ALIGN WITH SNAP-TO GRIDS

To set or clear the snap-to grid, click **View** and click **Snap To Grid**. A check mark indicates that an image or shape will "snap to" the grid; click the check mark to deselect a snap-to grid and prevent it from affecting the placement of an image or shape.

TIP

To change the color of the view box in the Navigator palette, click the **More** button and click **Palette Options**. In the Palette Options dialog box, click the **Color** down arrow, and click the **color** that you want to replace the current color. Or, you can click the **color swatch** icon on the dialog box, which will cause the Color Picker to be displayed, from which you can choose a color. Click **OK** when finished.

To move around in the image:

Drag the view box to the portion of the image you want to view.

–Or–

Click the image in the Navigator palette to place the view box where you want it.

USE THE STYLES AND EFFECTS PALETTE

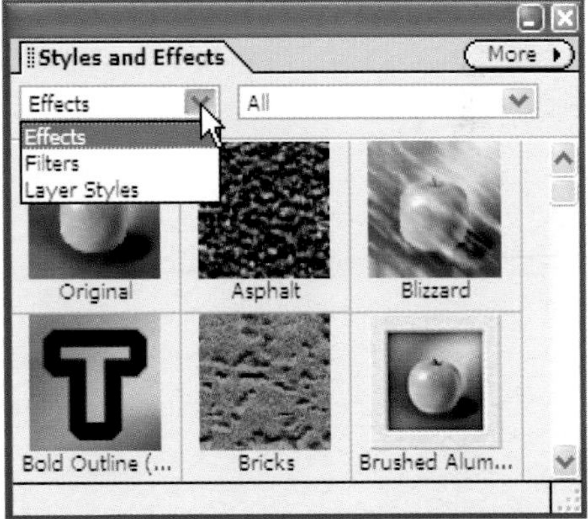

The Styles And Effects palette contains special effects that can be applied to an image. Chapters 4, 5, and 7 discuss the palette in more detail. If the palette is not already in the Palette Bin, click **Window** and click **Styles And Effects**. Click the **left** down arrow, and click **Effects**, **Filters**, or **Layer Styles**. Click the **right** down arrow, and choose the type of effect, filter, or layer style you want. Then click the relevant thumbnail, which gives you a small picture representing how the special effect, filter, or style will look applied to your image. Click the **More** button in the upper-right corner, and click **List View** to display your choices in a list as opposed to thumbnails.

QUICKSTEPS

USING THE PALETTE BIN

The Palette Bin is on the Standard Edit workspace.

SHOW OR HIDE THE PALETTE BIN

To show or hide the Palette Bin:

Click **Window** and click **Palette Bin**.

–Or–

Click the **Open** or **Close** buttons on the left of the Palette Bin.

Palette Bin

–Or–

Press **F7**.

SHOW OR HIDE FLOATING PALETTES

To hide or show floating palettes, press the **TAB** key.

ADD A PALETTE TO THE PALETTE BIN

Click **Window** and then click the name of the palette you want to add to the Palette Bin. If a palette name has a check mark next to it in the Window menu, it will appear in the Palette Bin or floating in the workspace, depending on the palette. You can add a floating palette to the Palette Bin by clicking the **More** button and then clicking **Place In Palette Bin**. Click the **Close** button in the upper-right corner as if to delete it. The floating palette is placed in the Palette Bin.

CHANGE THE PALETTE ORDER

To rearrange the order of palettes in the Palette Bin:

1. Click the title bar of the palette you want to move.
2. Drag the palette to the new location.

DELETE A PALETTE FROM THE PALETTE BIN

Click **Window** and click a palette name to remove the arrow next to the name. The palette will be instantly removed from the Palette Bin.

Continued...

USE THE UNDO HISTORY PALETTE

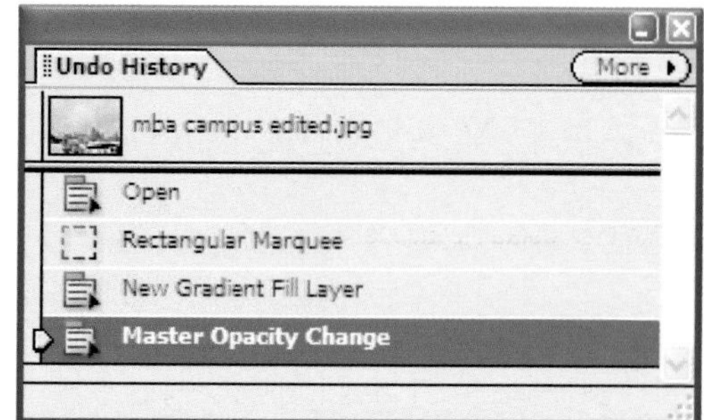

The Undo History palette contains a list of the changes that have affected the pixels of the image. If the Undo History palette is not already in the Palette Bin, click **Window** and click **Undo History**. Use this palette to return to previous changes and modify or remove alterations without losing all your work. Click a change to see that stage of modifications to the image. The most recent changes are at the bottom; the oldest are at the top. The topmost item is the original image with no changes. When you select a change, all subsequent changes created after it become unavailable. When you delete a change, all changes beneath it are also deleted.

Explore Preferences

Photoshop Elements contains several ways in which you can customize the product to suit your needs. There are nine preference areas dealing with everything from saving files to displaying colors and cursor icons. The following sections will discuss some of the more common preferences.

Set General Preferences

General preferences contain a collection of general-purpose settings, as seen in Figure 1-9.

1. Click **Edit**, click **Preferences**, and click **General**. The Preferences dialog box appears.
2. Click the **Color Picker** down arrow to choose the Color Picker style displayed in Photoshop Elements.
3. Click the **Step Back/Fwd** down arrow to choose the keyboard keys to press when you want to undo or redo your edits. The Undo command in the Edit menu will change accordingly to reflect this change.

USING THE PALETTE BIN *(Continued)*

RESET PALETTE LOCATIONS

In the Standard Edit workspace, click **Window** and then click **Reset Palette Locations**. The palettes are returned to their default locations.

FLOAT OR DOCK A PALETTE

To float a palette, drag it from the Palette Bin. To dock a palette (or place it back in the Palette Bin), click the **Close** button on the palette.

TIP

Saving a larger number of states, or changes, causes more memory to be used.

NOTE

If you are getting unexpected results when you try to set preferences, it may be because the preferences file is corrupted. You can create a new preferences file. Double-click the **desktop** icon to start Photoshop Elements; or click **Start**, click **Programs**, and then click **Adobe Photoshop Elements**. Immediately press and hold ALT+CTRL+SHIFT when the program begins to run. Click **Yes** when asked if you want to delete the current settings file. Restart Photoshop Elements to start with a fresh preferences file with default values.

Figure 1-9: General preferences are settings that allow you to control a range of functions, such as whether to use the Adobe Color Picker or to automatically hide the Photo Bin.

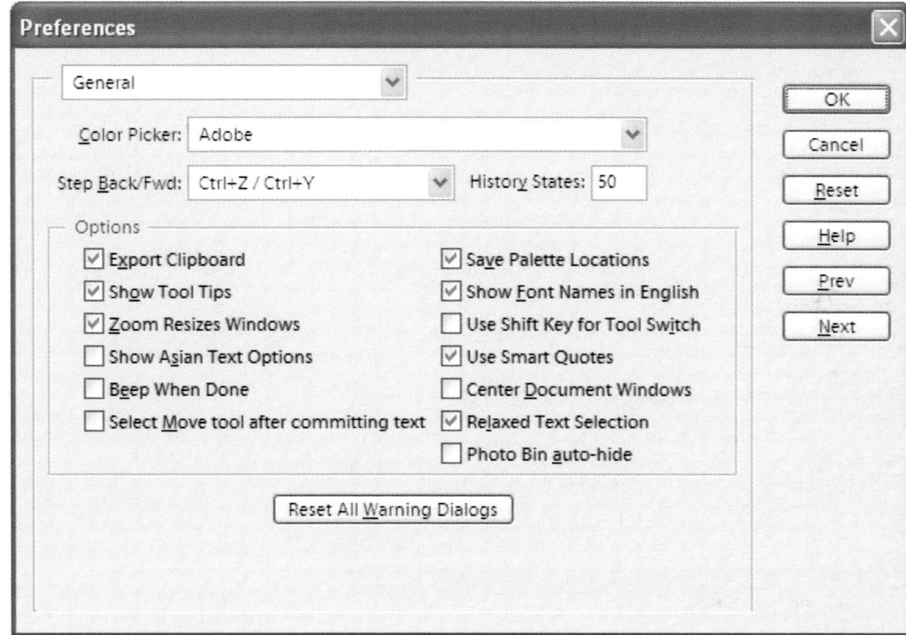

4. Click in the **History States** field, and type the number of changes, or states, that you want recorded in the History Undo palette.
5. In the Options area, select or deselect check boxes according to your preferences.
6. Click the **Reset All Warning Dialogs** button to redisplay any warning messages in which you clicked the Do Not Show This Message Again check box.
7. Click **OK** to save your changes. Click **Reset** to reset settings to original default values.

TIP

See Chapter 10 for information on how to change preferences pertaining to the File Browser.

NOTE

When in a Preferences dialog box, you can click **Next** to advance to the next Preferences dialog box.

Change File Preferences

When you bring up the Preferences dialog box pertaining to files, you can change such things as whether to save image thumbnails, whether to use uppercase or lowercase letters in file extensions, how many recent file names to record, whether to ignore camera data profiles when you download images from your camera, whether to maximize your file compatibility with PSD files, and whether to ask before saving layers in TIFF files or to flatten the image first.

1. Click **Edit**, click **Preferences**, and click **Saving Files**. The Preferences dialog box for files appears.
2. Change any options you desire.
3. Click **OK** to save your changes.

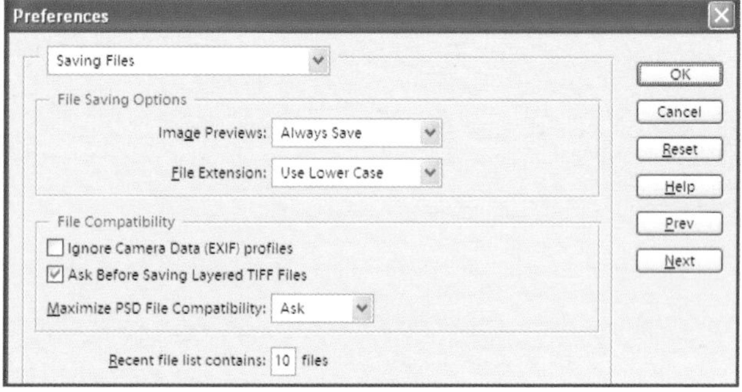

Change Cursor Displays

From the Preferences dialog box pertaining to cursors, you can choose between a standard display and a more precise display that uses a crosshairs or circular cursor, depending on what is selected; and, in the case of the Brush tool, use the brush size as the cursor.

1. Click **Edit**, click **Preferences**, and click **Display & Cursors**. The Preferences dialog box for cursors appears.
2. Change any options you desire. A preview of your changes is displayed.
3. Click **OK** to save your changes.

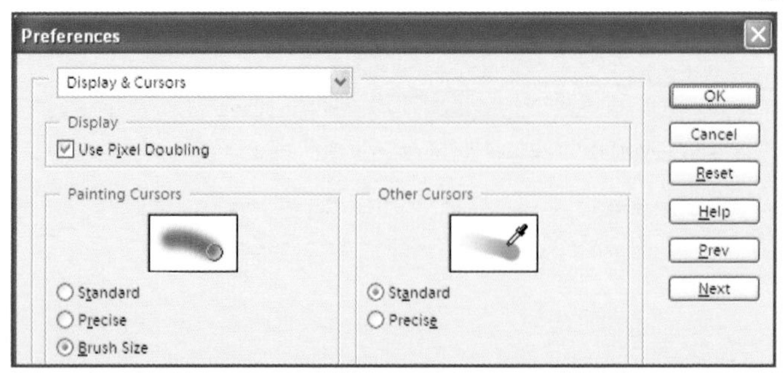

Change Plug-Ins and Scratch Disks

Plug-ins are additional programs used in Photoshop Elements that add capability. *Scratch disks* are any drive or partition of a drive used as a type of virtual memory when Photoshop Elements needs additional memory to work with images.

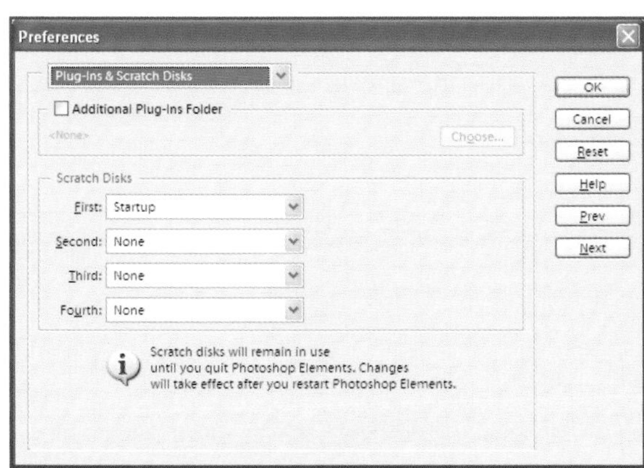

To modify plug-ins and scratch disks:

1. Click **Edit**, click **Preferences**, and click **Plug-Ins & Scratch Disks**. The Preferences dialog box for plug-ins and scratch disks appears.
2. Perform one or both of the following tasks:
   - Click **Additional Plug-Ins Folder** to find folders where plug-ins are stored. A dialog box will appear, from which you indicate where the folder may be found.
   - In the Scratch Disks area, click the **First** down arrow, and type the file path for the primary scratch disk. Click **Second**, **Third**, and **Fourth** if you want additional scratch disks to be used.
3. Click **OK** to save your changes.

Change Memory and Cache Usage

Photoshop Elements uses a memory cache to store thumbnails and image states for quick access. Use the Preferences dialog box pertaining to image cache and memory to change your settings.

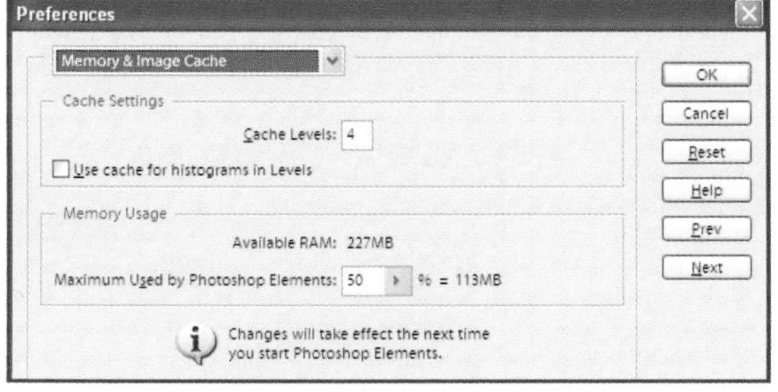

1. Click **Edit**, click **Preferences**, and click **Memory & Image Cache**. The Preferences dialog box for memory and image cache appears.
2. Select from the following options:
   - Click in the **Cache Levels** field, and type a number to increase or decrease the number of cache levels used to contain image data. If you increase the number, the response time will be improved but memory usage will be increased.
   - Click the **Use Cache For Histograms In Levels** check box to save states of an image in the cache. This increases the performance of the histogram in the Levels dialog box.

If you allocate too much RAM to Photoshop Elements, it will hinder the computer operating system running in the background.

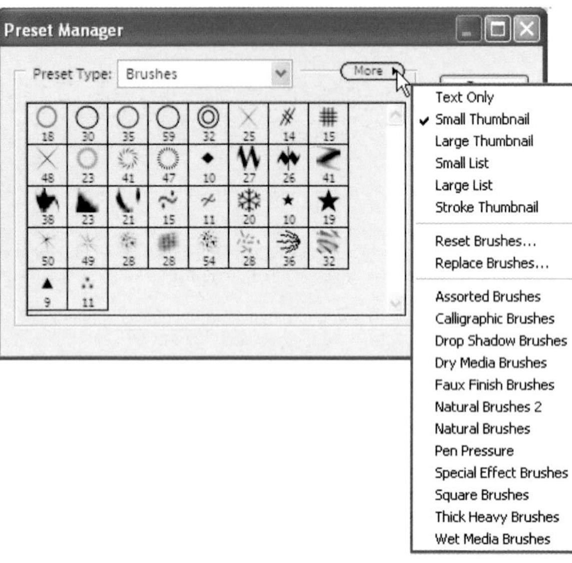

CAUTION

To delete a preset, click the preset and click **Delete**. No warning message is displayed; the preset will immediately disappear from the list.

- Click the **Maximum Used By Photoshop Elements** right arrow, and drag the slider to increase or decrease the percentage of available RAM memory Photoshop Elements will use. You can also type a value in the text box.

3. Click **OK** to save your changes.

Set Preset Manager Options

Photoshop Elements uses libraries of preset default effects for brush tools, color swatches, gradients, and patterns. You will see default presets when choosing one of these effects. You can change these defaults to one of a wide selection of presets available. You can also save and load libraries of your own to use.

To manage libraries of presets:

1. Click **Edit** and click **Preset Manager**. The Preset Manager is displayed.
2. Click the **Preset Type** down arrow, and click **Brushes**, **Swatches**, **Gradients**, or **Patterns**.
3. Choose from among the following options:
   - To load a library that comes with Photoshop Elements, click the **More** button and click one of the libraries in the bottom half of the menu.
   - To load a library or preset from a folder on your computer, click **Load** and browse to the folder location. Click the desired file name, and click **Load**.
   - To save a preset, click a preset to select it, and click **Save Set**. Type the file name and browse to the location where the preset is to be saved. Click **Save**.
   - To change the size of thumbnails or lists, click **More** and click a size of thumbnail or a list type.
   - To rename a preset, click a preset to select it, click **Rename**, type the new name, and click **OK**.
4. Click **Done** when you are finished.

How to...

- *Understand File Types*
- *Understanding Pixels, Resolution, and Dimension*
- *Change Resolution or Pixel Dimension*
- *Get Digital Camera Photos*
- *Scan Images*
- *Find or Import Images*
- *Use Video Stills*
- *Find Files With Photo Browser*
- *Renaming Files*
- *Moving and Zooming Files*
- *Start a Slide Show*
- *Using Photo Browser Icons*
- *Work with the Catalog*
- *Using Collections*
- *Place Photos in a Collection*
- *Work with Stacks*
- *Using Stacks and Version Sets*
- *Work with Version Sets*
- *Organize Images Using Tags*
- *Viewing Photo Properties*
- *Use Date View*
- *Process RAW Image Files*

Chapter 2

Acquiring, Organizing, and Managing Images

Chapter 2 covers the new feature in Photoshop Elements 3.0, the Organizer, that enables you to find, download, organize, and manage your images. The Organizer is where you can acquire images from scanners, digital cameras, video cameras, and files from your own or another person's computer. Once you have the images, you can organize them by adding tags or placing them in a collection. Tags allow you to place one or more notes on an image that identify how it is to be viewed. For instance, you can organize images by someone's name, by an event (such as a wedding), by a place, or by subject (such as pets).

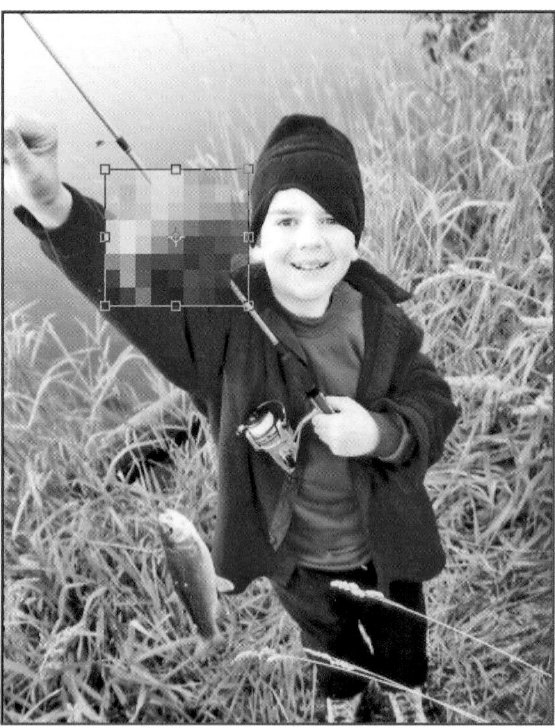

Figure 2-1: Bitmap images are made up of pixels, or hundreds of tiny dots, as seen in the magnified part of the image.

Acquire Images

You get images from a variety of places. You can download them from a scanner, digital camera, or card reader; from files and folders on your computer; from a mobile phone that also takes photos; from a network; or even from the Internet.

Understand File Types

Images used in Photoshop Elements can be *bitmap* or *vector-based*. An image might be a bitmap, vector graphic, or a combination of both. Chapter 7 contains additional information on bitmaps and vector graphics.

USE BITMAP IMAGES

Digital photos are bitmap images. They consist of pixels, or tiny dots. Figure 2-1 displays an image partly magnified so that you can see the pixels. You can see that if the image is enlarged too much, the enlarged pixels cause the image to appear distorted and blurred. See the "Understanding Pixels, Resolution, and Dimension" QuickFacts for how file size, resolution, and image dimension are related to the number of pixels.

You change a bitmap image by adding or deleting pixels, or by changing the color of the pixels. You can change pixels by applying color with paint brushes, applying color fills, and using filters and special effects to enhance bitmap images. Most file formats used in Photoshop Elements are bitmap, including BMP, PICT, GIF, JPEG, TIFF, and PNG.

USE VECTOR IMAGES

Vector images are created as points, lines, and curves based on mathematical formulas rather than as pixels. Clipart are often vector files. When a vector-based graphic is resized, it will not be distorted, which is the case with pixels (although complex fills within vector graphics may be distorted when enlarged). In addition, when a vector graphic is enlarged, the file size stays the same. Common vector file types are encapsulated PostScript (ESP, Adobe Illustrator (AI), and CorelDRAW (CDR).

QUICKFACTS

UNDERSTANDING PIXELS, RESOLUTION, AND DIMENSION

Three ways you can look at pixels are: how pixels determine file size (pixel dimension), how they impact image size for display and printing, and how they are related to resolution.

UNDERSTAND FILE SIZE AND PIXEL DIMENSION

When you capture an image with your digital camera, you capture a certain number of pixels, such as 2272 x 1504 (or 3,417,088 pixels), a typical size for photos. (At this number of pixels, the camera would be advertised as a 3.4-megapixel camera.) This is your pixel dimension—the height and width of an image in pixels. When you download a photo to Photoshop Elements, that number of pixels is stored on your hard disk. This stored number of pixels determines the file size at typically 8 to 16 bits per pixel. The pixel dimension will not change unless you add or delete pixels. (You can add or delete pixels from an image by resizing an image using resampling, a technique explained later in this chapter.)

UNDERSTAND RESOLUTION

Resolution determines the quality, or density, of the detail seen in the image. It is usually measured in pixels (ppi) or dots per inch (dpi), or how many pixels are displayed per inch in an image. The more pixels per inch in an image (the density), the higher the image quality. An image's resolution is one way to determine what size the image will be when printed or seen on a monitor (another way is to specify the image size in inches). You normally use a higher resolution for printing, for example, 300 ppi, whereas an image is typically viewed on a monitor at 72 ppi, a lower resolution (although it will be perfectly clear on the monitor). Thus, an image with a fixed number of pixels can be viewed with varying

Continued...

Vector graphics are created using the shape tools in Photoshop Elements, as described in Chapter 7, or using other similar products. However, when you view vector-based graphics on your monitor, you will see them as pixels, since the images are displayed that way on the digital-based screen. Since Photoshop Elements is a bitmap-oriented program, it will show the pixels when the image is enlarged, although the lines will not be blurred, as with bitmap images. See Figure 2-2 for an example.

Figure 2-2: A drawing is a vector-based graphic, and although the pixels in the enlarged sample are displayed, because Photoshop Elements is a bitmap-based program, you can see that the vector-based image is sharper than a bitmap image.

Change Resolution or Pixel Dimension

To view the resolution or dimension of an image so that you can change one or both, click the **Image** menu, click **Resize**, and click **Image Size**.

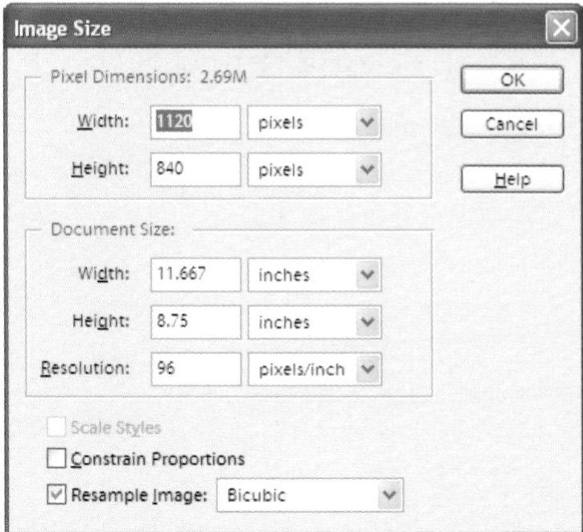

CHANGE DIMENSIONS OF AN IMAGE

To change the pixel dimensions of an image:

1. Click the **Image** menu, click **Resize**, and click **Image Size**.
2. Click the **Constrain Proportions** check box to ensure that the proportion of height to width will be changed relative to each other.

1 2 3 4 5 6 7 8 9 10

UNDERSTANDING PIXELS, RESOLUTION, AND DIMENSION

(Continued)

resolutions, depending on the needed quality, image size, and the device displaying the image. Resolution of the image file is determined by the device used to capture the image. You can specify this with scanners, but most cameras have a default resolution. You can change the resolution of the image file by changing the image size or the resolution using the Resize Image command, described in "Change Resolution or Pixel Dimension." When the image is displayed on a monitor or printer, the resolution will be changed to accommodate that device.

UNDERSTAND PIXEL DIMENSION VS. IMAGE SIZE

You normally describe a monitor in terms of its pixel dimension, such as 1024 x 768. (You choose the monitor display size in the Windows Display Properties dialog box.) This is related to the physical size of your monitor (for example, a 17" monitor) and the number of dpi (used interchangeably with ppi) set for the display. The file image is sized to fit the monitor on a pixel-by-pixel basis at the dpi set for the monitor. In Photoshop Elements, you can determine magnification while editing the image.

On a printer, the image size is described usually in inches, such as 5 x 4 inches. The printed image size, if not specified at printing, is a function of the file-image pixel dimension and the printing resolution. For example, if your image has been captured with a pixel dimension of 1500 x 1200 pixels and your image has an appropriate printing resolution, such as 300 ppi, the printed image size will be 5 x 4 inches (1500 divided by 300 ppi, and 1200 divided by 300 ppi). If you wanted a larger printed

Continued...

3. Accept the default selection **Resample Image** if you want the pixel dimensions changed to reflect the change in image size or resolution. Click the down arrow and choose a resample algorithm.

   –Or–

   Click **Resample Image** to deselect it for the pixel dimensions to remain constant.

4. In the Pixel Dimensions area, type a new width and/or height. The other dimensions will be automatically updated.

   –Or–

   In the Document Size area, change the width and/or height, and the pixel dimensions will be automatically changed.

CHANGE THE RESOLUTION OF AN IMAGE

To change the resolution of an image *without* changing the pixel dimensions (to print a different-sized image, for instance):

1. Click the **Image** menu, click **Resize**, and click **Image Size**.
2. Deselect **Resample Image**.
3. Type a new resolution and click **OK**.

To change the resolution *and* its pixel dimensions:

1. Click the **Image** menu, click **Resize**, and click **Image Size**.
2. Click **Resample Image**.
3. Type a new resolution. The pixel width and height are updated.
4. Click **OK**.

Get Digital Camera Photos

To get photos from a digital camera, you must first hook up your camera to the computer. The camera must be turned on.

1. To load the Organizer from the Edit work area, click the **Photo Browser** button.

UNDERSTANDING PIXELS, RESOLUTION, AND DIMENSION

(Continued)

image (or a less detailed image), you would choose a resolution of 150 ppi, which would print a lesser-quality image of 10 x 8 inches. Conversely, if you choose to print a specific-sized picture, your resolution would also change to maintain the relationship between pixels and inches. (If you are resizing the image within Photoshop Elements rather than as a printer option, you must consider the effects of resampling, explained later in the chapter. You can change the image size and not the resolution, or vice versa, with resampling. In this case, pixels would be added or deleted from the image. Resampling is the default setting for the Resize Image command; however, you have to careful since resampling to a higher pixel dimension at the same resolution will lead to distortions when Photoshop Elements redraws the pixels. For example, if you were to double the size of an image at the same resolution, the pixels would also double in size.)

TIP

When you enlarge an image by no more than ten percent and use the bicubic method with resampling, the resulting image will be fairly good.

2. From the Organizer menu, click **File**, click **Get Photos**, and then click **From Camera Or Card Reader**. The Adobe Photo Downloader is displayed.
3. If your camera is correctly connected and turned on and your Photoshop Elements camera preferences are set, the Adobe Downloader will automatically display thumbnails of the photos on your camera, as seen in Figure 2-3.

Figure 2-3: The Adobe Photo Downloader displays thumbnails of your photos, which you can select to download by clicking or clearing the check boxes under the thumbnail images.

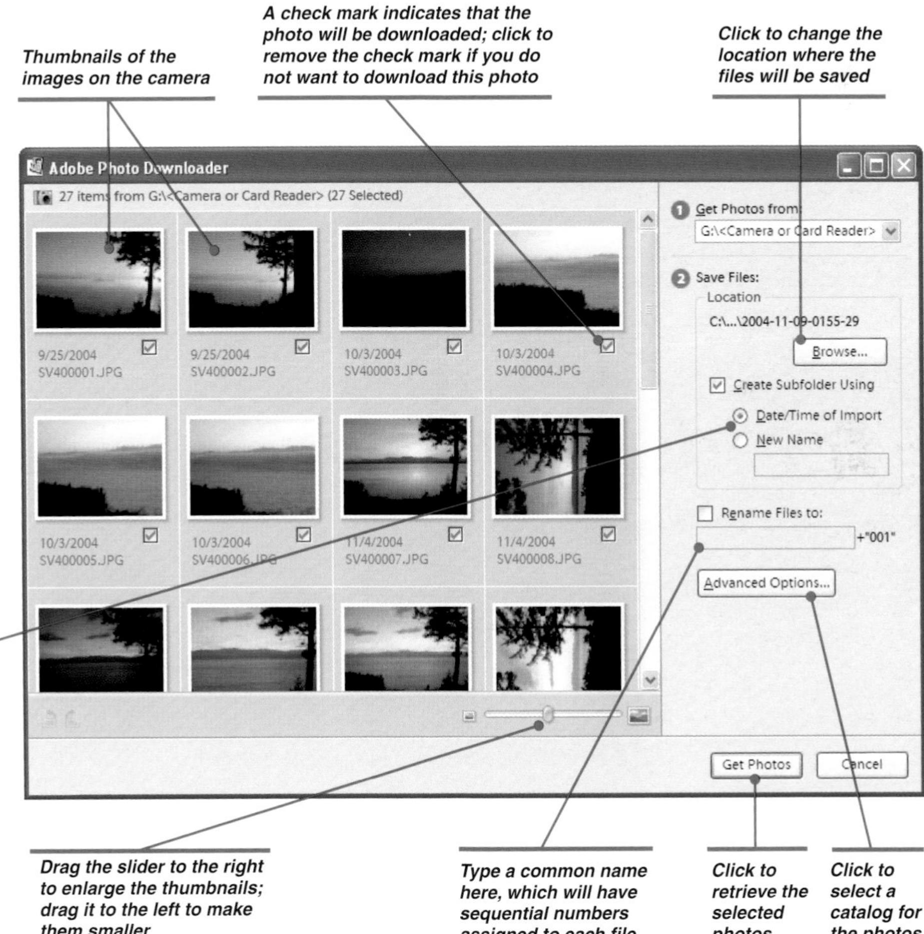
Thumbnails of the images on the camera
A check mark indicates that the photo will be downloaded; click to remove the check mark if you do not want to download this photo
Click to change the location where the files will be saved
Adobe Photo Downloader
27 items from G:\<Camera or Card Reader> (27 Selected)
Get Photos from:
G:\<Camera or Card Reader>
Save Files:
Location
C:\...\2004-11-09-0155-29
Browse...
Create Subfolder Using
Date/Time of Import
New Name
Rename Files to:
+"001"
Advanced Options...
9/25/2004 SV400001.JPG
9/25/2004 SV400002.JPG
10/3/2004 SV400003.JPG
10/3/2004 SV400004.JPG
10/3/2004 SV400005.JPG
10/3/2004 SV400006.JPG
11/4/2004 SV400007.JPG
11/4/2004 SV400008.JPG
Get Photos
Cancel
Choose between naming the files by date (the default) or by name
Drag the slider to the right to enlarge the thumbnails; drag it to the left to make them smaller
Type a common name here, which will have sequential numbers assigned to each file
Click to retrieve the selected photos
Click to select a catalog for the photos

1 2 3 4 5 6 7 8 9 10

NOTE

When you resize an image, you have an option to *resample* it. Resampling adds pixels to an image that is being enlarged and removes pixels from an image that is being reduced. Resampling is done using an algorithm that does its best to preserve the quality of the image, but an image in which the pixels are increased or decreased will not have the same quality as the original image. To change the size or resolution of an image, click the **Image** menu, click **Resize**, and click **Image Size**. On the Image Size dialog box, Resample Image is the default selection, so you must deselect this if you don't want to increase or decrease the number of pixels.

TIP

When resampling, select an algorithm, or interpolation method, that best determines how the added or removed pixels will impact the image: click **Bicubic** for most situations for a smooth transition; click **Bicubic Smoother** for resizing an image upward (making it larger); click **Bicubic Sharper** when resizing an image downward (making it smaller); click **Nearest Neighbor** for a faster, lower-quality image; and click **Bilinear** for a mid-quality image.

4. By default, all photos are selected to be downloaded to your computer. Click the check marks beneath the photos to deselect them and prevent them from being downloaded to your computer.
5. When the photos you want have been selected, click **Get Photos**.
6. A message is displayed stating that the files are being copied to your hard disk. When the files have been downloaded, the Organizer will display the following message.

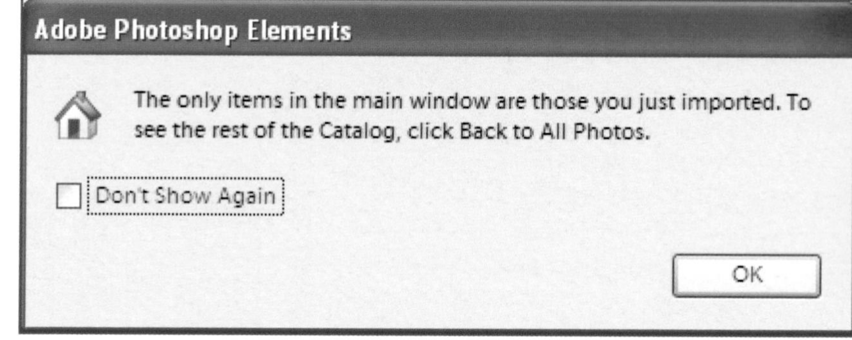

7. Click **OK**. You will be asked if you want to delete the photos from your camera or card reader.
8. Click **Yes** to delete them, or click **No** to retain the photos on your camera.

Scan Images

To scan an image from within Photoshop Elements:

1. Click the **Photo Browser** button. The Organizer is displayed. Photo Browser
2. From the Organizer toolbar, click the **Get Photos From Camera**, **Card Reader**, **Scanner**, **Or File System** button, and click **From Scanner**.

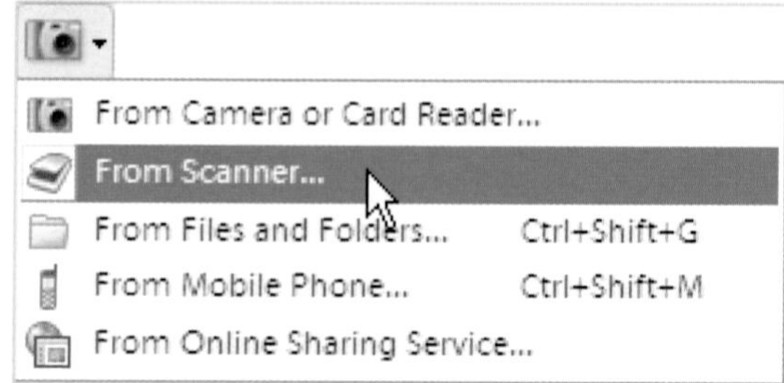

NOTE

When you get photos from scanners or digital cameras, you will also need a driver and perhaps software to handle the importing of the images. Windows has drivers that may accommodate your device, but you most likely will need to install the driver that comes with the device when you buy it. The software to handle the transfer of images will either be supported by the computer software you are using, as in Photoshop Elements, or you will have to install software that comes with the device, as you did with the driver. The Adobe Downloader will start by default when you connect a recognized camera or card reader to the computer.

NOTE

If you transfer a photo from the camera to a file on your hard drive or network, open the file as you normally would in Photoshop Elements.

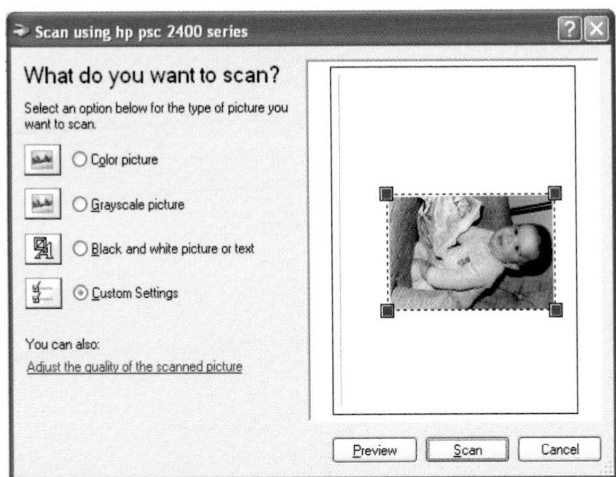

–Or –

Click the **File** menu, click **Get Photos**, and click **From Scanner**. The Get Photos From Scanner dialog box appears.

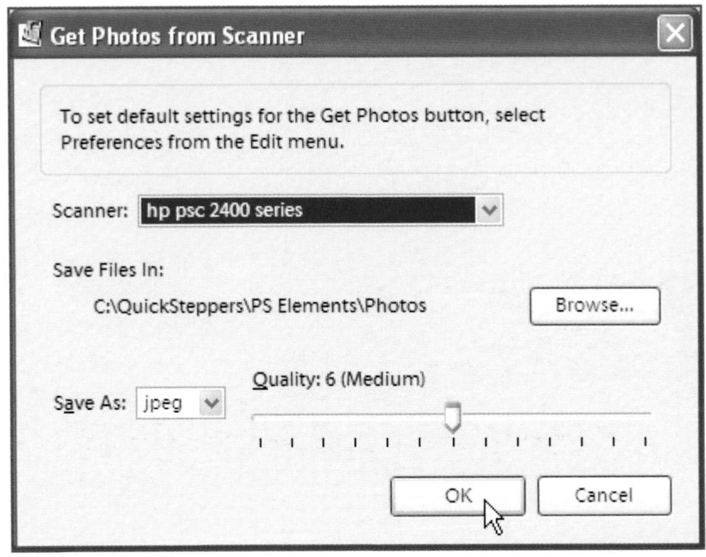

3. Click the **Scanner** down arrow, and select your scanner.
4. Click **Browse** to change where your scanned files will be saved. The default location is My Pictures\Adobe\Scanned Photos.
5. In the **Save As** area, click the down arrow and select the file type (JPEG, TIFF, or PNG).
6. If you want the image to be of a higher or lower quality, click the **Quality** slider and drag it to the right to increase the quality; drag it to the left to decrease the quality. Remember that the higher the quality, the higher resolution and the larger the file size.
7. Click **OK** to start the scan.
8. The scan software starts. The dialog box and steps you take at this point will differ depending on your scanner. For instance, you may be asked what you are scanning: color picture, grayscale picture, black and white, or a custom setting. You may also be able to adjust the quality of the image by adjusting the brightness and contrast or the resolution. You may be able to preview the image before starting the scan.

> **TIP**
>
> Scan the photograph for the highest resolution for which the image will be used. The standard for display on a computer monitor is 72 dpi. If the photo will be printed, scan at the same resolution as will be used when it is printed (for example, 300 dpi). Scanning at a higher resolution is acceptable; scanning at a lower resolution is not. You can always down-sample, or reduce the image to a lower resolution and pixel size, for e-mailing or displaying an image on the Web. Even so, more than 400 dpi is usually unnecessary unless you're planning to enlarge the image when you print it.

> **NOTE**
>
> If you choose to scan a file directly to your hard drive or network, open the file as you normally would in Photoshop Elements.

> **NOTE**
>
> To set the preferences for a camera or card reader, click the relevant option in the Preferences dialog box. You can specify the type of camera, whether to use Adobe Downloader, select a location to save the files, and create a subfolder for tracking import date and time.

9. Once you have finished scanning the image, it will open in Photoshop Elements. Click **OK** in response to the message notifying you that you can return to the catalog to see all your photos.

SET SCANNER PREFERENCES

To set your scanner preferences:

1. From the Organizer menu, click **Edit**, click **Preferences**, and click **Scanner**. The Preferences dialog box appears, as shown in Figure 2-4.
2. Click the **Scanner** down arrow, and select your scanner.
3. Click the **Save As** down arrow, and select one of the following file types:
   - **JPEG** (Joint Photographic Experts Group) is used for displaying photos on the Web. It has its own compression, and some quality may be lost, but files will be smaller.

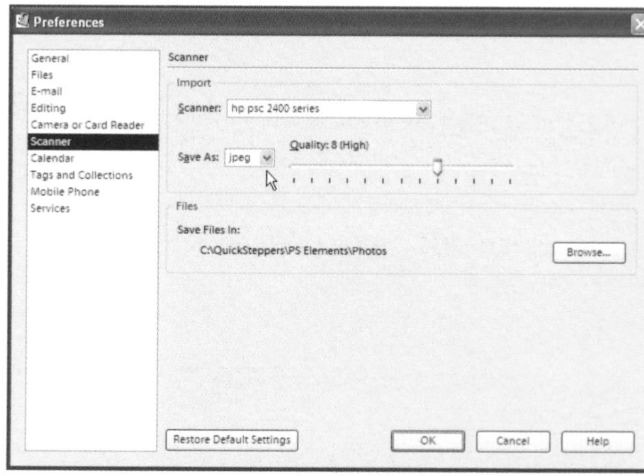

Figure 2-4: Use the Preferences dialog box to set defaults for your scanner and digital camera devices.

   - **TIFF** (Tagged Image File Format) is widely used for images that you will print, e-mail, display on the Web, and so on. Use this if you don't have a specific need for another file type. It is a larger file size than JPEG or PNG.
   - **PNG** (Portable Network Graphics), in the PNG 24-bit version, is similar to JPEG—high-quality photographic detail with compression.
4. Drag the **Quality** slider to the right to increase the quality; drag it to the left to decrease the quality.
5. Click **Browse** to change where the files will be saved.
6. Click **OK** to save the new preferences.

CAUTION

Be careful about increasing the resolution while increasing the image size, as it almost always results in distortion. If you want to increase the resolution, first deselect the **Resample Image** option and enter your new resolution. Then, if you want to increase the pixel dimension of the image with the higher resolution, resize the image again and this time click the **Resample Image** option using the **Bicubic** algorithm. Increase the pixel dimension by percentage, not pixels, and restrict the increase to no more than 110 percent. You can do this multiple times to get a larger image with little or no distortion if the original image is reasonably sharp.

TIP

You can select multiple contiguous file names by pressing **SHIFT** while you click the file name. To select noncontiguous files, press **CTRL** and click the file names.

Find or Import Images

To find images in your computer's files and folders:

1. From the Organizer menu, click **Files**, click **Get Photos**, and then click **From Files And Folders**. The Get Photos From Files And Folders dialog box appears, as shown in Figure 2-5.

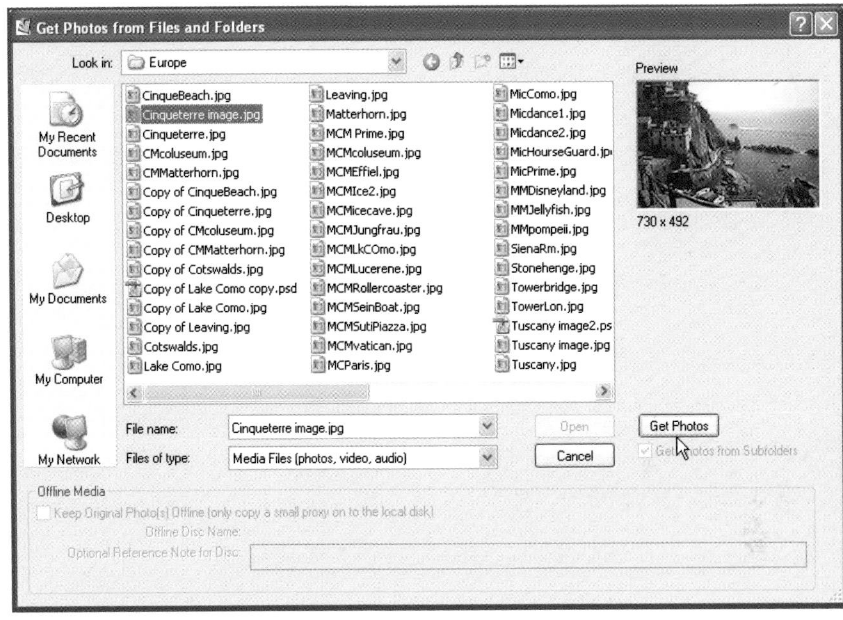

Figure 2-5: When you click a file name, its thumbnail image is displayed in the Preview pane.

2. Choose from among the following options:

- Click the **Look In** down arrow, and locate the folder that you want.
- Click **My Recent Documents** to find images you have worked with recently, and then click the file name to select it.
- Click **Desktop** to find images on your desktop, and then click the file name to select it.

You can also elect to search All Hard Disks, Drive C, or My Documents in the Get Photos By Searching dialog box.

- Click **My Documents** to find images stored in the My Documents folder, and double-click folder names until you find the file name of the image you want. Click it to select it.
- Click **My Computer** to search the folders and files on your computer; browse until you find the image file, and click it to select it.
- Click **My Network** to find photos on your network. Browse to the location where the image is stored. Click it to select it.

3. Click **Get Photos** to retrieve the photos. They are displayed in the Organizer.

FIND AND IMPORT PHOTOS

To find and import photos that are not in your catalog but that are on your computer or network:

1. From the Organizer menu, click **File**, click **Get Photos**, and then click **By Searching**. The Get Photos By Searching For Folders dialog box appears.
2. Choose between the following options:
   - **Exclude System And Program Folders** excludes system and program folders from the search.
   - **Exclude Files Smaller than __KB** excludes files that are under a certain size. Deselect this option to make sure you don't overlook small files. You can also change the default size by typing a new file size in the text box.
3. In the Look In area, click **Browse**. Find the file or folder you want to import in the Browse For Folder dialog box, and click **OK**.
4. Click **Search** to find the photos. Beneath the Search Results area, the number of files found in the folder are displayed.
5. Click **Select All** to see a preview, as seen in Figure 2-6.
6. Click **Import Folders** to add these photos to the catalog.

Figure 2-6: Find and import photos using the Search feature in the Get Photos By Searching dialog box within the Organizer to add photos to the catalog.

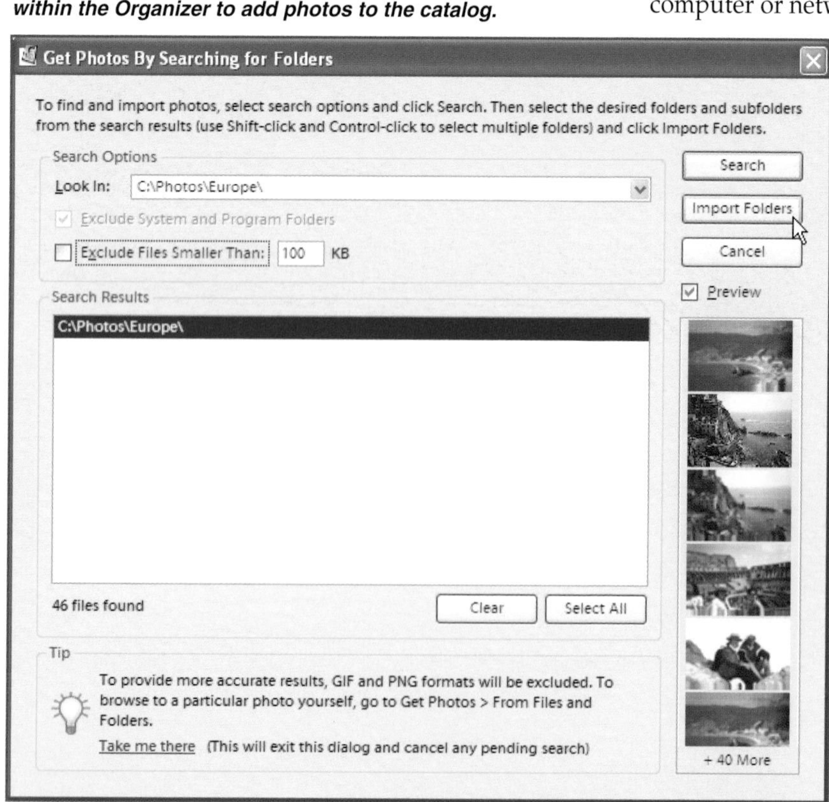

Use Video Stills

To capture a still photo from a video:

1. From the Standard Edit menu, click **File**, click **Import**, and click **Frame From Video**.
2. In the Frame From Video dialog box, click **Browse** to find the video file. Supported file formats are .mpg, .mpeg, .wmv, .asf, .avi, .and .mlv. (Mac OS supports QuickTime and .mpeg formats.) When you find the file, click it to select it, and click **Open**. The video is displayed in the dialog box, as seen in Figure 2-7.
3. Use a combination of these techniques to advance through the video:
   - Drag the slider to the frame you want.
   - Click the playback controls to play the video.

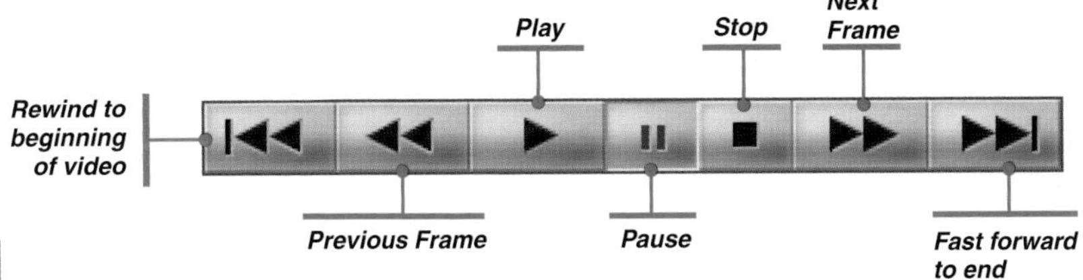

   - Press the **LEFT ARROW** or **RIGHT ARROW** key to nudge the video backwards or forwards through the frames, respectively.
   - Press **SPACEBAR** to capture a frame.
4. When you find the frame you want, click **Grab Frame**. The photo is displayed in the Editor.
5. When you are done, click **Done**. Your frame is displayed in the Edit area, where you can enhance and edit it as with any photo.

Figure 2-7: You can advance through a video frame by frame until you find the image you want, and then grab it for a still photo.

Organize Your Images

Photoshop Elements 3.0 has added an Organizer to its features. The Organizer has two main views: the Photo Browser and the Date View. Although you have access to some quick editing tools in the Organizer, you primarily manipulate the file rather than the image.

You can add a file to a catalog other than the default catalog (named Catalog—what a surprise!). However, be aware of what you are doing—having more than one catalog may not be the thing to do since you cannot view or work with photos in both catalogs at the same time; only one catalog at a time can be accessed. Instead, to differentiate photos, you can add them to collections instead of to a new catalog (recommended), tag them, and stack them. You can view files in a catalog by date, collection, stack of photos, version set of edited photos, or tag.

TIP

You can also access the Organizer from the Editor by clicking **Photo Browser** on the Shortcut toolbar.

Find Files with Photo Browser

To find a photo on your computer or network using the Photo Browser feature:

- After starting Photoshop Elements, click **View And Organize Photos**.

  –Or–

- While working with the Editor, click **Photo Browser**. The Organizer opens and displays the Photo Browser view, as seen in Figure 2-8.

  –Or–

- Use one of the techniques shown in Figure 2-8 to find an image or photo.

TIP

You can easily find photos using tags and collections. See "Organize Images Using Tags" and "Place Photos in a Collection" for more information.

Figure 2-8: Use the Photo Browser to find your images, and then catalog or attach tags to them.

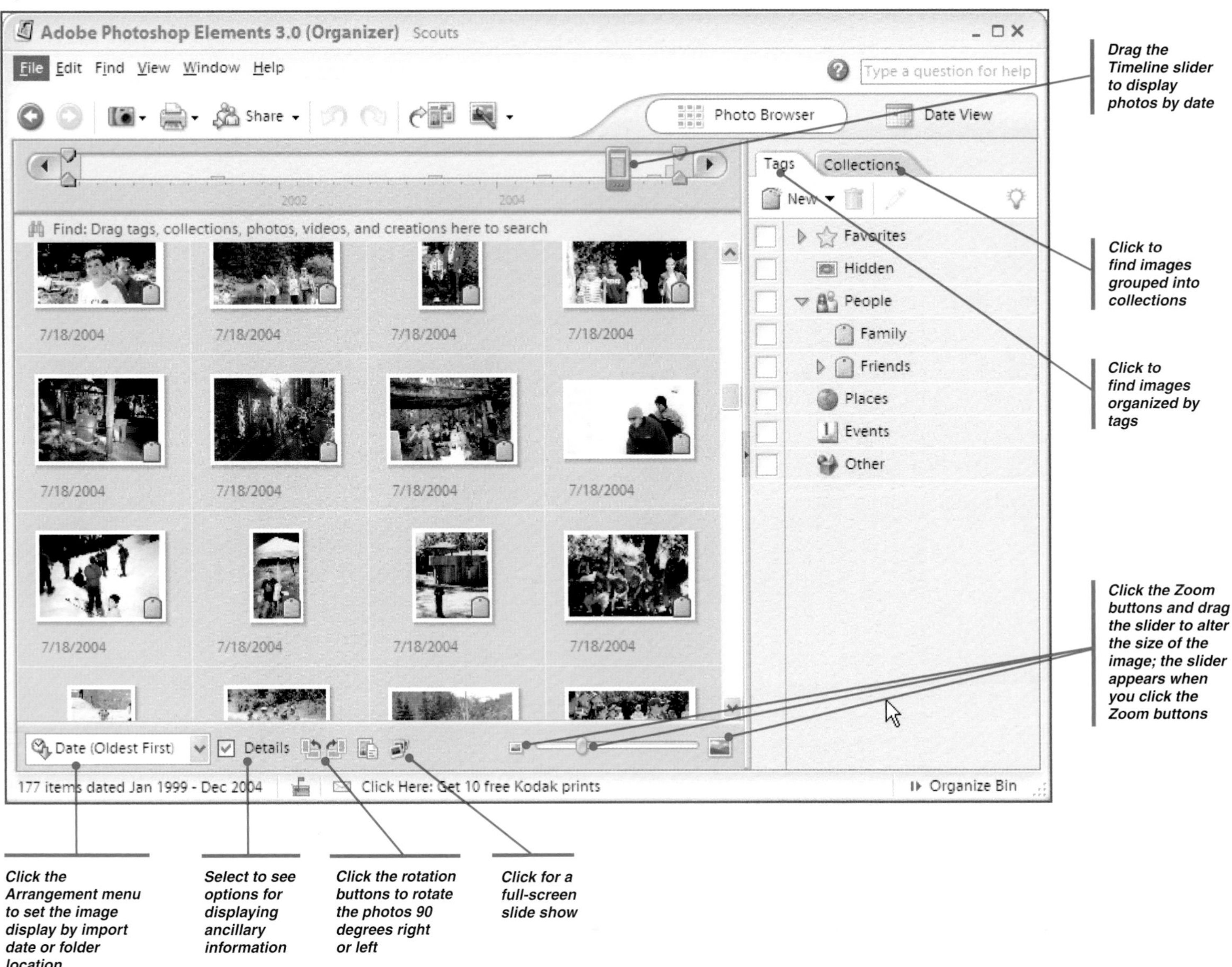
Adobe Photoshop Elements 3.0 (Organizer) Scouts
File Edit Find View Window Help
Type a question for help
Share
Photo Browser
Date View
Tags
Collections
Find: Drag tags, collections, photos, videos, and creations here to search
Favorites
Hidden
People
Family
Friends
Places
Events
Other
Date (Oldest First)
Details
177 items dated Jan 1999 - Dec 2004
Click Here: Get 10 free Kodak prints
Organize Bin
Drag the Timeline slider to display photos by date
Click to find images grouped into collections
Click to find images organized by tags
Click the Zoom buttons and drag the slider to alter the size of the image; the slider appears when you click the Zoom buttons
Click the Arrangement menu to set the image display by import date or folder location
Select to see options for displaying ancillary information
Click the rotation buttons to rotate the photos 90 degrees right or left
Click for a full-screen slide show

FIND FILES USING THE TIMELINE BAR

The Timeline bar, located under the Shortcut toolbar, is used to locate photos quickly by date, import batch, or folder location. The Timeline bar is tied to the Arrangement menu, located just above the Status bar. When you choose an arrangement option, the Timeline bar reflects that choice. The Timeline bar is organized by month and date; the height of the bars on the Timeline bar indicates how many photos are present at any given time, as can be seen in Figure 2-9.

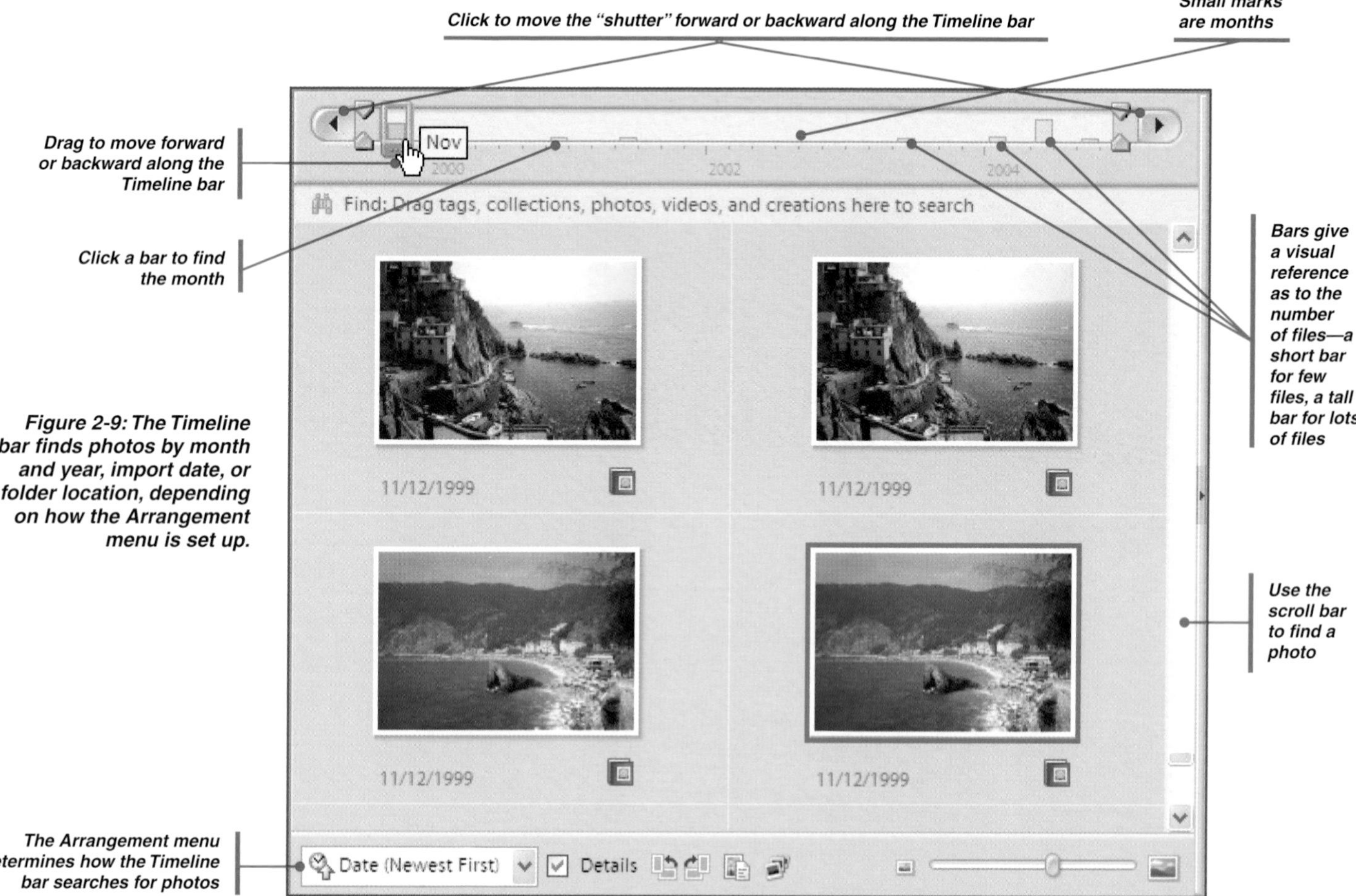
Click to move the "shutter" forward or backward along the Timeline bar
Small marks are months
Drag to move forward or backward along the Timeline bar
Click a bar to find the month
Nov
2000
2002
2004
Find: Drag tags, collections, photos, videos, and creations here to search
Bars give a visual reference as to the number of files—a short bar for few files, a tall bar for lots of files
11/12/1999
11/12/1999
11/12/1999
11/12/1999
Use the scroll bar to find a photo
The Arrangement menu determines how the Timeline bar searches for photos
Date (Newest First)
Details

Figure 2-9: The Timeline bar finds photos by month and year, import date, or folder location, depending on how the Arrangement menu is set up.

1. Click the **Arrangement** down arrow, and then click the option you want for the Timeline bar searches.
2. Click the Timeline month or place where you expect to find the photo you want. You may have to click and then scroll through the photos to find the specific one you want.

> **TIP**
>
> When you have clicked a bar (a month or folder name), you can then drag the "shutter" right or left along the Timeline bar.

USE THE FIND MENU TO LOCATE FILES

What if you have really difficult search criteria, such as all photos containing lime green, or all photos downloaded on January 1, 2005, or all photos with "Michael" in the caption? Don't despair; the Find menu offers many additional ways of finding files, as shown in Figure 2-10.

Find View Window Help	
Set Date Range...	Ctrl+Alt+F
Clear Date Range	Ctrl+Shift+F
By Caption or Note...	Ctrl+Shift+J
By Filename...	Ctrl+Shift+K
By History	▸
By Media Type	▸
Items with Unknown Date or Time	Ctrl+Shift+X
By Color Similarity with Selected Photo(s)	
Untagged Items	Ctrl+Shift+Q
Items not in any Collection	

Figure 2-10: The Find menu presents many ways to find photos and other media files if the quick and easy ways do not work for you.

> **NOTE**
>
> When you click a folder or month containing lots of photos, you can change the size of thumbnails to see more files at a time. Drag the thumbnail slider to the left to decrease the size of the thumbnails and increase the number displayed.

1. From the Organizer menu, click **Find** and select from among the following options:
   - **Set Date Range** finds photos taken between two dates. You may know approximately when you took the photo, but not exactly. This narrows the search.
   - **By Caption Or Note** finds a photo by a caption or note that you recorded on the photo. Perhaps you know it contains a particular word or phrase. You can match any part of a word or only the beginnings of words.
   - **By Filename** finds a specific file named in a way you remember, even if you can't remember where it is located. You don't have to know the file name exactly—you can search for file names containing certain characters.

QUICKSTEPS

RENAMING FILES

RENAME DOWNLOADED FILES

When you download photos from digital cameras or scanners, you may find that the file names are meaningless, containing a sequence of letters and numbers only a computer could love. To give your photos a name you can relate to:

1. In the Organizer, click a thumbnail to select it, click **File**, and then click **Rename**. The Rename dialog box appears.
2. Type the new name and click **OK**.

–Or–

1. Right-click the thumbnail image and click **Show Properties**. The Properties dialog box appears, as shown in Figure 2-11.
2. Highlight the name to select it, and then type the new name.
3. Click the **Close** button (the X in the upper-right corner) to close the dialog box.

RENAME A BATCH OF FILES

To rename a batch of files in the Organizer:

1. Select the files to be renamed. If the files are contiguous, press SHIFT and click the first and last files. If the files are noncontiguous, click CTRL and click the individual files.
2. Click **File** and then click **Rename**.
3. In the Rename dialog box under Common Base Name, type the name that will be common to the selected photos.
4. Click **OK**. Photoshop Elements will add a sequential number to each photo so that it will be unique, such as "Philmont Hike-1.jpg."

- **By History** finds photos imported or received on a date, e-mailed to someone, printed or exported on a date, ordered or shared online, used in a creation, or located in a Web Photo Gallery.
- **By Media Type** finds a file by its media type, such as photos, videos, audio files, creations, or audio captions.
- **Items With Unknown Date Or Time** finds files without any identifying time or date records.
- **By Color Similarity With Selected Photos** finds photos with similar coloring to a selected photo.
- **Untagged Items** finds all files that have not been tagged.
- **Items Not In Any Collection** finds files outside of any collections.

2. Enter the data required by your specific search dialog box, and click **OK**.

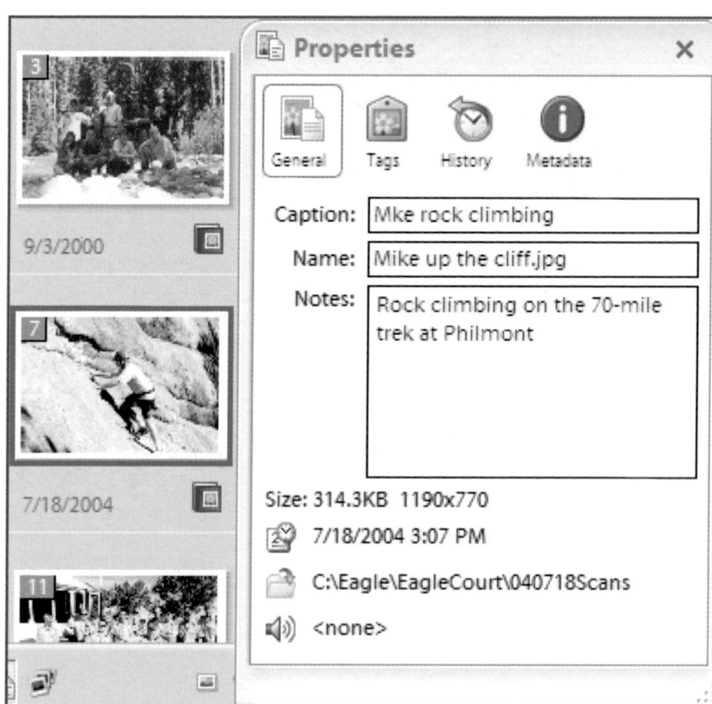

Figure 2-11: Right-click the thumbnail image, and click Show Properties to change the photo name.

MOVING AND ZOOMING FILES

MOVE FILES

To move files from one folder to another using the Organizer:

1. Click one or more images to select them.
2. Click **File** and then click **Move**. The Move Selected Items dialog box appears.
3. Click **Browse** to find the folder within which the photos will be moved, as shown in Figure 2-12. Select the folder and click **OK**.
4. Click **OK** in the Move Selected Items dialog box to move them.

USE THE ZOOM TOOL

To vary the size of the thumbnails in the Photo Browser, use the Zoom tool located above the Status bar. Use small thumbnails to scan through a selection of photos quickly; use large thumbnails to compare two photos for the best one or to check the details before you work with the photo in the Editor. Figure 2-13 shows the largest view. An example of smaller thumbnail images can be found in Figure 2-8:

- Drag the slider to vary the thumbnail size.

–Or–

- Click the **Small Thumbnail Size** button or the **Single Photo View** button, located on either side of the slider, to display the smallest and largest sizes.

NOTE

Photoshop Elements will add the file extension if you accidentally overwrite it.

Figure 2-12: Using the Move command in the Organizer for one or more photos retains the links in the catalog, as opposed to using Windows Explorer, for example, to move the files outside Photoshop Elements.

Click for single-photo view, as shown here

Click for smallest-sized thumbnails

Drag to vary the thumbnail size

Figure 2-13: Drag the Zoom slider to vary the size of the thumbnail display from the largest (shown here) to the smallest of six thumbnail images in one horizontal line.

TIP

If you find you have additional photos to move while in the Move Selected Items dialog box, click the **Add** button. The Add Photos dialog box appears, where you can locate and select multiple photos to add to those you want to move.

Start a Slide Show

The Photo Review feature, shown in Figure 2-14, is a great way to quickly go though your photos, making some changes; varying size to see them better; and rotating, deleting, and taking other actions. The photo is shown in full-screen size, which you can change. A toolbar is located on the top of the screen providing tools to manipulate the photos and run the slide show. Along the side of the screen are thumbnails of the other photos in the Photo Review.

1. In the Photo Browser, find the photo or photos that you want to show in the Photo Review, and click them to select them. Use **SHIFT** and click to select contiguous files; use **CTRL** and click to select noncontiguous files.
2. From the bottom of the photo pane, click the **Photo Review** button. The Photo Review dialog box appears with the following options:
   - **Background Music** Browse or select a choice from the list box.
   - **Page Duration** Click to determine how long each photo will be displayed before advancing to the next photo in the slide show.
   - **Include Captions** Click to display photo captions.
   - **Allow Photos To Resize** Click to enable photos to change size, if needed, to compare two photos at a time, for example.
   - **Allow Videos To Resize** Click to enable the videos to change size, if needed, for display requirements.
   - **Repeat Slide Show** Click to repeat the slide show after it has advanced through all the slides.
   - **Show This Dialog Each Time Photo Review Is Entered** Deselect to skip this dialog box.
3. Click **OK**. The slide show begins.
4. Click the tools in the toolbar to view the photos, and take any actions you want.
5. To revert to the Photo Browser, click **Stop** on the toolbar, or press **ESC**.

Figure 2-14: The Photo Review allows you to advance through a series of photos, manipulating the photos' sizes and rotation, as well making minor changes.

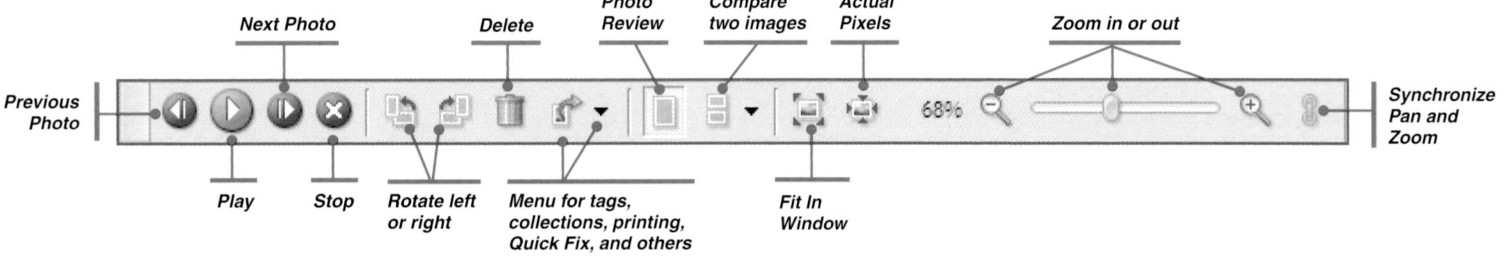

QUICKFACTS

USING PHOTO BROWSER ICONS

Some of the icons you will find in the Photoshop Elements Photo Browser include:

This is first in a stack of photos

This is a video clip

This is an offline image

Person-designated tag 

Place-designated tag

Event-designated tag 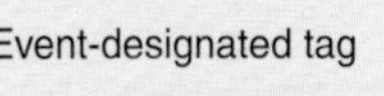

Other-designated tag

Contained within a collection

Contains an audio caption

REVERT TO A PREVIOUS IMAGE

To return to the previous image, click the **Back To Previous View** button on the Shortcut toolbar. To return to the current image, click **Forward To Next View**.

Work with the Catalog

Photos that you download to Photoshop Elements are automatically assigned to the primary catalog. The catalog does not contain images; it retains information, such as file name, date of creation, where the photo is located, notes or tags you've added, collections the photo is in, and more. All of your files will be retained in the same catalog unless you create a new one. You might do that if multiple users are accessing Photoshop Elements, or if you have a particular set of photos that you want to be permanently separated from the rest of your photos. In addition to photos, the catalog tracks other Photoshop creations, videos, and audio clips. Multiple catalogs can work against the efficiency of Photoshop Elements, but you may want to create them in some circumstances. In addition, you may want to back up or move files.

Catalog

Photoshop Elements keeps track of your photos through a Catalog.

Like a card catalog in a library, the Catalog is how Photoshop Elements tracks the location of files and remembers information about them.

Most people keep all their photos in one Catalog, which can have thousands of photos. You might want a separate Catalog for a special purpose, such as business photos. Each user of the program can have their own catalog.

New... Open... Save As... Recover...

☑ Import free music into all new catalogs

Cancel

CREATE A NEW CATALOG

1. In the Organizer click **File**, and click **Catalog**. The Catalog dialog box appears. 

1 2 3 4 5 6 7 8 9 10

TIP

When you create a new catalog, do not use "Catalog" for the file name since that is the default name that Photoshop Elements uses.

NOTE

If the links in your catalog are damaged, for instance, by a computer or power failure, you can repair them in the Organizer. Click **File** and then click **Catalog**. In the Catalog dialog box, click **Recover**. Click **OK** to proceed.

NOTE

You cannot move photo entries or tags from one catalog to another. You cannot open more than one catalog at a time, and you cannot search for entries across catalogs.

CAUTION

If you move a file outside of Photoshop Elements (using Windows Explorer, for instance), the catalog links to the file will be damaged and you will have a missing file. An error message displayed within Photoshop Elements when you try to view the image will allow you to browse to find the new location to restore the links in the catalog.

2. Click **New**. The New Catalog dialog box appears.
3. In the **Save In** drop-down list, accept the default location, or browse and find where you want the catalog to be stored.
4. Under File Name, type the name of the catalog.
5. Click **Save**.

OPEN ANOTHER CATALOG

1. In the Organizer, click **File** and click **Catalog**. The Catalog dialog box appears.
2. Click **Open**.
3. Browse to find the catalog if it is not in the default folder. Click **Open**.

CHANGE CATALOG LOCATION

1. In the Organizer, click **Edit**, click **Preferences**, and click **Files**. The Preferences dialog box appears.
2. In the Save Catalogs In area, click **Browse** to find the desired locations. The Browse For Folders dialog box appears. Find the folder name, click it, and click **OK**.

   –Or–

   Click **Make New Folder** to create a new folder for storing the catalog. Click **OK**.
3. Click **OK** when the folder and location are correct.

DELETE A PHOTO FROM A CATALOG

To delete a photo from a catalog:

1. Right-click a thumbnail image and click **Delete From Catalog**. The Confirm Deletion From Catalog dialog box appears.
2. To delete the file from the hard disk, click **Also Delete Selected Items From The Hard Disk**.
3. Click **OK**.

Place Photos in a Collection

Collections allow you to group photos according to a name that you select. You can have several collections that show the best copies of photos in your catalog. They are easily organized for display purposes.

CREATE A NEW COLLECTION OR COLLECTION GROUP

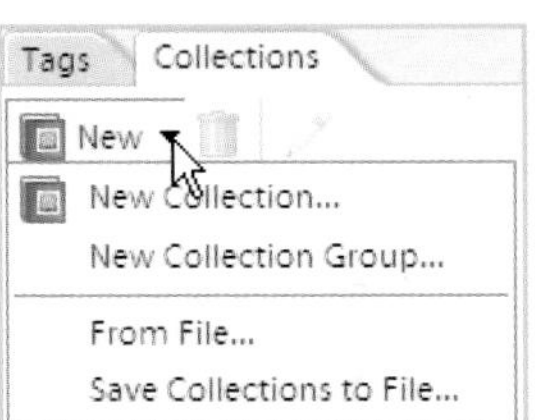

1. In the Organizer, click the **Collections** tab in the Organize Bin.
2. Click the **New** down arrow, and click **New Collection** or **New Collection Group**.
3. Select one of the following:
   - To set up a hierarchy of collections, click **New Collection Group**. In the Create Collection Group dialog box, type a name in the Collection Group Name field. If there is a parent to this group (a level above this one), select it from the Parent Collection Group list. Click **OK**.
   - To create a new collection, click **Create Collection**. If the collection is contained within another collection, click the **Group** down arrow, and click a name. Then type a name for the collection in the Name field. If you have notes, type them in the Note text box. Click **OK**.

DELETE A COLLECTION

To delete a collection:

1. Click the collection name in the Organize Bin to select it.
2. Click the **Delete** button on the Organize toolbar.
3. Click **Yes** to delete the collection.

NOTE

The first photo in a collection will become the icon for it. If you want to use a different icon, see "Change the Icon for a Collection."

QUICKFACTS

USING COLLECTIONS

Collections organize photos by displaying them as a group. You can determine what the collection will be; for instance, it can be the name of a person or an event such as a wedding. A photo can be in more than one collection and can be placed in a specific place in the collection. You can have two-tier collections in which a top-level collection contains subcollections, for example, a "Pets" collection that contains subcollections of "Domino," "Smoky," and "Tank," as individual pet collections. You can only view one collection at a time. Collections may or may not have a unique icon identifying them. See "Place Photos in a Collection" for more information.

CAUTION

Be sure to click the Delete button in the Organize Bin and do not press the **DELETE** key on your keyboard. Pressing the **DELETE** key will result in your photos being deleted instead of the collection. When you delete a collection using the Organize Bin Delete button, the photos are not deleted, only the collection links to them are.

ADD ONE OR MORE PHOTOS TO A COLLECTION

To add photos to a collection:

1. Display all the photos by clicking **Back To All Photos**, if necessary, to find the photos you want to add.
2. Click the photos to select them. To select contiguous photos, press **SHIFT** while you click the first and last photos. To select noncontiguous photos, press **CTRL** and click the photos to select them. They are highlighted with a blue border.
3. Click the name (not the check box) of one or more collections.
4. Perform one of these tasks:
   - Drag a highlighted photo to one or more collections.
   - Drag the collection name to one of the photos.

Even though only one photo is physically dragged to the collection, all selected photos are linked to it and deposited in the collection as well.

VIEW A COLLECTION

To see the photos in a collection:

1. In the Organizer, click **Window** and click **Organize Bin** to display the collections.
2. Click the **Collections** tab.
3. Click the check box next to the collection name. A binoculars icon is placed in the check box.

The photos will be displayed as thumbnails, as seen in Figure 2-15.

Figure 2-15: Place a check mark next to the collection name to display the photos in it. You'll see a binoculars icon next to the selected collection name.

Figure 2-16: The first photo in a collection is used as the icon, but it can be changed to another photo in the collection or to one on your computer or network.

CHANGE THE ICON FOR A COLLECTION

To change the identifying icon for a collection:

1. If the Organize Bin is not visible, from the Organizer menu, click **Window** and click **Organize Bin**.
2. Click the **Collections** tab. Click the collection name to select it (not the check box).
3. Click the **Edit** button in the Collection tab toolbar. The Edit Collections dialog box appears. 
4. Click **Edit Icon**. The Edit Collection Icon dialog box appears, as seen in Figure 2-16.
5. Perform one of the following actions:
   - Click **Find** to look through the collection of photos and find one to substitute for the current photo. When you find a photo, click it to select it, and click **OK**.
   - Click **Import** to find a photo not in the collection. The Import Image For Collection Icon dialog box appears. Find the file name, click it so its name is in the File Name text box, and click **Open**. The imported photo will become the icon only; it will not become a part of the collection.
6. Change the size of the icon by dragging the selection box to the size you want. Click **OK** and click **OK** again to close the Edit Collection dialog box.

Work with Stacks

Use stacks to organize photos of the same subject into one item so that you can easily find them again and determine which photo in the stack is the one you want to view or edit.

CREATE A STACK

To create a stack of photos:

1. In the Organizer, select the photos to be stacked.
2. Right-click a photo and click **Stack**.
3. Click **Stack Selected Photos**. The photos are stacked, and only the top photo is displayed. The Stack icon identifies the photos as stacked.

QUICKFACTS

USING STACKS AND VERSION SETS

USE STACKS TO ORGANIZE VERSIONS OF A PHOTO

Stacks are used to arrange similar photos, usually for the purpose of keeping multiple photos of the same or similar subject together. For example, you might want to have several photos of your house available. You can go through the photos to find the view that is best for your holiday card. The newest photo will be on top, although you can rearrange them if needed. You can also merge stacks into one. If you are searching for photos by tags, only the top photo will be displayed unless you expand the display. You must expand the stack in order to edit, attach a tag, e-mail, or otherwise work with a photo other than the top one (see "Work with Stacks").

USE VERSION SETS TO TRACK PHOTO EDITS

When you edit or otherwise make changes to your original photo, a copy is made unless you resave it under the original name and suppress the version-set default. Photoshop Elements saves these edited copies as *version sets*. A version set is a special type of stack consisting of edited versions of one photo. These help keep your photo organization more streamlined so that you don't have multiple copies of a photo scattered on your hard disk. You can go through the edited copies, finding the best one for your purposes. You can stack versions sets together into one stack, and they will retain their unique version-set stacks. A version set for a photo can exist within a stack made up of other photos. The newest photo becomes the top and visible photo unless you designate another one as first. See the section "Work with Version Sets" for more information.

SHOW PHOTOS IN THE STACK

To show the photos in a stack so they can be edited or tagged:

1. In the Organizer, right-click the photo and click **Stack**.
2. Click **Reveal Photo In Stack**. The Photos From Stack pane shows the photos in the stack.
3. When you are ready to return to the regular photo pane, click the **Back To All Photos** button.

Icon identifying the photos as stacked

CHANGE THE TOP PHOTO IN A STACK

To change the top photo in a stack:

1. In the Organizer, right-click the top photo in the stack, and click **Stack**.
2. Click **Reveal Photos In Stack**. The photos are displayed, as seen in Figure 2-17.
3. Right-click the photo you want to be the top one, click **Stack**, and then click **Set As Top Photo**.

DELETE PHOTOS IN A STACK

To delete photos in a stack:

1. In the Organizer, right-click the top photo in the stack, and click **Stack**.
2. Click **Reveal Photos In Stack** to display all the photos:
   - To delete a photo from the stack without deleting the stack, right-click the photo, click **Stack**, and click **Remove Photo From Stack**. The photo will not be deleted from the catalog or the computer.

Figure 2-17: Photos in a stack allow you to keep several photos of the same subject together so you can easily examine and compare them.

NOTE

If the Organize Bin is not visible, click **Window** and click the **Organize Bin** check box.

- To delete a photo from the stack *and* the computer, click the photo and press the **DELETE** key.
- To delete all photos in a stack except for the top one when viewing the top photo in the stack in normal view, right-click the top photo, click **Stack**, and click **Flatten Stack**. (If you want the photos also removed from the hard disk, click **Also Delete Photos From The Hard Disk**.) Click **OK**.

> **TIP**
>
> To delete all photos in a version set *except* for the original photo, in the Organizer, right-click the photo, click **Version Set**, and click **Revert To Original**.

Figure 2-18: *Version sets contain edited copies of one photo, and are a form of a stack, which you can manipulate by right-clicking the photo to view the context menu shown here.*

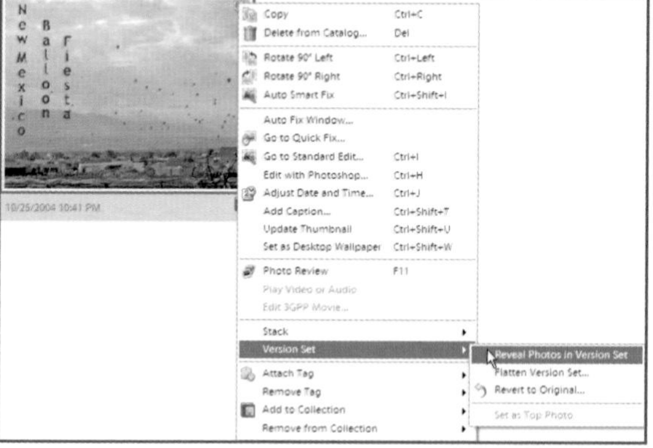

Work with Version Sets

Version sets group multiple copies of one photo. When you edit a photo and then save the edited file, it is automatically saved as a version set of the original photo. You can change this by deselecting that option in the Save As dialog box. Version sets are a form of a stack, and have many of the same commands, as seen in Figure 2-18. A version set is identified by this icon:

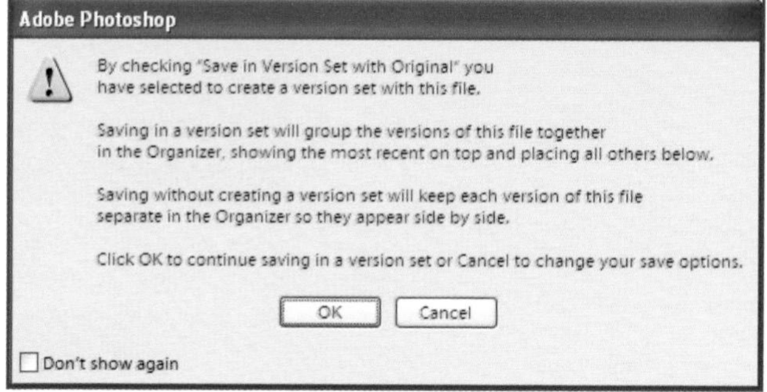

DISPLAY VERSION-SET PHOTOS

To display the photos contained in a version set:

1. In the Organizer, right-click the photo and click **Version Set**.
2. Click **Reveal Photos In Version Set**. The photos are displayed.

DELETE VERSION SETS

To delete all photos in a version set except for the top one by flattening it (reducing the stack to a single image):

1. In the Organizer, right-click the photo and click **Version Set**.
2. Click **Flatten Version Set**. You are warned that all photos will be deleted except for the top photo.

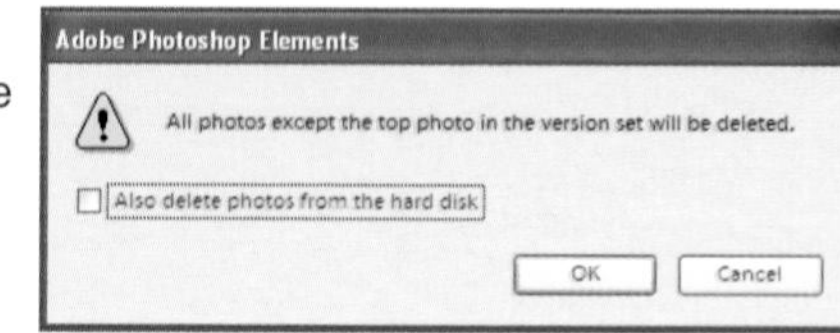

3. To delete the photos from your hard disk as well as the version set, select the **Also Delete Photos From The Hard Disk** check box.
4. Click **OK** to complete the flattening of the version set.

Organize Images Using Tags

You can tag photos with one or more names or phrases that identify the photo, or facilitate finding all photos related to that name or phrase. For example, you may want to tag all photos showing your pet, Fido. You can then display all tagged photos containing Fido, regardless of when the photo was taken or under what circumstances.

SET TAG PREFERENCES

1. In the Organizer, click the **Edit** menu, click **Preferences**, and click **Tags And Collections**. The Preferences dialog box for tags and collections appears, as shown in Figure 2-19.

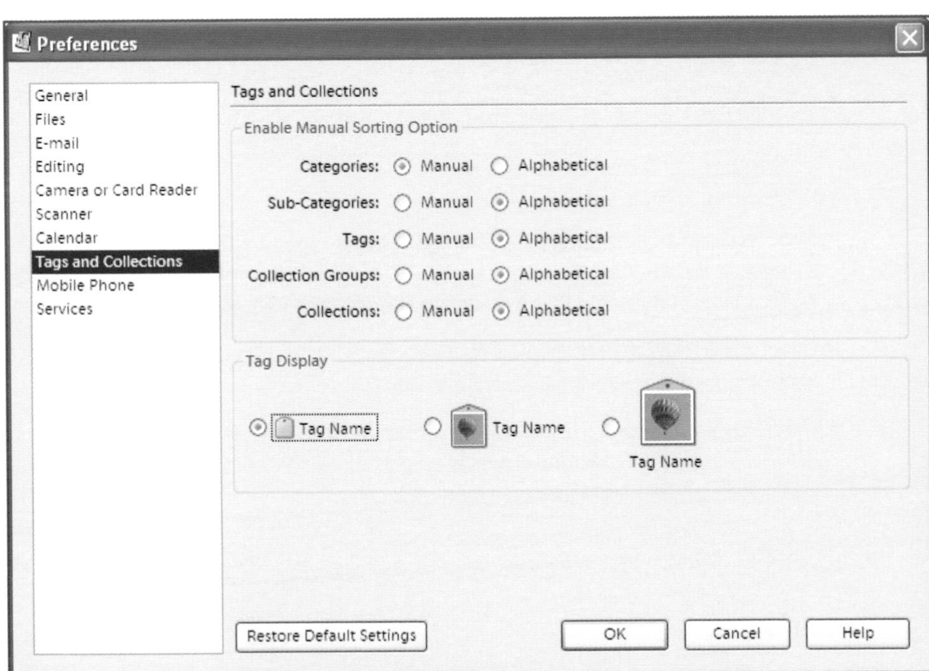

Figure 2-19: Set preferences for tags to be sorted alphabetically or manually, and select the size at which tags will be displayed.

2. Select from among the following options:
   - In the Enable Manual Sorting Options area, click the **Manual** option next to Tags to change the sort from alphabetical (the default) to manual. With manual sorting, you drag the tagged photos in the order you want them to be displayed. With alphabetical, the tags are automatically sorted by name.
   - In the Tag Display area, click the tag icon representing the size you want the tag to be.
   - To restore the original defaults for all the tags and collections options, click **Restore Default Settings**. Remember that this will restore all the options in the dialog box.
3. Click **OK** when finished. Your preferences are applied.

QUICKSTEPS

VIEWING PHOTO PROPERTIES

Properties for each photo can be displayed in the Photo Browser or the Organizer Bin.

DISPLAY AND CHANGE PROPERTIES

To display properties for a file:

1. In the Organizer, select a file. This can be done in either the Photo Browser or the Date View.
2. Right-click the file and click **Show Properties**. The Properties dialog box appears.

   –Or–

   Click the **Show Or Hide Properties** button on the toolbar beneath the Photo pane.

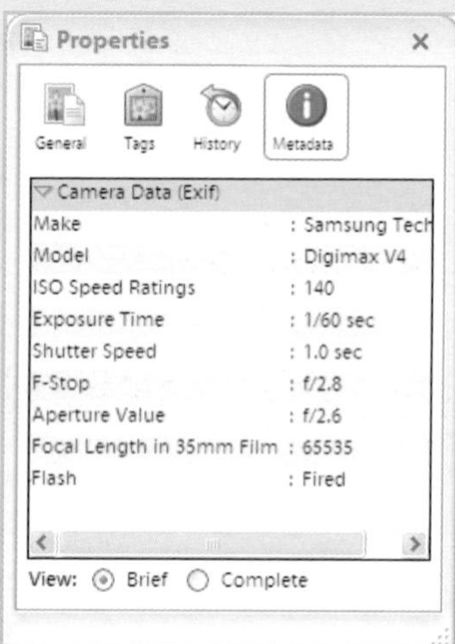

3. Select from among the following options:
   - Click **General** to see information such as file name, notes, size of the file, the time it was created, where the file is located, and any sound files that are attached to it. You can add a caption, change the file name, and add notes in this view.

Continued...

CREATE A TAG

1. In the Organizer, click the **Window** menu and click **Organizer Bin** if it is not visible.
2. Click the **Tags** tab in the Organizer Bin.
3. Click the **New** button in the Tags toolbar. Choose from among the following options:

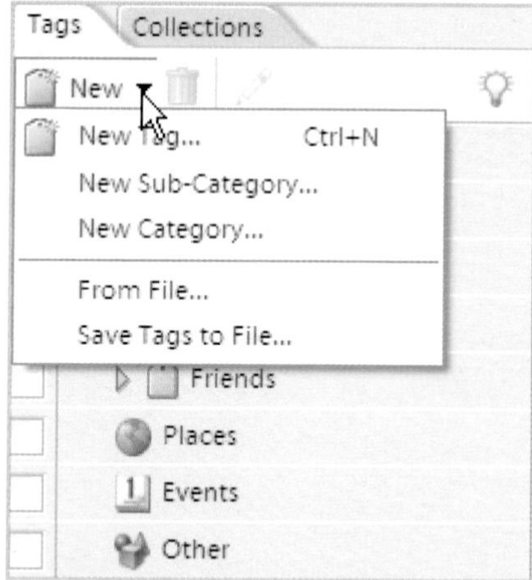

   - **New Tag** creates a new tag for a photo. Select the category (People, Places, Events, Other are the defaults. You can create others under New Sub-Category or New Category). Type the name, make any notes for the photo, and click **OK**.
   - **New Sub-Category** creates a category beneath another one. Type the subcategory name, choose the parent category, and click **OK**.
   - **New Category** creates a new category other than the People, Places, Events, or Other defaults. Click **Choose Color** to select a color for the new tag, type the category name, click a category icon, and click **OK**.
4. Click **OK** when the tag information is complete. The new tag or group appears in the Tag pane, where you can assign it to photos of your choice.

VIEWING PHOTO PROPERTIES

(Continued)

- Click **Tags** to see any tags that have been applied to the photo.
- Click **History** to see when the file was imported, edited, and other historic facts. You may see a thumbnail of the original version of the photo.
- Click **Metadata** (the default view) to see camera make, model, ISO speed, exposure time, shutter speed, and whether a flash was used. You can see either a summary of camera information by clicking the **Brief** View area (at the bottom of the dialog box) or a complete listing of all the data for the file, including brief camera information, plus the file name and creation data, photo dimensions, format, color mode, and more by clicking the **Complete** option in the View area.

4. Click the **Close** icon to close the dialog box.

DOCK PROPERTIES IN THE ORGANIZE BIN

If the photo's properties are not shown in the Organize Bin, you can restore the default setting.

1. Click **Window** and then click **Dock Properties In Organize Bin**.
2. Right-click the photo and click **Show Properties**. The Properties dialog box appears in the Organizer under the Tags And Collections pane.
3. Drag the handle on the top of the dialog box to reduce or increase its size so you can see information in the Tags And Collections pane.

TIP

The From File and Save Tags To File selections in the New menu allow you to save tags and restore them later. You can save tags for photos that may have been removed from the catalog temporarily or that you don't need right now. You can restore photos and tags later.

TAG A PHOTO

To place a tag on a photo:

1. In the Organizer, click the **Window** menu and click **Organizer Bin** if it is not visible.
2. Click the **Tags** tab in the Organizer Bin.
3. Create a tag for the photo if one doesn't already exist.
4. Drag the tag name in the Tags pane to the photo. The tag is displayed under the photo.

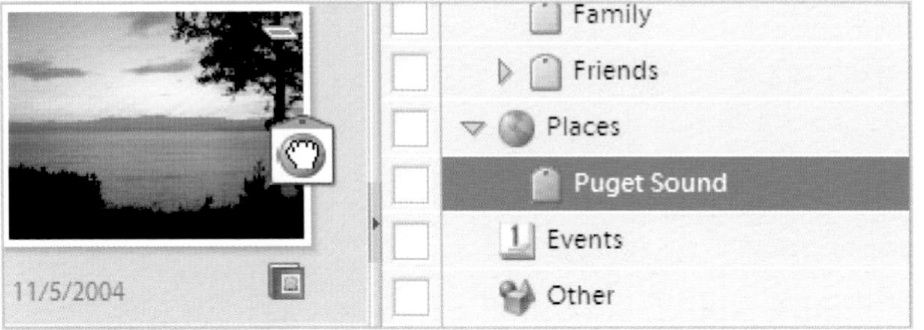

DISPLAY TAGGED PHOTOS

1. In the Organizer, click the **Window** menu and click **Organizer Bin** if it is not visible.
2. Click the **Tags** tab in the Organizer Bin.
3. Click the check box next to the tag name to display the tagged photos. A binoculars icon appears in the check box.

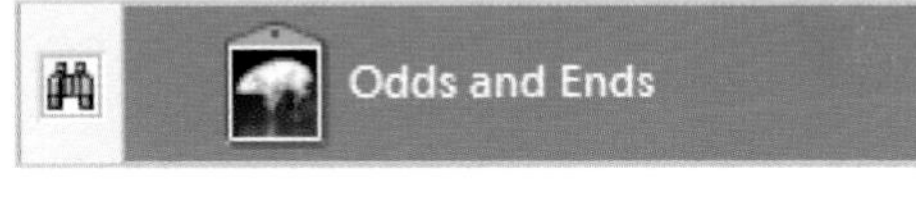

4. Click the **Back To All Photos** button, or click the tag name (the binoculars) to go back to all photos.

DELETE A TAG OR CATEGORY

To delete a tag or category:

1. In the Organizer, click the **Window** menu and click **Organizer Bin** if it is not visible.
2. Click the **Tags** tab in the Organizer Bin.
3. Click the tag or category name to select it.
4. Click the **Delete** icon on the toolbar.
5. Click **OK** to verify that you want to delete the tag.

TIP

You can remove a tag from a photo in one of two ways. If the tag is displayed below the photo, right-click the tag and click **Remove *tag name*** from the submenu. If the tag appears on the photo, click the photo or tag, and click **Remove Tag** from the context menu. Click the name of the tag to be removed from the submenu.

NOTE

To add copyright information to a file, open a file in the Editor, click **File**, and then click **File Info**. (You can also first find the file in the File Browser, click **File**, and then click **File Info**.) The dialog box for the file appears. Click the **Copyright Status** down arrow, and click an option from the menu. Type what you want to appear in the copyright notice, and type the copyright info URL (the web address where the copyright information can be found) as you want it to appear. If the photo contains a Digimarc watermark (acquired by you outside of Photoshop Elements), copyright information will already be contained in the dialog box.

Use Date View

Use the Date View to locate and view photos by date. You can locate and view photos by year, by month, and by day. Use the view that most closely approximates your idea of when the photo was taken or imported.

1. Click **Date View** from the Photo Browser or Editor. The Date View window opens with the default calendar view. Click the **Day** button beneath the calendar view. Figure 2-20 shows an example of the Day view.

Figure 2-20: The Day view in Date View shows all the photos that have been shot or imported on the selected day.

2. Click the current date bar, which in Figure 2-20 shows September 25, 2004. A Set Date dialog box appears. Enter the day, month, and year, and click **OK**.
3. To display the next or previous days, click the **right arrow** or **left arrow** buttons on the Day bar, respectively.

USE THE MONTH VIEW

1. Click the **Month** button on the bottom of the window. The Month view is displayed, as shown in Figure 2-21.

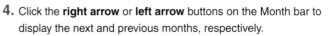

Figure 2-21: The Month view displays the photos imported or shot during the selected month.

2. To see the photo for a particular day, click the thumbnail in the calendar. The photo is displayed in the Preview pane on the right.
3. Click the **right arrow** or **left arrow** buttons on the Day bar to scroll back and forth through the days of the selected month.
4. Click the **right arrow** or **left arrow** buttons on the Month bar to display the next and previous months, respectively.

USE YEAR VIEW

1. Click the **Year** button on the bottom of the window. The Year view is displayed, as shown in Figure 2-22.
2. To see a photo for a selected year, click the thumbnail in the calendar. The photo is displayed in the Preview pane on the right.
3. Click the **right arrow** or **left arrow** buttons on the Day bar to scroll back and forth through the days of the selected month.
4. Click the **right arrow** or **left arrow** buttons on the Year bar to display the next and previous years, respectively.

Figure 2-22: The Year view displays the photos imported or shot during the selected year.

Process RAW Image Files

If your digital camera has the capability of capturing images in RAW format, you can use this format to capture all of the data recorded by your camera's image sensor. The resulting file is the digital equivalent of a film camera negative, which you then process before editing the image in Photoshop Elements. If you've experimented with the RAW format in the past, your only option for processing the image was the camera manufacturer's RAW processing software, which may or may not have been intuitive, or Photoshop 7.0 (with the optional RAW plug-in) or Photoshop CS. The RAW plug-in found

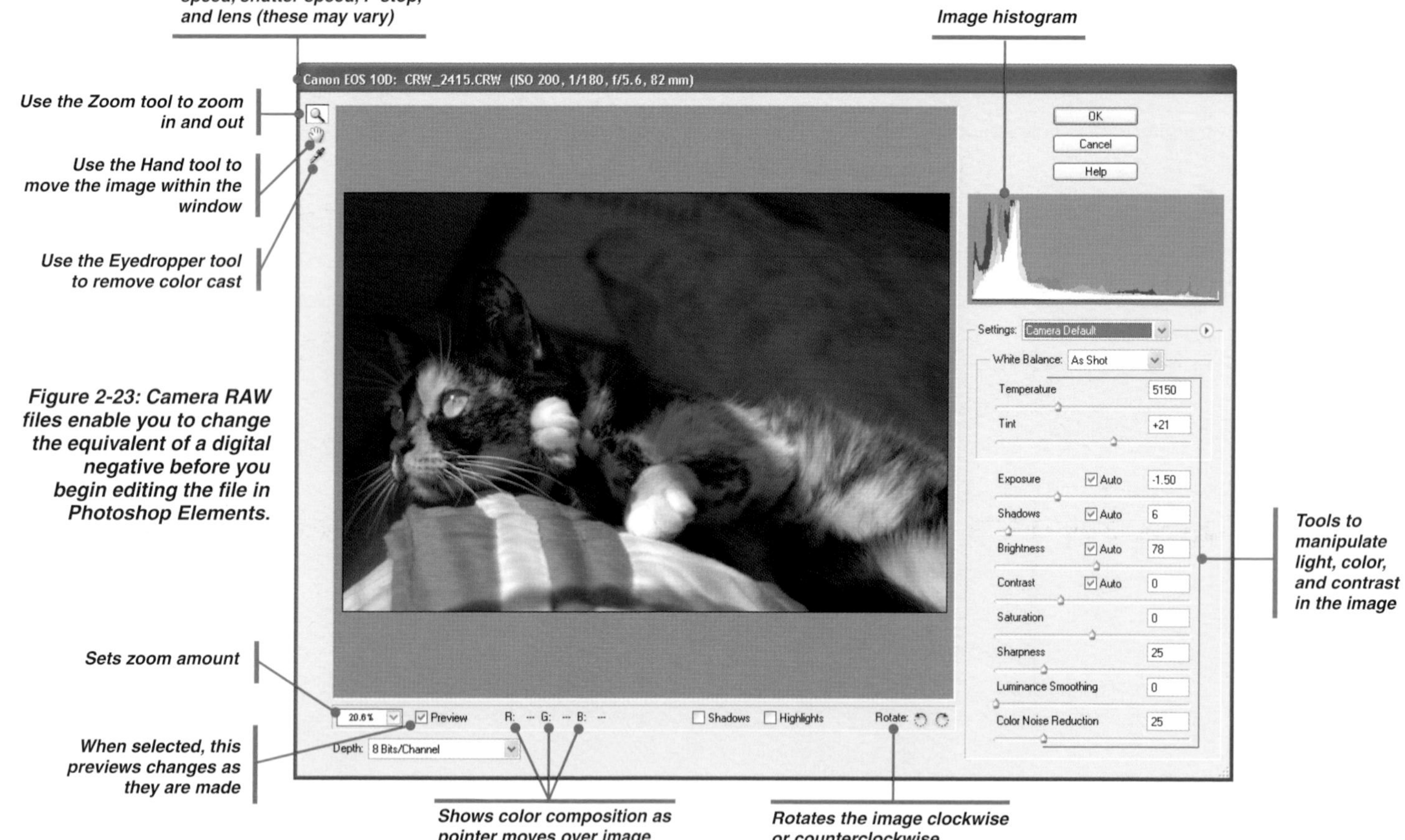

Figure 2-23: Camera RAW files enable you to change the equivalent of a digital negative before you begin editing the file in Photoshop Elements.

NOTE

If you choose 16 Bits/Channel, you have greater latitude when adjusting levels and applying color corrections in Photoshop Elements. A 16-bit image will also give you better color latitude when printing the image. However, some filters are not supported in 16-bit mode, and many other applications cannot read a 16-bit image. Unsupported filters and commands are unavailable in the applicable menu group. To apply a filter or command not supported in 16-bit mode or to save an image for use in another application, click the **Image** menu, click **Mode**, and then click **Convert To 8 Bits/Channel**.

in Photoshop Elements 3.0 is a derivative of the RAW add-on plug-in that was originally introduced with Photoshop 7.0.

Photoshop Elements does not support every camera's RAW file format. To find the digital cameras for which RAW files are supported by Photoshop Elements, go to http://www.adobe.com/products/photoshop/cameraraw.html.

Unlike JPG or GIF, RAW is not an acronym. Each camera manufacturer has its own proprietary file format and extension for its camera's RAW files, including RAW, RAF, CRF, NEF, RAF, ORF, and CRW.

The extension for thumbnail files is .thm. When importing a file from your camera to Photoshop Elements, do not select this format; instead select the actual RAW file for the specific camera used.

1. Click the **File** menu, click **Open**, and navigate to the RAW image you want to process.
2. Click **Open** to display the image in the RAW dialog box, as shown in Figure 2-23. The title bar displays the camera that captured the picture, camera settings, and the file name.
3. Choose an image bit depth from the Depth menu. Your options are 8 Bits/Channel (the default) or 16 Bits/Channel.
4. By default, Photoshop Elements analyzes the image and applies suggested processing settings, as noted by the Auto check boxes shown in Figure 2-23. To change the default, clear the check boxes and drag the sliders to process the image using custom settings as described in the following (if you decide you like the image with the automatic settings applied by Photoshop Elements, skip ahead to step 5):
   - **Settings** Click the appropriate setting for color, lighting, noise, and sharpening. Click **Selected Image** to retain the settings for the current file; click **Camera Default** to retain the settings set by the camera that took the picture; click **Previous Conversion** to retain the settings used for the last RAW image converted; or click **Custom** to establish new settings for this image. When processing a RAW image using custom settings, pay attention to the pixel distribution on the histogram in the upper-right corner of the dialog box. If you see a spike at either end of the histogram, you are clipping colors. (*Clipping colors* is when the colors are lost, or disappear, into all black or all white because of lighting or exposure effects.)

     Selected Image
     Camera Default
     Previous Conversion
     Custom

TIP

Select the **White Balance** tool (the eyedropper) in the upper-left corner of the RAW dialog box, and click an area in the image that you know is supposed to be pure white. This removes any color cast and changes the temperature and tints to neutral.

TIP

Place your cursor in the **Temperature** field, and hold the **SHIFT** and **UP ARROW** keys to increase the value by 500; hold the **SHIFT** and **DOWN ARROW** keys to decrease the value by 500. Release the **SHIFT** key to change the value by increments of 50. In the **Tint** field, hold the **SHIFT** and **UP ARROW** keys to increase the value by .10; hold the **SHIFT** and **DOWN ARROW** keys to decrease the value by .10. Release the **SHIFT** key to change the value by increments of .01.

TIP

Place your cursor in the **Exposure** field, and press the **SHIFT** and **UP ARROW** keys to increase exposure by .50; press the **SHIFT** and **DOWN ARROW** keys to decrease exposure by .50. Release the **SHIFT** key to change the value by increments of .05.

- **White Balance** Choose a white balance that reflects the lighting conditions under which the photo was taken. White balance alters the Temperature and Tint settings.
- **Temperature** and **Tint** Use these to fine-tune the white balance. Drag the **Temperature** slider to the right to warm the image with more yellow; drag the slider to the left to cool the image with more blue. Drag the **Tint** slider to the right to add a magenta tint to the image, which compensates for a green color-cast; drag the slider to the left to add a green tint to the image to compensate for a magenta color-cast.

As Shot
Auto
Daylight
Cloudy
Shade
Tungsten
Fluorescent
Flash
Custom

- **Exposure** Drag the **Exposure** slider to the left to darken the image, or drag it to the right to lighten the image. A setting of 1.0 is equivalent to setting the camera aperture one F-stop higher. A setting of –1.0 is equivalent to setting the camera aperture one F-stop lower. The Exposure slider will clip off light areas, forcing them to become white. Press **ALT** while dragging the Exposure slider to display any highlight colors, or dominant colors, that are being clipped. If you see areas of the image go totally white, these highlights are completely clipped to white and will reveal no detail.
- **Shadows** Drag the **Shadows** slider to the right to darken the shadows in the photo, or drag the slider to the left to lighten them. The Shadows slider will clip off dark areas, forcing them to become black. If you don't like the custom settings you've applied, press **ALT** to change the Cancel button into a Reset button. Click the **Reset** button to revert to the settings applied when the image was opened. Press **ALT** while dragging the Shadows slider to display any shadow colors that are being clipped. If you see areas of the image go totally black, these shadows are completely clipped to black and will reveal no detail.
- **Brightness** Adjust the overall brightness of the photo by dragging the **Brightness** slider to the left to darken it; drag it to the right to lighten it. Unlike the Exposure and Shadows sliders, the Brightness slider will not clip off dark and light areas.
- **Contrast** Adjust the overall contrast of the photo by dragging the **Contrast** slider to the left to decrease contrast; drag it to the right to increase contrast. This affects the midtones of an image.
- **Saturation** Adjust the overall saturation (color brightness) of the photo by dragging the **Saturation** slider to the left to decrease saturation; drag it to the right to increase saturation. For bright, vivid colors in an image, use a positive saturation. For duller colors, use a negative saturation.

TIP

While adjusting shadows, brightness, contrast, saturation, sharpness, luminance smoothing, and color noise reduction, place your cursor in the applicable text field, and press the **SHIFT** and **UP ARROW** keys to increase exposure by .10; hold the **SHIFT** and **DOWN ARROW** keys to decrease exposure by .10. Release the **SHIFT** key to change the value by increments of .01.

TIP

Click the **Shadows** and **Highlights** check boxes to display any shadows or highlights that are being clipped in the image preview. Shadows that are clipped to black contain no detail, whereas highlights that are clipped to white reveal no detail.

- **Sharpness** Increase the appearance of sharpness in the image by increasing the contrast on the edges of the image. If you see any artifacts in the form of white specks around edges in the image, you've applied too much sharpening. When adjusting image sharpness, choose **100%** from the Select Zoom Level drop-down list in the lower-left corner of the dialog box. Alternatively, you can click the **Zoom** tool, and zoom in on the image.
- **Luminance Smoothing** Drag the slider to remove any grayscale noise that may have occurred when shooting an image at a high ISO setting. Use the **Zoom** tool to reveal grayscale noise or colored specks.
- **Color Noise Reduction** Drag the slider to remove any noise in the form of colored specks that may have occurred when shooting an image at a high ISO setting. Use the **Zoom** tool to reveal grayscale noise or colored specks.

5. You can also make these changes to your photo:

   - **Image Rotation** Rotate the image clockwise or counterclockwise by clicking the rotate image buttons beneath the image.
   - **Depth** Set the bit depth for color channels between 8 and 16 bits per channel.
   - **RGB** When using the Zoom tool, Hand tool, or White Balance eyedropper, you will see numbers next to the letters that describe the red, green, and blue values of the pixels beneath the pointer.
   - **Shadows** Turn on the display of clipped shadows, shown in blue.
   - **Highlights** Turn on the display of clipped highlights, shown in red.

6. Click **OK** to process the image. After Photoshop Elements processes the image, it appears in the document window. You can now use the Photoshop Elements menu commands and tools to apply edits to the processed image before saving it in the desired file format.

How to...

Chapter 3 Making Selections

One of the most important aspects of Photoshop Elements is making selections, since it determines the accuracy and effectiveness of the modifications you will be making to an image. Without first selecting an area or subject, you cannot use many of the tools. Chapter 3 explains the use of the selection tools in creating, refining, and modifying your selections. Since a selection is also needed for cropping—an essential tool for modifying images—cropping is explained in this chapter as well.

Create Selections

Creating selections is really about defining exactly what will be edited or changed within an image. Or, you can make selections in one image to use in another image. When you select an area of an image, only that area can be changed until the selection is deselected. Photoshop Elements has four primary selection tools:

USING SHORTCUTS FOR SELECTING

The selection tools can be selected by typing a single letter on the keyboard. For selection tools in a group, move to each tool in turn by pressing the same letter. Photoshop Elements provides you with the following keyboard-shortcut options:

- **Marquee tools**: Press **M** on the keyboard once to select the previously used marquee tool; press **M** again to toggle between the Rectangular Selection tool and the Elliptical Marquee tool.
- **Lasso tools**: Press **L** on the keyboard once for the previously used Lasso tool; press **L** again to toggle between the Lasso tool, the Magnetic Lasso tool, and the Polygonal Lasso tool.
- **Magic Wand tool**: Press **W**.
- **Selection Brush tool**: Press **A**.
- **Crop tool**: Press **C**.
- **Move or rotate the selection**: Press **V**.
- **Zoom in on a selection**: Press **Z**.
- **Zoom out of a selection**: Press **ALT + Z**.
- **Select the Hand tool to pan through the image**: Press **H**.

- **The Marquee tools**, including the Rectangular Marquee tool, used to define a square or rectangular selection; and the Elliptical Marquee tool, used to define a circular or elliptical selection. Use these tools when the area you want to select is shaped like a square or rectangle, a circle or ellipse (respectively).

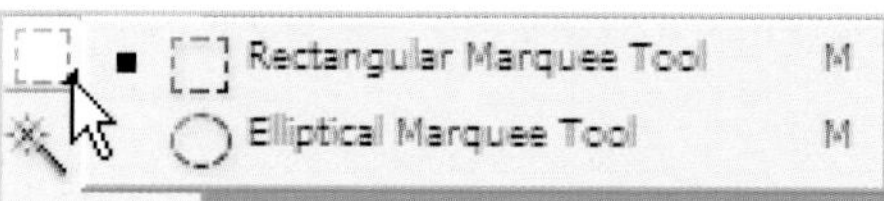

- **The Lasso tools**, including the Lasso tool, used to make a freehand-drawn selection; the Magnetic Lasso tool, used to make a selection that "snaps" to the edges of a shape; and the Polygonal Lasso tool, used to make a selection by connecting straight lines between points. Use one of the lasso tools when the selection you want is irregularly shaped: the Lasso tool works well with freeform shapes with a mixture of curves and straight lines; the Magnetic Lasso tool works well when you have distinct shapes or colors; and the Polygonal Lasso tool is used with shapes that are made up of many multidirectional straight lines.

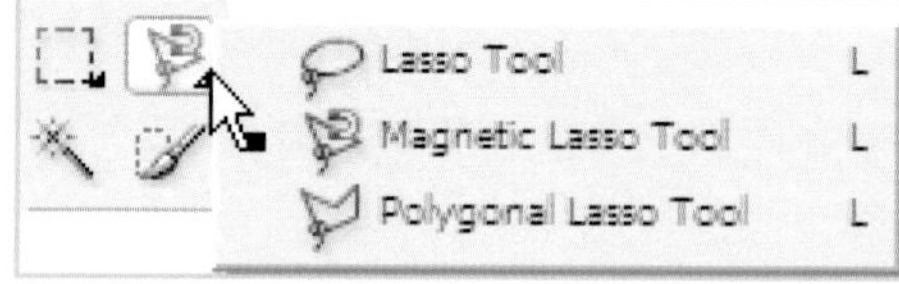

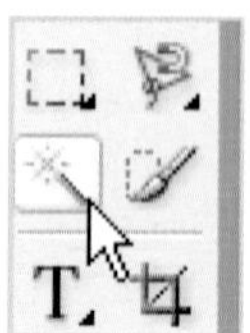

- **The Magic Wand tool** selects pixels on an image containing similar colors; you can control the degree of similarity that the colors must have.
- **The Selection Brush tool** paints areas you want to edit, or masks areas you don't want to edit by painting over them.

Select with Marquee Tools

The marquee selection tools create rectangular or elliptical selections.

MAKE A RECTANGULAR SELECTION

You can make a rectangular selection, as seen in Figure 3-1, with the Rectangular Marquee tool.

Figure 3-1: The Rectangular Marquee tool selects a square or rectangular area.

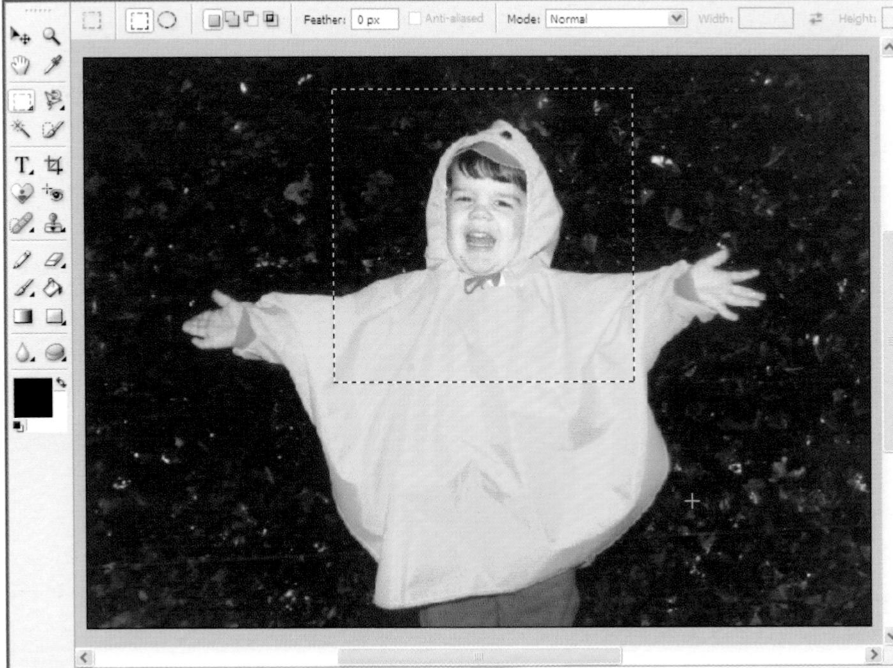

TIP

When making a selection with a marquee tool, you can hold down **SPACEBAR** to momentarily stop sizing the marquee and drag it to another area of the image. This helps when you have to fine-tune the positioning of the marquee.

1. If the Rectangular Marquee tool is not the current tool, click and hold the **Marquee tool** icon in the Toolbox palette. The Marquee Tool submenu appears. (You can also click the **triangle**, which indicates a submenu is available, in the lower-right corner to display the submenu.)

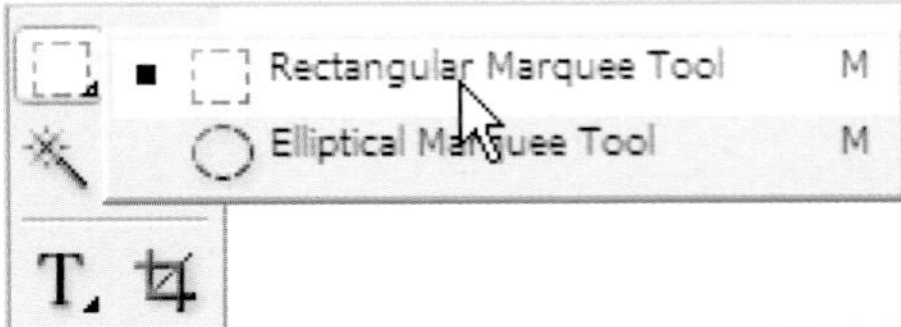

2. Click the **Rectangular Marquee** tool to select it.

NOTE

To place a marquee selection around the entire image, press **CTRL+A**.

3. Click within the image and drag to create the marquee selection.

   –Or–

   Hold **SHIFT** while dragging to constrain the selection to a square. Don't release the **SHIFT** key before you have completed the selection, or you will end up with a rectangle.

4. To adjust the position of the selection box, move the crosshairs pointer inside the selection. It will change into an icon of an arrow dragging a selection box; use it to drag the selection as needed.

MAKE AN ELLIPTICAL SELECTION

To make a circular or elliptical selection, as seen in Figure 3-2, with the Elliptical Marquee tool:

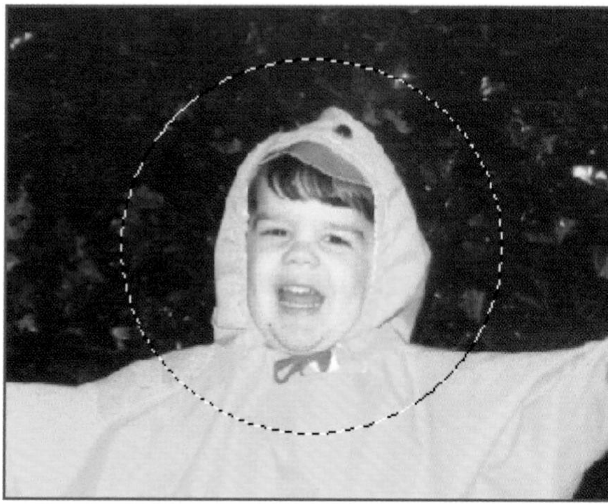

Figure 3-2: The Elliptical Marquee tool creates a circular or elliptical selection.

1. If the Elliptical Marquee tool is not the current tool, click the current **Marquee tool** icon in the Toolbox palette, and hold the mouse button down. The Marquee Tool submenu appears. (You can also click the **triangle**, which indicates a submenu is available, in the lower-right corner to display the submenu.)
2. Click the **Elliptical Marquee** tool to select it.

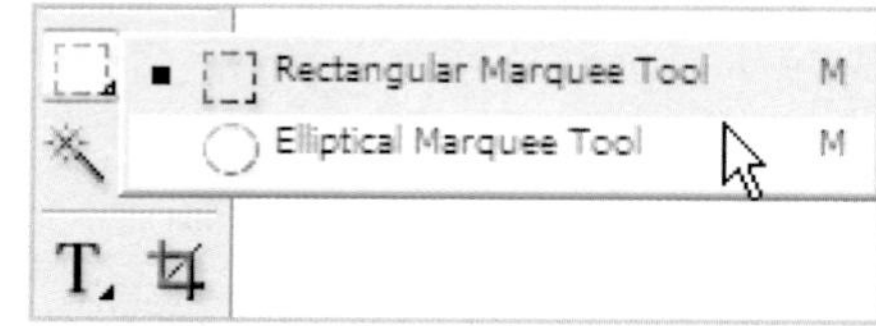

3. Click within the image and then drag to create the selection.

   –Or–

   Hold down the **SHIFT** key while dragging to constrain the selection to a circle. Don't release the **SHIFT** key before you have completed the selection, or you will end up with an ellipse.

4. To adjust the position of the selection circle, move the pointer inside the selection, and it will morph into an icon of an arrow dragging a selection; use it to drag the selection circle as needed.

CONSTRAINING YOUR SELECTIONS

MAKE A REGULAR SELECTION OF A FIXED SIZE

You can tell Photoshop Elements in advance exactly what size you want your rectangular or elliptical selection to be. With the Rectangular Marquee or Elliptical Marquee tool selected:

1. From the Options bar, click the **Mode** down arrow, and click **Fixed Size**. In the Options bar, the Width and Height text boxes will become available (they will initially be unavailable, but when you click Fixed Size, they will become available).

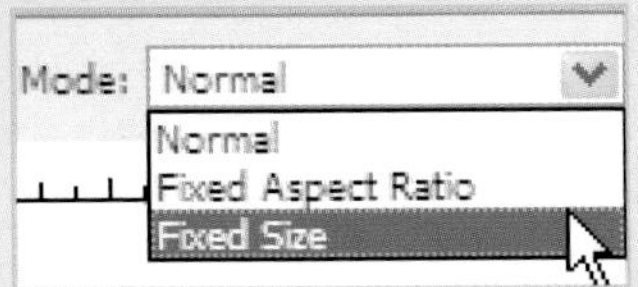

2. Type the width and height in pixels (px), inches (in), centimeters (cm), or millimeters (mm).
3. Click to set, or place, the upper-left corner of the selection, and drag to position it.

MAKE A SELECTION OF A FIXED-ASPECT RATIO

You can constrain the aspect ratio of a selection so that, for example, it is twice as tall as it is wide, regardless of the actual size of the area selected. If, for example, you want to make a selection that is twice as tall as it is wide, type 1 in the Width field, and type 2 in the Height field.

Then, with the Rectangular Marquee or Elliptical Marquee tool selected:

1. From the Options bar, click the **Mode** down arrow.
2. Click **Fixed Aspect Ratio**.
3. Fill in the **Width** and **Height** fields.
4. Click the image and drag to create the selection.

Select with Lasso Tools

Photoshop Elements has three different Lasso tools: the Lasso tool, the Polygonal Lasso tool, and the Magnetic Lasso tool.

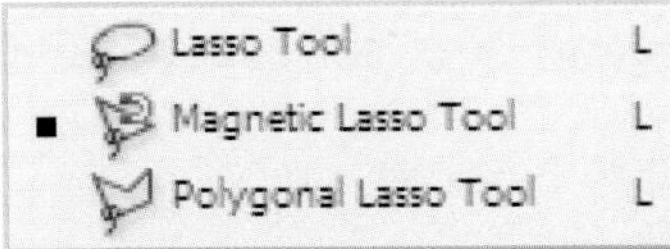

SKETCH A FREEHAND SELECTION

You can make a freehand sketch of the outline of your selection.

1. If the Lasso tool is not the current tool, click the current **Lasso tool** icon in the Toolbox palette, and hold the mouse button down. You can also click the **triangle**, which indicates a submenu is available, in the lower-right corner to display the submenu. The Lasso Tool submenu appears.
2. Click the **Lasso tool** to select it.

3. Click within the image and drag around the area you want to select as if you were drawing a selection.
4. Release the mouse button to close the selection.

You can fine-tune the way the Lasso tool works by changing its options, as shown in Figure 3-3.

SELECT AN AREA WITH THE POLYGONAL LASSO TOOL

Use the Polygonal Lasso tool to select a shape with straight edges. You create a selection made up of a number of straight segments.

1. If the Polygonal Lasso tool is not the current tool, click the current **Lasso tool** icon in the Toolbox palette, and hold the mouse button down. The Lasso Tool submenu appears. You can also click the **triangle**, which indicates a submenu is available, in the lower-right corner to display the submenu.

2. Click the **Polygon Lasso** tool to select it.
3. Click your image once to define the first point of your selection.
4. Move the mouse to a new position. A line segment follows the cursor.
5. Click to create the second point of your selection, move the pointer to define the third point, and continue to click and move.
6. Double-click to finish the selection.

You can fine-tune the way the Polygonal Lasso tool works by changing its options, shown in Figure 3-3.

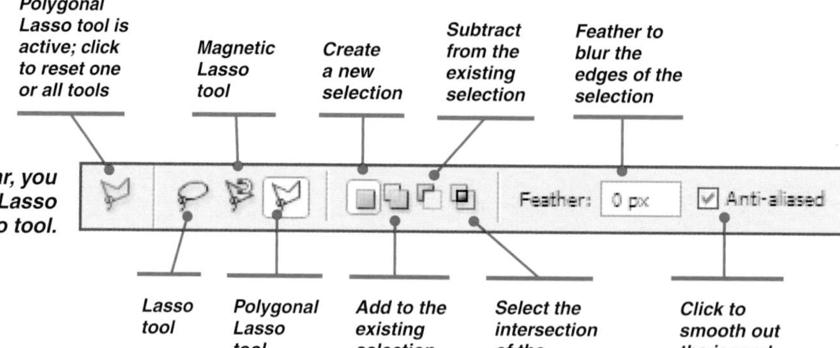

Polygonal Lasso tool is active; click to reset one or all tools
Magnetic Lasso tool
Create a new selection
Subtract from the existing selection
Feather to blur the edges of the selection
Feather:
0 px
Anti-aliased
Lasso tool
Polygonal Lasso tool
Add to the existing selection
Select the intersection of the existing selection and the new selection
Click to smooth out the jagged edges of selection

Figure 3-3: Using the Options bar, you can change certain features of the Lasso tool and the Polygonal Lasso tool.

TIP

You can combine selection tools in one selection. For instance, when making a selection with the Lasso tool or the Magnetic Lasso tool, hold down the **ALT** key and click to temporarily switch to the Polygonal Lasso tool. At this point, you can define the selection with points. When you release the **ALT** key, the Lasso or Magnetic Lasso tool will return, and you continue on with the selection, now defining the selection according to the active selection tool.

SELECT AN AREA WITH THE MAGNETIC LASSO TOOL

Use the Magnetic Lasso tool to select areas with sharp contrast, such as contrasting colors or shapes. The Magnetic Lasso tool will attempt to automatically follow and "snap to" the edges. You can fine-tune the way the Magnetic Lasso tool works by changing its options, as shown in Figure 3-4.

1. If the Magnetic Lasso tool is not the current tool, click the current **Lasso tool** icon in the Toolbox palette, and hold the mouse button down. The Lasso Tool submenu appears. You can also click the **triangle**, which indicates a submenu is available, in the lower-right corner to display the submenu.

2. Click the **Magnetic Lasso** tool to select it.
3. Click your image once to begin creating a magnetic-type selection.
4. Move the mouse to a new position. A line segment follows the cursor. Photoshop places small, square "anchors" as it goes.
5. Press the **BACKSPACE** key at any time to delete the last anchor.
6. Click the image at any time to force the Magnetic Lasso tool to place an anchor at the cursor location.
7. Double-click to finish the selection.

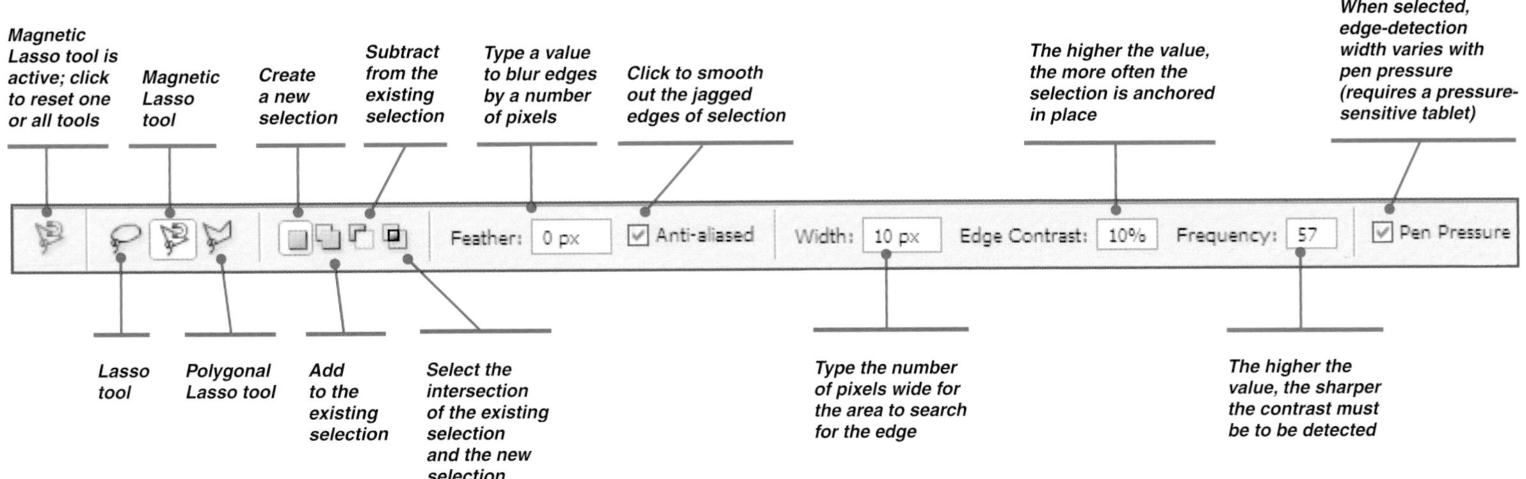

Magnetic Lasso tool is active; click to reset one or all tools
Magnetic Lasso tool
Create a new selection
Subtract from the existing selection
Type a value to blur edges by a number of pixels
Click to smooth out the jagged edges of selection
The higher the value, the more often the selection is anchored in place
When selected, edge-detection width varies with pen pressure (requires a pressure-sensitive tablet)
Feather: 0 px
Anti-aliased
Width: 10 px
Edge Contrast: 10%
Frequency: 57
Pen Pressure
Lasso tool
Polygonal Lasso tool
Add to the existing selection
Select the intersection of the existing selection and the new selection
Type the number of pixels wide for the area to search for the edge
The higher the value, the sharper the contrast must be to be detected

Figure 3-4: With the Options bar, you can change how the Magnetic Tool will function.

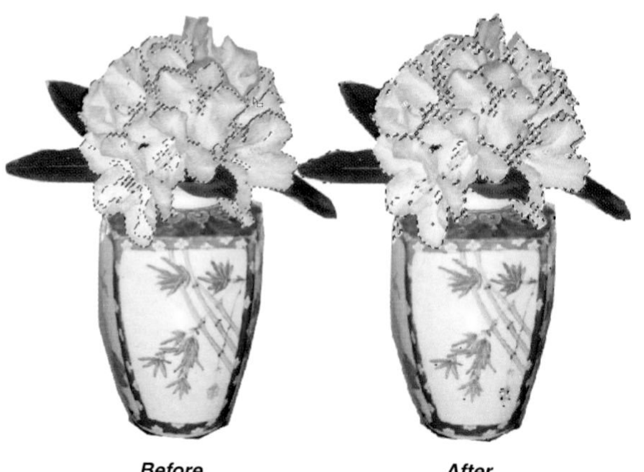

Before increasing tolerance, only a narow spectrum of color is selected.
After increasing tolerance, a greater spectrum of color is selected.
Before
After

Use the Magic Wand Tool

Marquee selections are great for selecting circles and squares and rectangles, but sometimes you need to select all the pixels of the same color, regardless of the shape. Then it's time for the Magic Wand tool.

SELECT AN AREA WITH THE MAGIC WAND TOOL

1. Click the **Magic Wand** tool from the Toolbox palette.
2. Set the **Tolerance** on the Magic Wand Options bar. When you first click the Magic Wand, it senses the hue, and the tolerance setting determines whether similar hues are selected. The larger the tolerance, the more colors will be selected. A tolerance of 32 is a good place to start. The "before" illustration of a vase and flowers has a tolerance of 32; the "after" illustration has a tolerance of 50.
3. Click to place a check mark in the **Anti-Alias** check box to soften edges of the selection.
4. Click to place a check mark in the **Contiguous** check box to select only adjoining pixels that meet the tolerance test. If you clear the check box, noncontiguous pixels will be selected. (See "Make Contiguous and Noncontiguous Selections with the Magic Wand Tool" for more information.)
5. Click within the area that you want to select.
6. If too many pixels are selected, reduce the tolerance. If too few pixels are selected, increase the tolerance. Click twice within the selection to reselect the area using the new tolerance levels. Press **SHIFT** while you click to select multiple selections.

The Magic Wand tool's Options bar, shown in Figure 3-5, gives you more control over the tool's selections.

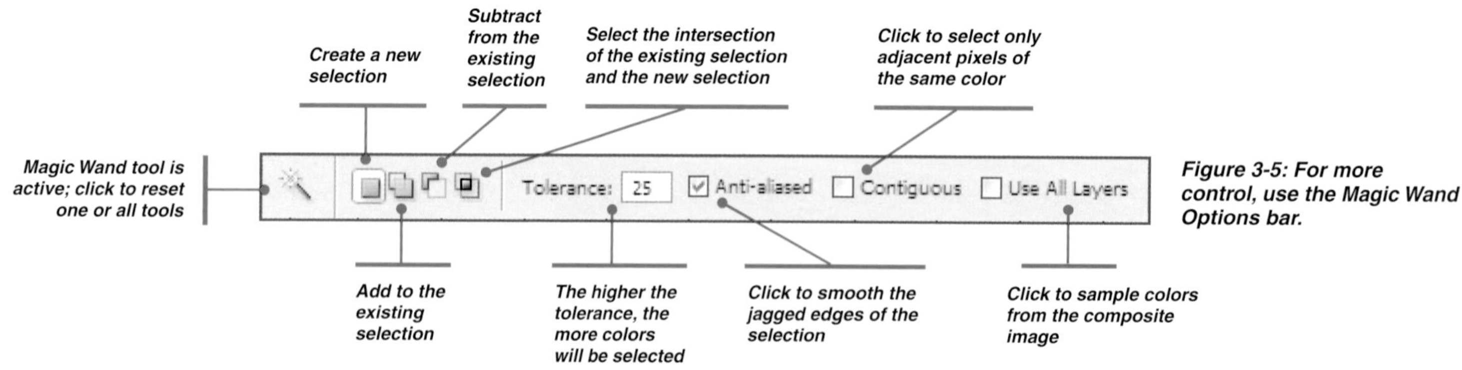

Figure 3-5: For more control, use the Magic Wand Options bar.

TIP

Once you have made color selections with the Magic Wand tool, you can adjust the color within the selection using one of the color tools that you may find by clicking **Enhance**, clicking **Adjust Color**, and then clicking **Adjust Hue/Saturation** or **Color Variations**.

MAKE CONTIGUOUS AND NONCONTIGUOUS SELECTIONS WITH THE MAGIC WAND TOOL

- If you click the **Contiguous** check box on the Magic Wand Options bar, the tool will only select a single contiguous area. Pixels of the same color elsewhere in the image will not be selected.

Only a single leaf is selected with a contiguous selection

- If you clear the **Contiguous** check box on the Magic Wand Options bar, the tool will select all pixels of the same color, regardless of their location within the image.

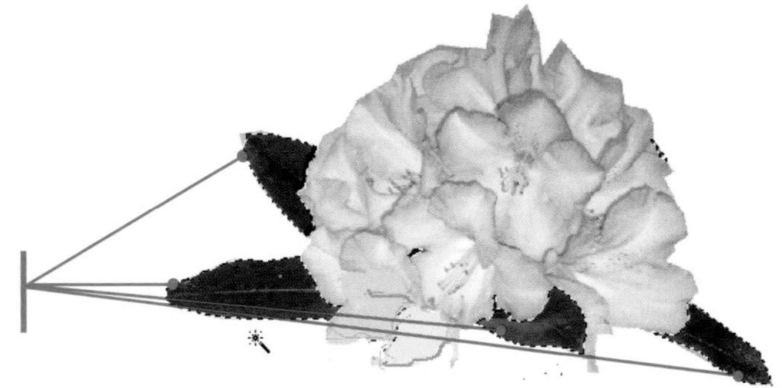

All green in the image is selected with a noncontiguous selection

Use the Selection Brush Tool

The Selection Brush tool enables you to make selections in an image by brushing over the area you want to select. You can use the Selection Brush tool after using other selection tools, such as the Marquee tools, to refine the selection process. Part of the Selection Brush tool's uniqueness lies in its ability to mask the selection so that you can see it clearly and modify the selection further if need be.

TIP

Press **ALT** while painting over the area you want to remove from the selection to undo the previous selection as you brush.

TIP

Use the Mask mode of the Selection Brush tool to paint over the area you want to select, switch to Selection mode, and then invert the selection. See "Invert a Selection" for more information.

USE THE SELECTION BRUSH TOOL

1. If you are using another selection tool, use it now to make your selection on the image.
2. Without clicking the Add To Selection icon, click the **Selection Brush Tool**.
3. From the Options bar, select one or more of the following options:
   - **Brush Presets**—Click a size and type of brush to use in making the selection. If you choose a "soft edges" brush, the selection will also have soft edges. If you want precise sizing for the brush, use the Brush Size and Hardness options instead.
   - **Brush Size**—Click the down arrow and click a size if the brush presets do not have the size you need.
   - **Mode**—Click **Selection** from the Mode drop-down list. The Mask option can be used to refine the selection and edit selected parts of an image.
   - **Hardness**—Click a percentage of hardness to define the brush preset more precisely. A higher percentage makes the selection edge harder. A lower percentage softens the edge.
4. With the Selection Brush tool, brush over the area to be included in the selection. If you have already selected an area with another selection tool, you can add to it or select an entirely different area; you don't need to press the **SHIFT** key. Figure 3-6 shows an example of making a selection with the Magic Wand tool and then using the Selection Brush tool to select a more precise area.

Figure 3-6: After using the Magic Wand or another selection tool, you can use the Selection Brush tool to refine the selection by brushing over the area, including the previously selected area, to include fragmented selections.

Figure 3-7: Switching between the Selection mode and the Mask mode allows you to correct and refine selections using the Selection Brush tool.

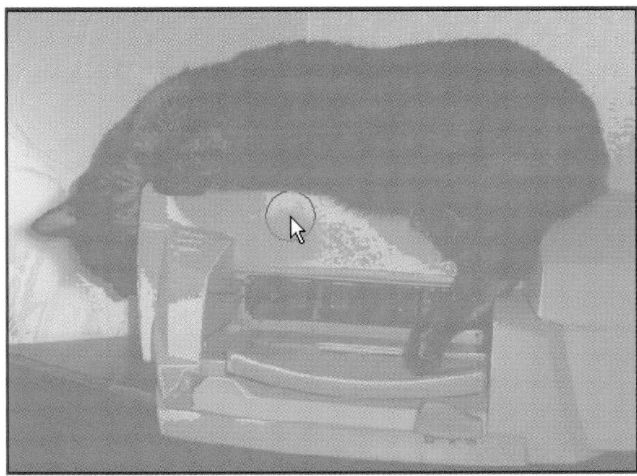

Figure 3-8: After working in Mask mode to get the selection as you want it, the finalized selection can then be edited as usual.

USE THE MASK MODE WITH THE SELECTION BRUSH TOOL

Using the Mask mode allows you to switch back and forth between selecting and excluding areas of an image. After you have selected an area, including the part you want to exclude:

1. Click the **Mode** down arrow, and click **Mask**. A layer of color covers the image, as seen in Figure 3-7.
2. Brush the areas you want to exclude from the selection. They are painted red.
3. To switch back to Selection mode, click the **Mode** down arrow, and click **Selection**.
4. Brush the areas you want included in the selection.
5. Continue to switch between the Selection and Mask modes until the selection is as you want it. Figure 3-8 shows an example of a completed selection.

Refine Selections

Once you have selected an area, you might want to refine it by making complex selections, adding to the selection, or subtracting from it. This section describes a variety of ways in which a selection can be modified.

Invert a Selection

Sometimes, the elements you *don't* want to work with are easier to select than the elements you *do* want, as in the case of a complex object on a simple background. In that case, select the background elements first and then invert the selection.

1. Use any combination of selection tools to select the background elements you do *not* ultimately want selected. An example is shown in Figures 3-9 and 3-10.

Figure 3-9: To select a complex object, it is sometime easier to select the simpler aspects and then inverse the selection, shown here with the sky selected using the Magic Wand tool.

Blue sky background selected with Magic Wand tool

2. From the menu bar, click **Select** and click **Invert**, or press **SHIFT+CTRL+I**, to invert the selection. Now everything that was selected is deselected, and everything that was deselected is selected.

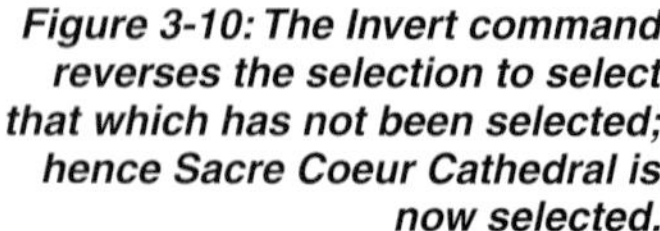

Figure 3-10: The Invert command reverses the selection to select that which has not been selected; hence Sacre Coeur Cathedral is now selected.

Selection inverted so that just the cathedral is selected

SAVING AND DESELECTING

You may have worked hours on a selection and want to save it to return to later, or you may want to clear, or deselect, a selection.

SAVE AND RETRIEVE A SELECTION

- To save a selection, click the **Select** menu and click **Save Selection**. In the Save Selection dialog box, type a name for the selection, and click **OK**. (If the selection is a modification of an existing saved selection, click the **Selection** down arrow, and click the name to override the previously saved selection with your modified version.)
- To retrieve a selection, open the image pertaining to the selection, click the **Select** menu and click **Load Selection**. In the Load Selection dialog box, click the **Selection** down arrow, click the name of the selection, and click **OK**.

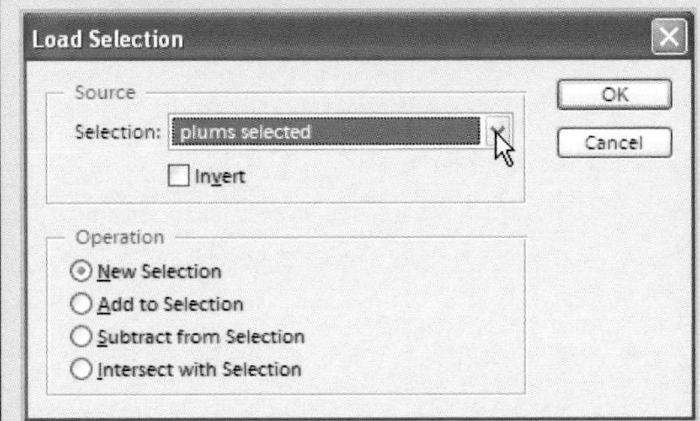

DESELECT AND RESELECT A SELECTION

- To deselect an active selection, click **Select** and click **Deselect**, or press **CTRL+D**.
- To reload the previously used selection for the current image, click **Select** and click **Reselect**, or press **SHIFT+CTRL+D**.

Add to a Selection

To add to an existing selection:

1. Choose any selection tool from the Toolbox palette except for the Selection Brush tool.
2. Hold down the **SHIFT** key, and make another selection.
3. Change tools at any time, and hold down the **SHIFT** key to continue adding to the current selection.

–Or–

1. Click the **Add To Selection** icon on the Options bar.
2. Select any selection tool (not the Selection Brush tool), and make a new selection.

Subtract from a Selection

To subtract from an existing selection:

1. Choose any selection tool from the Toolbox palette, including the Selection Brush tool.
2. Hold down the **ALT** key, and select the part of the active selection to be subtracted.
3. Change tools at any time, and hold down the **ALT** key to continue subtracting from the current selection.

–Or–

1. Click the **Subtract From Selection** icon on the Options bar.
2. Select any selection tool except for the Selection Brush Tool, and select a previous selection to undo it.

Select Intersections

This handy technique allows you to successfully select areas that are most easily defined by intersecting selections (the common area within two selections).

1. Make your first selection using any selection tool.
2. Select your second selection tool, if it is not the same as the first.

USING FEATHERING

Feathering softens a selection by blending the pixels in the selection into the neighboring pixels by the feather amount specified. The pixels at both edges of a selection are only *partially* selected. Feathering only goes one way—from the edge in—making the feathered selections partially transparent. If an effect or filter is applied to them, that filter or effect is also rendered partially transparent.

Without feathering

With feathering of 10 pixels

FEATHER AN EXISTING SELECTION

1. From the menu bar, click **Select** and then click **Feather**.
2. Type a value in the Feather Radius field between 0.2 and 250 pixels. The larger the number, the more the edges of the selection will be blurred.

CREATE A FEATHERED SELECTION WITH A SELECTION TOOL

1. Select any of the Lasso or Marquee tools.
2. Type a value in the Feather field between 0.2 and 250 pixels. The larger the number, the more the edges of the selection will be blurred. The size of the feather is generally determined by the area you've selected and the image size. For example, if you were making a selection around a subject's eye prior to applying sharpening to make the eyes stand out, you would create a feather of only 1 or 2 pixels in size. If you were selecting a person in a large image, you might increase the feather to 15 or 20 pixels.

3. Click the **Intersect With Selection** icon on the Options bar.
4. Make your second selection. The ultimate selection will be the intersection of the two.

Modify a Selection

You can modify a selection in a number of ways: repositioning, resizing, expanding, or contracting. From the menu bar, click **Image**, click **Transform**, and click **Free Transform**:

- To move the selected image, hold down the pointer and drag the selection to a new position. The selected image will be cut from the background.
- To resize the selection, drag the handles on the sides and corners of the selection.
- Click outside the selection until you see a curved double-arrow pointer, and drag it to rotate the selection.

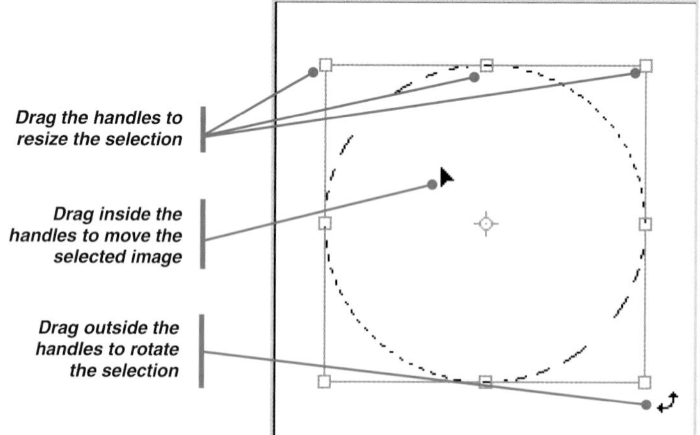

Drag the handles to resize the selection
Drag inside the handles to move the selected image
Drag outside the handles to rotate the selection

QUICKSTEPS

USING ANTI-ALIASING

Anti-aliasing smoothes the jagged edges of a selection. It works by blending the color of the pixels at the very edge of the selection with the background pixels. An element selected and copied without anti-aliasing and then pasted in front of a different-colored background will display an unsightly, ragged edge.

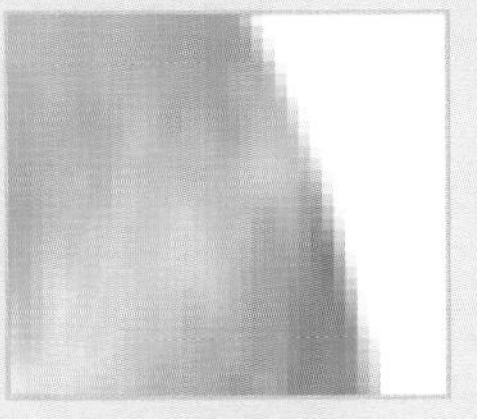

Anti-aliasing helps minimize this problem by blending the edges to soften and integrate the pasted image and the background. You'll usually want to enable anti-aliasing on the Options bar of whatever type of selection tool you're using. Place a check mark in the **Anti-Aliased** check box on the selection tool's Options bar to select it. ☑ Anti-aliased

NOTE

You cannot apply anti-aliasing to an existing selection. It must be applied after a selection tool is selected and before the selection is made.

Work with Selections

You can add a border to a selection, expand or contract selections, and make multiple selections.

ADD A BORDER TO A SELECTION

When you add a border to a selection, you specify the border size in pixels. For example, if you specify a 15-pixel border, the selected area comprises a 15-pixel border of the previous selection. That is, only the pixels between the two selection borders are selected.

1. From the menu bar, click **Select**, click **Modify**, and then click **Border**.
2. Type the size of the border in pixels, and click **OK**. Photoshop creates a new border selection centered on the original selection.

EXPAND OR CONTRACT A SELECTION

To expand a selection:

1. From the menu bar, click **Select**, click **Modify**, and then click **Expand**.
2. Type the number of pixels by which to expand the selection.
3. Click **OK**.

To contract a selection:

1. From the menu bar, click **Select**, click **Modify**, and then click **Contract**.
2. Type the number of pixels by which to contract the selection.
3. Click **OK**.

QUICKSTEPS

USING GROW AND SIMILAR

The Grow and Similar commands expand the current selection by adding pixels of similar color to those already selected.

Original selection

Selection expanded with the Grow command

THE GROW COMMAND

Although the initial selection does not have to be made using the Magic Wand tool, the Grow command expands the selection to include any adjacent pixels that fall within the Tolerance range specified in the Magic Wand Options bar. With a selection active:

From the menu bar, click **Select** and then click **Grow**. Similarly colored adjacent pixels are selected.

THE SIMILAR COMMAND

The Similar command expands the selection to include *any* pixels throughout the image that fall within the Magic Wand's Tolerance range, whether those pixels are adjacent to the current selection or not. If it selects too many, as in Figure 3-12, you can use the Selection Brush tool to mask the unwanted pixels in the selection. You can also press **ALT**, and drag over the unwanted selections.

With a selection active:

From the menu bar, click **Select** and then click **Similar**. Similarly colored pixels are selected throughout the image.

MAKE MULTIPLE SELECTIONS

To make multiple selections using any combination of selection tools:

1. Choose a selection tool, such as the Marquee tool, from the Toolbox palette.
2. Make your first selection.
3. Press **SHIFT** and make another selection.
4. Change tools at any time, and press **SHIFT** to continue adding to the current selection. Figure 3-11 shows an example.

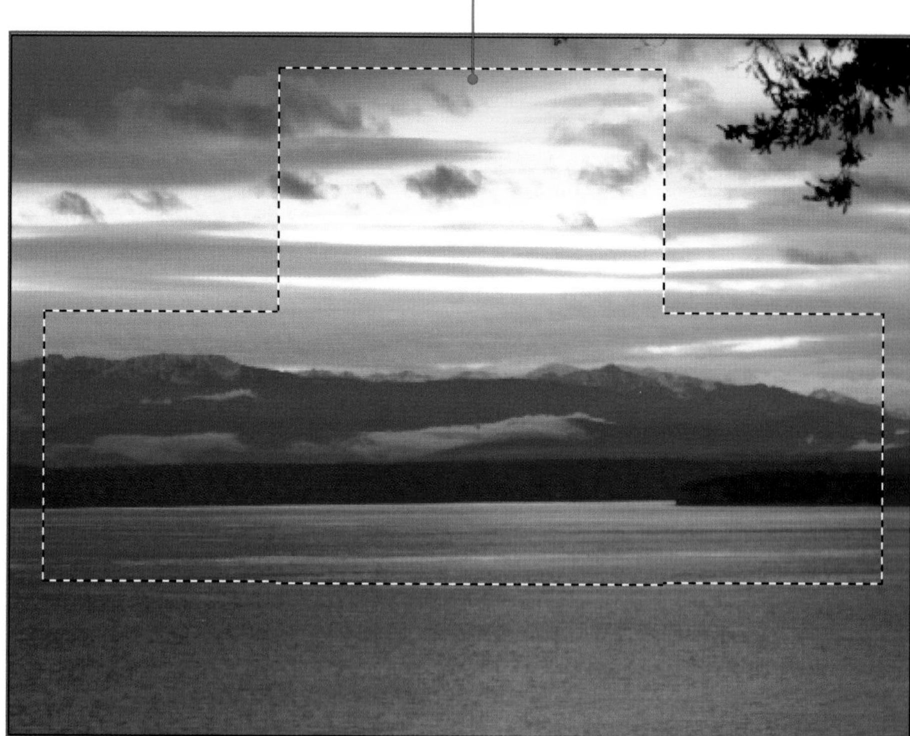
Selection expanded with the Grow command

Figure 3-11:** **You can add to your original selection by holding down the SHIFT key while you make another selection.

Figure 3-12: One consequence of the Similar command is that too much may be selected, allowing you to simply delete the unwanted pixels in the selection.

Selection expanded with the Similar command

NOTE

If you delete selected pixels while working on the background layer, they are replaced with the current background layer.

NOTE

You can crop an image to a nonrectangular selection as well. The image will be cropped to the smallest rectangular dimensions that include all selected pixels.

Crop a Selection

Cropping cuts off unwanted areas on the outside of an image. Photoshop Elements has a Crop tool, but it is often convenient to crop an image to fit a selection using the menu option.

1. Click the **Rectangular Marquee** tool in the Toolbox palette.
2. Click a point and drag to select a rectangular area of an image.
3. If necessary, move or redo the selection.
4. When you are ready to crop the selection, click **Image** and then click **Crop**. The area outside of the selection is discarded. There is no indicated area, only the boundary of the selection outline.

Delete Contents of Selections

If a selection is active, pressing DELETE only deletes pixels within the selection. You can use selections to quickly and safely erase large parts of an image.

1. Use one or more selection tools to select the area you want to delete. You can select the part of the image you want to keep, click **Select**, and then click **Invert** to select everything else in the image you want to delete.

2. Press DELETE to delete the selected area.
3. Click the **Eraser** tool to clean up the image.

TIP

If you try to transform a selection using the Move tool, you transform the pixels in the selection as well.

NOTE

The pixels defined in the Feather field will create an outside edge around the cropped image. For instance, if you have defined a feathering of 20 pixels, there will be a rim around the cropped image 20 pixels wide.

TIP

If you change your mind, you can undo any action by clicking **Edit** and then **Undo**. (This applies to any action you want to undo; the Undo command changes its name according to the command, for instance, Undo Crop.)

Copy Selection Contents

In addition to copying something from one place on your image to another, you can also copy to another layer or document. You can copy a selection to a layer and experiment with different blending modes to repair an image or achieve special effects. See Chapter 7 for additional information on how to use blending modes with layers.

COPY SELECTION CONTENTS TO A NEW LAYER

To copy the contents of a selection to a new layer:

1. Use any combination of selection tools to select the elements you want to extract from the background.
2. Press CTRL+J to copy the contents of the selection to a new, blank layer.

Since the copy will be positioned on a new layer directly above the original, the results of this process will not be apparent at first. To see the copy by itself:

1. Click the **Window** menu and then click **Layers** to open the Layers palette.
2. In the Layers palette, click the **eyeball** icon at the left of the background layer to hide the background layer. The new copy, without background, becomes apparent.

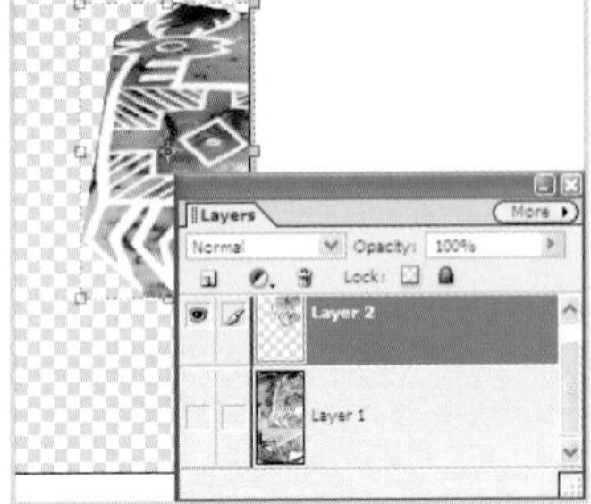

You'll learn more about layers in Chapter 4.

COPY SELECTION CONTENTS TO A NEW DOCUMENT

To copy the contents of a selection to a new document:

1. Use any combination of selection tools to select the elements you want to extract from the background.
2. Press CTRL+C to copy the contents of the selection to the Clipboard.
3. From the menu bar, click **File**, click **New**, and then click **Image From Clipboard** to create a new document. By default, Photoshop Elements sizes the new document to fit the contents of the Clipboard.

QUICKSTEPS

MOVING AND DUPLICATING SELECTION CONTENTS

MOVE THE CONTENTS OF A SELECTION

With a selection active:

1. Click the **Move** tool in the Toolbox palette.
2. Drag within the selection to move the contents.

DUPLICATE THE CONTENTS OF A SELECTION

With a selection active:

1. Click the **Move** tool in the Toolbox palette.
2. Press ALT and drag within the selection to duplicate the contents.

   –Or–

   Drag the duplicated contents into another image that is open in the workspace.

Use the Magic Eraser Tool

The Magic Eraser tool works like a combination of the Magic Wand tool and the DELETE key. It selects an area of similar color and deletes it.

1. If the Magic Eraser tool is not the currently active tool, click the current **Eraser** tool in the Toolbox palette, and hold the mouse button down. The Eraser tool submenu appears. (You can also click the **triangle**, which indicates a submenu is available, in the lower-right corner to display the submenu.)
2. Click the **Magic Eraser** tool to select it.

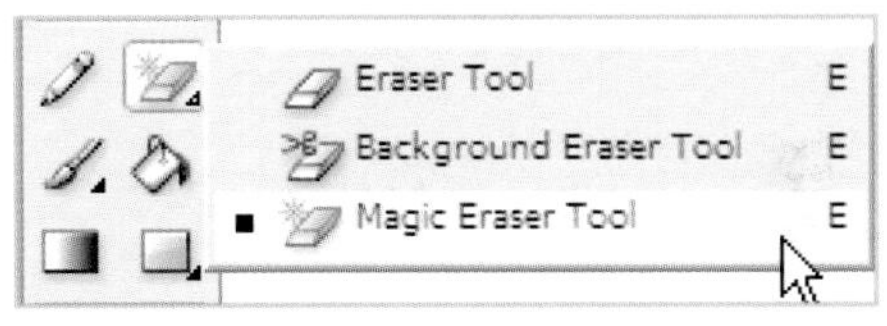

3. Set the **Tolerance** level in the Options bar. The higher the tolerance, the wider the range of colors that will be deleted. A good starting tolerance level is 32.
4. Leave the **Anti-Aliased** check box selected to blur the line between the erased selection and the background image.
5. Leave the **Contiguous** check box selected to erase only adjoining pixels. Click the **Contiguous** check box to clear it and deselect and erase similar hues of color anywhere in the image.
6. Click **Use All Layers** to erase the selected hue from all layers.
7. Click the **Opacity** right arrow, and drag the slider to increase or decrease the visibility of the layers beneath the erased area.
8. Click a background area in your image to delete it. Only pixels in a selected area will be deleted.

Use the Background Eraser Tool

The Background Eraser tool erases areas of similar color and turns the background transparent. When you first click inside the image with the Background Eraser tool, it samples the background color. As you drag the tool, the pointer changes into a circle with a plus sign. The plus sign indicates where the "hot spot" is, or where the color to be erased is being sensed. Use the Background Eraser tool to erase the background from around a foreground element. If you use this tool on the background layer, it automatically becomes a copy layer.

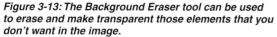

TIP

To decrease the brush size, press the **LEFT BRACKET** key ([); press the **RIGHT BRACKET** key (]) to increase the size.

Figure 3-13: The Background Eraser tool can be used to erase and make transparent those elements that you don't want in the image.

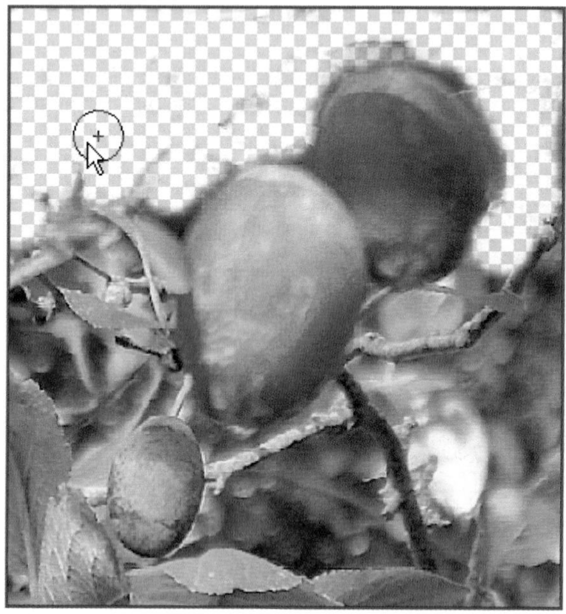

1. If the Background Eraser tool is not the current tool, click the current **Eraser** tool in the Toolbox palette, and hold the mouse button down. The Eraser tool submenu appears. (You can also click the **triangle**, which indicates a submenu is available, in the lower-right corner to display the submenu.)
2. Click the **Background Eraser** tool to select it.
3. Click the **Limits** down arrow, and click **Contiguous** for selected colors that are touching each other, or click **Discontiguous** for areas that are under the circle but not touching.
4. Click the **Brush Preset** down arrow to alter the diameter, hardness, spacing, angle, roundness or pen pressure, and size for the brush.
5. Click **Tolerance** and drag the slider to increase or decrease the variance from the original hue that will be selected.
6. Click the **Tolerance** down arrow, and drag the slider to the percentage of tolerance you want. This determines the sensitivity to color that the tool will detect when erasing. A higher percentage allows a broader variance of color to be erased; a lower percentage reduces the color variance that will be erased.
7. Click in an area you want to erase to sample the background color.
8. Without releasing the mouse button, drag the tool over the background to erase pixels of similar color, as seen in Figure 3-13.
9. To erase multiple areas or multiple colors, repeat steps 5 and 6.

The Background Eraser tool has a number of options that you can adjust for better results, as shown in Figure 3-14.

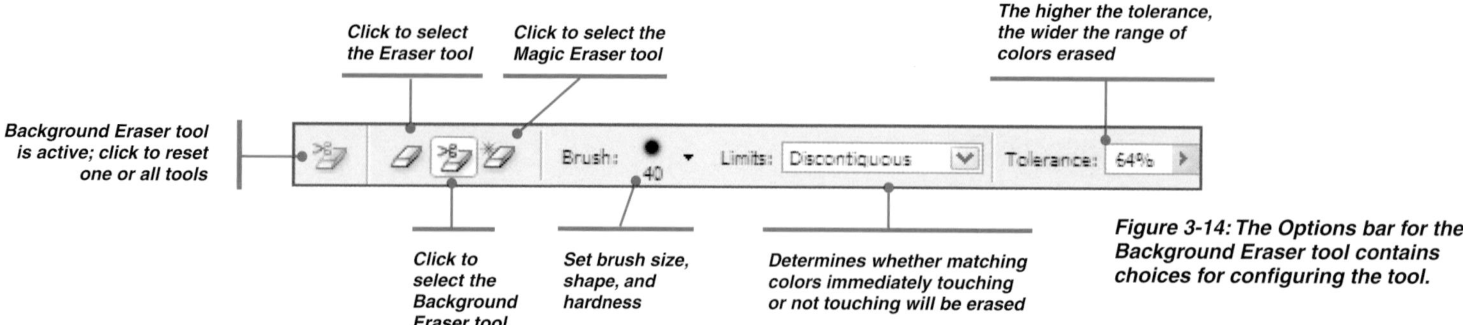

Click to select the Eraser tool
Click to select the Magic Eraser tool
The higher the tolerance, the wider the range of colors erased
Background Eraser tool is active; click to reset one or all tools
Brush:
40
Limits:
Discontiguous
Tolerance:
64%
Click to select the Background Eraser tool
Set brush size, shape, and hardness
Determines whether matching colors immediately touching or not touching will be erased

Figure 3-14: The Options bar for the Background Eraser tool contains choices for configuring the tool.

How to...

Chapter 4
Using Layers

Layers are one of the primary tools that Photoshop Elements offers to help you achieve advanced effects. With layers, you can build complex compositions while still maintaining control of the individual elements. You can use layers to keep your possibilities open so that you can change your mind without undoing hours of work. Think of layers as a combination of photographs and overhead transparencies that can be stacked one on top of the other. You can hide all or part of a layer by varying a layer's transparency or opacity; by using special effects, such as blending modes or filters; or by using masks. Layers can cast shadows and create other effects, too, as you'll see in this chapter.

Work with Layers

Photoshop Elements contains a Layers palette to create, copy, delete, rearrange, and add special effects to your layers. You'll do most of your manipulation of layers via the Layers palette, shown in Figure 4-1.

QUICKFACTS

UNDERSTANDING LAYERS

Layers are stacked elements of an image. In addition to image layers, you may have special layers called adjustment layers, fill layers, and text layers. You can edit the layers by rearranging them; by adding color or type; and by enhancing them with special effects, such as fills, gradients, borders, or layer styles. You work on one layer at a time, and when several layers are as you want them, you can group them together, or link them.

Only the selected layer is active at a time. When you are attempting to edit a layer, it is important to make sure that the layer you want is active, or you'll get an error message or will be unable to perform the edit. Layers can be locked against any changes being made. Background layers are automatically locked—they cannot be moved in the stack unless they are unlocked. When you are finished editing an image, you will probably want to flatten all layers, merge some layers, or simplify adjustment or text layers. These functions reduce the size of the file and make the changes permanent.

When you *flatten* an image, you reduce all layers to a single layer. You can merge some layers into one layer while leaving other layers intact, which allows you to reduce the file size while retaining the layers with which you are still working. Simplifying is done using adjustment layers, text layers, or shape layers. When you *simplify* layers, you convert them to image layers. After the conversion, you can no longer edit the layers with text or shape tools, but you can apply filters or use the painting tools. Most tasks you want to do with layers can be done from the Layer menu or from the Layers palette.

Figure 4-1: The Layers palette allows you to manipulate and control layers.

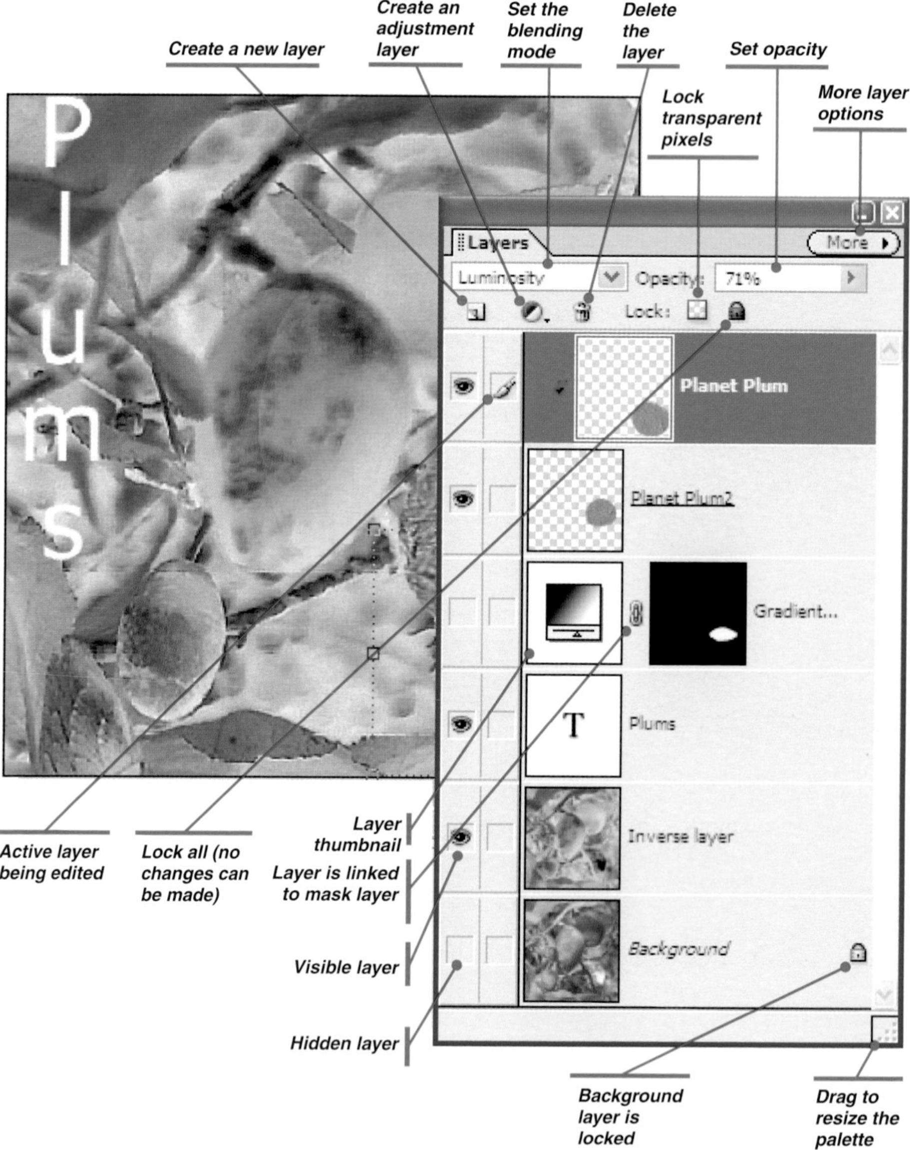

TIP

To name a layer in the New Layer dialog box, simply type over the highlighted default name. Or, you can accept the default name by clicking **OK**.

TIP

To rename a layer, double-click the layer's name in the Layers palette, and type a new name.

TIP

Use layers as a form of quick and easy backup. Before making changes to your work, copy it to a new layer. Make the changes on the new layer, and if you don't like them, simply delete the layer.

Create New Layers

You can create layers in a variety of ways. You can create a new, blank layer; duplicate a layer; create a layer from a selection; or create adjustment and fill layers.

CREATE A NEW LAYER

To create a new, blank layer:

Click the **Create New Layer** button at the top of the Layers palette.

–Or–

Click the **Layer** menu, click **New**, and click **Layer**. The New Layer dialog box appears.

–Or–

Press SHIFT+CTRL+N.

COPY AN EXISTING LAYER

You can also create a new layer by copying an existing layer.

In the Layers palette, click and drag the source layer (the pointer changes to a fist) to the **Create A New Layer** button, located at the top of the Layers palette, and then release the mouse button.

–Or–

Right-click the layer to be copied, and click **Duplicate Layer**. Type the new name and click **OK.**

–Or–

Click **Layer**, click **Duplicate Layer**, type a new name, and click **OK**.

–Or–

Press CTRL+J.

Photoshop creates a new layer that is an exact copy of the original. The new layer appears immediately above the source layer in the Layers palette.

CREATE A NEW LAYER FROM A SELECTION

You can create a new layer by copying only the selected portions of an existing layer. This is a useful way to separate a selected element or elements from the background while leaving your original image intact.

NOTE

If a selection is active, the Layer Via Copy command (**CTRL+J**) copies the selected portions to a new layer. If there is no active selection, the command copies the entire layer.

To create a new layer from a selection:

1. Select the portions of a layer that you wish to copy.
2. Click the **Layer** menu, click **New**, and click **Layer Via Copy**.

   –Or–

   Press **CTRL+J**.

Rearrange Layer Order

The order of layers in the Layers palette can determine your final result, as shown in Figures 4-2a and 4-2b. What is revealed in an image may depend on the order of the layers (opacity affects this as well).

Figure 4-2a: If the special effects layer is above the full image layer, the special effects are visible.

Figure 4-2b: If the special effects layer is beneath the full image layer, the special effects are hidden.

NOTE

The original background layer cannot be moved unless you double-click the **Lock** icon. This allows you to rename the layer, which unlocks it. After this, you can freely move the renamed background layer.

To change the order of layers:

Drag a layer up or down to a new position on the Layers palette.

–Or–

1. Click the layer in the Layers palette that you want to move.
2. Click the **Layer** menu and click **Arrange**.

TIP

If you accidentally delete a layer, you can restore it by pressing **CTRL+Z** or clicking the **Edit** menu and clicking **Undo Delete Layer**.

QUICKSTEPS

HIDING AND REVEALING LAYERS

In a document with multiple layers, you might want to temporarily hide individual layers.

TEMPORARILY HIDE A LAYER

To temporarily hide a layer:

Click the **eye** icon located to the far left of the layer thumbnail in the Layers palette. The eye icon disappears, and the layer is hidden.

REVEAL A HIDDEN LAYER

To reveal a hidden layer:

Click the empty space located to the far left of the layer thumbnail in the Layers palette. The eye icon reappears, and the layer is revealed.

3. Select one of the following options:
   - **Bring To Front** moves the layer to the top of the palette or to the top of the stack of layers.
   - **Bring Forward** moves the layer up the stack by one layer.
   - **Send Backward** moves the layer down the stack by one layer.
   - **Send To Back** moves the layer to the bottom of the Layers palette or to the bottom of the stack of layers.

Delete a Layer

1. Click a layer thumbnail in the Layers palette.
2. Drag the layer to the **Delete Layer** button, located at the top of the palette.

   –Or–

   Right-click the layer's name in the Layers palette, and click **Delete Layer**.

Lock or Unlock Layers

Background layers are locked to protect against certain editing changes. You can unlock a layer by renaming it.

To unlock a layer from the Layers palette:

1. Double-click the **padlock** icon on the layer. The New Layer dialog box appears.
2. Type the new name or accept the default, and click **OK**. The layer is unlocked.

Rename a Layer

To rename a layer:

1. Double-click the layer to be renamed in the Layers palette. The New Layer dialog box appears.
2. Type a new name or accept the default suggested, and click **OK**.

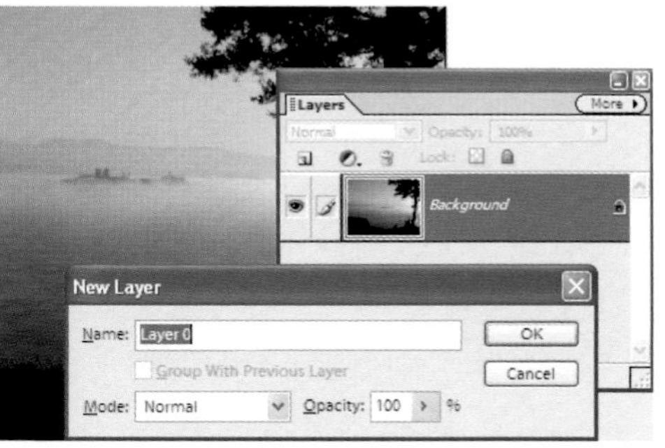

LINKING AND UNLINKING LAYERS

Layers that are linked move, rotate, and transform together. For example, if you move the contents of a layer 50 pixels to the left, the contents of all layers linked to that layer will also move 50 pixels to the left.

LINK LAYERS

To link another layer to the currently selected layer:

On a layer other than the currently selected layer, click the blank area immediately to the left of the layer thumbnail. A chain icon appears.

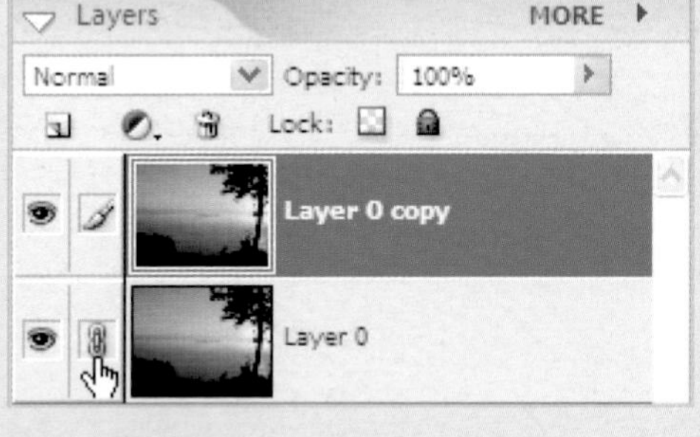

UNLINK LAYERS

To unlink layers:

Click the **chain** icon to the left of the thumbnail in the Layers palette to break the link with the currently selected layer.

NOTE

The Merge Down command will not be available if the bottom layer is a text layer or a shape layer.

Duplicate a Layer

To create an exact copy of a layer:

1. In the Layers palette, click the layer you want to duplicate.
2. Click **Layer** and click **Duplicate Layer**. The Duplicate Layer dialog box appears.

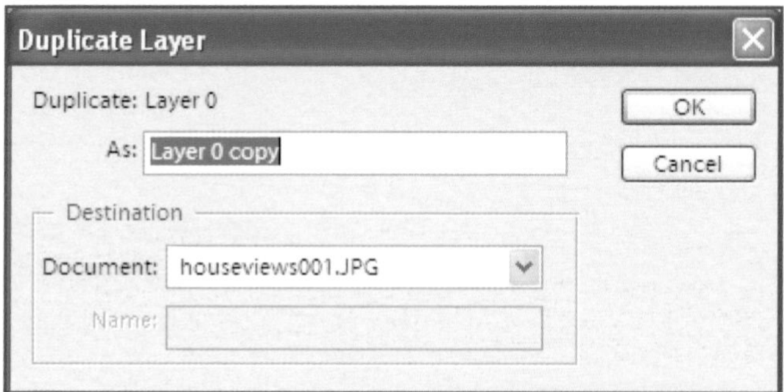

3. Type a new name or accept the default name, and click **OK**.

   –Or–

   Press **CTRL+J** to duplicate the layer.

Flatten an Image

When you are finished working with your layers and ready to finalize an image, you flatten it to get rid of all the layers, which reduces the file size.

To flatten all layers into a single layer:

Click the **Layer** menu and click **Flatten Image**.

–Or–

1. In the Layers palette, click the **More** right arrow in the upper-right area of the Layers palette. The Palette options menu appears.
2. Click **Flatten Image**.

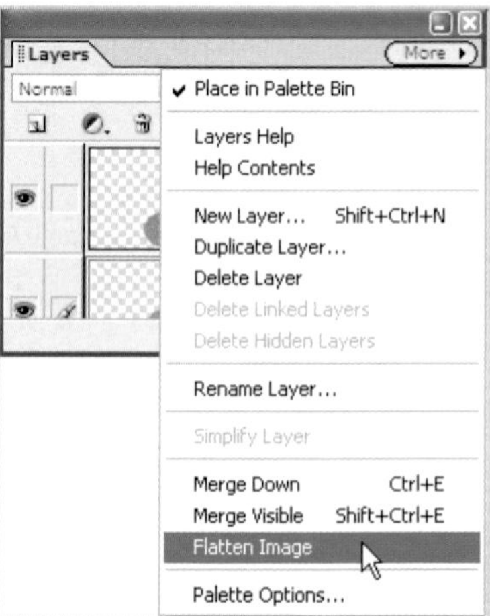

QUICKSTEPS

MERGING LAYERS

You can combine two or more layers into a single layer. This reduces the file size and makes the image easier to handle; however, this is a permanent change and when merged, layers can no longer be separately manipulated (unless you immediately undo the merge by clicking **Edit** and then clicking **Undo Merge** or by pressing **CTRL+Z** before performing any other commands). You can merge layers in several ways.

MERGE A LAYER WITH THE LAYER BENEATH IT

1. In the Layers palette, select the topmost of the two layers you want to merge.
2. Click the **More** right arrow, located in the upper-right area of the Layers palette, and click **Merge Down**.

   –Or–

   Press **CTRL+E**.

MERGE LINKED LAYERS

You can merge all linked layers into a single layer:

1. In the Layers palette, click one of the linked layers to select it.
2. Click the **More** right arrow, located in the upper-right area of the Layers palette, and click **Merge Linked**.

   –Or–

   Click the **Layer** menu and click **Merge Linked**.

Continued...

Copy Merged Layers

You might want to copy a merged version of a layered document—a version that looks the same but that does not contain multiple layers—to the Clipboard.

1. Click **Select** and then click **All** to select the whole document, or press **CTRL+A**.
2. Click **Edit** and click **Copy Merged**, or press **SHIFT+CTRL+C**.
3. Click the **File** menu, click **New**, and click **Image From Clipboard**.

When you paste the contents of the Clipboard into a new document, the contents now consist of only a single layer (see Figure 4-3a and Figure 4-3b for a comparison).

Figure 4-3a: Before carrying out the Copy Merged command, this document is made up of many interacting layers.

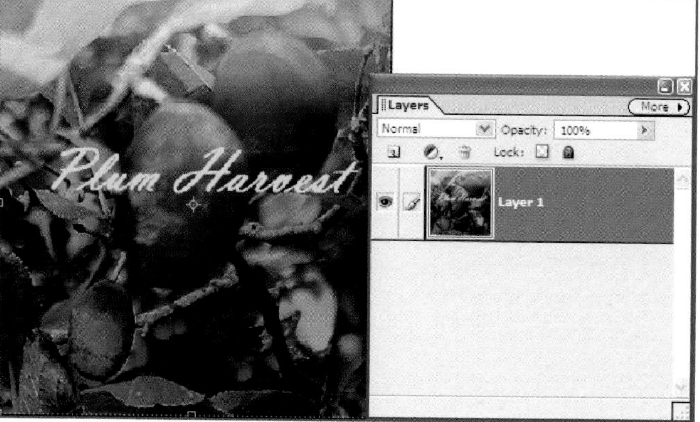

Figure 4-3b: When the merged document is copied to the Clipboard, it can be pasted to a new document or to another program as a single layer.

1 2 3 4 5 6 7 8 9 10

MERGING LAYERS (Continued)

MERGE VISIBLE LAYERS

You can merge layers to simplify the Layers palette when you've done all the editing you're going to do on several layers. Make the layers visible and then merge the visible layers into one layer.

To merge all visible layers into a single layer:

1. In the Layers palette, click one of the visible layers to select it.
2. Click the **Layer** menu and click **Merge Visible**.

–Or–

1. Click the **More** right arrow, located in the upper-right area of the Layers palette.
2. Click **Merge Visible**.

NOTE

Hidden layers cannot be modified or copied.

TIP

When dragging a layer from one document to another, hold down the **SHIFT** key to center the new layer within the document.

PASTE FROM ANOTHER APPLICATION TO A NEW LAYER IN PHOTOSHOP ELEMENTS

1. Open a previously existing image or a new, blank file in Photoshop Elements.
2. Switch to another application, such as a web browser, and select and copy an image.
3. Return to Photoshop Elements, click **Edit**, and click **Paste**. The new image is pasted into the Photoshop Elements document on a new layer.

PASTE A NEW LAYER FROM ANOTHER PHOTOSHOP ELEMENTS DOCUMENT

1. Open two images in Photoshop Elements.
2. Click **Window**, click **Images**, and then click **Tile** to display both images at once.
3. Click the **Move** tool in the Toolbox.
4. Click within the first document to select it.
5. Click **Select** and click **All**, or press **CTRL+A**, to select the entire image.
6. Click **Edit** and click **Copy**, or click **Copy Merged** if the image contains multiple layers.
7. Click within the second document to select it.
8. Click **Edit** and click **Paste**, or press **CTRL+V**, to paste the first image into a new layer in the second document.

COPY A LAYER USING DRAG

You can drag layers directly from one Photoshop Elements document to another.

1. Open two documents within the same window by opening the two files and then clicking **Window**, clicking **Images**, and clicking **Tile**.
2. Click in the first document to select it.
3. In the Layers palette, drag the layer you want to copy, and place it anywhere in the second document. A copy of that layer appears in the second document.

Use Layer Techniques for Color, Tones, Patterns, and Gradients

NOTE

When you create an adjustment layer, it will be named according to type, for example, Gradient Map or Brightness/Contrast.

Adjustment layers and fill layers are special layers used to add tonal changes, color changes, and other special effects to an image. These layers do not contain images—only the definitions that describe the special effects used in the image layer. You have many choices when it comes to special effects, as you'll see in this section.

Create an Adjustment Layer

Layers don't always contain images or fills; they can also be adjustment layers. Adjustment layers allow you to make adjustments to an image without making any permanent changes to it. You can create several adjustment layers for an image, and in this way test various special effects for an image without committing to one. Your original image is preserved, and you can tweak the adjustment further at any time.

1. Open an image in Photoshop Elements.
2. Click **Layer** and then click **New Adjustment Layer**. From the menu that appears, shown in Figure 4-4, click one of the following commands:

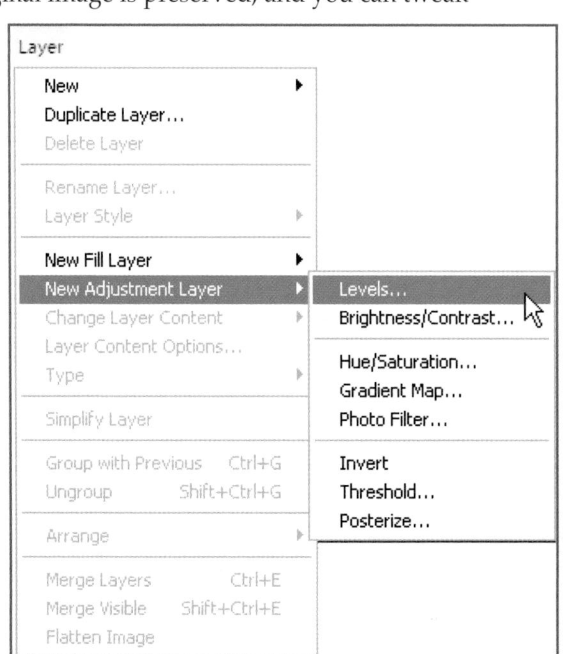

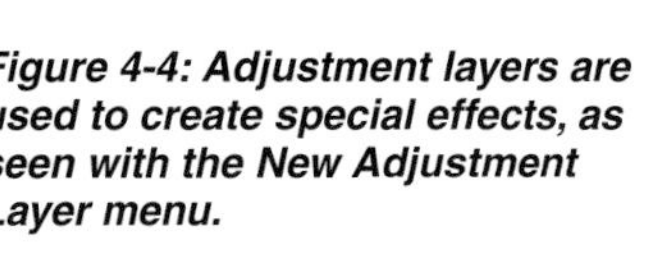

Figure 4-4: Adjustment layers are used to create special effects, as seen with the New Adjustment Layer menu.

USING LAYER ICONS

Some of the icons you'll find in the Layers palette in Photoshop Elements include:

- The eye icon indicates that a layer is visible. Click the eye icon to hide the layer, or click the blank leftmost box where the icon was to reveal the layer.
- The brush icon is available when you create a shape layer or a text layer, or create a new blank layer and then use the drawing tools, or paste an image into the layer.
- The chain icon indicates that a layer is linked to the selected layer.
- The padlock icon indicates that a layer is locked. If the layer is a background layer, double-click to it to rename it and unlock the layer. If the lock icon is displayed as a result of clicking the Lock All button on the top of the Layers palette, click the Lock All icon to unlock all layers.
- The folder icon indicates that a layer has been imported from Adobe Photoshop CS and contains layer sets. A layer set is a group, or folder, of layers that are only created in Photoshop CS. You cannot open or edit the imported layer sets with Photoshop Elements.
- The square icon with a circle in the middle indicates the presence of a layer mask or that there is painting on a layer.
- The circle icon with a white line through the middle indicates that a layer style has been applied.

- **Levels** adjusts color and tones (see "Use Levels to Adjust Color").
- **Brightness/Contrast** adjusts the overall brightness of an image and the contrast within it.
- **Hue/Saturation** adjusts the color and intensity of an image (see "Use Hue/Saturation to Adjust Intensity" for more information).
- **Gradient Map** creates a gradient color that is applied to a layer (see "Use Gradient to Adjust Layer Background").
- **Photo Filter** places a filter of a selected color or temperature over the image.
- **Invert** produces a negative color image.
- **Threshold** converts the image to black and white.
- **Posterize** creates an image in which the colors are posterized, or simplified, by converting areas of similar color to a solid color, making the image look like a poster as opposed to a photo.

3. After making a choice, the New Layer dialog box appears. Click **OK**.
4. A dialog box for the selected command may allow you to adjust the image. Some commands, for example, Invert, do not have such controls. When you are finished, click **OK**.

USE LEVELS TO ADJUST COLOR

1. Open an image.
2. Click **Layer**, click **New Adjustment Layer**, and click **Levels**.
3. The New Layer dialog box appears. Click **OK**.
4. The Levels dialog box appears. Manipulate the dialog box as follows:
   - Drag the **middle slider** (the gray one), located beneath the histogram, to adjust the brightness of the middle tones. Drag far enough to one side to make the image significantly darker or lighter. You can also type a value in the middle Input Levels text box, which is set at 1.0 by default.
   - Drag the **left slider** (the black one), located under the histogram, to adjust the shadows of the image. All pixels located in the levels to the left of the slider are clipped to black. You can also type a value in the left Input Levels text box, which is set at 0 by default.

To change the attributes of an adjustment or fill layer, select the layer to be changed in the Layers palette. Click **Layer** and then click **Change Layer Content**. From the menu that is displayed, click the adjustment or fill option that you want.

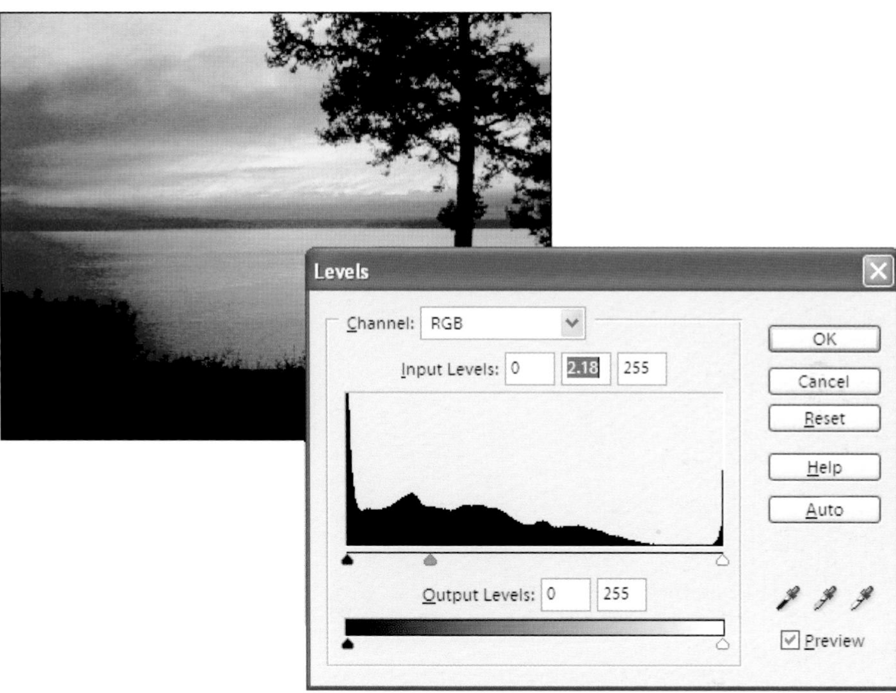

- Drag the **right slider** (the white one) to adjust the highlights of the image. All pixels located in the levels to the right of the slider are clipped to white. You can also type a value in the right Input Levels text box, which is set at 255 by default.
- Click the **Channel** down arrow to select between adjusting RGB color to modify all color channels, or click **Red**, **Green**, or **Blue** to modify a specific color channel. A grayscale image will only have a Gray channel available.
- Drag the **left slider** located at the bottom of the dialog box to darken the entire image, or drag the **right slider** to lighten it.

5. Click **OK**.

1
2
3
4
5
6
7
8
9
10

TIP

If a layer's mask thumbnail is white, the file size will not be greatly increased, so you don't need to merge these adjustment layers to conserve space.

TIP

To select just the non-transparent pixels of a layer, press **CTRL** and click the layer in the Layers palette.

The image looks different, but the original photo layer is actually untouched. To see this, in the Layers palette, click the **eye** icon, located to the left of the adjustment layer, to temporarily hide it. The photo returns to normal, as shown in Figure 4-5.

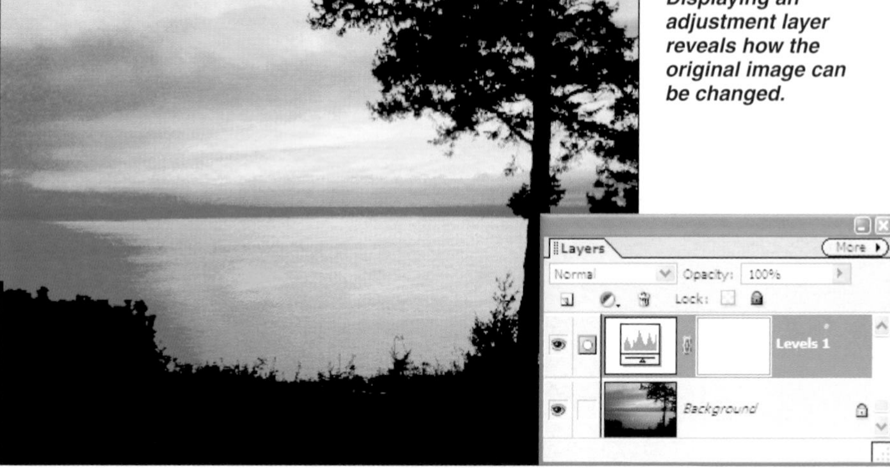

Figure 4-5a: Displaying an adjustment layer reveals how the original image can be changed.

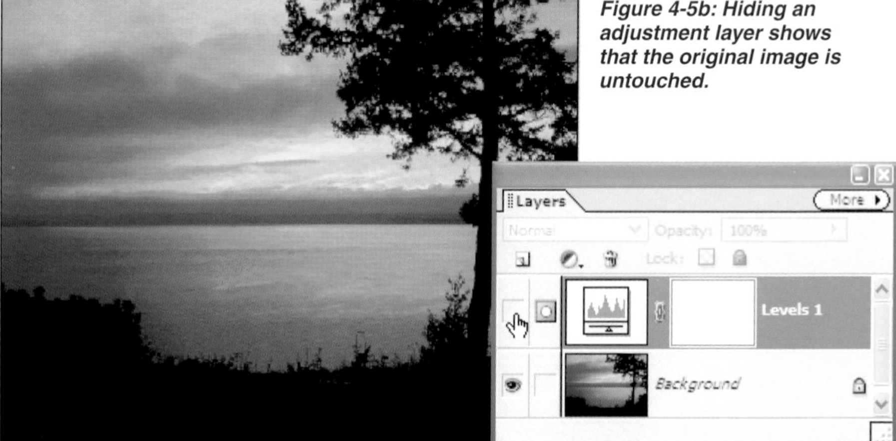

Figure 4-5b: Hiding an adjustment layer shows that the original image is untouched.

> **TIP**
>
> To lessen the effect of an adjustment layer, or to make it less intense, lower the adjustment layer's opacity, displayed in the Layers palette, by clicking the **Opacity** right arrow and dragging the slider.

> **NOTE**
>
> If you click the **Group With Previous Layer** check box on the New Layer dialog box when creating an adjustment layer, the new adjustment layer will only affect the layer directly beneath it. The Group With Previous Layer command is only available on the Layer menu when the adjustment layer is selected.

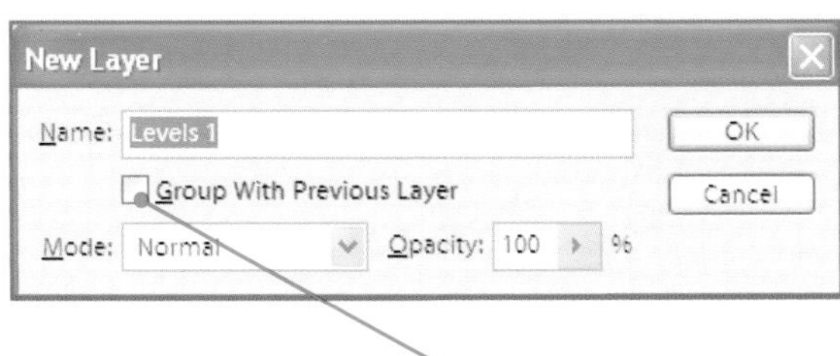

Click here to limit the new adjustment layer's effects to the layer directly beneath it

CHANGE AN ADJUSTMENT LAYER

In the Layers palette, double-click the layer thumbnail to reopen the appropriate dialog box (for example, the Levels dialog box).

DELETE AN ADJUSTMENT LAYER

In the Layers palette, click the adjustment layer you want to delete, and drag it to the **trashcan** icon at the top of the palette.

USE HUE/SATURATION TO ADJUST INTENSITY

1. Open an image.
2. Click **Layer**, click **New Adjustment Layer**, and click **Hue/Saturation**.
3. The New Layer dialog box appears. Click **OK**.
4. The Hue/Saturation dialog box appears. Manipulate it in one of the following ways to intensify your color:

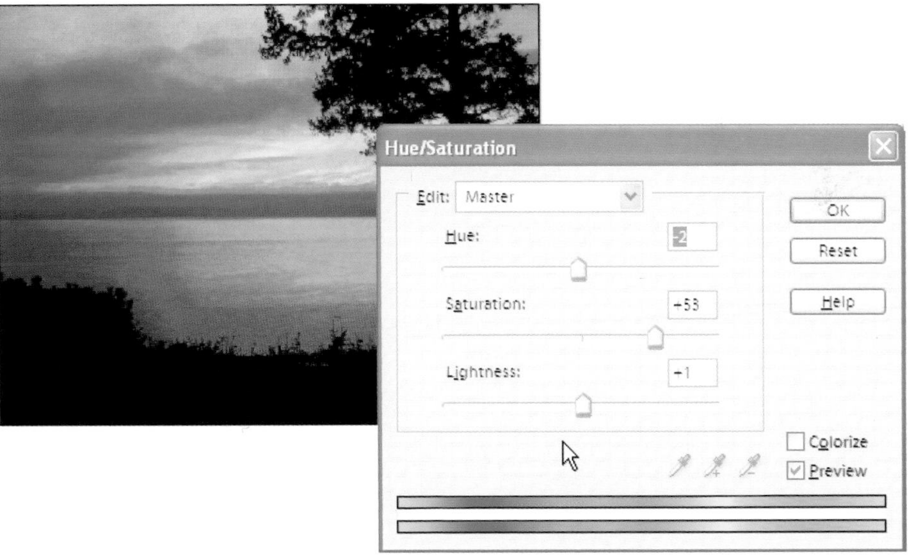

1 2 3 4 5 6 7 8 9 10

1 2 3 4 5 6 7 8 9 10

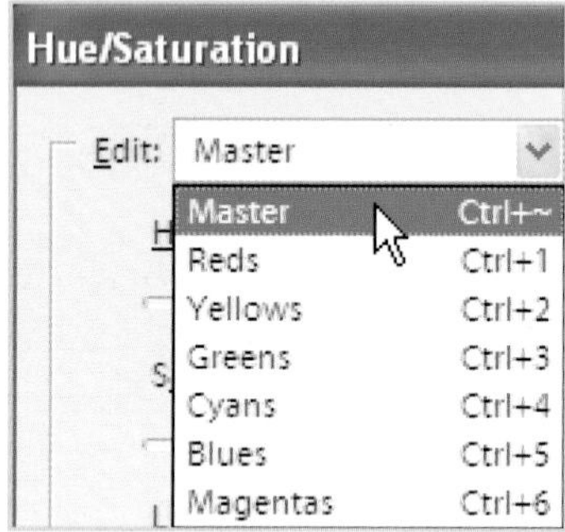

- Click the **Edit** down arrow, and click **Master** for all colors, or click an individual color to change it using the dialog box controls.
- Drag the **Hue** slider to change the color in the image.
- Drag the **Saturation** slider to change the intensity of the color.
- Drag the **Lightness** slider to vary the lightness of the overall image.

5. When you are finished, click **OK**. The adjustment layer is displayed in the Layers palette.

TIP

See Chapter 5 for more information on how to use the Hue/Saturation feature.

USE GRADIENT TO ADJUST LAYER BACKGROUNDS

1. Open an image.
2. Click **Layer**, click **New Adjustment Layer**, and click **Gradient**.
3. The New Layer dialog box appears. Click **OK**. The Gradient Map dialog box appears.
4. Click the **Gradient** down arrow, and click a gradient option, as shown in Figure 4-6.

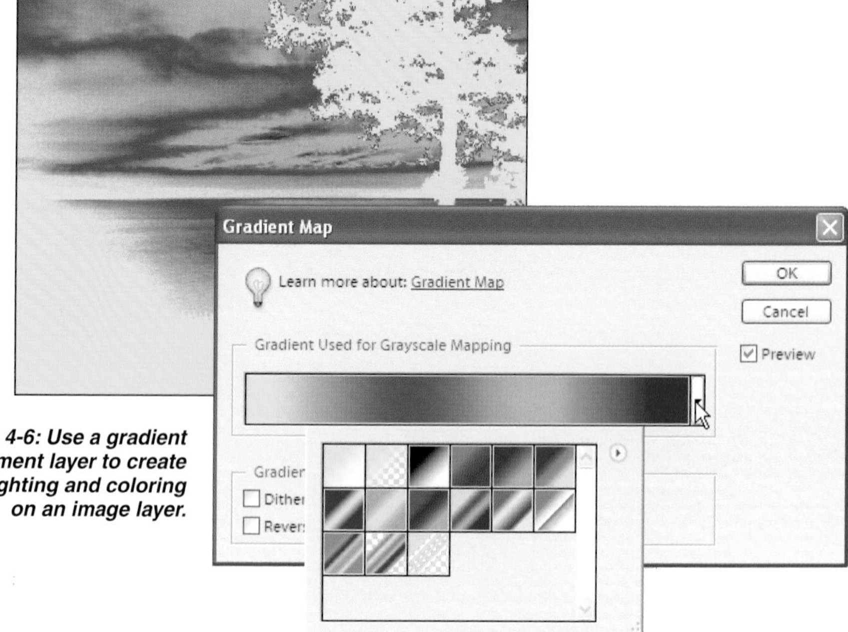

Figure 4-6: Use a gradient adjustment layer to create special lighting and coloring on an image layer.

5. When you are finished, click **OK**. The adjustment layer is displayed in the Layers palette.

USE AN ADJUSTMENT LAYER TO INVERT AN IMAGE

1. Open an image.
2. Click **Layer**, click **New Adjustment Layer**, and click **Invert**. The New Layer dialog box appears. Click **OK**. Or, click the **Create Adjustment Layer** icon on the Layers palette, and click **Invert**. Your image will immediately be displayed in inverted colors.

MAKE AN IMAGE BLACK AND WHITE USING AN ADJUSTMENT LAYER

1. Open an image.
2. Click **Layer**, click **New Adjustment Layer**, and click **Threshold**.
3. The New Layer dialog box appears. Click **OK**.
4. The Threshold dialog box appears with your image converted to black and white. Drag the slider to the right to remove white (increase blackness); drag it to the left to remove black (increase whiteness).
5. Click **OK** when the image is as you want it. The adjustment layer is displayed in the Layers palette.

NOTE

When you use the Invert command, the pixels are changed to an inverse value on the 0-255 color scale. For example, if a color has a value of 240, its inverse is 15.

TIP

Blending modes and opacity will have a huge effect on the Invert feature. Try using the Difference blending mode, and then roll the opacity back to about 40 percent when experimenting with an inverted layer.

QUICKFACTS

USING LAYER SHORTCUT COMMANDS

Photoshop Elements has the following command buttons available on the Layers palette:

- **Create A New Layer** adds a new layer to the image. Drag an existing layer to this button to create a duplicate layer.
- **Create A New Adjustment Or Fill Layer** adds an adjustment or fill layer to the image.
- **Delete A Layer** removes a layer from the Layers palette. If you do this, you do not get a message asking you to confirm the deletion; the layer is simply deleted.
- **Lock Transparent Layers** prevents transparent layers from being edited.
- **Lock All Layers** prevents all layers in the image from being edited.

POSTERIZE AN IMAGE WITH AN ADJUSTMENT LAYER

1. Open an image.
2. Click **Layer**, click **New Adjustment Layer**, and click **Posterize**.
3. The New Layer dialog box appears. Click **OK**.
4. The Posterize dialog box appears with your image displayed in a posterized fashion. Type a number between 2 and 255—typing a lower number creates a more dramatic look, whereas typing a higher number lessens the effect. Typing 255 creates no visible effect.

5. Click **OK** when the image is as you want it. The adjustment layer is displayed in the Layers palette.

> **NOTE**
>
> Blending modes, discussed in detail in Chapter 5, allow you to create certain special effects. When you combine blending modes with opacity, you can create some rather interesting effects. To select a blending mode, click a layer. Then, on the Layers palette, click the leftmost down arrow, and select a blending mode.

> **NOTE**
>
> Up to 50 states are retained by default in the Undo History palette. You can change that amount by clicking **Edit**, clicking **Preferences**, and clicking **General**. Type the number of states you want to be saved in the History States text box.

> **TIP**
>
> In the Undo History palette, the oldest states are listed first and the newest states are listed last.

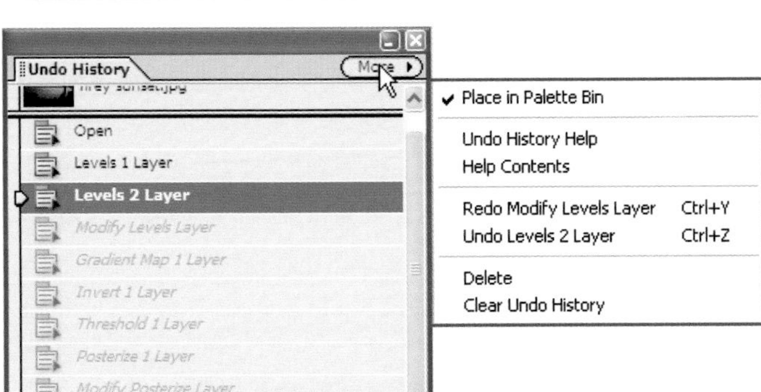

Use Opacity

You can control how much of a layer's content is revealed or hidden by varying the opacity. When you set opacity to 100 percent, for instance, the layer beneath is completely hidden. If you set opacity to 50 percent, the layer beneath is 50 percent revealed. Chapter 5 discusses opacity in further detail.

To set opacity:

1. Click a layer in the Layers palette.
2. On the Layers palette, click the **Opacity** right arrow, and perform one of the following actions:
   - Drag the slider to the left to increase transparency and reveal what is beneath.
   - Drag the slider to the right to decrease transparency and hide what is beneath.

As you drag, the percent will be displayed in the Opacity text box.

Undo History

As you change the pixels of an image by using a command on it, a state of the image is created. That state is captured in the Undo History palette. Changes that do not affect the pixels of the image, such as zooming in on an image, are not captured in the Undo History palette. You can revert to any state at will.

Click **Window** and click **Undo History**. The Undo History palette is displayed in the Layers palette:

- To revert to a previous state, click the desired state in the Undo History list. To revert to the original image, click the topmost state in the list.
- To delete a state, right-click it and click **Delete**. All states following the one to be deleted will also be deleted. (Use the Undo command on the Edit menu to recover them if needed.)
- To see additional commands for the Undo History palette, click the **More** down arrow in the upper-right area of the palette.

TIP

One way to allow some effects to show through is to vary the opacity of the brush, which will change black to a grayscale color. For instance, an opacity of 50 percent is the equivalent of R (128), G (128), and B (128)—the middle tone on the grayscale color model.

LIMIT ADJUSTMENT OR FILL LAYER EFFECTS WITH A MASK

You can protect areas of an image from the effects of an adjustment or fill layer by using a mask. When you paint with black, the adjustment will be painted away; the painted area will be unaffected by the adjustments or fill effects. If you paint with white, the area will be exposed to the adjustment or fill effects. Various shades of gray will allow some of the effects to show through; the darker the shade of gray, the less the effects will be seen in the image.

1. Open an image and create an adjustment or fill layer with the effects you want. In the Layers palette, the adjustment or fill layer will have a white thumbnail indicating that a mask for the layer exists. You cannot paint on the adjustment or fill layer; you must paint on the mask.

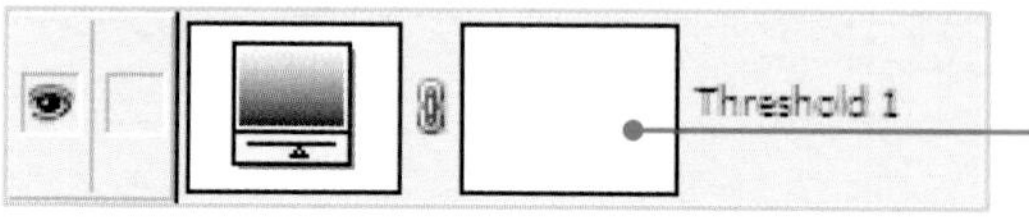

Click to activate the mask for the layer. Press SHIFT and click to turn it off.

2. If you have not already done so, make the foreground color black (or white or gray, or change the opacity of the brush, if you want to allow part or all of the effects to be seen).
3. Click the **white mask** thumbnail to select the mask.
4. Click a brush and define its size. If you select a soft-edged brush, you will prevent a harsh edge at the end of the mask, similar to a feathering effect.
5. Brush over the part of the image you want to protect from the effects of the adjustment or fill layer. An example can be seen in Figure 4-7.

Use Fill Layers

A *fill layer* is a special type of adjustment layer that allows a solid-color fill, a pattern, or a gradient color design to be integrated into an image. Fill layers affect the layers stacked above them, but not beneath them.

Figure 4-7: Painting a mask on an adjustment or fill layer allows you to control what part of the image is protected from the adjustment or fill effects, as seen here.

1. Open an image and in the Layers palette, select the layer that will be above the fill layer.
2. Click **Layer** and click **New Fill Layer**. From the menu that appears, select one of the following:
   - **Solid Color** fills a layer with a solid color you select from the Color Picker.
   - **Gradient** fills a layer with a gradient pattern that you select from a preset menu of gradients.
   - **Pattern** fills the layer with a pattern that you select from a menu of preset designs.

FILL A LAYER WITH SOLID COLOR

To fill a layer with solid color:

1. Open an image and select it in the Layers palette.
2. Click **Layer**, click **New Fill Layer**, and click **Solid Color**. The New Layer dialog box appears. Click **OK**. The Color Picker dialog box appears, as seen in Figure 4-8.

   –Or–

Figure 4-8: The Color Picker is used when you create a solid-color fill layer.

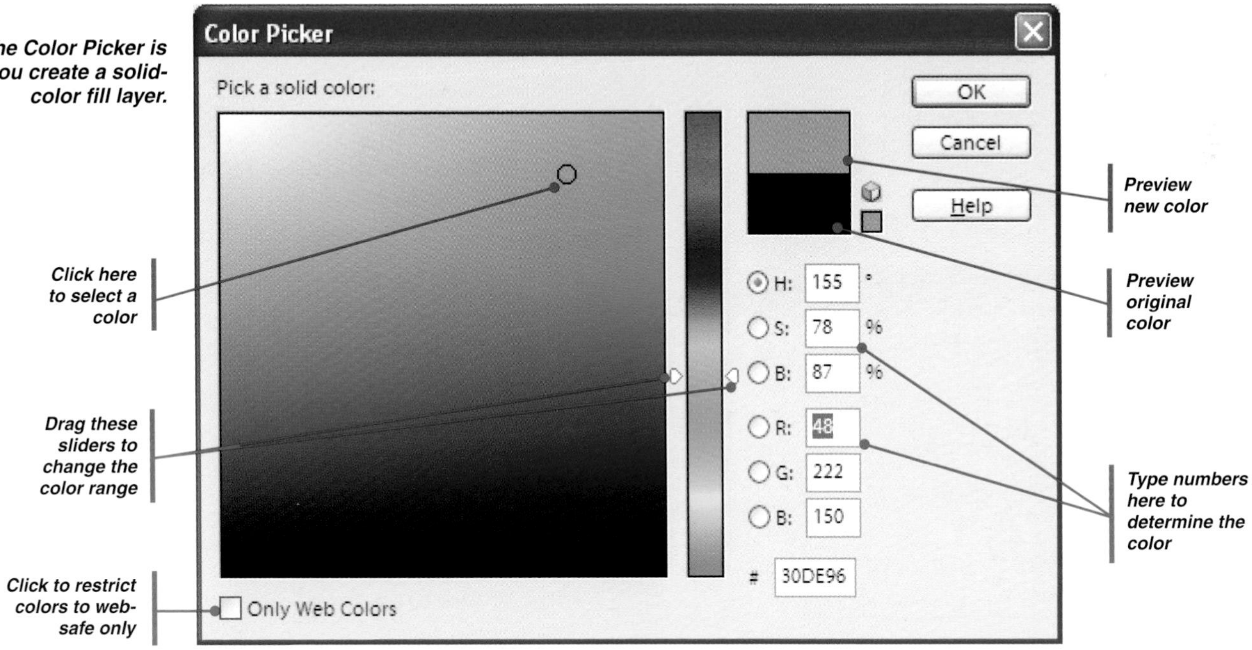

> **TIP**
>
> Click the **Opacity** button on the Layers palette, and drag the slider to increase or decrease the opacity and transparency of the fill layer.

Click the **Adjustment Layer** icon in the Layers palette, and click **Solid Color**. The Color Picker dialog box appears.

3. You can select a color in one of three ways:
   - Click in the **Pick A Solid Color** area to select a color. The color is displayed in the upper preview box.
   - Drag the sliders on the color bar up or down to select a color. The current color is displayed in the upper preview box.
   - Type numbers that precisely determine the color you want in the respective fields. The H field pertains to hue; the S field pertains to saturation; the B field pertains to brightness; the R field pertains to red; the G field pertains to green; and the B field pertains to blue.
4. Click **OK** to accept the color selection.

FILL A LAYER WITH GRADIENT COLOR

1. Open an image and select it in the Layers palette.
2. Click **Layer**, click **New Fill Layer**, and click **Gradient**. The New Layer dialog box appears. Click **OK**. The Gradient Fill dialog box appears.

   –Or–

   Click the **Adjustment Layer** icon in the Layers palette, and click **Gradient**. The Gradient Fill dialog box appears.

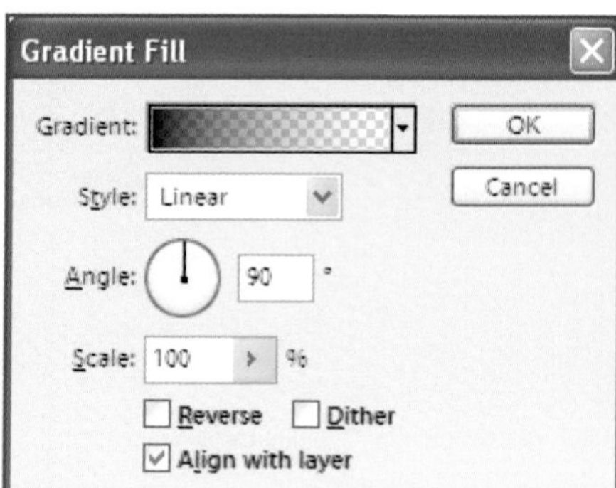

3. Click the **Gradient** down arrow, and select the gradient fill you want.
4. Select from among the following options:
   - **Style** defines how the gradient design will be distributed on the image.
   - **Angle** defines the angle of the design.
   - **Scale** enlarges or reduces the size of the gradient design.

- **Reverse** reverses the style orientation. For instance, if Radial is chosen, the gradient pattern will usually be concentrated in the center of the image with the edges showing a lesser effect. Clicking Reverse concentrates the pattern around the edges of the image and less towards the center.
- **Dither** blends adjacent colors in the gradient to reduce banding.
- **Align With Layer** connects the gradient fill to the dimensions of the layer.

5. Click **OK**. The fill layer is displayed in the Layers palette above the image.

FILL A LAYER WITH A PATTERN

1. Open an image and select it in the Layers palette.
2. Click **Layer**, click **New Fill Layer**, and click **Pattern**. The New Layer dialog box appears. Click **OK**. The Pattern Fill dialog box appears.

   –Or–

   Click the **Adjustment Layer** icon on the Layers palette, and click **Pattern**. The Pattern Fill dialog box appears.
3. Click the **Pattern** down arrow, and select the pattern fill you want.
4. Select from among the following options:
   - **Scale** enlarges or reduces the size of the pattern design.
   - **Link With Layer** connects the pattern to the fill layer.
   - **Snap To Origin** snaps the origin (usually the upper-left corner) of the pattern to the origin of the image.
5. Click **OK**. The fill layer is displayed in the Layers palette above the image.

Simplify a Layer

When you have fashioned the layer to your satisfaction with text layers, adjustment layers, or fill layers, you simplify the layer to reduce the file size and enable the use of filters and painting tools. Simplifying converts a type layer, fill layer, pattern layer, gradient level, or shape level into an image layer. After you simplify a layer, the icon identifying the style is replaced with the effect thumbnail. You are no longer able to edit or change the fill or adjustment in the layer.

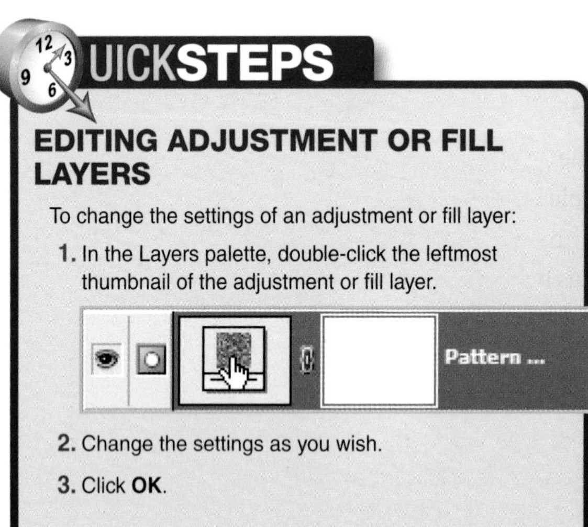

QUICKSTEPS

EDITING ADJUSTMENT OR FILL LAYERS

To change the settings of an adjustment or fill layer:

1. In the Layers palette, double-click the leftmost thumbnail of the adjustment or fill layer.
2. Change the settings as you wish.
3. Click **OK**.

Right-click the layer and click **Simplify Layer**.

–Or–

Select the adjustment or fill layer, and then click the **Layer** menu and click **Simplify Layer**. The special effect or style is merged into the layer.

Before the layer is simplified

After the layer is simplified

Work with Layer Styles

Layer styles present opportunities to add interesting effects to layers; however, layer styles cannot be effectively displayed on all layers. The styles and effects take place around the edges of layer content, so if you have a layer that is the same size as your background (the layer is full), the effect will not be visible, as can be seen in Figures 4-9a and 4-9b.

Figure 4-9a: Applying a style to the layer containing the photo has no discernable effect.

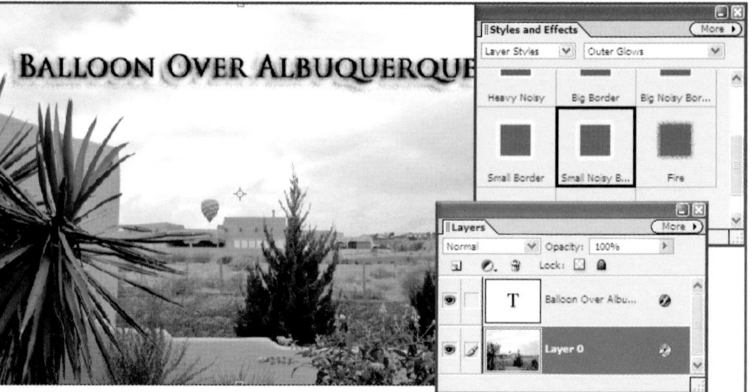

Figure 4-9b: The same style applied to a type layer is perfectly visible.

QUICKSTEPS

WORKING WITH LAYER STYLES

CLEAR LAYER STYLES

Sometimes, you might want to erase what you've done and start over. To remove all styles on a layer:

1. Click the layer in the Layers palette to select it.
2. Click the **Layer** menu, click **Layer Styles**, and click **Clear Layer Style**.

   –Or–

   Right-click the layer and click **Clear Layer Style**.

CHANGE LAYER STYLES

To change the settings for a layer style:

1. Click a layer to select it.
2. Click **Layer**, click **Layer Style**, and click **Style Settings**. The Style Settings dialog box appears.

   –Or–

   Double-click the **Layer Styles** icon on the desired layer in the Layers palette.
3. Make your desired changes and click **OK**.

Apply a Layer Style

Photoshop Elements has a wide selection of layer styles available in the Styles And Effects palette, as can be seen in Figure 4-10. Layer styles have a cumulative effect, so if you add several effects to a layer, the image will show them all. If you have multiple shapes or text objects in a layer, all objects will have the same style. Locked layers or background layers cannot be assigned a layer style or effect.

Click here to open the Styles And Effects palette

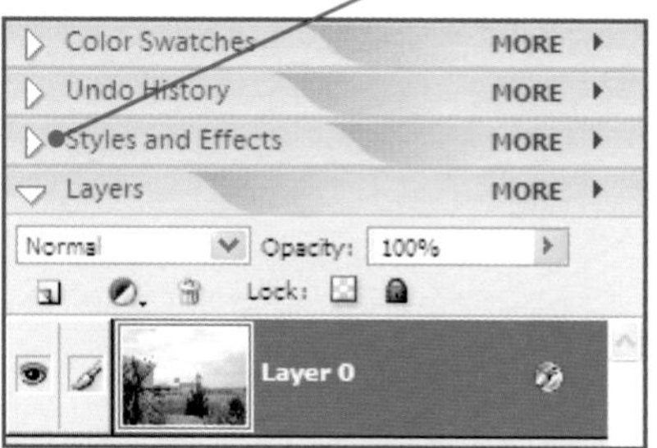

1. Select the layer on the Layers palette to which the style will be applied.
2. Open the Styles And Effects palette. If it is not displayed in the Palette Bin, click **Window** and click **Styles And Effects**. If it is displayed, click the left-pointing arrow in the title bar to open it.
3. Click the **left** down arrow, and click **Layer Styles** from the list.
4. Click the **right** down arrow, and click the style you want, such as that shown in Figure 4-10.

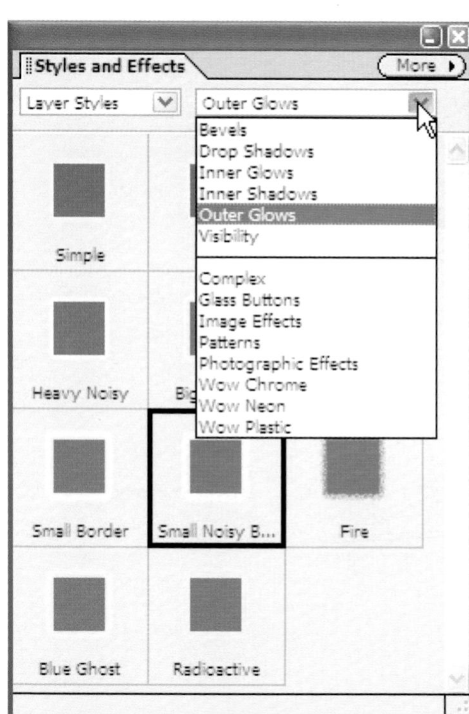

Figure 4-10: You can access many layer effects from the Layer Style dialog box.

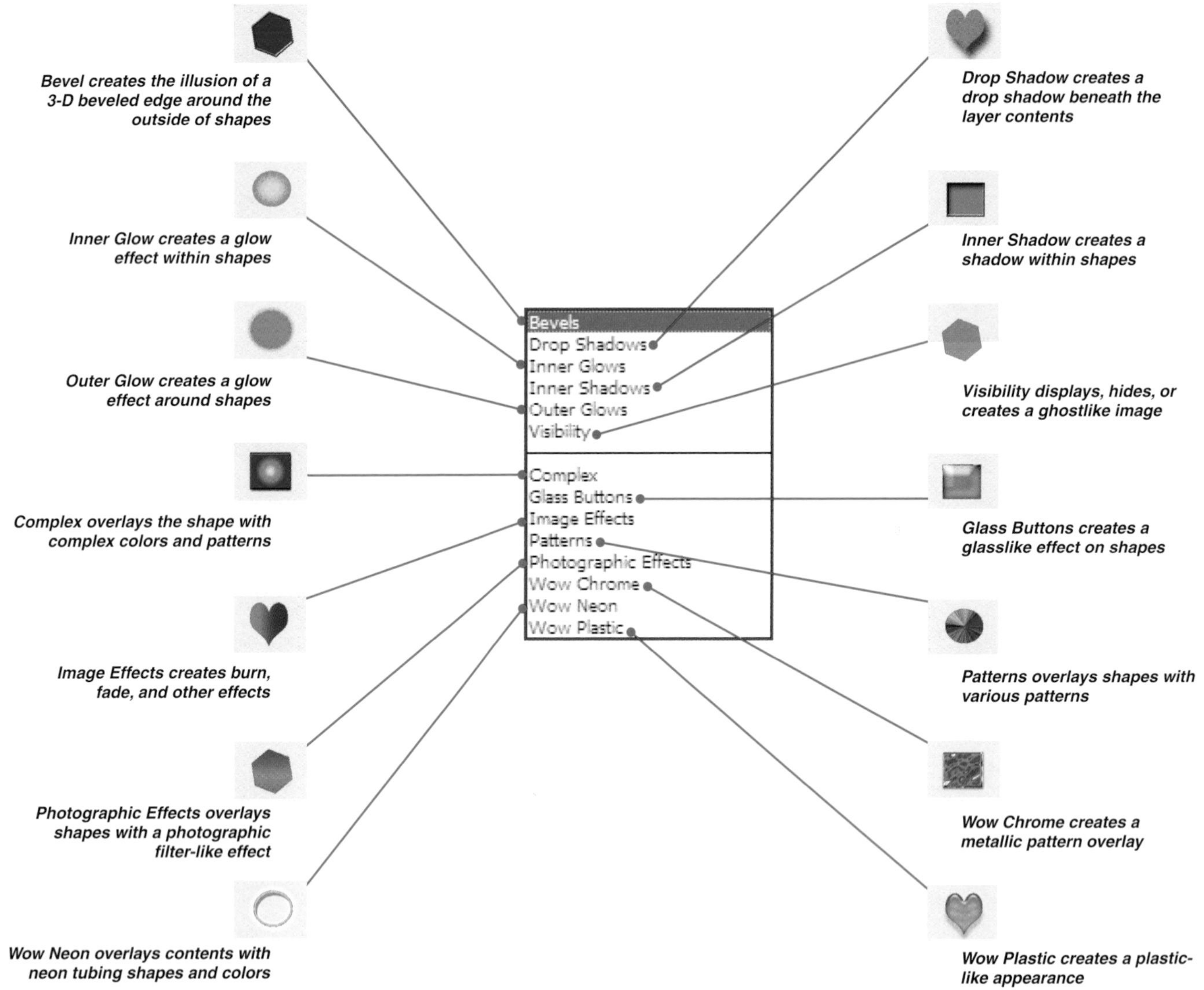

Bevels
Drop Shadows
Inner Glows
Inner Shadows
Outer Glows
Visibility

Complex
Glass Buttons
Image Effects
Patterns
Photographic Effects
Wow Chrome
Wow Neon
Wow Plastic

Bevel creates the illusion of a 3-D beveled edge around the outside of shapes

Inner Glow creates a glow effect within shapes

Outer Glow creates a glow effect around shapes

Complex overlays the shape with complex colors and patterns

Image Effects creates burn, fade, and other effects

Photographic Effects overlays shapes with a photographic filter-like effect

Wow Neon overlays contents with neon tubing shapes and colors

Drop Shadow creates a drop shadow beneath the layer contents

Inner Shadow creates a shadow within shapes

Visibility displays, hides, or creates a ghostlike image

Glass Buttons creates a glasslike effect on shapes

Patterns overlays shapes with various patterns

Wow Chrome creates a metallic pattern overlay

Wow Plastic creates a plastic-like appearance

How to...

- *Use Auto Corrections*
- *Adjust Lighting*
- *Eliminating Red Eye*
- *Sharpen Images*
- *Use the Clone Stamp Tool to Repair Backgrounds*
- *Using a Digital Tablet*
- *Clone Pixels from Another Image*
- *Apply Patterns*
- *Using the Brush to Repair Images*
- *Correct Backlighting*
- *Removing Dust and Scratches*
- *Soften Images with the Smudge and Blur Tools*
- *Visually Correct Images with the Color Variations Command*
- *Enhancing Images with Adjustment Layers*
- *Remove Color Casts*
- *Adjust Hue and Saturation*
- *Using Photo Filters*
- *Replace Color*
- *Use the Color Replacement Tool*
- *Make Tonal Adjustments*

Chapter 5 Retouching and Repairing Images

Whether you shoot digital images or scan images into Photoshop Elements, the resulting image is likely to need some work. The image may need to be retouched or repaired, or you may need to correct for certain deficiencies, such as color balance, a noticeable color cast, or an image that is not as sharp as it could be. In this chapter, you'll learn to use Photoshop Elements to enhance and repair images.

Make Quick Enhancements

Photoshop Elements gives you several options to quickly repair or enhance an image. You can take advantage of Photoshop Elements' automated enhancements to adjust *levels* (the distribution of pixels between shadow and highlight areas), adjust image contrast, and adjust color.

> **NOTE**
>
> You can also correct image deficiencies in Standard Edit mode from the Enhance menu. As a rule, you have more options when working in Standard Edit mode. If you find your edits in Quick Fix mode are not getting the job done, click the **Reset** button above the image, and then switch to Standard Edit mode.

Use Auto Corrections

When you need to quickly correct an image, you can take advantage of Photoshop Elements' Quick Fix pane. From here, you can use the Smart Fix Auto option, Auto Lighting Levels, Auto Lighting Contrast, or Auto Color corrections features found in the Palette Bin. To use Photoshop Elements' auto-corrections features:

1. Open the image you need to repair or enhance.
2. Click the **Quick Fix** button to display the Quick Fix pane. When you open the Quick Fix pane, you see your image in the document pane to the left of the Palette Bin, as shown in Figure 5-1.
3. Click the **View** down arrow, and click one of the following options: **Before**, **After**, **Before And After (Portrait)**, or **Before And After (Landscape)**. Figure 5-2 shows an image previewed in Before And After (Portrait).

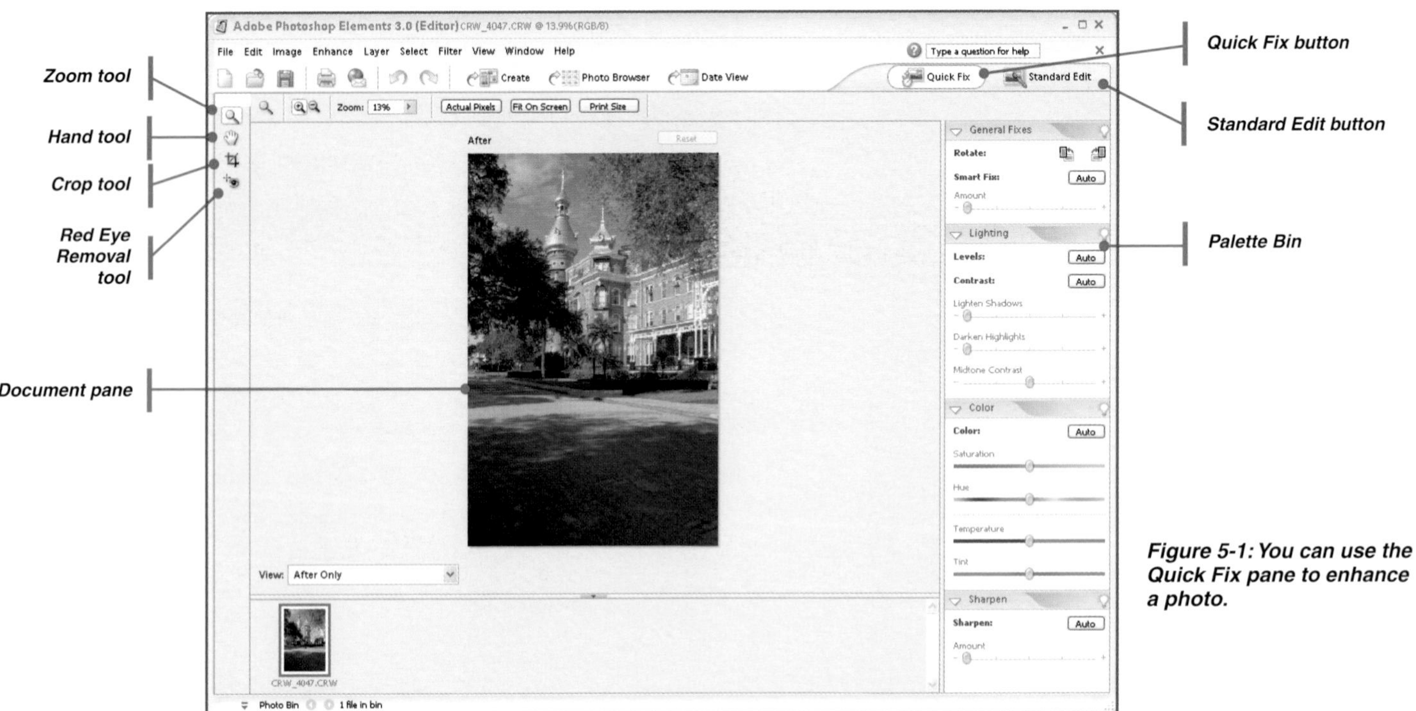

Figure 5-1: You can use the Quick Fix pane to enhance a photo.

TIP

With the Hand or Zoom tool selected, click **Actual Pixels** to view the image at its current pixel size; click **Fit On Screen** to size the image to the workspace; or click **Print Size** to view the image at the size it will be printed. Alternatively, you can press **CTRL+0** to size the image to the screen, or press **CTRL+ALT+0** to view an image at its actual pixel size.

Figure 5-2: You can preview your image before and after corrections are made.

USE AUTO SMART FIX

You can use the Auto Smart Fix feature to adjust the lighting and color in an image. Use this auto-correction feature to correct overall color balance and to adjust highlights and shadows.

1. Open the image you need to repair, and click the **Quick Fix** button to display the Quick Fix pane.
2. In the General Fixes section of the Palette Bin, click **Auto** to apply Auto Smart Fix. In most cases, this will correct the image.
3. Drag the **Amount** slider to increase the amount of correction, as shown. As you drag the slider, your image will automatically update.
4. Click **Commit** to apply the change. Alternatively, you can press **ENTER** to commit the change, or click **Cancel** if you decide not to apply the change. Figure 5-3 shows an image of a flower both before and after it was enhanced using Auto Smart Fix.

Cancel *Commit*
General Fixes
Rotate:
Smart Fix: Auto
Amount

Figure 5-3: You can quickly correct an image using Auto Smart Fix.

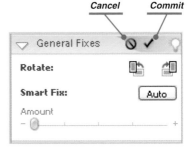

Adjust Lighting

The palettes in the Quick Fix pane also contain options you can use to adjust lighting. You have two options for adjusting lighting: Auto Levels and Auto Contrast. You can have Photoshop Elements perform these tasks automatically, or you can manually adjust levels by lightening shadows if detail is lacking in dark areas of the photo, or by manually darkening highlights if detail is lacking in bright areas of the photo. You can also manually adjust the amount of contrast applied to the midrange values in the image.

MANUALLY ADJUST LEVELS

If you prefer to visually adjust levels rather than leaving it to Photoshop Elements' automation, you can manually adjust levels.

1. Open the image you need to adjust, and click the **Quick Fix** button to display the Quick Fix pane.
2. In the Lighting section, click the **Auto** button to the right of the Levels title to let Photoshop Elements adjust the levels. In most cases this will get the job done. However, you can also manually adjust the levels by following steps 3 and 4.
3. Drag the **Lighten Shadows** slider to add detail to shadowed areas of the image.
4. Drag the **Darken Highlights** slider to add detail to the bright areas of the image. The following image shows the sliders being used in conjunction to manually adjust the levels of an image.
5. Click **Commit** to apply the change. Alternatively, you can press **ENTER**.

TIP

Click **Auto** to apply the Smart Fix corrections Photoshop Elements thinks your image needs.

USE AUTO CONTRAST

If your image lacks detail, it lacks contrast. To quickly adjust image contrast:

1. Open the image you want to adjust, and click the **Quick Fix** button to display the Quick Fix pane.
2. In the Lighting palette, click the **Auto** button to the right of the Contrast area, as shown in the illustration.

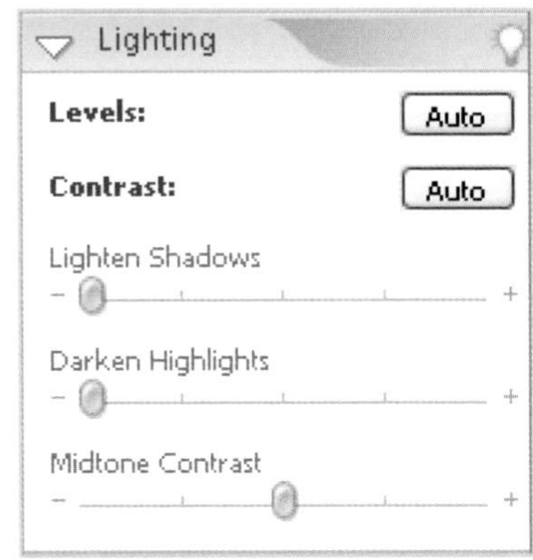

3. Click **Commit** to apply the change. Alternatively, you can press ENTER.

> **NOTE**
>
> As you drag the sliders, your image updates accordingly.

> **TIP**
>
> If your image is too light and lacks detail, drag the **Darken Highlights** slider to the right and the **Midtone Contrast** slider to the right. This combination will darken the image and increase contrast around the edges of the image.

MANUALLY ADJUST CONTRAST

If Auto Contrast does not get the job done, or if you prefer to manually adjust the contrast:

1. Open the image you want to adjust, and click the **Quick Fix** button.
2. In the Lighting section, drag the **Midtone Contrast** slider to the right to increase the contrast, or drag it to the left to decrease the contrast.
3. Click **Commit** to apply the changes. Alternatively, you can press ENTER.

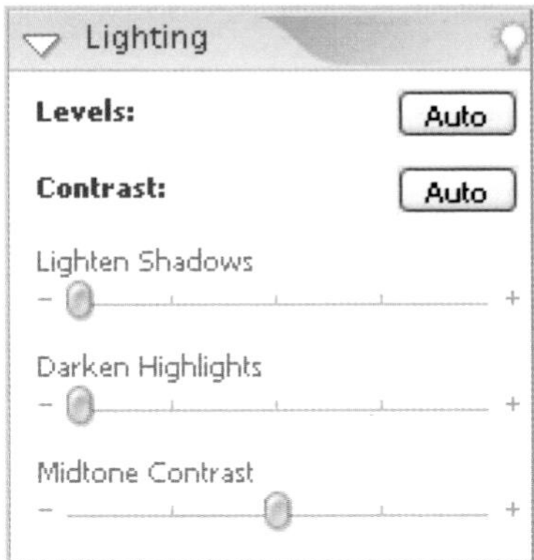

USE AUTO-COLOR CORRECTIONS

Many images you capture with a digital camera or scan into your computer need color correction. In the Color section of the Quick Fix pane, you can color-correct an image and, if need be, manually tweak the color correction.

1. Open the image you want to adjust, and click the **Quick Fix** button to display the Quick Fix pane.
2. In the Color section, click the **Auto** button. If the image still isn't color-corrected to your satisfaction, perform steps 3–7.
3. Drag the **Saturation** slider to the right to saturate, or deepen, the image color; drag it to the left to desaturate the image color.
4. Drag the **Hue** slider to add color to the image. Notice that the color bar under the Hue slider is color-coded. As you drag the slider over a particular color, it is added to the image, which adds that hue to all colors in the image.
5. Drag the **Temperature** slider to the right to warm the image (add more reds and oranges); drag it to the left to cool the image (add more blues).
6. Drag the **Tint** slider to the right to add a magenta tint to image colors; drag it to the left to add a green tint to the colors.
7. Click **Commit** to apply the changes. Alternatively, you can press **ENTER** to apply the changes. Figure 5-4 shows a photograph that was enhanced using Auto Levels and Auto Color Correction.

Figure 5-4: You can color-correct your images using the Auto Levels and Auto Color Correction commands.

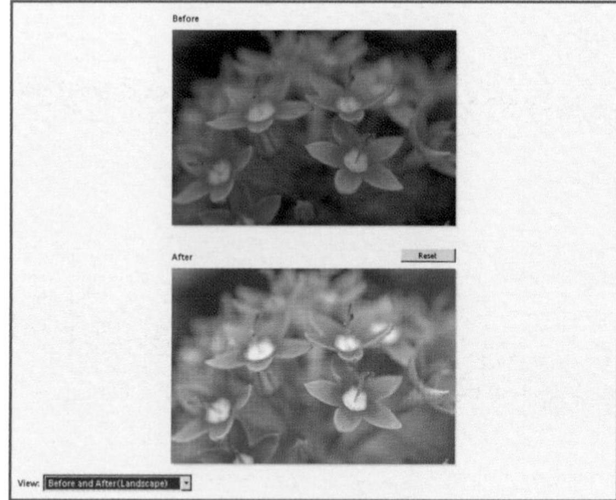

CAUTION

If you sharpen the image too much, artifacts will appear in the form of colored dots.

AUTO-SHARPEN AN IMAGE

You can automatically sharpen an image that lacks detail. When you sharpen an image, you increase the contrast of the pixels that define the edges of objects in your image.

1. Open the image you want to adjust, and click the **Quick Fix** button to display the Quick Fix pane.

QUICKSTEPS

ELIMINATING RED EYE

Red eye occurs when camera flash bounces off the retina of a person's eye, causing a red glow. The same phenomenon occurs when taking flash pictures of animals—instead of appearing red, the eye appears to have a ghostly glow. You can easily correct red eye within Photoshop Elements.

1. Open the image you want to adjust, and click the **Quick Fix** button to display the Quick Fix pane.
2. Use the **Zoom** tool to zoom in on the subject's eyes.
3. Click the **Red Eye Removal** tool.
4. Drag diagonally across the subject's pupil, as shown in the illustration.
5. Repeat for the other eye. Figure 5-5 shows an image where the Red Eye Removal tool was used to remove red eye from an image.

2. In the Sharpen section, click the **Auto** button.
3. Drag the **Amount** slider to add additional sharpening to the image.

4. Click **Commit** to apply the changes. Alternatively, you can press ENTER.

Work in Standard Edit Mode

When you need to make only a few adjustments on an image, your best bet is to work in Quick Fix mode. However, if you need to make extensive changes to an image, or if you want to get a bit artistic, you need to switch to Standard Edit mode to access all of Photoshop Elements' tools, which are neatly aligned on the left side of the workspace. When you select a tool, the Options toolbar (located above the Document pane) changes accordingly. To switch to Standard Edit mode, as shown in Figure 5-6, click the **Standard Edit** button in the upper-right corner of the screen.

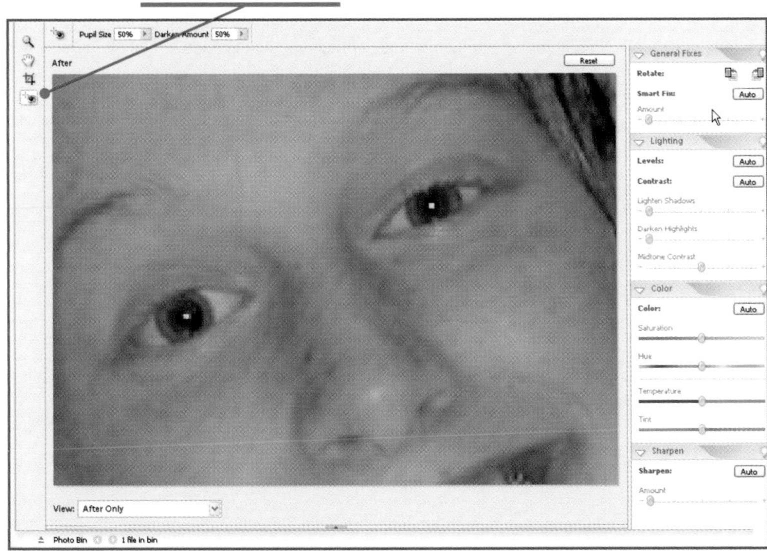

Figure 5-5: You can remove red eye from images using the Red Eye Removal tool.

1 2 3 4 5 6 7 8 9 10

Figure 5-6: You can manually edit an image in Standard Edit mode.

Options toolbar sets parameters for the selected tool

Tools toolbar contains tools to make selections and enhance or repair the image

Standard Edit button (accessed from the Organizer or Quick Fix Edit pane)

Palette Bin contains palettes for selecting color, adding styles or layers, and more

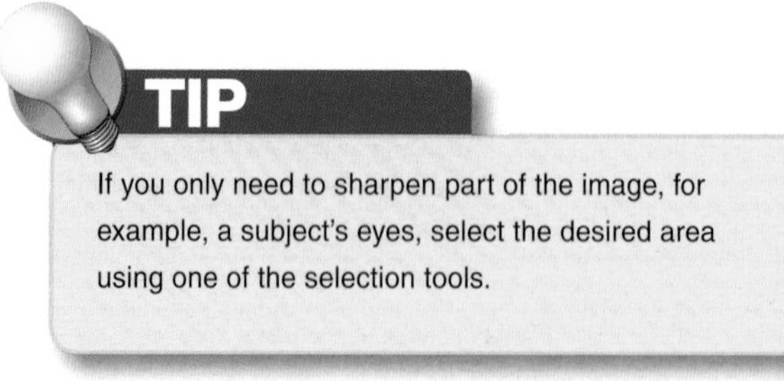

TIP

If you only need to sharpen part of the image, for example, a subject's eyes, select the desired area using one of the selection tools.

Sharpen Images

Some digital cameras don't produce a very sharp image. Some scanners are also notorious for creating soft images. You can sharpen images in Photoshop Elements using several different filters. However, if you need precise control when sharpening an image, your best bet is the Unsharpen Mask filter. The name may seem a bit confusing. What the filter actually does is increase the contrast of unsharp, or soft, edges (hence the name) in your image, which makes the images look notably sharper.

1. Open the image you want to sharpen.
2. Click the **Filter** menu, click **Sharpen**, and then click **Unsharp Mask**. The Unsharp Mask dialog box is displayed.

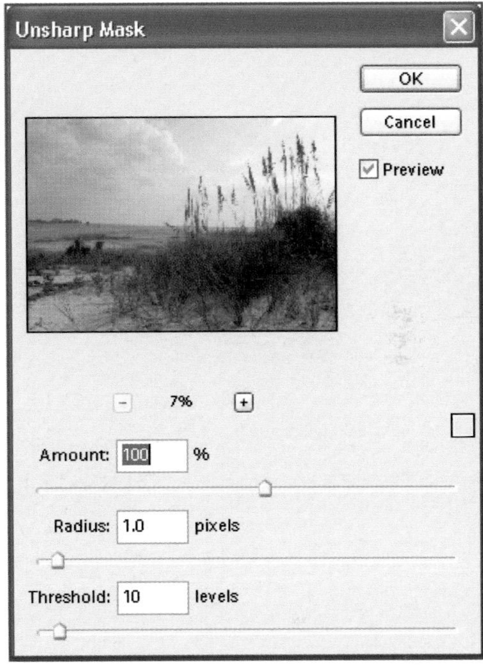

3. Drag the **Amount** slider to the right to determine the percentage of sharpening you want to apply to the image. Alternatively, you can type a value between 1 and 500 in the Amount text field. Typically, a value between 100 and 150 percent works well for a high-resolution image that will be printed, and a value between 45 and 100 works well for a low-resolution image for monitor or Web site viewing. As you drag the slider, you can see what the sharpened image will look like in the preview window provided the Preview option is selected (it is selected by default). If you notice artifacts (colored specks) around the edges in the image, you've over-sharpened. Drag the slider to the left until the artifacts disappear.
4. Drag the **Radius** slider to determine the distance in pixels that sharpening is applied from the edges in your image. In most instances the default value of 1 is perfect, although you may need a larger value when sharpening an image with large geometric shapes, such as buildings. If you decide to increase the radius, pay attention to your image. If you increase the radius too much, you'll create artifacts in the image.
5. Drag the **Threshold** slider to determine how different pixels must be before they are sharpened. This equates to levels in the histogram. For example, if a pixel has a level of 0 (solid black) and you specify a threshold of 2, pixels with a level of 1 or 2 that are adjacent to pixels with a threshold level of 0 will be sharpened. In most instances, the default value of 0 levels is perfect, as it sharpens all pixels in the image. However, if you're sharpening portraits or images with large areas of flesh tones, experiment with values between 2 and 20 to avoid introducing artifacts to the flesh tones.

TIP

Click the **Preview** check box in the Unsharp Mask dialog box to disable the preview of your image, and then click the check box again. This will show you the difference before and after the command is applied. It's also an easy way to spot any artifacts in the event you've applied too much sharpening.

TIP

If you're not happy with the results, click **Edit** and then click **Undo Unsharp Mask** before doing anything else.

Figure 5-7: You can enhance details in an image using the Unsharp Mask command.

6. Click **OK** to sharpen the image. Figure 5-7 shows an example of what can be achieved with the Unsharp Mask filter. The image on the left shows a photograph that needs sharpening, while the image on the right shows the image after the Unsharp Mask command is applied.

Use the Clone Stamp Tool to Repair Backgrounds

When you capture an image with your digital camera, you may find sometimes that despite your best efforts, something undesirable appears in your scene, such as sparse patches of grass, that detracts from the overall image. When this happens, you can use the Clone Stamp tool to copy an area from another part of your image and paste it over the undesirable object.

1. Open the image containing the object you need to remove.
2. Click the **Clone Stamp** tool.
3. From the Options toolbar, click **Brush** and select a brush type from the Brush pop-up menu, as shown in Figure 5-8.

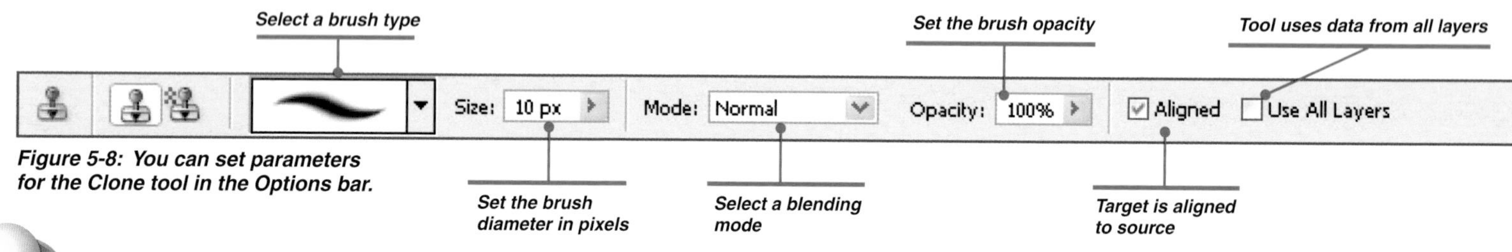

Figure 5-8: You can set parameters for the Clone tool in the Options bar.

TIP

Create a selection around the object you want to remove, and use the Clone Stamp tool to add a bit of background, such as the sky found on either side of the unwanted object. You can then clone from outside the selection into the selection. This technique prevents you from inadvertently copying over part of your subject.

4. Drag the **Size** slider to set the brush size. Alternatively, you can press the **RIGHT BRACKET** (]) key to increase the size of the brush or the **LEFT BRACKET** key ([) to decrease the size of the brush.
5. Select the desired blending mode from the Mode menu. Each blending mode produces a slightly different blend of the cloned pixels with the original pixels. For example, if you click the Darken blend mode, the cloned pixels darken the original pixels. Normal blend mode replaces the original pixels. Blending modes will be covered in detail in Chapter 7.

TIP

To achieve a natural result, clone from several different areas in order to prevent repeating a pattern, which is an obvious giveaway that the image has been altered.

QUICKFACTS

USING A DIGITAL TABLET

You'll have an easier time creating accurate selections or working with brush tools if you use a digital tablet. *Digital tablets* are devices that connect to a USB (Universal Serial Bus) port on your computer and have a stylus shaped like a pen. You draw on the digital tablet to create a selection in your image with one of the selection tools. The tablet is pressure-sensitive, which means you can control certain parameters, such as brush opacity or thickness, by applying more or less pressure to the tablet. Working with a digital tablet is intuitive because most people have been using pens and pencils for the majority of their lives. It's much easier to create a precise selection using a stylus and digital tablet than it is using a mouse. Digital tablets are sold at most stores that sell computers and, as of this writing, are priced as low as $99.00. The following image shows a digital tablet and stylus in use.

6. Drag the **Opacity** slider to determine how much of the original image appears when you clone an area. The default setting of 100 replaces the original image with cloned pixels wherever you use the tool.
7. The **Aligned** option is selected by default. Leave this option selected to have the sampled area (source pixels) move in conjunction with the target area into which you paint the cloned pixels. Click the **Use All Layers** check box to clone pixels from all layers in the image into the currently selected layer.
8. Press **ALT** and click in the area in your photo from which you want to clone.
9. Drag inside the selection to copy over the object you don't want in the image.
10. Click **Select** and click **Deselect** to remove the selection. The following illustration shows an image before and after it was enhanced using the Clone Stamp tool to replace the dead grass in the foreground of the photo.

1 2 3 4 5 6 7 8 9 10

Clone Pixels from Another Image

At times it's desirable to clone pixels from another image. For example, if you need to replace a less-than-lush lawn, you can clone pixels from an image that contains a picture-perfect lawn, such as a carefully manicured golf course.

1. Open the target and source images while working in Standard Edit mode.
2. Click the **Clone Stamp** tool and set the tool's parameters as outlined in the "Use the Clone Stamp Tool to Repair Backgrounds" section.
3. Click **Window**, click **Images**, and then click **Tile**.
4. Press ALT and click inside the area of the source image from which you want to clone the pixels.
5. Click inside the target image to which you want the pixels cloned, and drag the area in the image into which you want the pixels cloned. The illustration on the left shows grass being cloned from the bottom image to the top image.

Apply Patterns

You can also clone a pattern into an area of an image. This option is handy when you have a large area, such as a brick wall, you want removed from your image. Use the Pattern Stamp tool to clone a pattern into a photograph.

1. Open the image containing the background to which you want to apply a pattern.
2. Click the **Pattern Stamp** tool.
3. From the Options toolbar, click the **Brush** down arrow, and click a brush type, as shown in Figure 5-9.

Figure 5-9: You can set parameters for the Pattern Stamp tool in the Options bar.

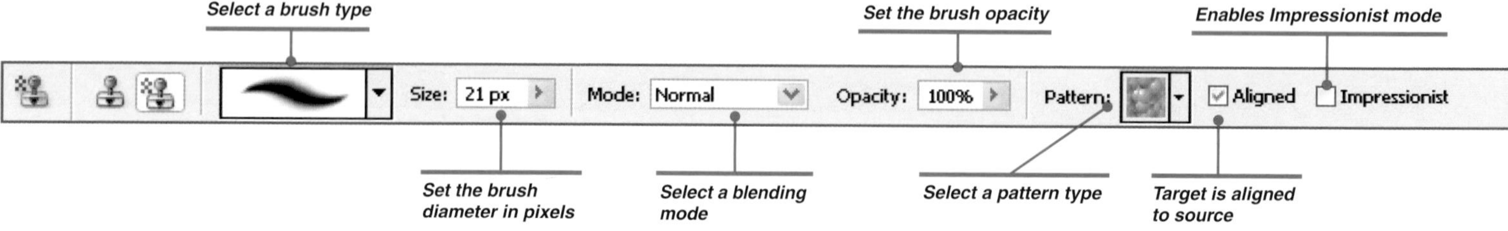

QUICKFACTS

USING THE BRUSH TO REPAIR IMAGES

The Brush tool can be used to add artistic splashes of color to any image (see Chapter 7). It can also be used to repair an image. For example, if you're editing an old, faded photograph you scanned into your computer, you can bring some of the color back by painting over the faded areas with a similar color while working in Color mode. Reduce the opacity of the brush to let some of the underlying color shine through. You can also use the Brush tool as a *dodging* tool (lighten pixels to reveal detail in darkened areas) and a *burning* tool (darken pixels in washed-out areas). Paint a blank layer using the Soft Light blending mode to achieve professional dodging or burning results. Choose a brush with a soft edge, and lower brush opacity to 30 percent to gradually dodge or burn as you paint the layer. Paint white where you need to lighten the image and restore details (dodge); paint black where you need to darken the image (burn).

TIP

To keep your original photo unchanged, copy the background layer, and apply all your edits to the duplicated layer. If the results are unacceptable, delete the duplicate layer to return to your original image.

4. Drag the **Size** slider to select a brush size. Alternatively, you can press the **RIGHT BRACKET** (]) key to increase the size of the brush or the **LEFT BRACKET** key ([) to decrease the size of the brush.
5. Click the **Mode** down arrow, and click a blending mode. Each blending mode produces a slightly different blend of the cloned pixels with the original pixels. For example, if you click the Darken blend mode, the cloned pixels darken the original pixels. Normal blend mode replaces the original pixels. Blending modes will be covered in detail in Chapter 7.
6. Accept the default opacity of **100%**, or type a lower value to let some of the original background show through the pattern. Alternatively, you can drag the **Opacity** slider to set the value.
7. Click the **Pattern** down arrow, and click a pattern.
8. Accept the default option (**Aligned**), and Photoshop Elements aligns the pattern as you paint, creating a seamless pattern.
9. Click the **Impressionist** check box, and the pattern is applied as if it were painted by an Impressionist painter.
10. Drag inside the image to replace the background with a pattern.

Correct Backlighting

In Photoshop Elements 2, you used the Fill Flash command to repair images in which the subject was backlit and camera fill flash was not used. Photoshop Elements 3 instead boasts a Shadow/Highlights command that takes care of two digital photography problems: a subject that is dark due to backlighting, and a subject that is dark because fill flash was needed but not used.

1. Open an image that contains a backlit subject.
2. Click **Enhance**, click **Adjust Lighting**, and then click **Shadows/Highlights**. The Shadows/Highlights dialog box appears. The default setting lightens shadows by 50 percent.

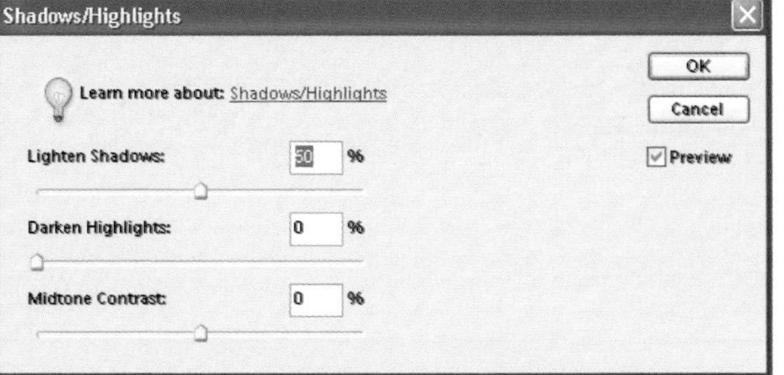

1 2 3 4 5 6 7 8 9 10

REMOVING DUST AND SCRATCHES

If you're working with old photos that have damage in the form of dust specks or scratches, you can easily remove them using the Dust & Scratches filter. The filter performs its magic by blurring dissimilar pixels.

1. Open the image you want to repair.
2. Click **Filters**, click **Noise**, and click **Dust & Scratches**. The Dust & Scratches dialog box is displayed.

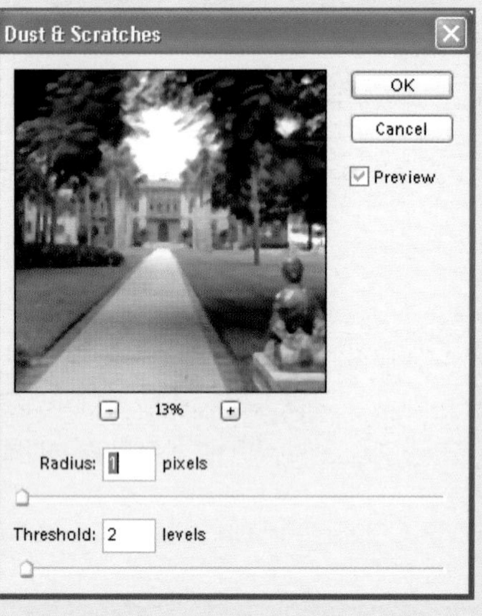

3. Drag the **Radius** slider to the right until the "noise" begins to disappear. Alternatively, you can type a value between 1 and 16 in the Radius text field. Don't select a value higher than needed, as you'll excessively blur the image.
4. Drag the **Threshold** slider to the right to specify the highest possible value that eliminates the dust marks and scratches. This setting determines how dissimilar pixels must be before the filter will eliminate them.
5. Click **OK** to apply the repair.

3. If needed, drag the **Lighten Shadows** slider to the right to further lighten the shadows, or drag it to the left to darken the shadows.
4. If needed, drag the **Darken Highlights** slider to the right to darken the brightest areas of the image.
5. If needed, drag the **Midtone Contrast** slider to the right to add contrast to the midtones in the photo, or drag it to the left to decrease the contrast.
6. Click **OK** to apply the change.

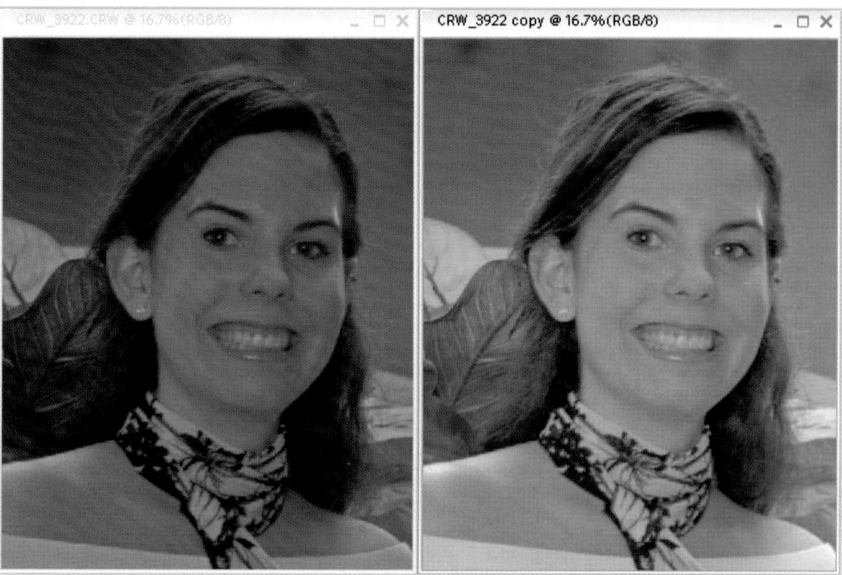

Soften Images with the Smudge and Blur Tools

Sometimes when you paste a selection into an image, you end up with a harsh edge that makes the image look unrealistic. Other times you may inadvertently add a harsh edge while editing an image. You can easily remove a harsh edge using the Smudge and Blur tools. The Smudge tool moves pixels, which results in a blending effect. You can use the Blur tool to soften a harsh edge or, for that matter, to blur an unwanted object in an image so that it is no longer recognizable, such as a garbage can.

> **TIP**
>
> If you're smudging a large area, choose a soft-edged brush so the transition between the smudged area and adjacent pixels isn't too harsh.

USE THE SMUDGE TOOL

Use the Smudge tool to smear pixels that you want to blend. The tool picks up colored pixels and moves them in the direction you drag. You can set the strength of the tool and choose the brush size, blending mode, and so on.

1. Click the **Smudge** tool while working in Standard Edit mode. 
2. From the Options toolbar, click the **Brush** down arrow, and select a brush type, as shown in Figure 5-10.

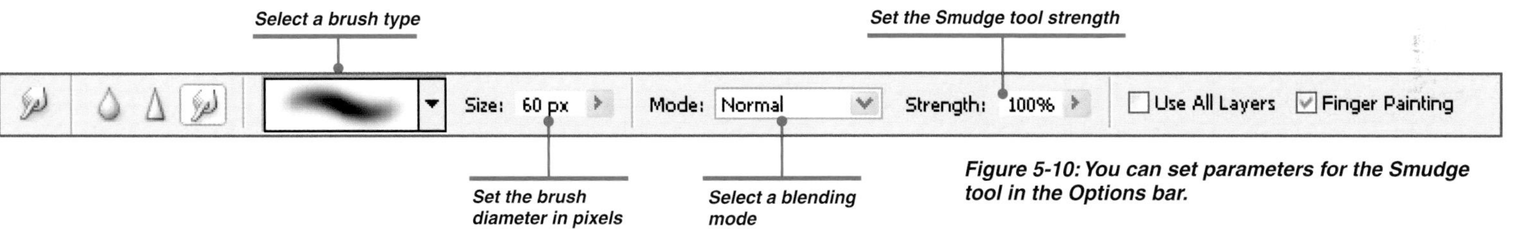

Figure 5-10: You can set parameters for the Smudge tool in the Options bar.

3. Drag the **Size** slider to set the brush size.
4. Click the **Mode** down arrow, and click a blending mode.
5. Drag the **Strength** slider to specify the strength of the tool. Alternatively, you can type a value between 1 percent (to barely move the pixels) and 100 percent (to use the tool at maximum strength).
6. Click the **Use All Layers** check box to use data from all the layers on the current layer you are smudging.

> **TIP**
>
> If you're blurring a large area, select the appropriate brush size, but make sure the brush type you choose has soft edges so there won't be a harsh transition between the area you blur and adjacent pixels.

USE THE BLUR TOOL

You can also smooth edges using the Blur tool. When you use the Blur tool, you don't move pixels; you blur the pixels you drag the tool across. You can choose the brush type, size, blending mode, and whether the tool blurs across layers.

Figure 5-11: You can set parameters for the Blur tool in the Options bar.

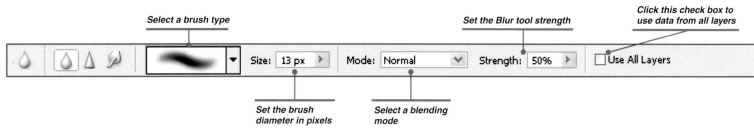

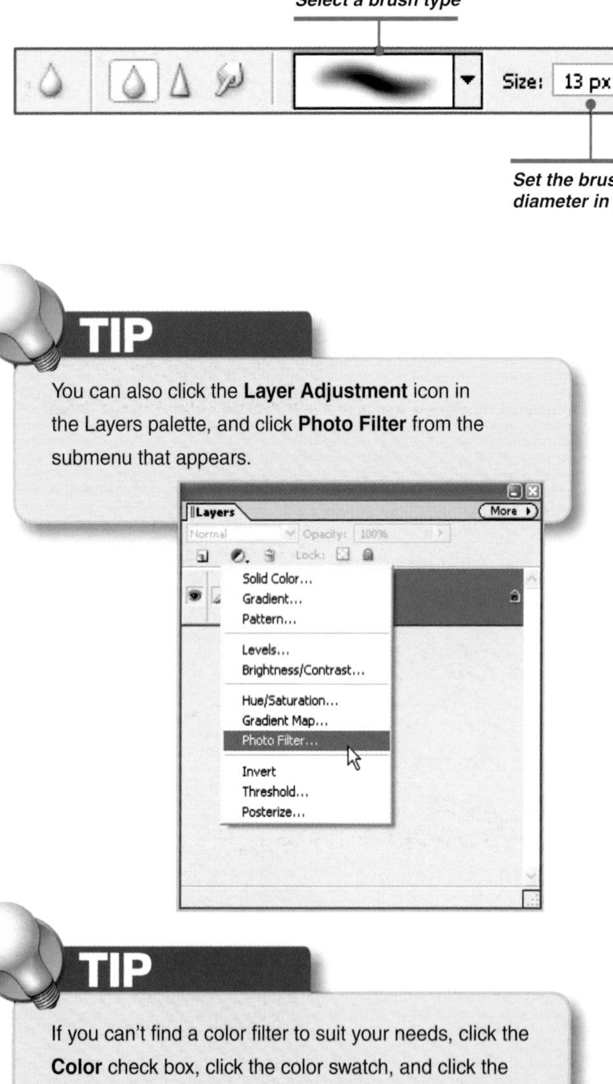

TIP

You can also click the **Layer Adjustment** icon in the Layers palette, and click **Photo Filter** from the submenu that appears.

TIP

If you can't find a color filter to suit your needs, click the **Color** check box, click the color swatch, and click the desired color from the Color Picker.

1. Click the **Blur** tool while working in Standard Edit mode.
2. From the Options toolbar, click the **Brush** down arrow, and click a brush type with a soft edge, as shown in Figure 5-11.
3. Drag the **Size** slider to set the brush size. Alternatively, you can type the desired value in the Size field.
4. Click the **Mode** down arrow, and click a blending mode.
5. Accept the default strength (**100%**), or type a different value in the Strength field. Alternatively, you can drag the **Strength** slider to set a value between 1 and 100 percent.
6. Click the **Use All Layers** check box to use data from all the layers on the current layer you are blurring.
7. Click the **Finger Painting** check box to smudge the current foreground color into your the image.
8. Drag across the pixels you want to smudge.

Work with Color

Another task you can perform with Photoshop Elements is adjusting color. You can use menu commands to color-correct images, change tonal value, remove color casts, and adjust image hue and saturation. You often use several of these commands in conjunction. You can also apply multiple color corrections using the Color Variations command.

Visually Correct Images with the Color Variations Command

If you're visually oriented and don't like dealing with curves, histograms, or levels, Photoshop Elements 3 has a wonderful command that lets you eyeball a color correction. This gem of an image adjustment command is known as Color Variations. With Color Variations, you can remove a color cast or highlight by clicking a variation of the original image and then comparing the original to the modified version.

1. Open the image you want to edit, and then to switch to Standard Edit mode by clicking the **Standard Edit** button; or, in the Organizer, click the **Edit** button and click **Go To Standard Edit**.
2. Click **Enhance**, click **Adjust Colors**, and then click **Color Variations**. The Color Variations dialog box appears, shown in Figure 5-12.
3. Select the type of adjustments you'd like to make:
   - **Midtones**, **Shadows**, and **Highlights** adjust the middle, dark, and light tones in your image, respectively.
   - **Saturation** increases or decreases the hue of the image.
4. Drag the **Amount** slider to determine the degree of correction you want to apply. As you drag the slider, the variation thumbnails change. Drag the slider to the left to produce subtle changes; drag the slider to the right to produce pronounced changes.

TIP

When working with color variations, start with the default Amount setting to make your initial adjustments, and then drag the slider to the left when making your final adjustments.

TIP

To restore the "after" thumbnail to the original image and remove any prior variation adjustments, click **Reset Image**.

NOTE

In the Color Variations dialog box, you can click a variation thumbnail multiple times to increase the effects of the action.

1 2 3 4 5 6 7 8 9 10

1 2 3 4 5 6 7 8 9 10

QUICKSTEPS

ENHANCING IMAGES WITH ADJUSTMENT LAYERS

When you edit an image and apply a command, pixels are modified. When you apply other commands, additional pixels are modified. If, after applying several commands, you decide that you applied a command in error, you can use the Undo History palette to restore the image to the step prior to the command you applied in error. When you do this, however, you lose all edits from that point forward. You can alleviate this problem by using adjustment layers. Adjustment layers are advantageous in that they can be deleted without affecting other modifications to an image. You can also save them and make them a permanent part of the image. When you apply an adjustment layer to an image, you can use many of the commands previously discussed in this chapter. If you decide that you need to tweak a command, you can easily do so by activating the layer and modifying the parameters.

1. Open the image you want to modify, and then switch to Standard Edit mode.
2. If only part of your image needs editing, create a selection using the applicable selection tool.
3. Click the **Window** menu and then click **Layers**. The Layers palette is displayed.
4. Click **Create Adjustment Layer**, and click one of the following options:
   - Click **Levels** to adjust the lightness or darkness in the image.
   - Click **Gradient Map** to choose from preset gradients that cover the selected pixels in the adjustment layer.

Continued...

5. To adjust the image, do one of the following:
   - To add a color to an image, click the appropriate increase variation-thumbnail. For example, to add red to an image, click the **Increase Red** variation thumbnail.
   - To remove a color cast from an image, click the opposite variation-thumbnail. For example, if the image has a green cast, click the **Decrease Green** variation thumbnail.
   - To adjust the saturation, click the **Saturation** option and then click the **Less Saturation** variation thumbnail to decrease saturation; click the **More Saturation** variation thumbnail to increase saturation.
6. Click **OK** to apply the changes.

Figure 5-12: You can use the Color Variations command to correct the color of an image.

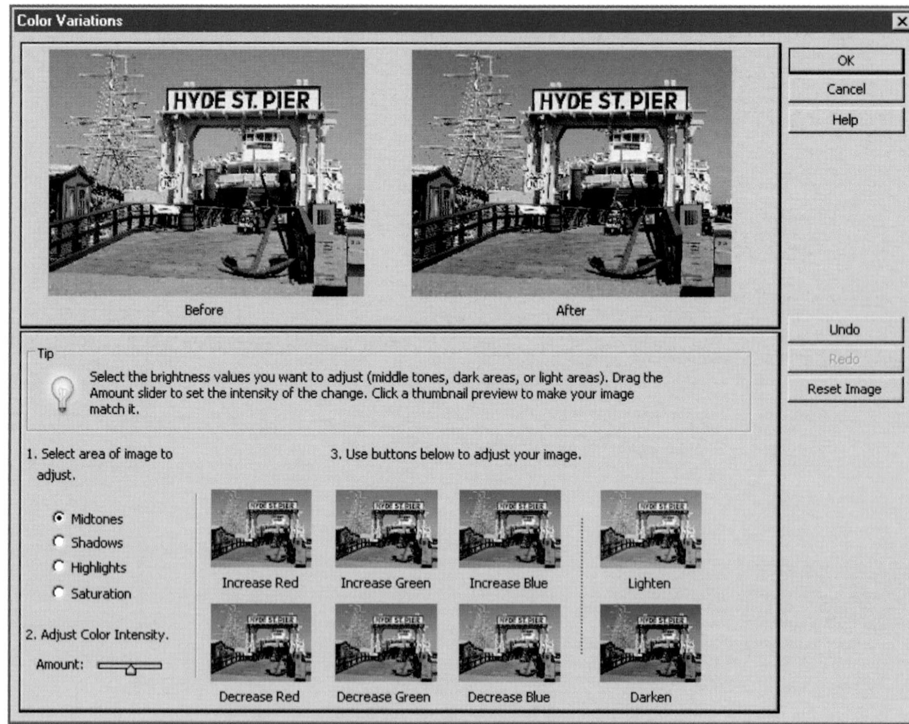

ENHANCING IMAGES WITH ADJUSTMENT LAYERS *(Continued)*

- **Photo Filter** to add a filter effect to the image or selection (see "Using Photo Filters").
- **Brightness/Contrast** to brighten or darken the image, or to add contrast or soften the image.
- **Hue/Saturation** to vary the tint or intensity of all colors or of a selected color.
- **Invert** to turn the selection into a negative-like image by inverting the brightness values.
- **Threshold** to convert grayscale or color images to black and white. Drag the slider to select the desired level. All pixels above that level are converted to white, whereas all pixels below the specified level are converted to black.
- **Posterize** to diminish the color in an image, creating a posterized image. The lower the number, the more dramatic the change.

5. Make the desired changes and click **OK** to close the dialog box. After applying an adjustment layer, it appears in the Layers list.
6. Add other adjustment layers as needed.
7. Double-click any adjustment layer to open the applicable dialog box. You can edit an adjustment layer at any time.
8. After you finish editing the image, click the **Layer** menu and click **Flatten**.

Remove Color Casts

When you scan an image or capture an image from a digital camera, it may contain a color cast. You can often remove a color cast by applying the Auto Levels command. However, if there is still a slight color cast, you can correct this using the Remove Color Cast command.

1. Open the image you want to edit, and then switch to Standard Edit mode.
2. Click **Enhance**, click **Adjust Color**, and then click **Remove Color Cast**. The Remove Color Cast dialog box appears.

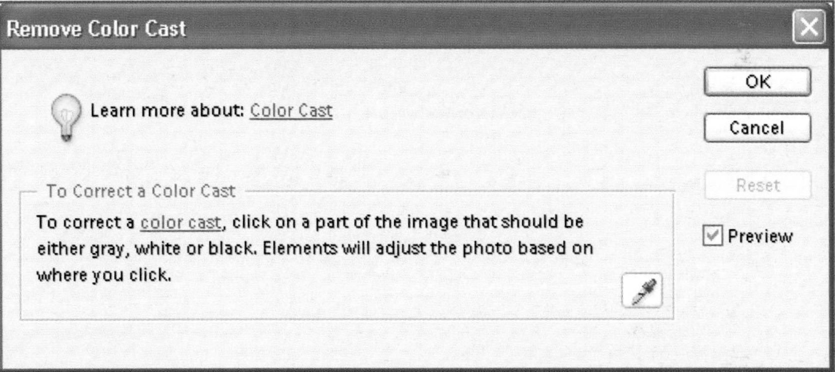

3. Click the **eyedropper** icon and then click an area inside the image that should be black, neutral gray, or white. After you click inside the image, the image changes. If the color cast is still apparent, click a different area within the image. As long as you have the Preview check box selected, the image updates every time you click inside the image.
4. Click **OK** to apply the changes.

TIP

If, after repeated clicks, you've changed the image so that it's difficult to find black, gray, or white, click **Reset** to remove the effects of the tool and start over with the original image.

Adjust Hue and Saturation

Use the Hue/Saturation command to adjust the hue and saturation for an entire image or for a specific color component. This command is an excellent tool to correct color deficiencies. You can also use this command to change the hue of specific colors and achieve special effects, such as converting an image to grayscale, which is covered in Chapter 7.

USING PHOTO FILTERS

If you're an avid 35-mm photographer, you may have used photo filters to warm or cool an image. Another popular photo filter you may have used is a color filter to tint an image. In Photoshop Elements you can apply the same filters digitally to cool, warm, or tint an image.

1. Open the desired image.
2. Click **Layer**, click **New Adjustment Layer**, and then click **Photo Filter**. The New Layer dialog box appears.
3. Accept the default layer name, or type a different name, and then click **OK**. The Photo Filter dialog box appears.
4. Click the **Filter** down arrow, and click one of the following options:
   - **Warming Filter (85)** warms up the color tones in a cool image that has a bluish color cast.
   - **Cooling Filter (80)** cools an image that has a yellowish cast by making the colors bluer.
   - **Warming Filter (81)** warms the color tones of a bluish image by making them more yellow.
   - **Cooling Filter (85)** cools an image with a yellow cast by making the colors bluer.
   - **Color Filters** tints an image. You can remove a color cast from an image by selecting a filter with a complimentary color. You can also use a color filter for special effects, such as applying a red tint over the image.
   - **Underwater Filter** makes an image appear as though it was photographed underwater by applying an aquamarine tint to the image. You can change that color of the tint and vary the opacity to achieve the desired result.
5. Drag the **Density** slider to determine how much color is applied to the image. Alternatively, you can type a value in the Percentage text box. Select a higher density for a more pronounced effect.
6. Click **OK** to apply the filter.
7. When you are satisfied with the adjustments, click **More**, click the **Layer** menu, and click **Flatten Image** to make the changes permanent.

CHANGE HUE OR SATURATION FOR THE ENTIRE IMAGE

1. In Standard Edit mode, open the image for which you want to adjust the hue.
2. Click **Enhance**, click **Adjust Color**, and then click **Adjust Hue/Saturation**. The Hue/Saturation dialog box appears.

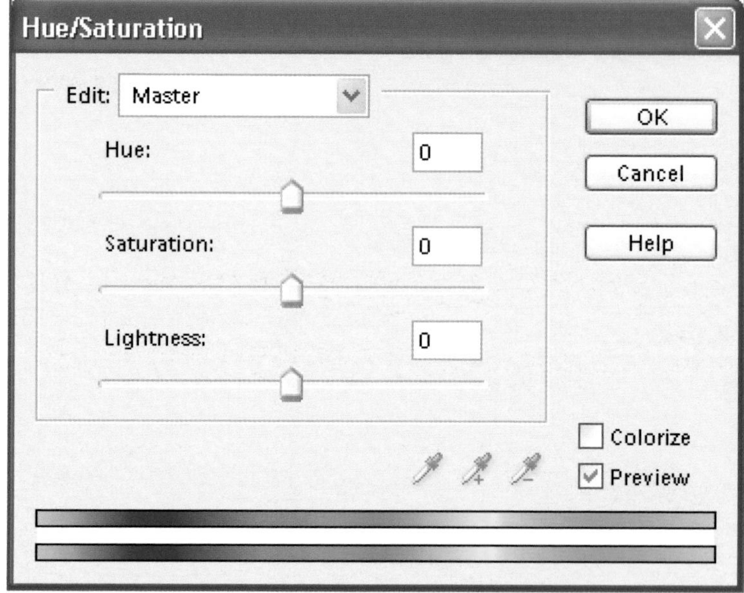

3. In the Edit list box, accept the selected default option (**Master**).
4. Drag the **Hue** slider until the colors appear as desired. Alternatively, you can type a value in the Hue text field.
5. Drag the **Saturation** slider to achieve the desired result. Drag to the right to increase saturation; drag to the left to decrease saturation. Alternatively, you can type a value in the Saturation text field.
6. Drag the **Lightness** slider to the left to darken the image; drag it to the right to lighten the image. Alternatively, you can type a value in the Lightness text field.
7. Click **OK** to apply the settings.

NOTE

When adding a photo filter to an image, accept the default option (**Preserve Luminosity**) unless you want the image to be darkened by the filter.

TIP

To adjust the hue or saturation for part of an image, select the area using the applicable selection tool.

TIP

To reset the settings in just about any Photoshop Elements dialog box, press **ALT** to momentarily convert the Cancel button to a Reset button. Click the **Reset** button prior to releasing the **ALT** key.

TIP

You can use the Hue/Saturation command to brighten a subject's teeth. Use the **Lasso** tool to select the teeth, and apply a **1**-pixel feather. Drag the **Lightness** slider to achieve a value between 9 and 11 for best results.

CHANGE HUE OR SATURATION FOR A SPECIFIC COLOR

1. Open the image for which you want to adjust the hue or saturation.
2. Click **Enhance**, click **Adjust Color**, and then click **Adjust Hue/Saturation**. The Hue/Saturation dialog box appears.
3. From the Edit drop-down list, click the desired color. The Hue/Saturation dialog box changes to the configuration shown here. Notice that a range of colors has been selected in the dialog box.

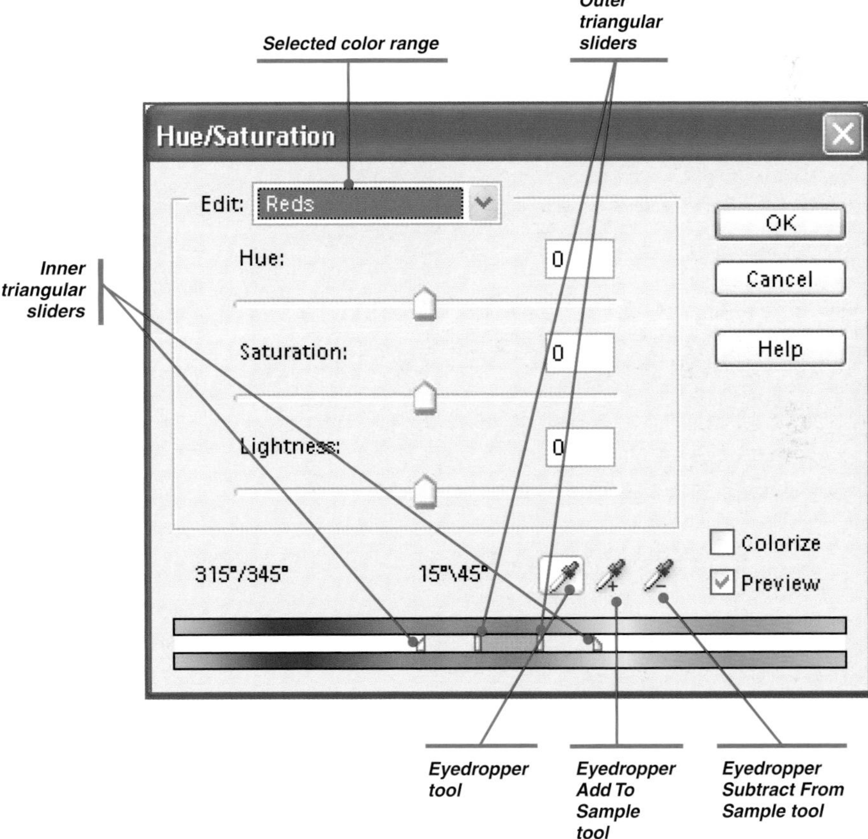

1 2 3 4 5 6 7 8 9 10

1 2 3 4 5 6 7 8 9 10

TIP

To adjust the hue or saturation for part of an image, select the area using the applicable selection tool.

TIP

Press **CTRL**, click in the color range selected, and drag the color bar to select a different range of color.

TIP

With the Eyedropper tool selected, press **SHIFT** to add colors to the range, or press **ALT** to decrease the range of color.

TIP

You can also click the **Color** swatch located to the right of the eyedroppers to open the Color Picker. You can then click inside the actual image to determine the color to be replaced.

4. Modify the range of colors by doing one of the following:
   - Drag the **inner triangular** sliders to change the range of colors.
   - Drag the **outer triangular** sliders to increase or decrease the range falloff. This setting determines how many similar colors will be affected by your edits.
   - Click the **Eyedropper** tool and click inside the image to specify the color range for which you want to change hue or saturation. This sets the selected color range in the Hue/Saturation dialog box.
   - Click the **Eyedropper Add To Sample** tool, and click inside the image to add colors to the range.
   - Click the **Eyedropper Subtract From Sample** tool, and click inside the image to remove colors from the range.
5. Drag the **Hue** slider to change the color of the range. If needed, drag the **Saturation** and/or **Lightness** sliders to change the saturation and/or lightness of the color range.
6. You can modify additional colors by selecting them from the Edit list, or click **OK** to apply your changes.

Replace Color

You can quickly replace areas of solid color in an image. This technique is handy when you want to create special effects, such as changing the color of a house wall from red to blue, or when you want to create a special effect, such as changing the color of the sky in an image you are editing.

1. In Standard Edit mode, open the image you want to edit.
2. Click **Enhance**, click **Adjust Color**, and then click **Replace Color**. The Replace Color dialog box appears, as shown in Figure 5-13.
3. Click one of the following display options:
   - **Image** displays the actual image.
   - **Selection** displays the area of color you are replacing.

Figure 5-13: You can replace a color in an image.

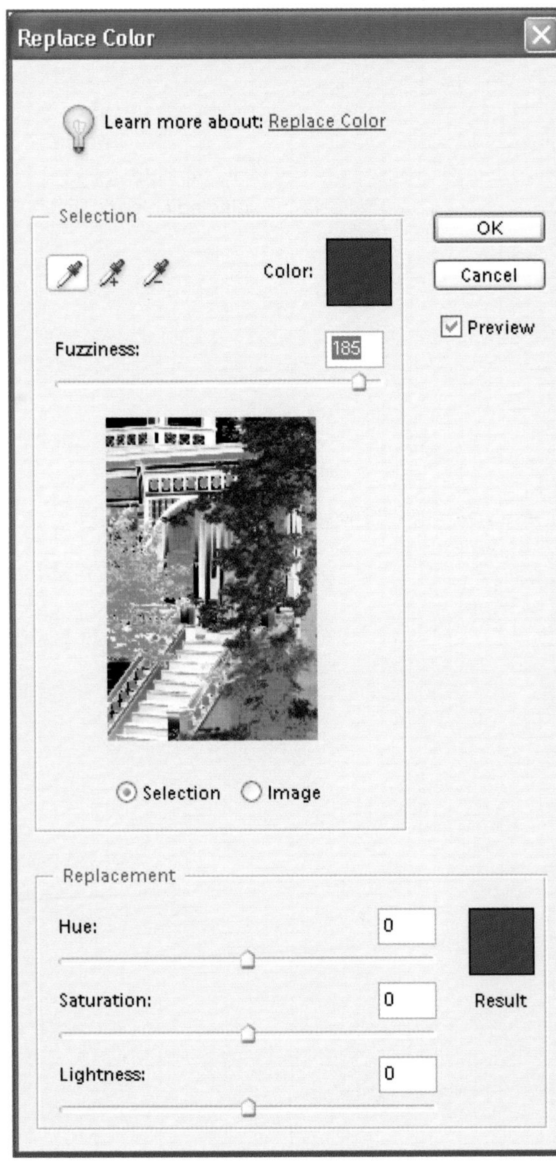

4. Click the **eyedropper** icon on the left, and click inside the display to select the color you want to replace.
5. Click the **eyedropper** icon in the middle (with the plus sign), and click inside the display to add colors to be replaced.
6. Click the **eyedropper** icon on the right (with the minus sign), and click inside the display to remove colors that you don't want replaced.
7. Drag the **Fuzziness** slider to determine how similar colors are to be treated. Drag the slider to the left to replace only colors that are closely related to the selection; drag it to the right to replace a wider variety of colors.
8. Drag the **Hue**, **Saturation**, and **Lightness** sliders to specify the replacement color. Alternatively, you can click the **Result** color swatch, and click the replacement color from the Color Picker.
9. Click **OK** to replace the color.

Use the Color Replacement Tool

If you have an image in which you want to replace one color with another, you can use the Color Replacement tool to achieve this. This tool enables you to replace existing color with the current foreground color while allowing underlying textures, such as wrinkles and wood grain, to show through.

1. Click the foreground color swatch to open the Color Picker.
2. Click the desired foreground color from the Color Picker.
3. Click the **Color Replacement** tool.
4. From the Options bar, click **Brush** and click a brush style.
5. Click one of the following Sampling options:
   - **Continuous** samples color continuously as you drag the tool over your image.
   - **Once** samples the color where you first click and only replaces that color as you drag the tool.
   - **Background Swatch** replaces the current background color with the current foreground color as you drag the tool.

TIP

If you don't like the selection you've made, press **ALT** to convert the Cancel button to a Reset button. Click the **Reset** button while pressing **ALT**.

TIP

To convert a color image to black and white, click **Enhance**, click **Adjust Color**, and click **Remove Color**.

6. Click one of the following Limits options:
   - **Discontiguous** replaces color wherever it is found, regardless of location, as you drag the tool inside your image.
   - **Contiguous** replaces color only when it is found in pixels contiguous with the color where you first clicked inside the image.
7. Type a tolerance value between 0 and 255. Specify a lower value to replace colors that are close to the color you first clicked; specify a higher value to replace a wider range of colors. Alternatively, you can drag the **Tolerance** slider to specify a value.
8. To create a smooth edge in the areas where you replace color, accept the default option (**Anti-Aliased**). If you deselect this option, the edges where you replace color may look jagged.
9. Click the color inside the image that you want to replace.
10. Drag over the desired area to replace the color.

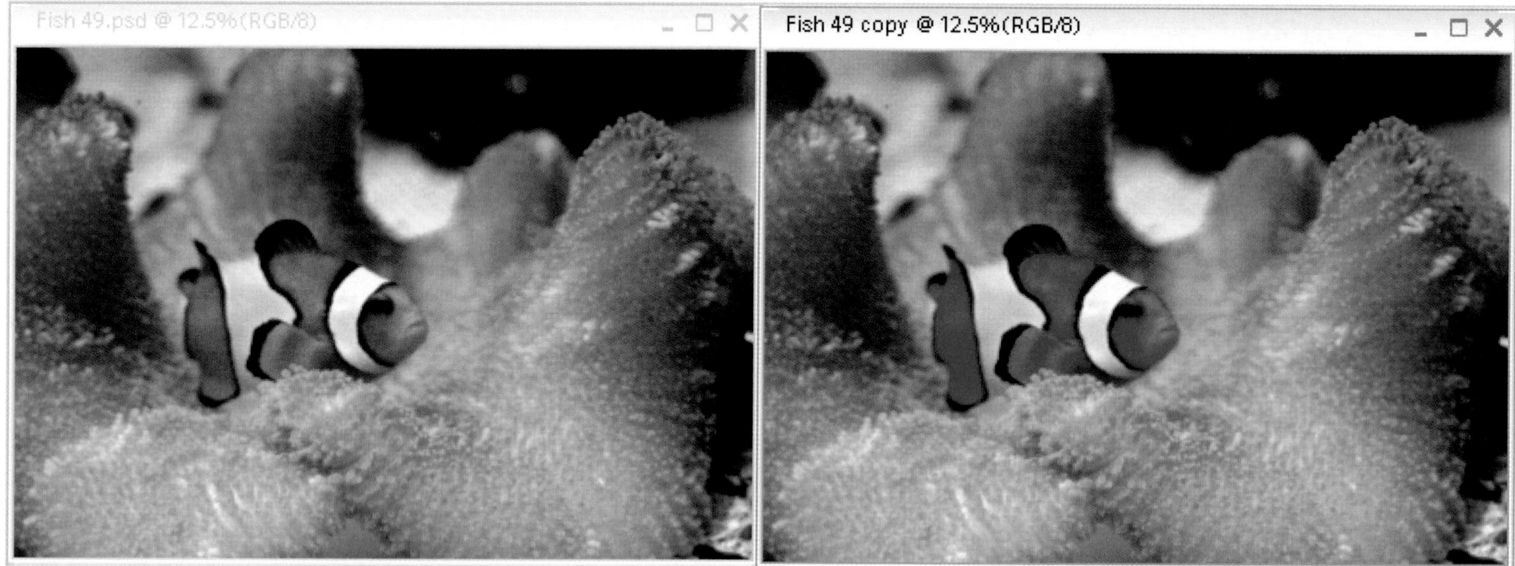

TIP

Hold down the **ALT** key to see if you are clipping any colors to white or black. If you see any colors start to appear when dragging the White input color slider, these colors will be clipped to white and appear blown out. If you see any colors appear when dragging the Black input color slider, these colors will be clipped to black and you'll lose detail in these parts of the image.

Make Tonal Adjustments

If your image lacks detail in certain areas, such as shadows, midtones, or highlights, you can correct this deficiency by adjusting these color values using the Levels command. When you adjust levels, you can adjust the black point (clip shadows to black), gray point (clip midtones to gray), or white point (clip highlights to white) to correct deficiencies in these tonal values.

You can also adjust the shadow and highlight values by dragging the input sliders at the bottom of the Levels dialog box. You can adjust levels for the entire image (red, green, and blue channels) or for an individual channel. Within the Levels dialog box is a histogram, which is a graph of how pixels are distributed from shadows to highlights. If there are sharp peaks in the histogram, this indicates a heavy distribution of pixels in that tonal range. Flat areas of the histogram indicate few pixels in that tonal range.

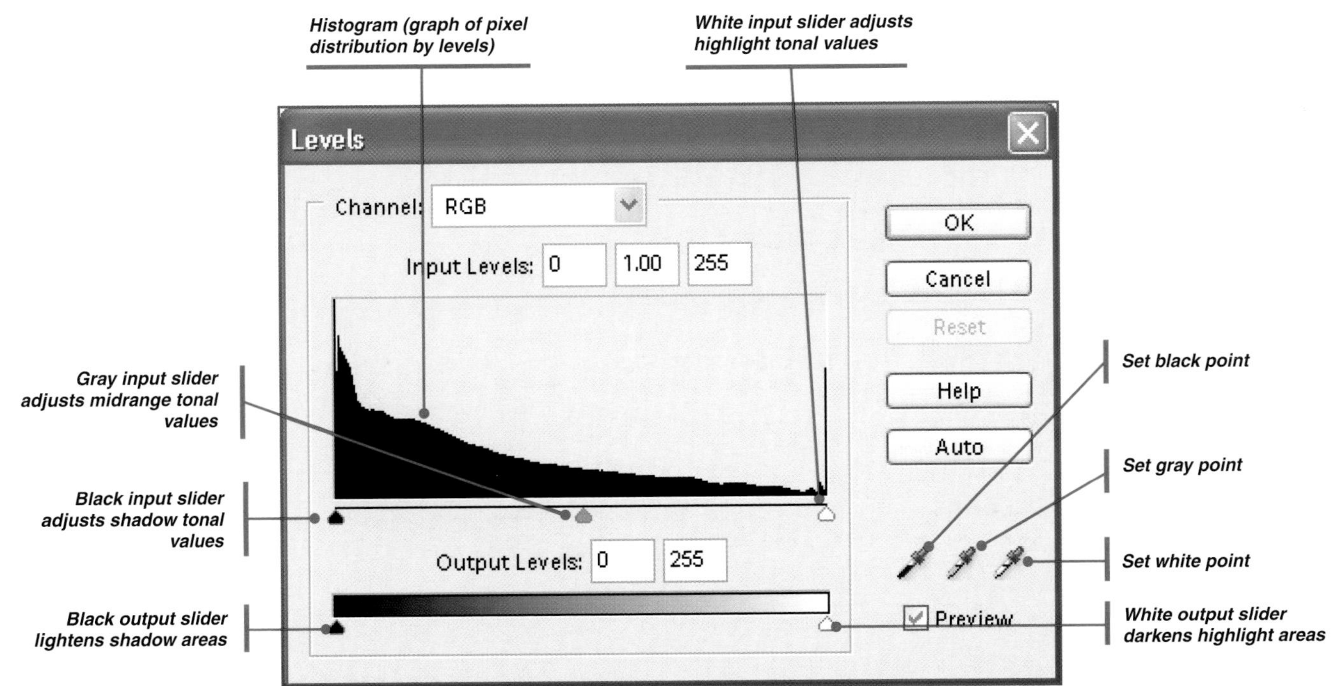

1 2 3 4 5 6 7 8 9 10

NOTE

When you change the black and white outputs of the image, you are reducing the tonal range.

TIP

If you know which objects in your image are supposed to be jet black, neutral gray, and bright white, you can adjust levels by clicking the **Set Black Point** eyedropper on the darkest black, clicking the **Set Gray Point** eyedropper on a neutral gray, and clicking the **Set White Point** eyedropper on the brightest white in the image.

TIP

If you see black spikes followed by white spikes in the histogram, you have clipped colors from your image. Click **Reset** to restore the histogram to the original levels when you first initiated the command.

1. In Standard Edit mode, click **Enhance**, click **Adjust Lighting**, and then click **Levels**. The Levels dialog box appears.
2. To change levels in all image channels, accept the default option (**RGB**). Otherwise, click the **Channels** down arrow, and click **Red**, **Green**, or **Blue** to change the specific levels.
3. Drag the **Black** and **White** input sliders to set the shadow and highlight tonal values, respectively. As you drag either slider, the Gray slider is moved to preserve the tonal range ratio.
4. Drag the **Gray** slider to set the midtone values without altering the shadow or highlight tonal values.
5. Drag the **Black** output slider to lighten the shadow areas of the image.
6. Drag the **White** output slider to darken the highlight areas of the image.
7. Click **OK** to apply the changes. Figure 5-14 shows an image before and after applying the Levels command.

Figure 5-14: You can adjust tonal levels using the Levels command.

How to...

- *Understanding Modes of Color*
  - *Embed a Color Profile*
  - *Calibrate Your Monitor with a Colorimeter*
- *Changing to Grayscale Mode*
  - *Set Image Color Mode*
- *Understanding Foreground vs. Background Colors*
- *Calibrating Your Monitor*
  - *Use the Color Picker*
  - *Change Color Models*
  - *Use Web-Safe Colors*
  - *Use the Swatches Palette*
  - *Use the Eyedropper Tool*
  - *Adjust Color Tolerance for Color Sampling*
- *Understanding Opacity*
  - *Tint and Age Pictures*

Chapter 6

Using Color

Whether you scan images into Photoshop Elements, capture digital images from your camera, or work with images you download from the Web, color is one of the most important considerations when editing images. You choose a color mode depending on the intended destination of your edited image. In this chapter you'll learn to work with all the color modes available to you in Photoshop Elements.

Set Up Your Standards

Before you begin doing any serious image editing in Photoshop Elements, you should get the application and your system in order so you can achieve the best results. In this regard, you'll need to calibrate your monitor so you can make wise color decisions. Another task you'll need to accomplish is choosing your color settings, which will vary depending on the intended destination of your final edits.

UNDERSTANDING MODES OF COLOR

When you edit images in Photoshop Elements, you have a great deal of latitude and can tailor color settings for the intended destination of the image. The color mode you choose is determined by the type of image you are creating and whether the image will be displayed on the Web, printed, or used as part of a multimedia presentation, such as a VCD (Video CD). In Photoshop Elements, you can choose from the following color modes:

- **Bitmap** This image mode uses two colors to define the image, black and white. When you convert an image to bitmap mode, you choose the manner in which black and white are mixed to determine the final image. This mode is best used for images displayed on portable devices that can only display 1-bit color (black and white), such as older PDA (Personal Digital Assistant) devices.
- **Grayscale** This image mode uses 256 shades of gray, from 0 (black) to 255 (white), to define an image. This mode is useful when you want to display images on non-color devices, or you want a grayscale representation of an image.
- **Indexed Color** This color mode uses a palette of 256 colors to display an image. This mode is commonly used for images with large areas of solid color that are displayed on a web site. It is also used for full-color images that have large areas of text. When you convert an image to indexed color, Photoshop Elements builds a CLUT (color lookup table) that stores and indexes the colors from the image. If an original color is not present in the indexed color palette, Photoshop Elements mixes (or *dithers*) the colors to create a reasonable facsimile of the original color. Indexed color palettes can produce a smaller file size for images intended for the Web.
- **RGB Color** This is the default color mode for images you scan into your computer and images you download from your digital camera. In this color mode, Photoshop Elements mixes varying amounts

Continued...

Choose Your Color Management Settings

When you edit an image you can choose whether or not to have Photoshop Elements embed an ICC (International Color Consortium) profile with your image. You have two profiles from which to choose: sRGB, which is predominantly used for images displayed on computer monitors and web sites, or Adobe 1998, which features an expanded color range optimized for images that will be printed.

Embed a Color Profile

As part of the editing process, you can determine whether or not to *embed* a color profile with the image. When you embed a color profile, you can make accurate color decisions, because the color profile is suited for the device on which the image will be displayed or printed.

1. Open the image with which you want to embed a color profile.
2. Click the **Edit** menu and click **Color Settings**. The Color Settings dialog box appears.
3. Click one of the following options to choose the desired color setting:
   - **No Color Management** does not embed an ICC profile with the image. This color setting is used when an image will be printed by a device that manages color.
   - **Limited Color Management** embeds an sRGB color profile with your image. This color profile is capable of reproducing the color range of a computer color monitor, and is used for images that will be displayed on web sites.
   - **Full Color Management** embeds the Adobe RGB (1998) color profile with your image. This option is best for images printed on an inkjet color printer. If you have one of the newer photo-quality printers, this color mode will give you the best results.
4. Click **OK** to apply the selected color settings.

UNDERSTANDING MODES OF COLOR *(Continued)*

of red, green, and blue to determine the color of each pixel in an image. Each color has 256 shades, from black (0) to white (255). For example, a dark red color might be represented as follows: R=235, G=35, and B=56. Pure red would be represented as R=255, G=0, and B=0; pure green would be represented as R=0, G=255, and B=0; whereas pure blue would be represented by R=0, G=0, and B=255. Pure black is R=0, G=0, and B=0; and pure white is R=255, G=255, and B=255.

CAUTION

If you intend to display a photorealistic image on the Web, your best bet is always RGB color mode. If you convert the image to indexed color mode, the file size may be larger due to the fact that Photoshop Elements will resort to extensive dithering to try and create a reasonable facsimile of the original, which almost always bloats the file size.

TIP

You can change color settings whenever you edit an image for a different destination.

Calibrate Your Monitor with a Colorimeter

Adobe Gamma is a good way to calibrate your monitor (see "Calibrating Your Monitor"), but the results vary because the software relies on the user's subjective interpretation. A *colorimeter* (hardware that measures the color output of a computer screen) will give you more accurate results when editing your photos in Photoshop Elements. In the past, a hardware and software package to calibrate a computer monitor was too expensive for nonprofessional photographers; however, this has recently changed. ColorVision (www.colorvision.com) has a package called ColorPlus (works only with Windows) that consists of software and a colorimeter that connects to a USB (Universal Serial Bus) port on your computer and enables you to accurately measure and calibrate an LCD (liquid crystal display) or CRT (cathode-ray tube) monitor. The market price for ColorPlus as of this writing is approximately $100.

1. Install ColorPlus software according to the manufacturer's instructions.
2. Connect the colorimeter to a USB port on your computer.
3. Start ColorPlus. After starting the application, the Introduction page appears, as shown in Figure 6-1.

Figure 6-1: You can accurately calibrate your monitor with a colorimeter.

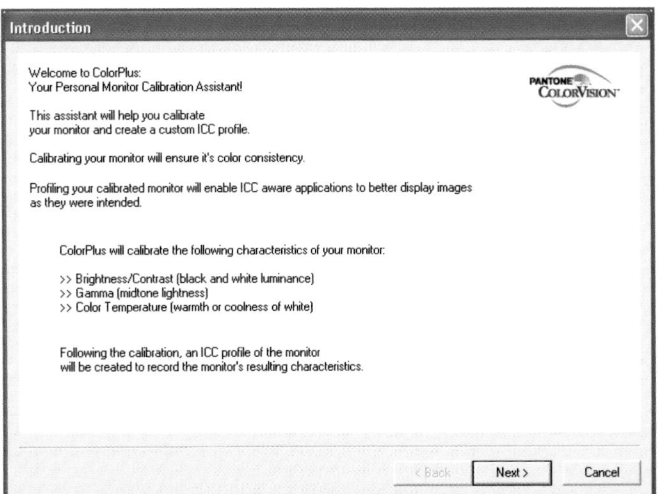

Introduction
Welcome to ColorPlus:
Your Personal Monitor Calibration Assistant!
PANTONE COLORVISION
This assistant will help you calibrate
your monitor and create a custom ICC profile.
Calibrating your monitor will ensure it's color consistency.
Profiling your calibrated monitor will enable ICC aware applications to better display images
as they were intended.
ColorPlus will calibrate the following characteristics of your monitor:
>> Brightness/Contrast (black and white luminance)
>> Gamma (midtone lightness)
>> Color Temperature (warmth or coolness of white)
Following the calibration, an ICC profile of the monitor
will be created to record the monitor's resulting characteristics.
< Back
Next >
Cancel

TIP

Disable any antivirus software when installing ColorPlus (or, for that matter, when installing any software).

If you are calibrating an LCD monitor, download the latest patch for ColorPlus. If you attempt to calibrate an LCD monitor using ColorPlus 1, the application will crash after taking color measurements.

4. Click **Next**. The Select Monitor Type dialog box appears.

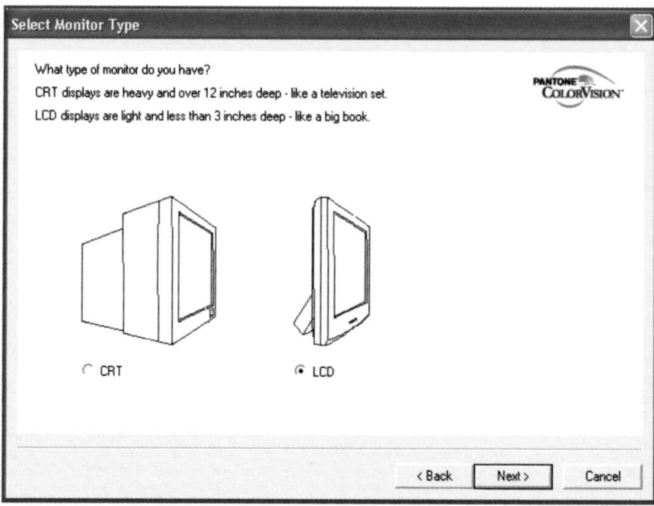

5. Select the type of monitor you are calibrating, and then click **Next**. The Measuring Display Characteristics dialog box appears. This dialog box instructs you on how to install the proper baffle (a device that regulates the flow of light) for the monitor you are calibrating. Figure 6-2 shows the page that appears when you calibrate an LCD monitor.

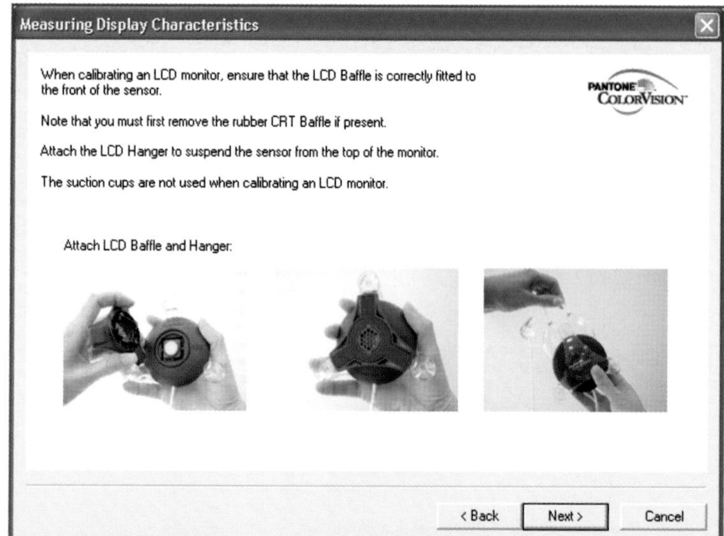

Measuring Display Characteristics
When calibrating an LCD monitor, ensure that the LCD Baffle is correctly fitted to the front of the sensor.
Note that you must first remove the rubber CRT Baffle if present.
Attach the LCD Hanger to suspend the sensor from the top of the monitor.
The suction cups are not used when calibrating an LCD monitor.
PANTONE COLORVISION
Attach LCD Baffle and Hanger:
< Back
Next >
Cancel

***Figure 6-2:** You must install the proper baffle for the colorimeter.*

TIP

The color and brightness of a monitor will change as it ages. Calibrate your monitor at least once a month to compensate for the inevitable aging process to ensure that your monitor accurately displays colors.

CAUTION

For best results, connect the colorimeter to a USB port on the back of your computer, not to a USB hub.

CAUTION

If you are calibrating an LCD monitor, do not attach the suction cups to the monitor, as you may damage the screen. The suction cups are designed for a CRT monitor. If you are calibrating an LCD monitor, tilt the monitor back to ensure that the colorimeter is flat against the screen.

6. Attach the proper baffle to the colorimeter, and click **Next**. The Measuring Characteristics dialog box appears, which shows a template of the colorimeter.
7. Align the colorimeter with the template.

8. Click **Next**. The colorimeter works in conjunction with the software to calibrate your monitor. You'll see several screens appear in succession as the colorimeter takes measurements to adjust the brightness, contrast, and white point of your monitor. This process takes about 20 minutes.
9. After the colorimeter finishes its measurements, you'll be prompted to remove the colorimeter from your monitor. You can then view an image that shows the results before and after calibration. After you accept the calibration, the software writes a color profile that is automatically loaded every time you start your computer.

1
2
3
4
5
6
7
8
9
10

QUICKSTEPS

CHANGING TO GRAYSCALE MODE

You can convert an image to grayscale mode, which makes the resulting image look like it was photographed using black-and-white film.

1. In Standard Edit mode, open the image you want to convert to grayscale mode.

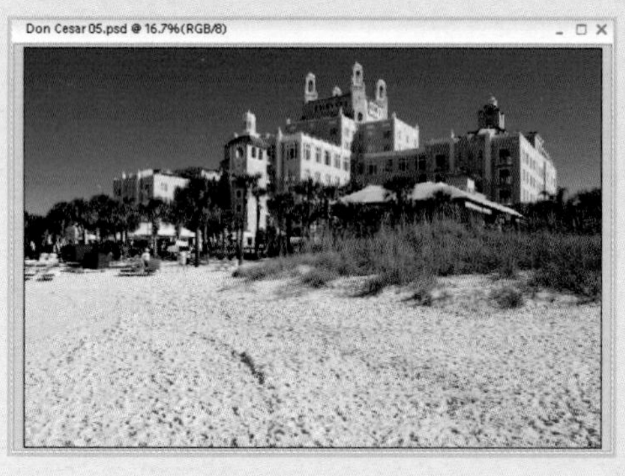
Don Cesar 05.psd @ 16.7%(RGB/8)

2. Click **Image**, click **Mode**, and then click **Grayscale**. Photoshop Elements displays a dialog box asking you to discard all color information.
3. Click **OK** to convert the image to grayscale.

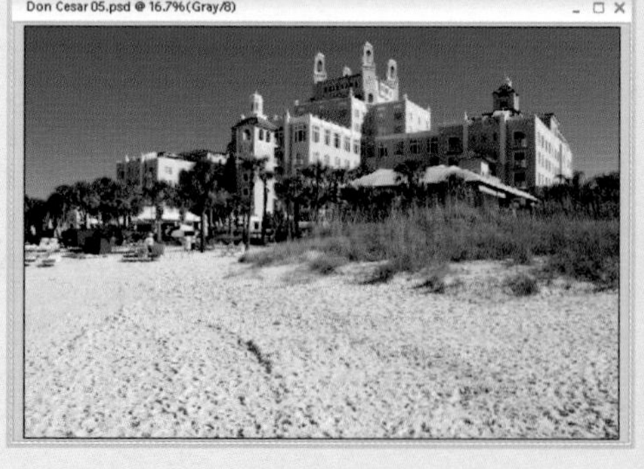
Don Cesar 05.psd @ 16.7%(Gray/8)

Set Image Color Mode

Most images you open in Photoshop Elements use the default RGB color mode. If you are creating an image for the Web or for a PDA device, however, you may need to change the color mode to suit the intended destination.

CHANGE TO BITMAP MODE

When you convert an image to bitmap mode, it is converted to 1-bit color (black and white).

1. In Standard Edit mode, open the image you want to convert to bitmap mode.

BAker Beach 29.psd @ 16.7%(RGB/8)

2. Click **Image**, click **Mode**, and then click **Bitmap**. If the image is not a grayscale image, the following dialog box appears.

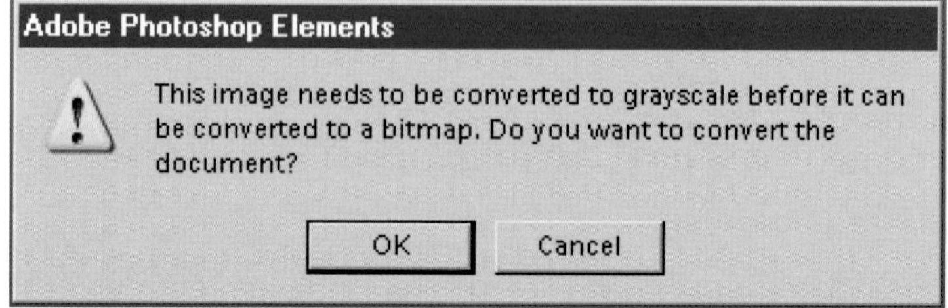
Adobe Photoshop Elements
This image needs to be converted to grayscale before it can be converted to a bitmap. Do you want to convert the document?
OK
Cancel

3. Click **OK**. The Bitmap dialog box appears.

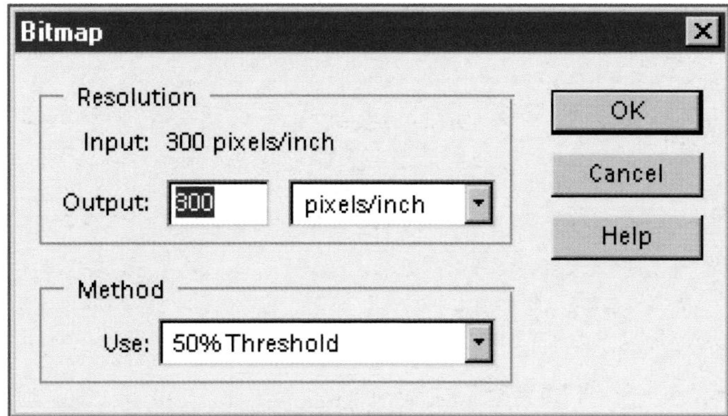

4. Type the desired resolution in the Output field.
5. Select the desired method from the following choices:
   - **50 % Threshold** converts pixels at or above the mid-gray threshold level (128) to white and converts pixels below that level to black, resulting in a high-contrast bitmap image.

NOTE

By default, resolution is measured in pixels/inch. If desired, choose pixel/cm (centimeter) from the drop-down menu to the right of the Output field.

1 2 3 4 5 6 7 8 9 10

- **Pattern Dither** converts the image into a geometric pattern of black and white dots to approximate the grayscale values of the image.

- **Diffusion Dither** analyzes each pixel in the image, starting with the upper-left corner. Pixels that are at or above the mid-gray threshold level of 128 are converted to white, while those below are converted to black. The end result mimics an old-fashioned, black-and-white photo with lots of grain.

CAUTION

When you discard all color information and print the grayscale image, some of the color heads on your printer will not fire, and the resulting print may not look as you had hoped.

TIP

Choose the Diffusion Dither method of converting an image to bitmap mode when you want the image to look like a photograph instead of a line drawing.

CHANGE TO INDEXED COLOR MODE

An image prior to being converted to indexed color mode.

You can convert an image to indexed color mode, which limits the palette to 256 colors. This option is used when you want to save an image as a GIF file for display on the Web.

1. In Standard Edit mode, open the image you want to convert to indexed color mode.
2. Click **Image**, click **Mode**, and then click **Indexed Color**. The Indexed Color dialog box appears.

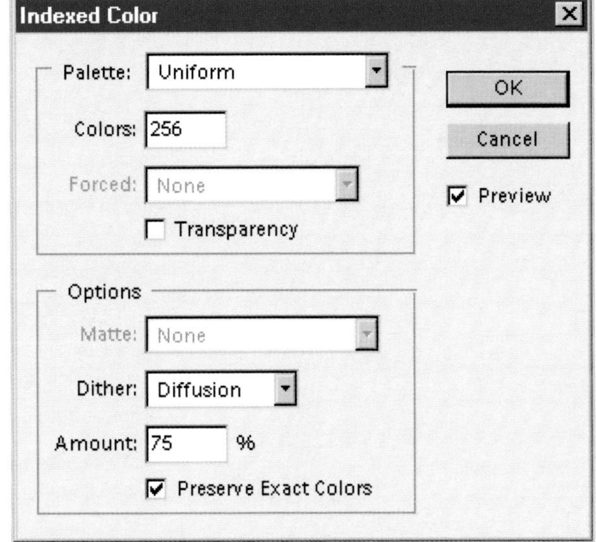

An image after being converted to indexed color mode.

3. Click one of the following options from the Palette drop-down list:
   - **Exact** creates a color palette using the exact colors in the RGB image. This option is unavailable if the image has more than 256 colors.
   - **System (Mac OS)** uses the Macintosh operating system 8-bit color palette. Colors not available from the palette will be dithered to produce a reasonable facsimile of the original color.
   - **System (Windows)** uses the Windows operating system 8-bit color palette. Colors not available from the palette will be dithered to produce a reasonable facsimile of the original color.

QUICKSTEPS

UNDERSTANDING FOREGROUND VS. BACKGROUND COLORS

In the lower-left corner of the toolbar are the Foreground and Background color swatches. You can choose the colors for the swatches from the Color Picker or from these color swatches. The default foreground color is black, and the default background color is white. The foreground color is used when using the Paint or Pencil tool to add color to a document.

1. Click the **Foreground Color** swatch to set the foreground color using the Color Picker.

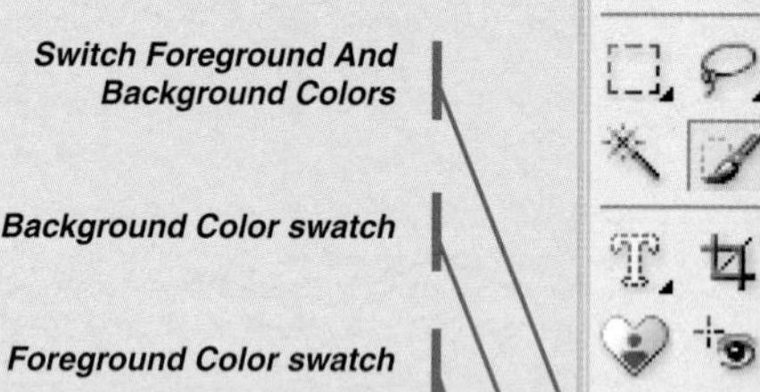

2. Click the **Background Color** swatch to set the background color using the Color Picker.
3. Click the **Default Foreground And Background Colors** icon to revert the swatches to black and white. Alternatively, you can press the D key.
4. Click the **Switch Foreground And Background Colors** icon to switch the current foreground color with the current background color. Alternatively, you can press the X key.

- **Web** uses the web-safe, 216-color palette, which uses colors available to both Windows and Macintosh palettes. Colors not available from the palette will be dithered to produce a reasonable facsimile of the original color. (See Chapter 9 for more information on web-safe colors.)
- **Uniform** creates the color palette by sampling the RGB color cube. Depending on the number of colors in the original image, the color palette will have 8, 27, 64, 125, or 216 colors.
- **Local (Perceptual)** creates a color palette that favors colors to which the human eye has greater sensitivity, such as the reds and oranges that are used to create flesh tones.
- **Local (Selective)** creates a color palette similar to the Perceptual palette using broad areas of color while preserving web-safe colors. The resulting image has better color integrity than other indexed color modes.
- **Local (Adaptive)** creates a color palette by sampling the image and using the predominant colors in the image. For example, if you're converting an image of a mountain scene with a large area of trees that reflects into a mountain lake, the palette will be predominantly greens and blues.
- **Custom** creates a palette using the Color Table dialog box that appears when this option is clicked, displaying the current adaptive palette. You can edit this color table, load a previously saved color table, or choose a table from the drop-down list.
- **Previous** uses the color palette last used when an image was converted to indexed color mode.

4. If available, specify the number of colors to be used when converting the image. You can specify up to 256 colors. Note that this option is not available for the two System or Web palettes.
5. If available, choose an option from the **Forced** drop-down list. This option forces certain colors to be included in the color table. You can choose **Black And White**, which adds pure black and white to the palette; **Primaries**, which adds red, green, and blue to the palette; **Web**, which adds the 216 colors from the web-safe palette; or **Custom**, which displays the Forced Colors palette, from which you can edit the existing colors in the palette.
6. Click **Transparency** if you want transparent parts of the image to remain transparent when the image is converted to indexed color mode. When this option is deselected, transparent areas are filled with the matte color (if selected) or with white.

CALIBRATING YOUR MONITOR

When you edit images in an application like Photoshop Elements, you're making decisions based on what you see on your computer monitor. What you get when you actually print the image, however, may be a different story. You can calibrate your monitor so that the colors you see on the screen will closely match what you get when you print the image. Adobe Photoshop Elements ships with a utility called Adobe Gamma, which leads you through the process of making adjustments to the brightness, gamma, and white point of the monitor. On a computer running Windows, you can access the Adobe Gamma utility (pictured here) through the Control Panel.

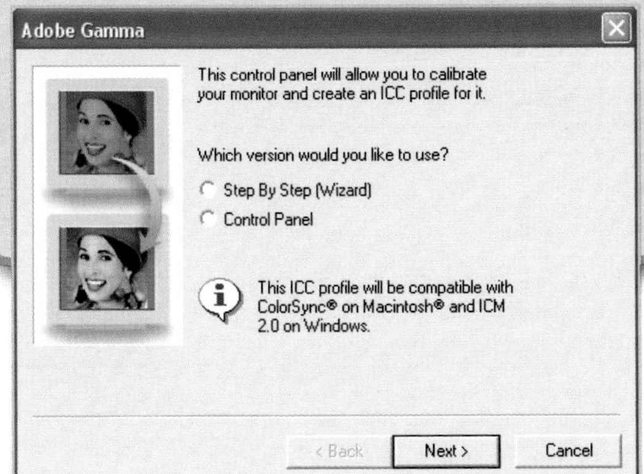

7. If the **Matte** option is available, you can specify the color used for the anti-alias sharp edges that are adjacent to transparent areas of the image. (If the Transparency option is also selected, the matte color fills all transparent areas of the image.)
8. Click an option on the **Dither** drop-down list. Dithering is used to approximate colors in the original image that are not found in the indexed color palette:
   - **None** Dithering is not used. Colors in the original image not found in the indexed palette are snapped to the closest match.
   - **Diffusion** Click this option to preserve details such as fine lines and text.
   - **Pattern** Click this option to create a half-tone pattern that simulates colors not found in the indexed color palette.
   - **Noise** Click this option to prevent seam-like patterns from appearing when the image is sliced for use in a web page.
9. If you clicked Diffusion from the Dither drop-down list, choose an **Amount** value. This option specifies the percentage of image colors that will be dithered. The default value is 75 percent. Higher values will increase file size.
10. Click the **Preserve Exact Colors** check box to prevent colors in the color table from being dithered.
11. Click **OK** to convert the image to indexed color mode.

CHANGE TO RGB MODE

By default, all images you edit in Photoshop Elements are in RGB color mode. If, however, you open a color image that is a GIF file with an indexed color palette, you can convert it to RGB color mode. Note that this will convert the image to RGB mode, but it will not increase the quality of the image.

1. In Standard Edit mode, open the image you want to convert to RGB mode.
2. Click **Image**, click **Mode**, and then click **RGB**.

NOTE

The Hexadecimal Color Value field shows the hexadecimal equivalent of the current color. If you've selected a color that is not in the web-safe palette, the Web Safe Alert cube appears. Directly below the Web Safe Alert cube is a color swatch of the closest web-safe match for the color. Click the rectangle to convert the current color to a web-safe color.

Choose Colors

An image without color is often rather drab. When you edit images in Photoshop Elements, you can paint color into an image, add text with colors that compliment the image, fill shapes with colorful gradients, and so on. As discussed previously, you can use the foreground and background color swatches to quickly choose a color. In the upcoming sections, you'll learn how to fill the foreground and background color swatches with the colors you want to paint into your image, or fill text or shapes in the document.

Use the Color Picker

When you work with color in Photoshop Elements, you use the Color Picker tool to set foreground and background colors, as well as to choose colors for other objects, such as gradients. You can then choose colors by selecting a hue and then fine-tuning the hue to arrive at the desired color.

1. Click a foreground, background, or gradient color. The Color Picker dialog box appears.

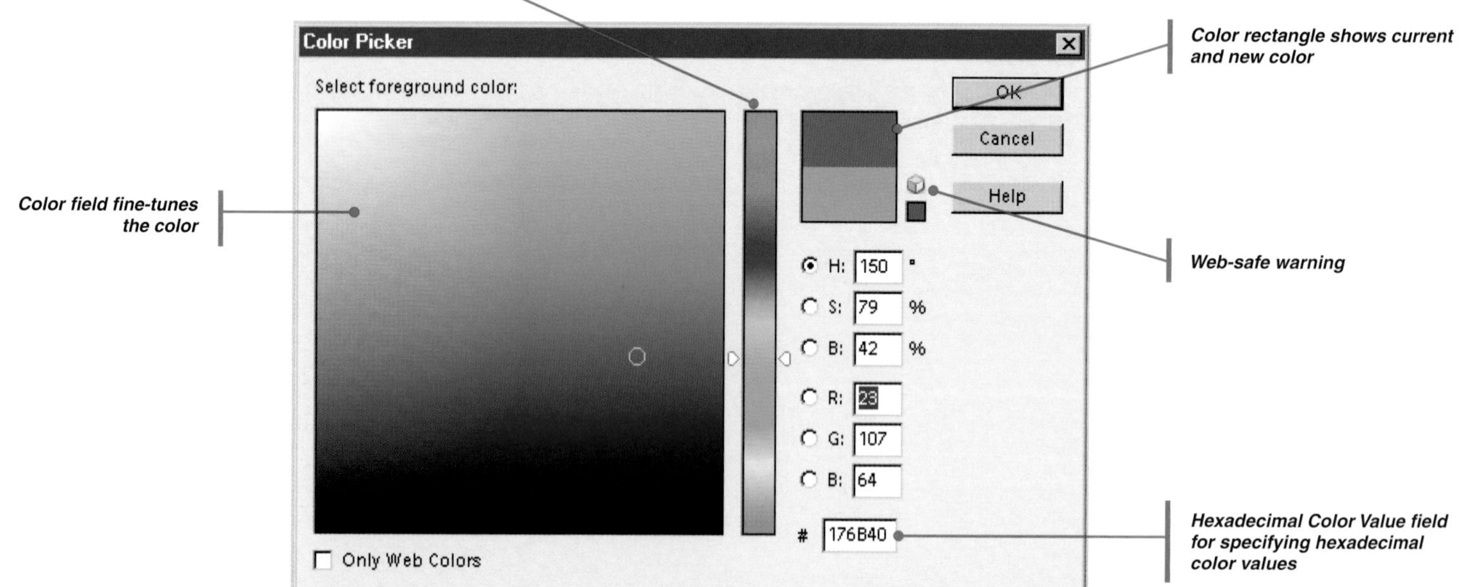

TIP

Move your cursor outside of the Color Picker, and the cursor changes to an eyedropper. Click anywhere inside the image you are currently editing to mix a perfect match for that color.

TIP

If you're matching a color from one of the color models, and your image is destined to be displayed on the Web in the GIF format, make sure the Web Safe Alert cube does not appear. If it does, click the cube to snap the mixed color to web safe.

2. Click inside the **Color** slider, or drag the white triangles to set the hue.
3. Click and drag inside the **Color** field to fine-tune the color. As you drag inside the Color field, a circle follows your cursor to indicate the currently selected color. The upper half of the color rectangle updates to show the currently selected color, while the bottom half shows the previously selected color.
4. Click **OK** to select the color.

Change Color Models

In addition to specifying a color by setting the Color slider and clicking inside the Color field, you can also choose colors with mathematical precision by entering known values to match colors from the HSB (Hue, Saturation, and Brightness) or RGB color models.

SPECIFY AN HSB COLOR

1. Click a foreground, background, or gradient color. The Color Picker dialog box appears.
2. Type a value between 0 and 360 in the H (hue) field. This corresponds to the color's location on the color wheel.
3. Type a value between 0 and 100 in the S (saturation) field.
4. Type a value between 0 and 100 in the B (brightness) field.
5. Click **OK** to exit the Color Picker.

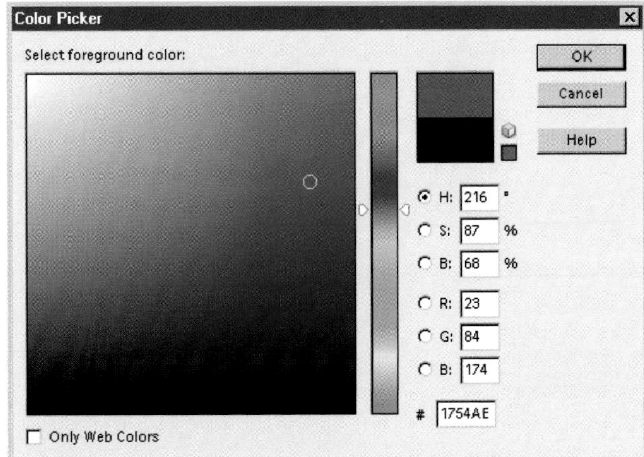

TIP

If you're mixing colors for an image that will be displayed on a DVD disc displayed on an NTSC (National Television System Committee) television set, do not specify a color darker than R=16, B=16, G=16, or brighter than R=234, G=234, B=234. These are NTSC- safe colors. NTSC is the television standard for North America.

TIP

To match a known web-safe color value, type the hexadecimal value in the Hexadecimal Color Value field.

SPECIFY AN RGB COLOR

1. Click a foreground, background, or gradient color. The Color Picker dialog box appears.
2. Type a value between 0 and 255 in the R field. This specifies the amount of red in the color mix.
3. Type a value between 0 and 255 in the G field. This specifies the amount of green in the color mix.
4. Type a value between 0 and 255 in the B field. This specifies the amount of blue in the color mix.

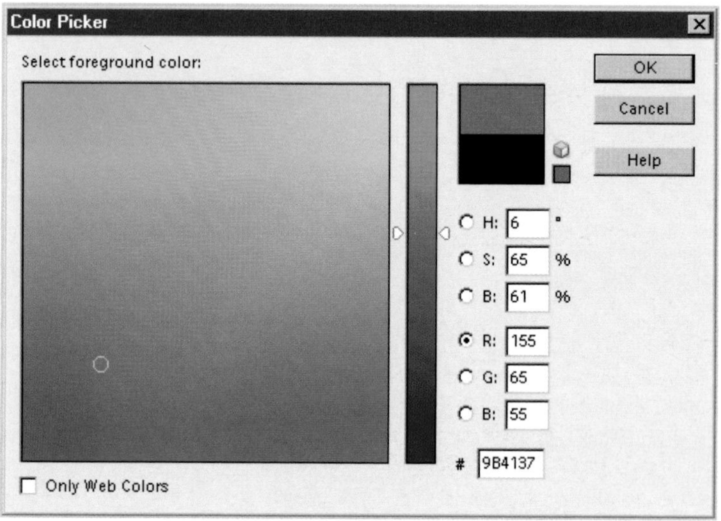

5. Click **OK** to exit the Color Picker.

Use Web-Safe Colors

When you edit images or create images that will be displayed on a web site, using web-safe colors will ensure that the image looks the same on both platforms. Web-safe colors are specified in hexadecimal format.

1. Click a foreground, background, or gradient color. The Color Picker dialog box appears.

2. Click the **Only Web Colors** check box. The Color field becomes a series of blocks instead of continuous colors. Each block represents a web-safe color.

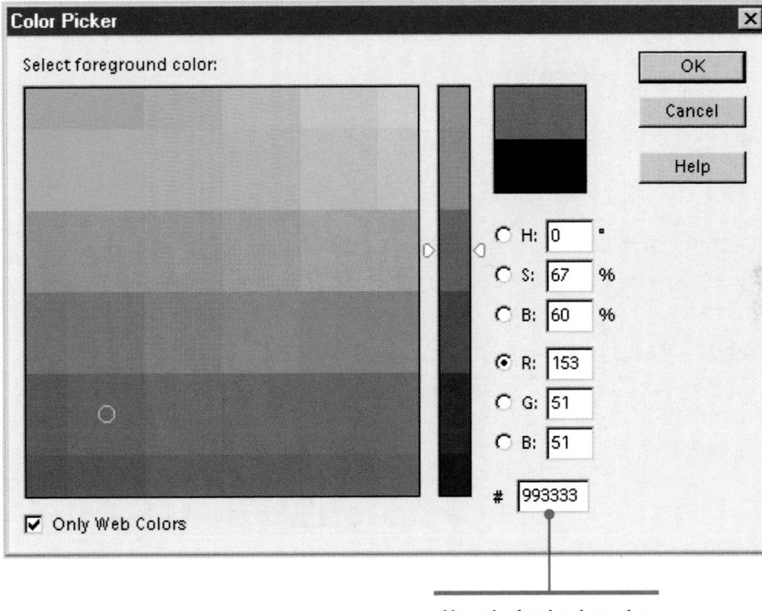

Hexadecimal color value

3. Drag the **Color** slider to specify a hue. The Color slider is also comprised of blocks, which are web-safe hues. As you select the web-safe color, the hexadecimal value is automatically updated.
4. Drag inside the **Color** field to select a color from the hue range.
5. Click **OK** to exit the Color Picker.

TIP

To set the background color, click the **Switch Foreground And Background Colors** icon, and then click the desired color in the Swatches palette. Click the **Switch Foreground And Background Colors** icon again to revert the selected foreground color to the background color.

Use the Swatches Palette

The Photoshop Elements Swatches palette is comprised of color swatches. You can use the Swatches palette to load a palette of colors you will use in an image. You can also use the Swatches palette to create custom swatches of colors that you frequently use.

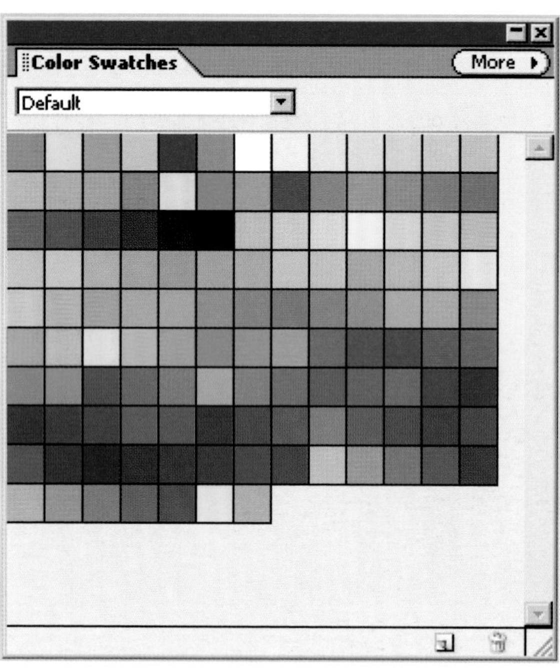

CHOOSE A COLOR FROM THE SWATCHES PALETTE

1. Click **Window** and then click **Color Swatches**.
2. Click the desired swatch in the Swatches Palette to set the foreground color.

LOAD A COLOR SWATCH LIBRARY

1. Click **Window** and then click **Swatches**.
2. Click the desired library from the Swatches drop-down list:

- **Default** This palette contains 132 colors, including the standard RGB colors (red, yellow, green, cyan, blue, and magenta), standard CMYK colors (red, yellow, green, cyan, blue, and magenta), grayscale (20 shades, from white to black), plus other color derivatives, such as dark cyan blue and darker cyan blue.
- **Mac OS** This palette contains 132 colors used by the Macintosh operating system.
- **Photo Filter Colors** This palette contains 18 colors used by popular photo filters, such as an orange that matches the Warming Filter (85) and a blue that matches the Cooling Filter (80).
- **Web Hues** This palette contains the 216 colors of the web-safe palette arranged by hue.
- **Web Safe Colors** This palette contains 216 colors of the web-safe palette arranged from black to white.
- **Web Spectrum** This palette contains 341 colors that can be displayed safely by a web browser. Note that this palette contains colors not found in the web-safe palette.

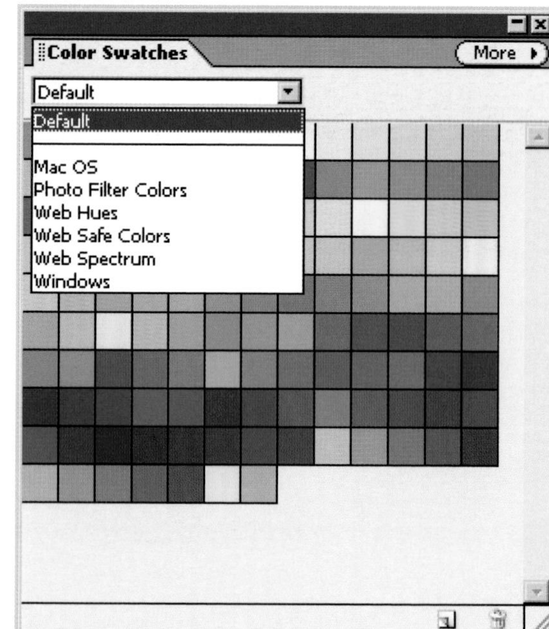

TIP

If you use Photoshop Elements for business purposes, create a custom swatch library for the colors you commonly use with a client's artwork. Save the custom color library using the client's company name.

BUILD A CUSTOM COLOR SWATCH LIBRARY

1. Click **Window** and then click **Swatches**.
2. Load the desired color swatch library as outlined previously (see "Load a Color Swatch Library"). Load a library that contains colors you'll want to use in your custom library.
3. To add a color to your custom library, mix the color, in the foreground color swatch, and perform one of the following tasks:

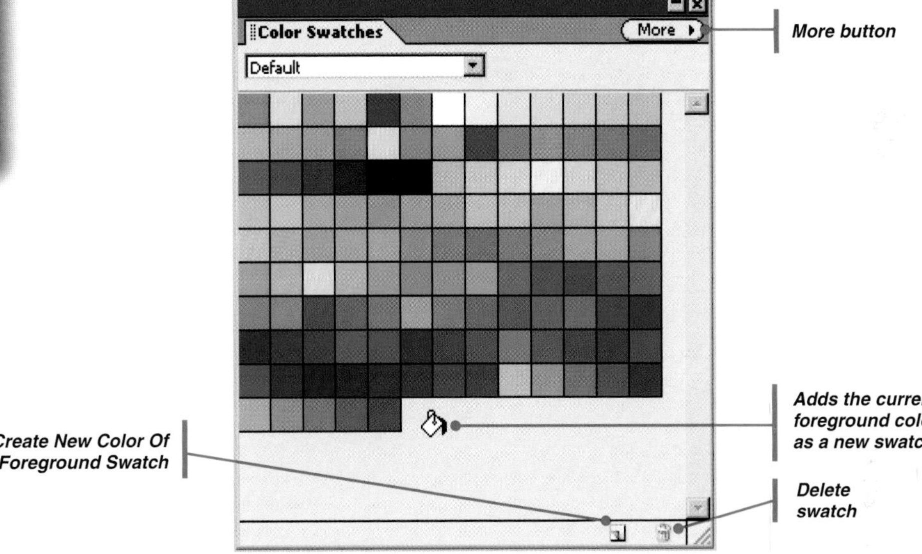

- Click the **Create New Color Of Foreground Swatch** icon.
- Click **More** and then click **New Color Swatch**. The New Color Swatch dialog box appears. Type a name for the new color, and click **OK**.

- Position your cursor over an empty spot in the bottom of the Swatches palette. When the cursor becomes a paint bucket, click to open the Color Swatch Name dialog box. Type a name for the swatch, and click **OK**.

TIP

To create a faux matte for an image, click the **Eyedropper** tool and then click an area in your image to sample the color you want to fill the background color swatch. Click **Image**, click **Resize**, and then click **Canvas Size**. The Canvas Size dialog box appears. Extend the canvas by the desired amount, and choose **Background** for the canvas extension color. Click **OK**. This technique works best when you sample a predominant color in the image or a color from the image's center of interest. The canvas extension color creates a border for the image with a harmonious color that draws the viewer's attention to the center of interest.

TIP

Click the **Eyedropper** tool and then sample a color in your image to fill the foreground color swatch with the sampled color.

TIP

Press SHIFT + I to quickly select the Eyedropper tool.

4. To delete a selected color from the Swatches palette, drag it to the **Delete Swatch** icon (it looks like a trashcan).
5. Click **OK** to verify that you want to delete the color swatch.
6. To identify a color, hold your cursor over the desired swatch, and a tool tip appears identifying the color by name.
7. To rename a color, right-click it and then click **Rename Color** from the context menu that appears.
8. To save a custom color palette, click **More** and then click **Save Color Swatches**. The Save dialog box appears.
9. Type a name for the custom color swatch library, and then click **OK**. If you specify the folder path My Programs\Adobe\Photoshop Elements 3.0\Preset\, the new color swatch is added to the Swatches folder and will appear on the Swatches drop-down list the next time you start Photoshop Elements.

Use the Eyedropper Tool

You use the Eyedropper tool to sample colors from within the image you're editing. You can use sampled color to fill the foreground or background swatches, or to specify a color for a gradient.

1. Click the **Foreground** or **Background** color swatch. This opens the Color Picker and activates the Eyedropper tool.
2. Click inside the image to sample a color.
3. Click **OK** to close the Color Picker dialog box. The applicable swatch is filled with the sampled color.

Adjust Color Tolerance for Color Sampling

When you use the Eyedropper tool to sample color, you can specify the area from which the color is sampled. By default, the tool samples the color under the pixel you click while using the Eyedropper tool. You can, however, increase the sample size, which enables you to sample the average color under the sample area.

NOTE

The selected sample size is used by the Eyedropper tool until you change the setting.

QUICKFACTS

UNDERSTANDING OPACITY

When you select the Brush tool or Pencil tool, the opacity of the tool determines how much of the area over which you paint is visible. At an opacity setting of 100 percent, the tool completely eclipses the underlying pixels. If, however, you select an opacity setting of less than 100 percent, some of the underlying image will be visible after you use the tool. Opacity also comes into play when you're painting on a mask. If you paint black at 100 percent opacity on an adjustment layer mask (which by default is white), the areas over which you paint reveal the original image without the effects of the adjustment layer. If you paint on the mask with a lower opacity, you mix some of the effects of the adjustment layer with the original image. You can also lower the opacity of the adjustment layer to vary the intensity of the adjustment. Opacity also has an effect when you're working with layers. The default opacity for a layer is 100 percent, which completely hides the pixels in the underlying layer. Lower the layer opacity to reveal part of the underlying layer, as shown in Figure 6-3.

1. Click the **Eyedropper** tool.
2. Click the **Options** menu, click the **Sample Size** down arrow, and click one of the following options:
   - **Point Sample** samples the color directly under the pointer.
   - **3 x 3 Average** samples the average color in an area 3 pixels by 3 pixels.
   - **5 x 5 Average** samples the average color in an area 5 pixels by 5 pixels.

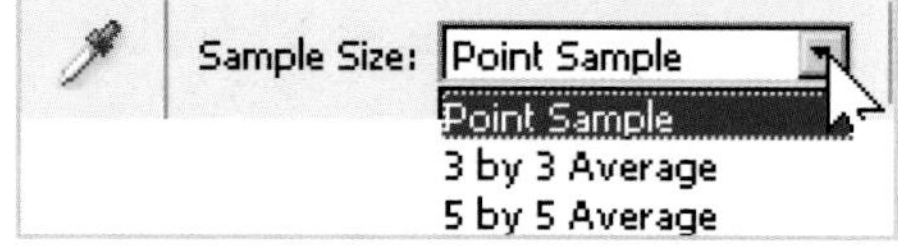

Figure 6-3: Lower opacity to reveal underlying layers.

Tint and Age Pictures

Photoshop Elements provides you with several different ways to tint and age a picture. This section shows you how to convert an image to grayscale without losing color data. Then you'll apply a sepia tint to the image and make it look old-fashioned and slightly grainy.

CONVERT THE IMAGE TO GRAYSCALE

1. Open the image that you want to tint and age.
2. Click **Window** and then click **Layers**. The Layers palette is displayed.
3. Click the **Adjustment Layers** icon, and then click **Brightness/Contrast**. The Brightness/Contrast dialog box appears.
4. Decrease the brightness and increase the contrast, as shown in Figure 6-4.

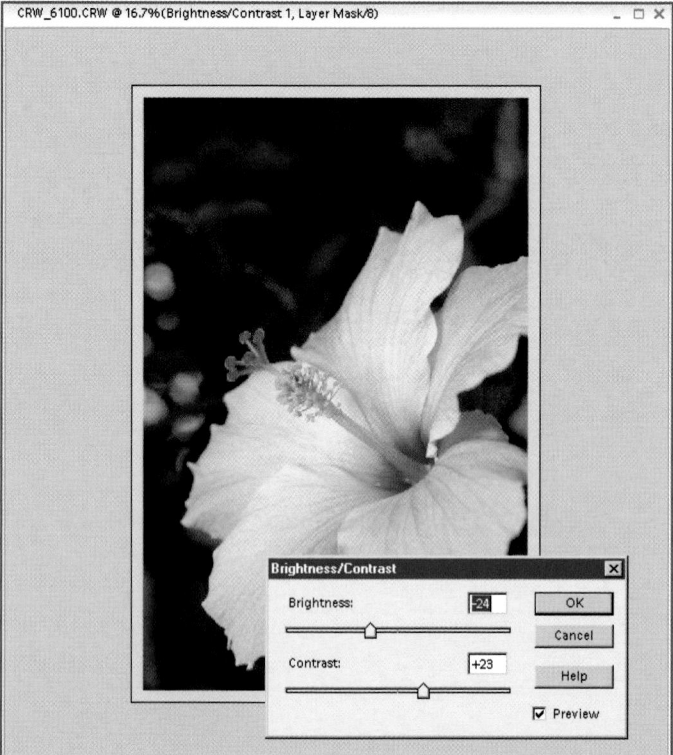

Figure 6-4: Adjust brightness and contrast prior to converting an image to grayscale.

TIP

When you're doing extensive work with layers, you may want to float the Layers palette to a more convenient location.

NOTE

At this stage, you can edit the Brightness/Contrast and the first Hue/Saturation adjustment layers until you get the rich black highlights and sharp contrast of a well-exposed grayscale image. If desired, you can adjust other color ranges in the first Hue/Saturation layer.

TIP

If you want to tint an image with a different color, choose the desired color from the Filter drop-down menu.

5. Click **OK** to apply the adjustment layer and close the dialog box.
6. Click the **Adjustment Layers** icon, and then click **Hue/Saturation**. The Hue/Saturation dialog box appears.
7. Click the **Edit** down arrow, and click a predominant color in the image that you want to accentuate. In the case of the flower image, pink was the predominant color, so the Magenta hue was selected.
8. Drag the **Saturation** slider to saturate the predominant color.
9. Click **OK** to apply the adjustment layer and close the dialog box.
10. Click the **Adjustment Layers** icon, and then click the **Hue/Saturation** icon. The Hue/Saturation dialog box appears, creating a second hue/saturation adjustment layer.
11. Drag the **Saturation** slider to the far left to desaturate the color from the image, as shown in Figure 6-5.
12. Click **OK** to apply the adjustment layer and close the dialog box.

ADD A SEPIA TONE TO THE IMAGE

1. Click the **Adjustment Layers** icon, and then click **Photo Filter**. The Photo Filter dialog box is displayed.
2. Click the **Filter** down arrow, and then click **Sepia**.
3. If desired, drag the **Density** slider to the right to strengthen the filter's effect.
4. Click **OK** to apply the adjustment layer and close the dialog box.
5. Click the **Photo Filter 1** layer in the Layers palette.
6. In the Layers palette, click the **Mode** down arrow, and then click **Multiply**.

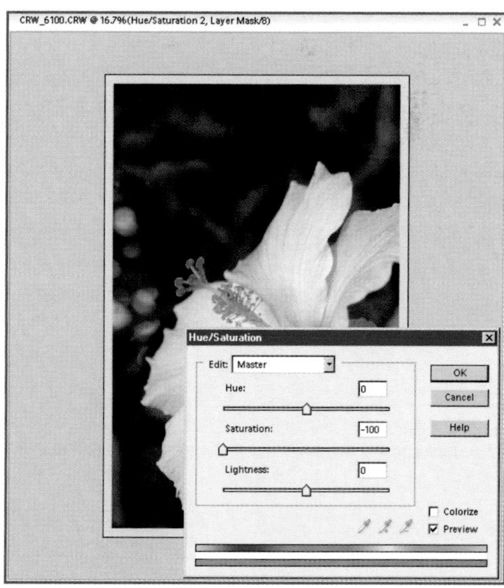

Figure 6-5: Desaturate the image if you want to convert it to grayscale.

1 2 3 4 5 6 7 8 9 10

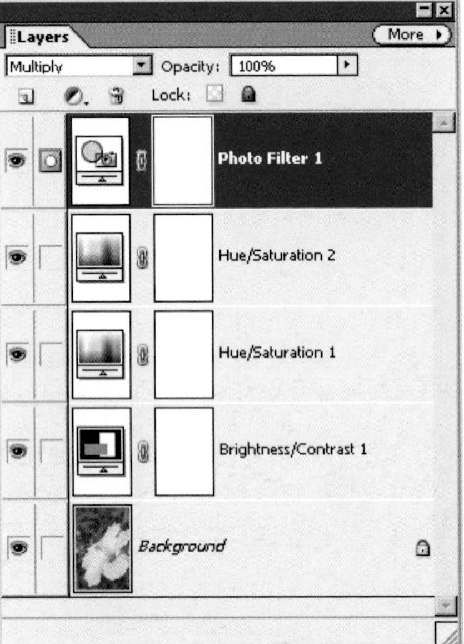

Image after adding sepia tone and film grain

7. Apply any final edits to the adjustment layers to adjust the contrast and make the grayscale conversion pop out.
8. Click **Layer** and then click **Flatten Image**.

ADD FILM GRAIN TO THE IMAGE

1. Click **Filter**, click **Artistic**, and then click **Film Grain**.
2. Drag the **Grain** slider to **6**, drag the **Highlight Area** slider to **1**, and drag the **Intensity** slider to **10**, as shown in Figure 6-6.

Figure 6-6: Add film grain to the image to complete the old-fashioned effect.

3. Click **OK** to apply the filter and exit the dialog box.

How to...

- Understanding Vector Drawings vs. Bitmaps
- Set Blending Modes
- Using Paint Tools
- Rescuing Underexposed or Overexposed Images
- Set Brush Opacity
- Set Brush Dynamics
- Set Tablet Support
- Create a Custom Brush
- Manage the Brush Library
- Framing Images
- Add Drop Shadows to Layers
- Add Fancy Borders
- Create Images that Look Like Paintings
- Blur Images
- Create a Zoom Blur
- Distort Images
- Add a Motion Blur Effect
- Add a Lens Flare
- Cut Out an Image
- Liquefy an Image
- Create a Vignette

Chapter 7 Painting, Drawing, and Special Effects

As previously discussed, you can use Photoshop Elements to touch up and restore images, but you can also use it to add an artistic touch to images. You can paint on images, paint on layers, or use filters to create special effects. This chapter will explore some of the effects you can achieve using the powerful Photoshop Elements toolset.

Use Paint or Pencil Tools

If you want to add a splash of color to an image, you can do so using the Brush or Pencil tools. The Brush tool can be used to achieve rather artistic-looking effects. For example, you can choose a brush that mimics a bristle brush, a smooth camel-hair brush, and so on. When you draw with the Pencil tool, you end up with a hard line reminiscent of what you get when drawing with a mechanical pencil. Each tool has its place. The easiest way to master either tool is by experimenting with them and becoming familiar with their use.

UNDERSTANDING VECTOR DRAWINGS VS. BITMAPS

When you edit images in Photoshop Elements, you begin by opening a bitmap image, which is comprised of individual dots of colors known as *pixels*. A pixel is resolution-dependent. When you open an image, it has a given number of pixels. When you change the pixel size of the document, Photoshop Elements resamples the pixels. It may help to think of resampling as similar to redrawing. If you double the pixel dimensions of a document, you are telling Photoshop Elements to double the size of each pixel in the document. Invariably, image degradation will occur when you increase the size of a document to a large degree. As a rule of thumb, you can achieve good results if you upsize an image by ten percent using the bicubic resampling method.

When you add shapes, paths, text, or paint on an image, you add vector-based graphics. *Vector-based graphics* are comprised of points (connected by straight lines) and curves. Complex shapes have multiple points. Vector graphics are not resolution-dependent, as the locations of the points are mathematically determined. When you change the size of a vector graphic, the points, lines, and curves are mathematically recalculated to reflect the new size; therefore, no degradation occurs. When you flatten an image or save a document, vector graphics are converted to bitmaps, a process known as *rasterizing.*

TIP

You can increase the brush size while painting by pressing the **LEFT BRACKET** ([) key; decrease the brush size by pressing the **RIGHT BRACKET** (]) key.

Set Blending Modes

When you use the Brush tool or Pencil tool, you are adding pixels of color to an image. You can determine the manner in which the pixels react with the existing colors of pixels on a layer by choosing a blend mode. The blend mode you choose also determines how the pixels of color on a layer interact with those of the underlying layer, as you will see in the upcoming sections.

USE THE NORMAL BLEND MODE

When you choose the Normal blend mode with a tool that uses a brush preset, the pixels of color you paint on the image eclipse the underlying pixels of color. When you use the Normal blend mode for a layer, the underlying layer is completely eclipsed, as shown in the illustration. The letters are on a separate layer and obscure the background. You can work around this by masking certain parts of the layer to reveal the underlying pixels.

USE THE DISSOLVE BLEND MODE

When you use the Dissolve blend mode for a brush or a layer, the underlying pixels randomly replace the pixels you brush or place on an overlying layer. This blending mode works best using the Brush tool with a large brush size. You can see this effect around the edges of the letters in the illustration.

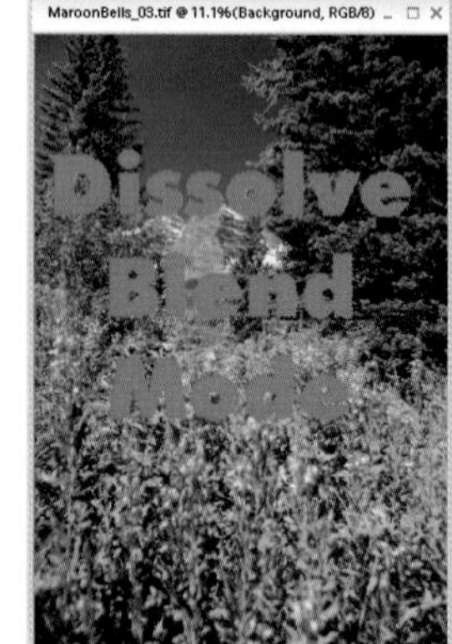

QUICKSTEPS

USING PAINT TOOLS

When you decide to add color to an image using the Brush tool, you must first set up the tool to suit the image onto which you're painting. When you set up the tool, the choices you make are dependent upon your desired outcome. This section shows the steps you take to set up the tool. The following sections explain the available options when using the Brush or Pencil tool.

1. Set the foreground and background colors by clicking each swatch and choosing the desired color from the Color Picker. These will be the colors you intend to paint onto your image. You can switch between the foreground and background colors by pressing the x key.
2. Click the **Brush** tool.
3. From the Options bar, click the **Brush** down arrow, as shown in Figure 7-1, and select a brush. The menu shows a stroke created with each brush type. When the stroke looks fuzzy near the edges, this designates a brush that will paint a soft edge.
4. Click the **Size** arrow and drag the slider to set the brush size. Alternatively, type the desired brush size into the Size field.
5. Click the **Mode** down arrow, and click the desired blending mode (see "Set Blending Modes" for more information).
6. Click the **Opacity** arrow and drag the slider to set the brush opacity. Alternatively, you can type a value in the Opacity field. (See "Set Brush Opacity.")
7. Click the **airbrush** icon to give the Brush tool airbrush capabilities.
8. Click the **Tablet Options** down arrow to reveal the options that can be controlled by the amount of pressure you put on your digital stylus. (See "Set Tablet Support.")

Continued...

Figure 7-1: Set brush parameters in the Options bar.

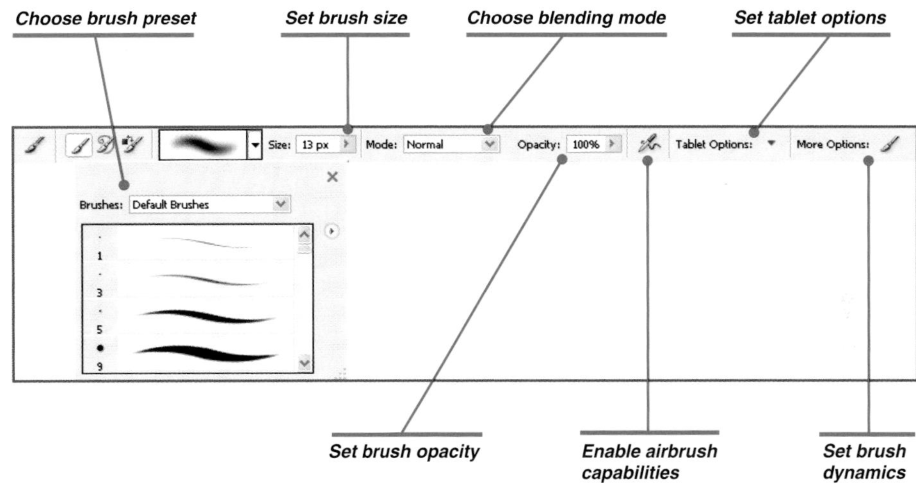

USE THE DARKEN BLEND MODE

When you use the Darken blend mode for a brush or layer, Photoshop Elements analyzes the pixels of color being painted or added to a layer and uses whichever color is the darkest, shown in the illustration in the transition from dark blue in the sky in the letters "Darken" to the varying colors in the flowers and plants shown in the words "Blend Mode."

USING PAINT TOOLS *(Continued)*

9. Click the **More Options** icon to reveal a menu that enables you to tailor the Brush tool even further based on the job at hand.
10. Drag inside the image to create a brush stroke.

USE THE MULTIPLY BLEND MODE

When you use the Multiply blend mode for a brush or layer, Photoshop Elements multiplies the brush color or layer color by the underlying pixels, which always results in a darker color, as seen in the darker letters in the illustration on the right.

USE THE COLOR BURN BLEND MODE

When you use the Color Burn blend mode for a brush or layer, Photoshop Elements darkens the underlying pixels of color based on the color being painted on an image or added to a layer. In the illustration on the right, notice how the words "Color Burn Blend Mode," which are applied on a separate layer using the Color Burn blend mode, darken the colors of the image on the underlying layer.

NOTE

Painting with white or adding white to a layer does not change the underlying pixels when using the Color Burn or Linear Burn blend modes.

USE THE LINEAR BURN BLEND MODE

When you use the Linear Burn blend mode for a brush or layer, Photoshop Elements decreases the brightness of the underlying pixels based on the color being painted on an image or added to a layer. You can see how the colors showing through the words in the illustration are not as bright as the colors surrounding the letters.

NOTE

The opacity of the brush or the layer works in conjunction with the blending mode to determine the overall effect. For example, if you paint pixels of color using the Normal blend mode but your brush opacity is 50 percent, the end result will blend 50 percent of the underlying pixels with the painted pixels.

NOTE

Painting with pure white using the Soft Light blend mode significantly lightens the underlying pixels; painting with pure black significantly darkens the underlying pixels.

USE THE OVERLAY BLEND MODE

When you use the Overlay blend mode for a brush or layer, Photoshop Elements preserves the underlying pixels of color and overlays the color being painted on an image or added to a layer. The end result either darkens or lightens the underlying pixels depending on the color being painted or added. You can see how some of the letters are darker while others are lighter in the illustration.

USE THE SOFT LIGHT BLEND MODE

When you use the Soft Light blend mode for a brush or layer, Photoshop Elements darkens or lightens the underlying pixels of color based on the color being painted on an image or added to a layer. If the color being painted or added to a layer is darker than 50 percent gray, the pixels are darkened; if the color is lighter than 50 percent gray, the pixels are lightened. You can see that red darkens the underlying pixels in the illustration on the right.

USE THE HARD LIGHT BLEND MODE

When you use the Hard Light blend mode for a brush or layer, Photoshop Elements either multiplies or screens the underlying pixels of color based on the color being painted on an image or added to a layer. If you paint with a color lighter than 50 percent gray, the pixels are screened, or lightened, which is a wonderful way to accentuate highlights in an image. If you paint with a color darker than 50 percent gray, the pixels are

QUICKSTEPS

RESCUING UNDEREXPOSED OR OVEREXPOSED IMAGES

If you have dark, underexposed photos or washed-out, overexposed photos, don't discard them. You may be able to save them using the Shadows/Highlight command and using layers and blending modes.

RESCUE UNDEREXPOSED IMAGES

To rescue an underexposed image:

1. Open an image that's underexposed.
2. Click **Window** and then click **Layers**. The Layers palette is displayed.
3. Drag the background layer to the **Create New Layer** icon to create a duplicate copy.
4. Click the new layer to select it.
5. Click the **Screen** blending mode. The image is brightened.
6. If the image is now overexposed, lower the opacity of the layer by clicking the **Opacity** arrow and dragging the slider to the left.

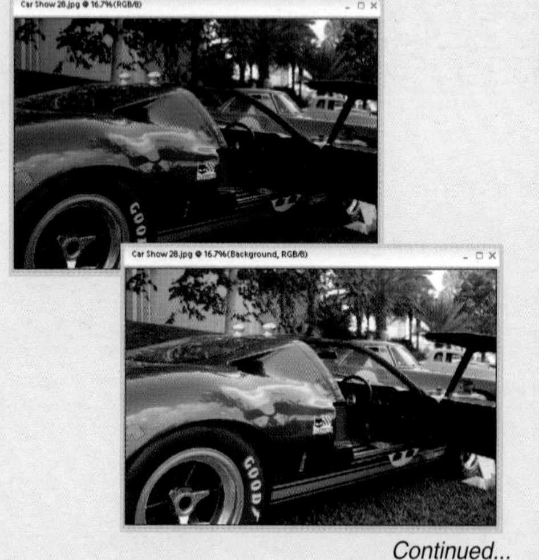

Continued...

multiplied, which effectively darkens the underlying pixels—a great way to restore washed-out areas of an image.

USE THE LINEAR LIGHT BLEND MODE

When you use the Linear Light blend mode for a brush or layer, Photoshop Elements increases or decreases the brightness of the underlying pixels of color based on the color being painted on an image or added to a layer. If you paint with a color lighter than 50 percent gray, the brightness is increased, which effectively lightens the underlying pixels. If you paint with a color darker than 50 percent gray, the brightness is decreased, which effectively darkens the underlying pixels.

USE THE VIVID LIGHT BLEND MODE

When you use the Vivid Light blend mode for a brush or layer, Photoshop Elements increases or decreases the contrast of the underlying pixels of color based on the color being painted on an image or added to a layer. If you paint with a color lighter than 50 percent gray, the contrast is decreased, which effectively lightens the underlying pixels. If you paint with a color darker than 50 percent gray, the contrast is increased, which effectively darkens the underlying pixels. Using the Vivid Light blend mode is similar to dodging and burning an image with the Dodge and Burn tools.

RESCUING UNDEREXPOSED OR OVEREXPOSED IMAGES *(Continued)*

RESCUE OVEREXPOSED IMAGES

To rescue an image that's overexposed:

1. Open an image that's overexposed.
2. If the Layers palette is not displayed in the Palette Bin, click **Window** and then click **Layers**.
3. Drag the background layer to the **Create New Layer** icon to duplicate the layer.
4. Click the new layer.
5. Click the **Mode** down arrow for the layer, and then click **Multiply**.
6. If the resulting image is now too dark, lower the opacity of the layer.

USE THE PIN LIGHT BLEND MODE

When you use the Pin Light blend mode for a brush or layer, Photoshop Elements uses the colors of the underlying pixels to determine the blended color. If the underlying color is lighter than 50 percent gray and you paint with a darker color, these pixels are replaced; if you paint with a lighter color, the pixels are not replaced. If the underlying color is darker than 50 percent gray and you paint with a lighter color, these pixels are replaced; if you paint with a darker color, the pixels are not replaced.

USE THE HARD MIX BLEND MODE

When you use the Hard Mix blend mode for a brush or layer, Photoshop Elements reduces the underlying colors to black, red, green, blue, yellow, cyan, or magenta, depending on the base colors and the blend color. You can see how red has changed the underlying colors in the illustration on the right.

USE THE DIFFERENCE BLEND MODE

When you use the Difference blend mode for a brush or layer, Photoshop Elements analyzes the underlying color and the color you are painting on an image or adding to a layer. The resulting blend subtracts either the blend color from the underlying color or the underlying color from the blend color, depending on the brightness value of each. Painting with white inverts the underlying color, while painting with black has no effect on the underlying pixels. Notice in the illustration how the underlying pixel color is changed based on the bright red color of the words "Difference Blend Mode." The gray colors of the mountains are changed to light green, and the purple columbines become a medium blue.

USE THE EXCLUSION BLEND MODE

When you use the Exclusion blend mode for a brush or layer, the end result is similar to that using the Difference blend mode, but the contrast is lower. Compare the illustration on the left to the preceding one, and you can see the subtle difference in the colors of the mountain where the text covers it.

USE THE HUE BLEND MODE

When you use the Hue blend mode for a brush or layer, Photoshop Elements blends the luminance and saturation of the underlying color with the hue of the blend color.

USE THE SATURATION BLEND MODE

When you use the Saturation blend mode for a brush or layer, Photoshop Elements blends the luminance and hue of the underlying pixels with the saturation value of the blend color.

USE THE COLOR BLEND MODE

When you use the Color blend mode for a brush or layer, Photoshop Elements mixes the blend color with the luminance and saturation of the underlying pixels. The resulting blend preserves the details of the underlying pixels but replaces the color of the underlying pixels with the color being applied to the image or layer. This mode is useful for simulating hand-tinting of grayscale photos.

USE THE LUMINOSITY BLEND MODE

When you use the Luminosity blend mode for a brush or layer, Photoshop Elements blends the hue and saturation of the underlying pixels with the luminance of the blend color.

TIP

While painting inside your image, you can change opacity on the fly by typing a number. Type 0 to change the opacity to 100 percent; type 1 to change the opacity to 10 percent; type 2 to change the opacity to 20 percent; and so on.

Set Brush Opacity

Each brush has an opacity control that determines how the brush affects the underlying pixels of color. When you set the opacity to 100 percent, the brush stroke is opaque and the underlying pixels are not visible. If you choose an opacity value of less than 100 percent, more of the underlying pixels are visible. Other tools have similar controls. For example, the Blur tool has a strength setting that determines the effect the tool has on the underlying pixels.

1. Click the desired tool from the toolbar. For this example, we'll use the Brush tool.
2. In the Options bar, click the **Opacity** arrow and drag the slider. Alternatively, you can type the desired value in the Opacity field. Specify a value close to 100, and the brush will be opaque. Specify a value close to 0, and the brush will almost be transparent.

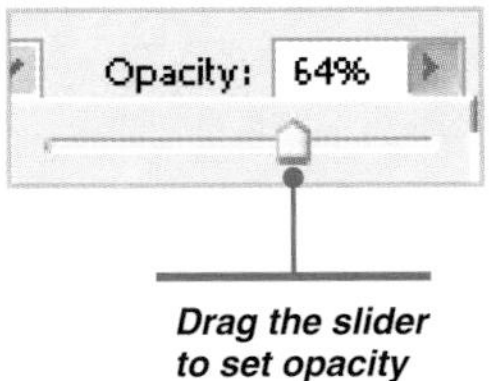

Drag the slider to set opacity

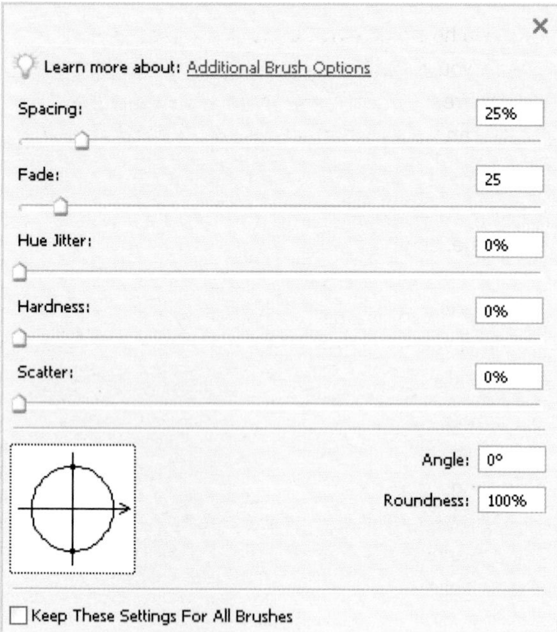

Set Brush Dynamics

You can change the way the Brush tool behaves by changing the brush dynamics. When you do this, you change the way paint is applied to your image.

1. Click the **Brush** tool in the toolbar.
2. In the Options bar, click the **More Options** icon (it looks like a paintbrush) to reveal the menu on the left.
3. Drag the **Spacing** slider to set the distance between marks in a brush stroke. By default, this setting is all the way to the left, which creates a continuous brush stroke. Drag the slider to the right to increase the space between marks and create an effect similar to that when painting dots of color.

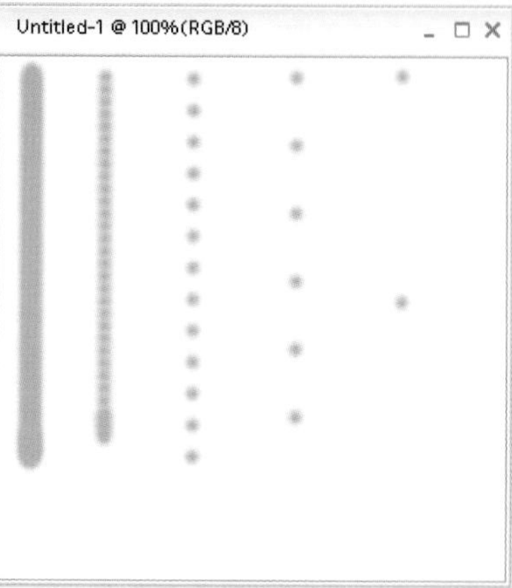

4. Drag the **Fade** slider to determine the number of steps before the stroke fades away to nothing. Each step is equivalent to a brush mark. A low value causes the brush stroke to fade quickly, while a higher value causes the stroke to fade slowly. A value of 0 causes no fade. A value of 10 causes the stroke to fade away in ten steps. Alternatively, you can type a value between 0 and 9999 in the Fade field.

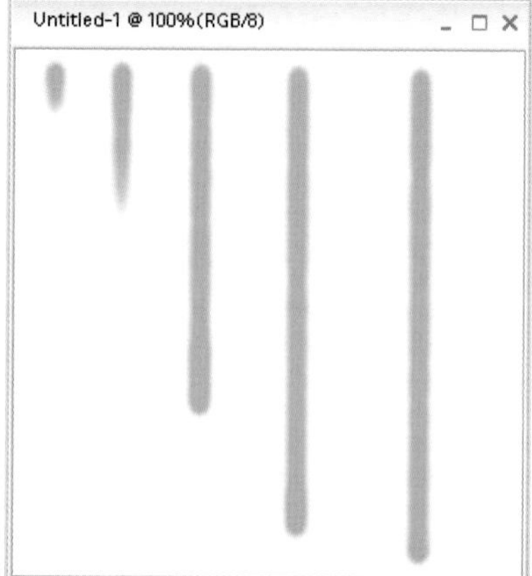

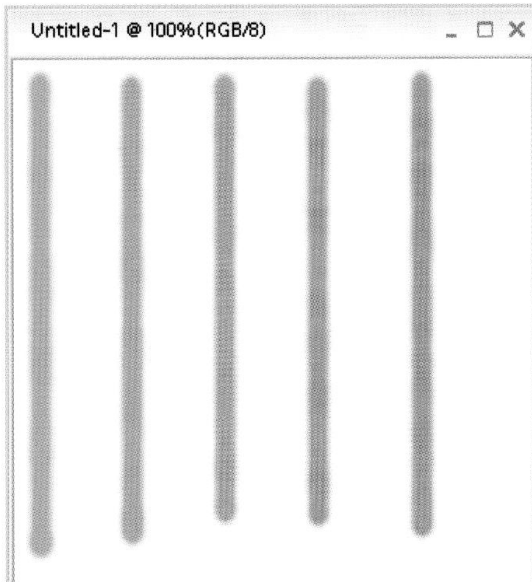

Hue Jitter slider

Scatter slider

5. Drag the **Hue Jitter** slider to determine how much the hue varies between the foreground and background colors as you paint. The default setting of 0 causes no hue jitter, while higher values produce frequent switching between foreground and background colors. Alternatively, you can type a value between 0 and 100 in the Hue Jitter field.
6. Drag the **Hardness** slider to determine whether the brush stroke has a soft or hard edge. Low values create a brush stroke with a soft edge, while high values create a brush stroke with a hard edge. Alternatively, you can type a value between 0 and 100 in the Hardness field.
7. Drag the **Scatter** slider to determine how the pixels of paint are scattered. Low values create a dense stroke with little paint scattering, while high values create a paint stroke with an increased area due to a wider scattering of pixels. Alternatively, you can type a value between 0 and 100 in the Scatter field.

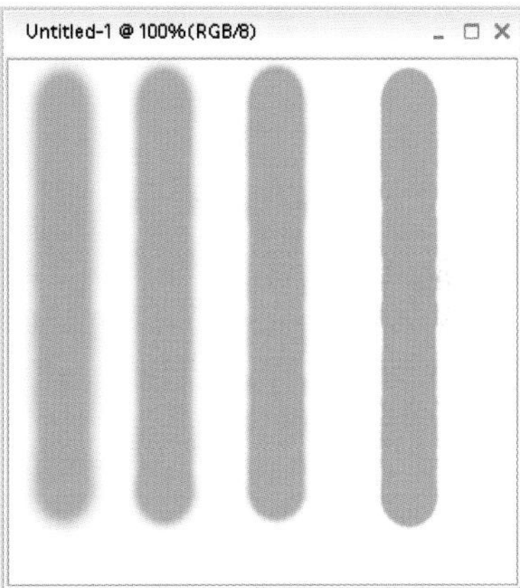

Hardness slider

8. Drag the **Angle** arrow head to set the number of degrees by which an elliptical brush's longitudinal axis is offset from horizontal. Alternatively, you can type a value between 0 and 360 in the Angle field. Drag a dot at the end of the circle to change the brush shape from round to elliptical. Alternatively, you can type a value between 0 and 100 in the Roundness field. An angled stroke painted with an elliptical brush looks like it was created with a calligraphic pen.
9. Click the **Keep These Settings For All Brushes** check box, and Photoshop Elements applies the settings to other brushes you choose from the Brushes drop-down list.

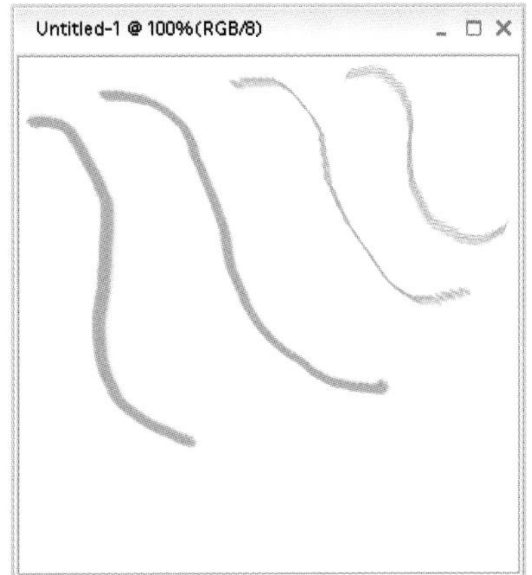

Angle arrow head

1 2 3 4 5 6 7 8 9 10

Set Tablet Support

If you paint with a digital tablet, such as those manufactured by Wacom, you can add a wonderful degree of realism to your painting. Painting with a tablet is more natural than painting with a mouse. In addition, the amount of pressure you exert when you press the stylus to the tablet varies the brush stroke. By default, the brush size changes from narrow to wide as you exert more pressure. When you modify your tablet options, stylus pressure affects other parameters, such as brush roundness and hue jitter. For example, if you click the Hue Jitter tablet option, increasing the pressure of your stylus on the tablet causes the foreground and background colors to switch (jitter) more frequently. You can set your tablet-support options to vary other brush dynamics as well.

1. Click the **Brush** tool in the toolbar.
2. In the Options bar, click the **Tablet Options** down arrow.
3. Click the **Size** check box (selected by default) to disable tablet control over brush size.

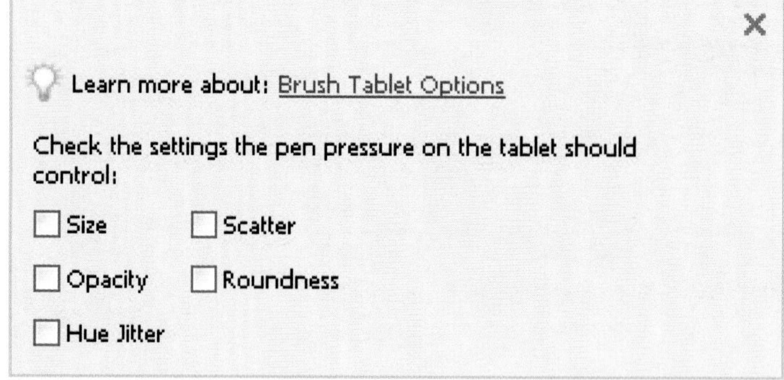

4. Click the **Scatter** check box to enable tablet control over brush scatter.
5. Click the **Opacity** check box to enable tablet control over brush opacity.
6. Click the **Roundness** check box to enable tablet control over brush roundness.
7. Click the **Hue Jitter** check box to enable tablet control over hue jitter between foreground and background colors.

TIP

To master your digital tablet, create a blank document with a white background, and then load your favorite colors in the foreground and background swatches. Experiment with different brushes and vary the pressure you exert on the stylus as you paint. After you fill up the document with brush strokes, press **CTRL+A**, and then press **DELETE** to clear the canvas and begin painting anew. Creative play is the quickest way to master painting with a digital tablet.

Create a Custom Brush

Photoshop Elements has a wide variety of preset brushes from which to choose. You can, however, alter a preset brush by modifying brush dynamics and then save the brush as a preset brush.

1. Click the **Brush** tool.
2. Click the **Show Selected Brush Presets** down arrow, and choose a preset brush.
3. Modify the brush size, blend mode, and opacity.
4. Click the **More Options** icon to modify brush dynamics, as outlined in the "Set Brush Dynamics" section of this chapter.
5. Click the **Brush** down arrow, and then click the arrow to the right of the uppermost preset thumbnail to reveal the Brush options menu.

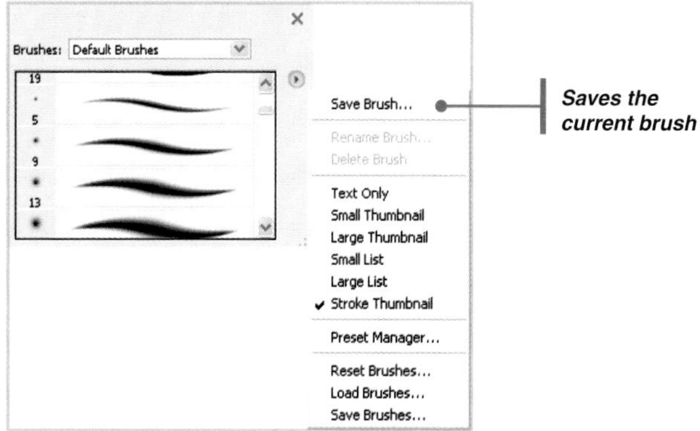

6. Click **Save Brush**. The Brush Name dialog box appears.
7. Type a name for your brush, and click **OK**.

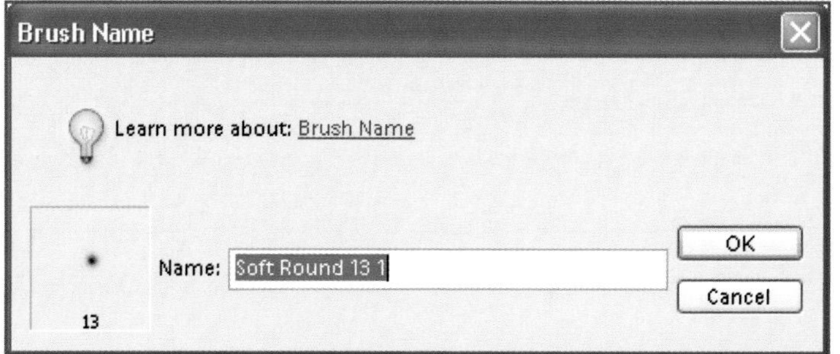

TIP

Choose a brush preset with the relevant size and softness for your needs.

NOTE

Your new brush appears at the bottom of the preset list for the brush library to which it was added. Hold your cursor over the brush thumbnail to reveal a tool tip with the brush name.

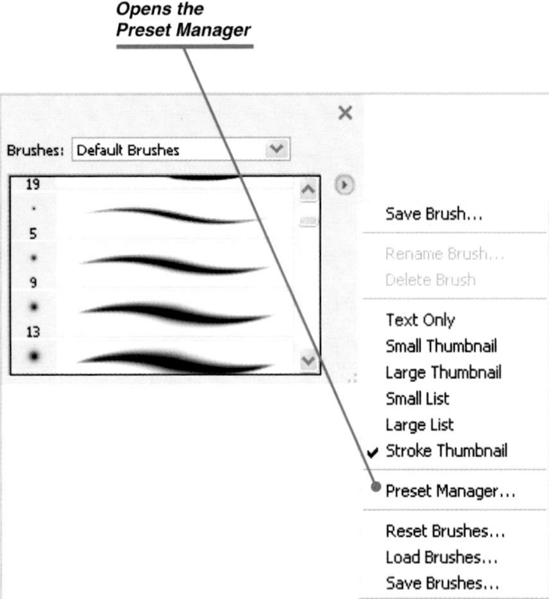

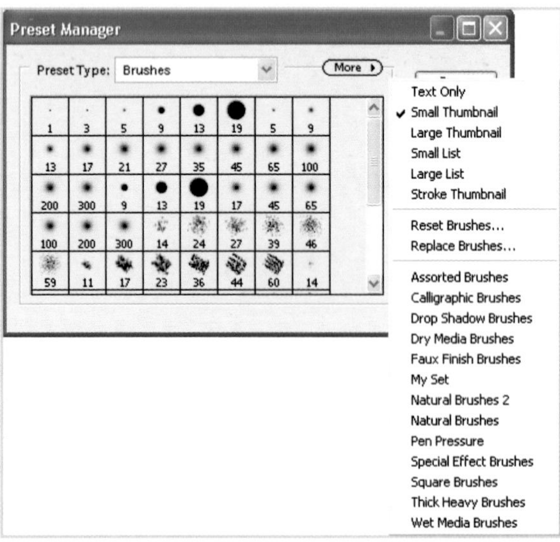

Manage the Brush Library

When you install Photoshop Elements, the default brush library is selected. You can, however, load other libraries and modify libraries by deleting brushes and adding custom brushes. This flexibility enables you to load the brush library that suits your current needs.

LOAD A BRUSH LIBRARY

When you load a brush library using the Preset Manager, you replace the existing library; whereas if you load a brush library from the Brush Options menu, you add the brushes to the currently loaded library.

1. Click the **Brush** tool in the toolbar.
2. Click the **Brush** down arrow, and then click the arrow to the right of the uppermost preset thumbnail to reveal the Brush options menu.
3. Click **Preset Manager**. The Preset Manager dialog box appears.

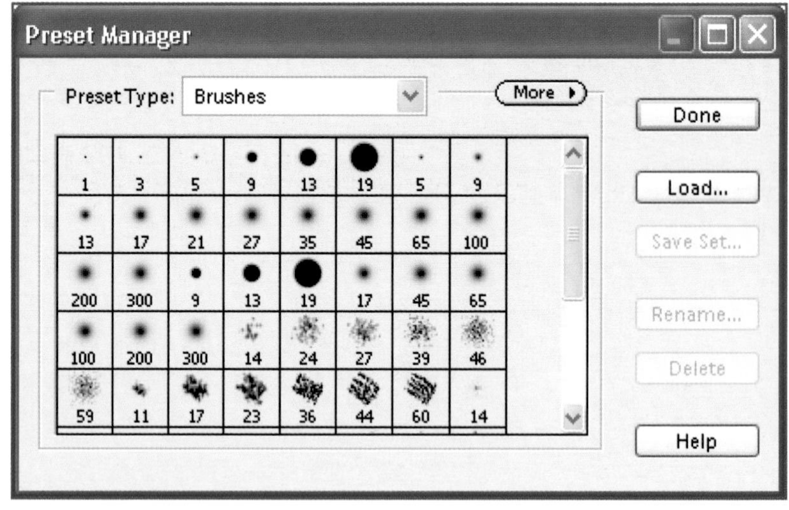

4. Click the **More** button.
5. Click the brush library you want to load.
6. Click **Done** to close the Preset Manager.

> **TIP**
>
> To reset brushes to the default set, click the **Brushes** down arrow, click the arrow to the right of the uppermost preset thumbnail to open the Brush Options menu, and then click **Reset Brushes**.

> **NOTE**
>
> When you delete a brush, you only remove it from view; it is still part of the preset library. You can restore the brush by reloading the library in which it is stored.

> **TIP**
>
> You can select multiple brushes in the Preset Manager and then delete them all at once.

APPEND A BRUSH LIBRARY

In addition to replacing one brush library with another, you can add the brushes from another library to the currently loaded brushes.

1. Click the **Brush** tool in the toolbar.
2. Click the **Show Selected Brush Preset**s down arrow, click the **Brush Options** menu, and then click **Preset Manager**.

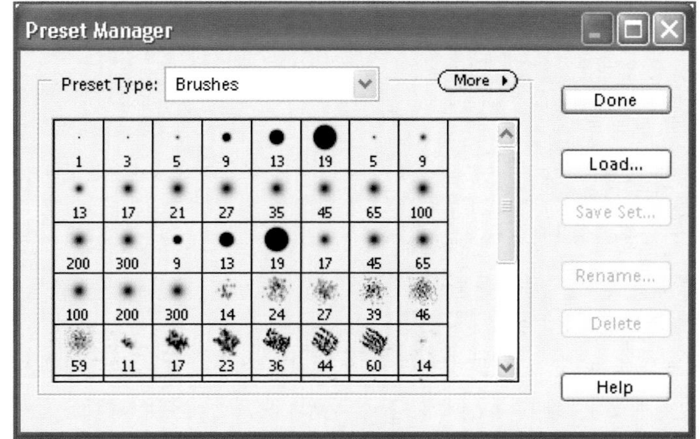

3. Click **Load.** The Load dialog box appears.
4. Click the preset library you want to add to the currently loaded brush library.
5. Click **Load**.

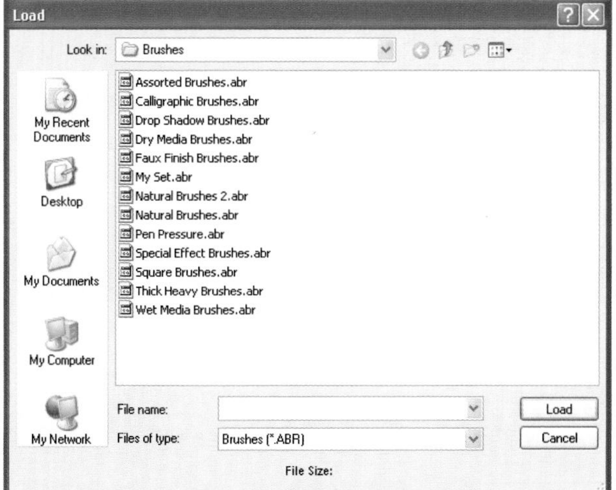

ORGANIZE A BRUSH LIBRARY

When you start using brushes for editing and adding color to your images, you may find you work with some brushes more than others. You can speed up your workflow considerably if you delete the brushes you're not using and then save the currently loaded brushes as a library.

1. Click the **Brush** tool in the toolbar.
2. Click the **Show Selected Brush Presets** down arrow, click the **Brush Options** menu, and then click **Preset Manager**.

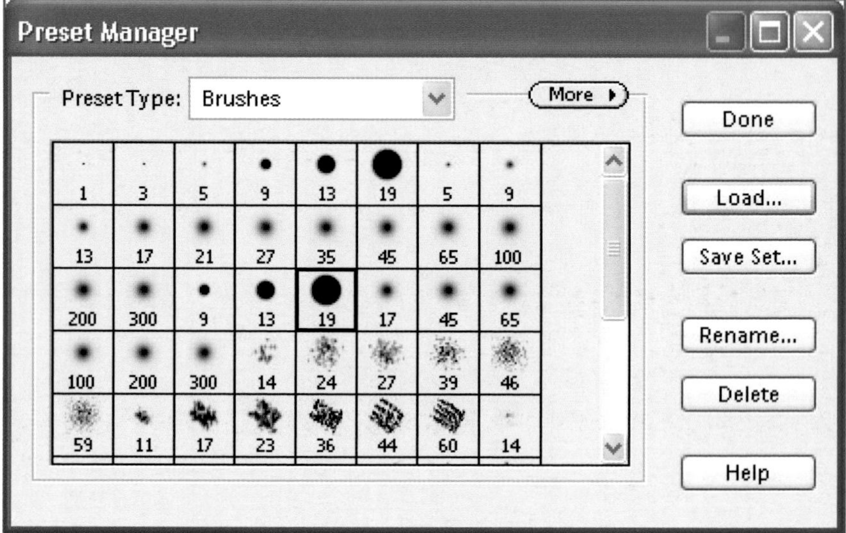

3. Load the desired brush library, or append the brush library, as outlined in the previous sections.
4. Click a **brush** icon and do one of the following:
   - Click **Rename** to open the Brush Rename dialog box. Type a new name and then click **OK**.
   - Click **Delete** to remove the brush from those currently loaded.
5. After you've deleted the brushes you don't want, click **Save Set**. The Save dialog box is displayed.
6. Type a name for your custom library.

TIP

After saving a custom library, you can load it at any time by following the steps in the "Load a Brush Library" section of this chapter.

NOTE

A warning dialog box appears if the frame you want to apply requires a selection or needs to be flattened.

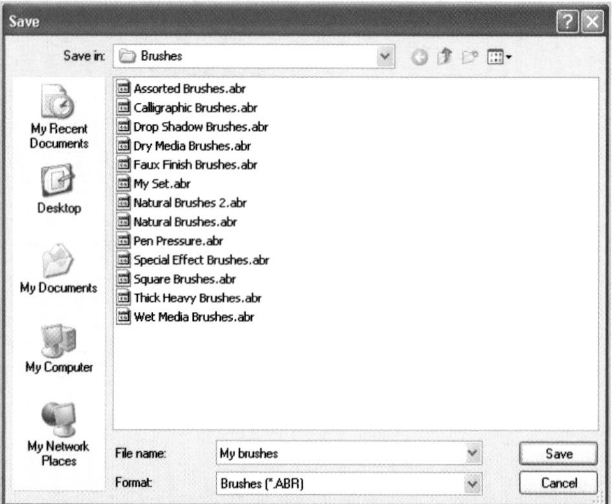

QUICKSTEPS

FRAMING IMAGES

You can easily put an image in a frame from the Frames section of the Styles And Effects palette. You can create a conventional wood frame or something with real panache, such as a recessed frame. For certain frames, such as the Vignette, you'll need to create a selection (see the section "Create a Vignette").

1. Open the image to which you want to add a frame.
2. Click **Window** and then click **Styles And Effects**. The Styles And Effects palette is displayed.
3. In the Styles And Effects palette, click the down arrow for the drop-down list on the left, and then click **Effects**.
4. Click the down arrow for the drop-down list on the right, and then click **Frames**. The Frames library is displayed.
5. Drag the desired frame onto your image. The following image shows the Photo Corners frame applied to an image.

7. Click **Save** to add your custom library to the Photoshop Elements Brushes folder.
8. Click **Done** to exit the Preset Manager.

Use Special Effects

Photoshop Elements ships with a plethora of special effects in the Styles And Effects palette. You can use effects on layers or apply effects to an entire image. In the upcoming sections, you'll learn to apply some basic effects. To become a master at special effects, expand on the knowledge you've learned here by experimenting with different effects.

Add Drop Shadows to Layers

Adding drop shadows to layers is a wonderful way to make individual images pop out when you're creating an image collage. Drop shadows can also be applied to text.

1. Click **Window** and then click **Layers**. The Layers palette is displayed.
2. Click the layer to which you want to apply the drop shadow.
3. Click **Window** and then click **Styles And Effects**. The Styles And Effects palette is displayed.
4. Click the **Category** down arrow, and click **Layer Styles**.
5. Click the currently selected **Layer Style Library** down arrow, and click **Drop Shadows**. The Drop Shadows Style Library is displayed.
6. Click the desired style to apply it to the layer. Figure 7-2 shows a photo collage in which each image has a drop shadow.

1
2
3
4
5
6
7
8
9
10

Figure 7-2: You can spice up a photo collage with drop shadows.

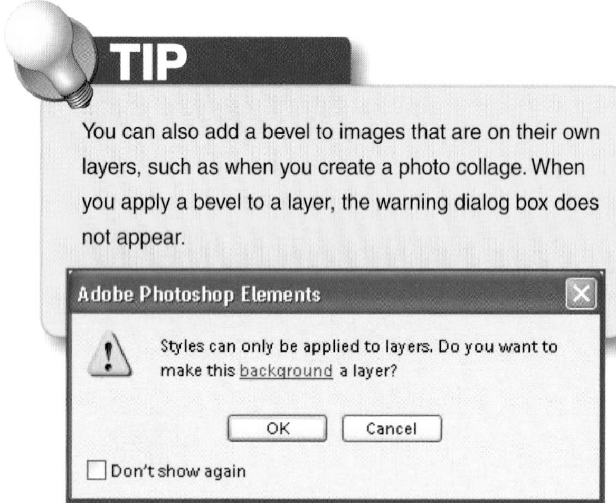

TIP

You can also add a bevel to images that are on their own layers, such as when you create a photo collage. When you apply a bevel to a layer, the warning dialog box does not appear.

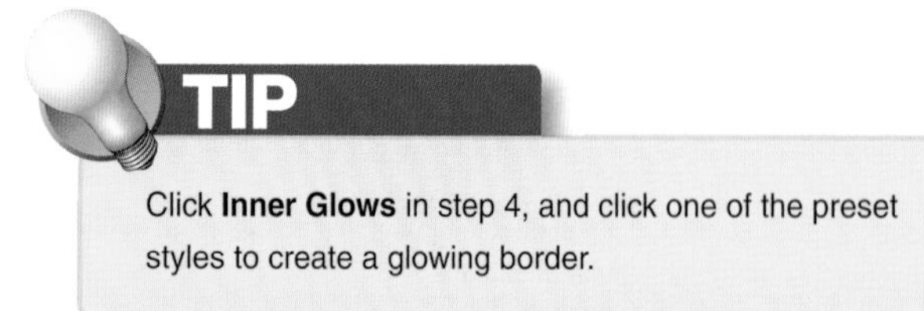

TIP

Click **Inner Glows** in step 4, and click one of the preset styles to create a glowing border.

Add Fancy Borders

You can also use styles to create a custom background for your image. If you want beveled edges or a glowing border surrounding your image, you can achieve either effect by using the Styles And Effects palette.

1. Open the image to which you want to add a border.
2. Click **Window** and click **Styles And Effects**. The Styles And Effects palette is displayed.
3. In the Styles And Effects palette, click the down arrow for the drop-down list on the left, and then click **Layer Styles**.
4. Click the down arrow for the drop-down list on the right, and click **Bevels**.
5. Click one of the preset styles. A dialog box is displayed, warning you that styles can only be applied to layers.
6. Click **OK**. The New Layer dialog box is displayed.
7. Type a different name for the new layer.
8. Click **OK** to convert the background to a layer and apply the bevel.

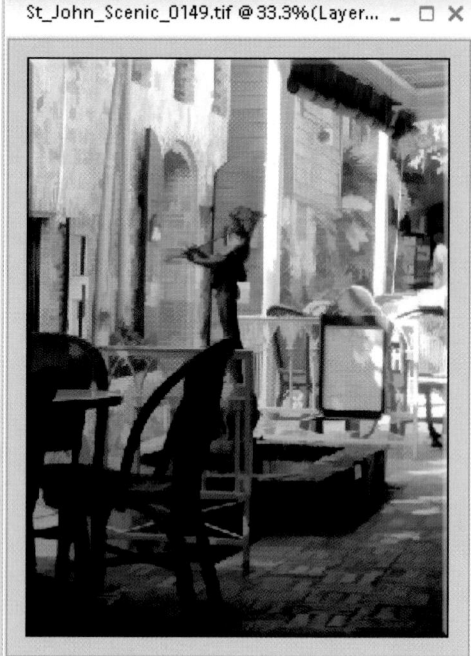

Use Filters

Photoshop Elements ships with a treasure trove of filters. As mentioned in previous chapters, you can use filters to sharpen images and can use multiple filters, if desired. If you really want to be organized, consider duplicating the background layer and applying all your filters to the duplicate layer. This way, you can immediately compare the enhanced version to the original by hiding the duplicate layer. When you apply filters to duplicate layers, you can delete them if you don't like the result; your original image remains on the background layer.

You can add filters using menu commands or from the Filter section of the Styles And Effects palette, as shown in Figure 7-3. Note that this figure is displayed with the palette floating in the workspace to view all of the available filters. Upcoming sections will explore filters and techniques you can use to add pizzazz to your images.

Figure 7-3: Use the Styles And Effects palette to apply filters to your images.

Figure 7-4: You can apply a filter to convert an image into a chalk-and-charcoal sketch.

Create Images that Look Like Paintings

Photoshop Elements has several filters you can use to add a painterly touch to your images. If you're a frustrated watercolor artist, or you like to dabble with colored pencils, but just can't seem to make it work, you'll love the Artistic and Sketch filters. The following steps will give you an idea of what you can do with them. In this procedure, you'll take it one step further by applying the filter on its own layer and using the Opacity control to let some of the original image shine through.

1. Open the photo you want to transform into a an image that looks like a painting.
2. Click **Windows** and click **Layers**. The Layers palette appears.
3. Drag the background layer to the **Create New Layer** icon.
4. Double-click the new layer and type Chalk & Charcoal to rename the layer.
5. Click the **Chalk & Charcoal** layer.
6. Click **Filter**, click **Sketch**, and then click **Chalk & Charcoal**. The Chalk & Charcoal dialog box appears, as shown in Figure 7-4.
7. Drag the relevant sliders to achieve the desired look.
8. Click **OK** to apply the filter.
9. In the Layers palette, click the **Opacity** arrow for the layer, and drag the slider to **80** percent.
10. Click the **More** button in the Layers palette, and then click **Flatten Image**.

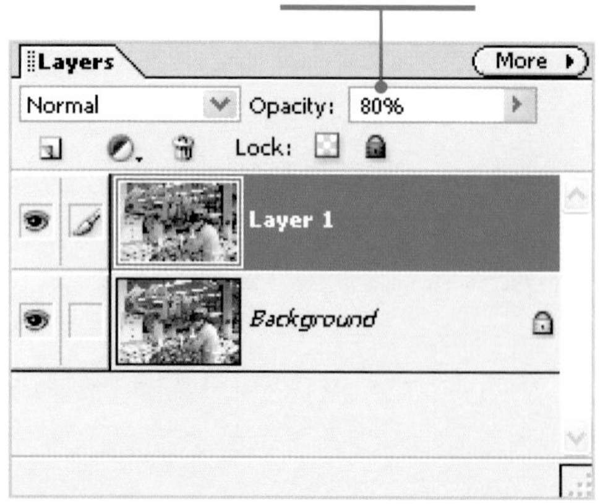

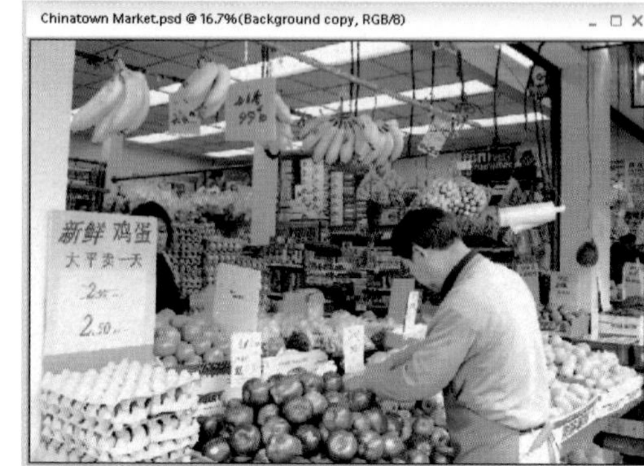

Blur Images

Sometimes there are details in your images that you'd rather not show. For example, if there's a garbage can in clear focus of the group portrait you photographed of your family, don't worry. You can easily make the detail unnoticeable by blurring it. The Gaussian Blur filter is ideal for this sort of job.

1. Create a selection around the object you want to blur out of the picture.
2. Feather the selection. The actual size of the feather depends on the size of your image. Your goal is to create a soft blend between the blurred object and the rest of the image.
3. Click **Filter**, click **Blur**, and then click **Gaussian Blur.** The Gaussian Blur dialog box is displayed.

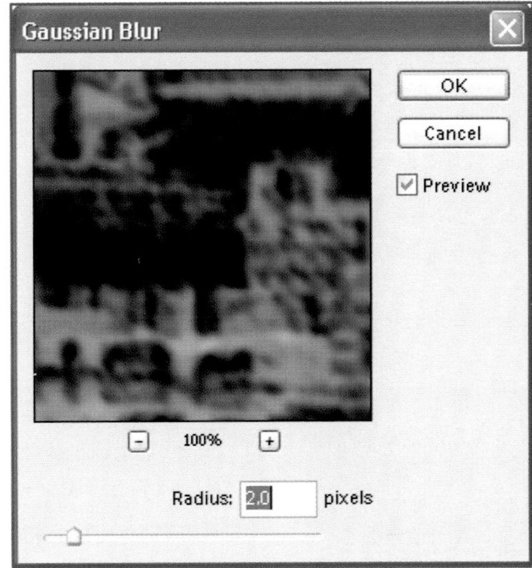

4. Drag the **Radius** slider to set the blur distance. Alternatively, you can type the desired valued in the Radius field. This value tells Photoshop Elements the distance from each pixel that the blur is to be applied.
5. Click **OK** to apply the blur. Figure 7-5 shows a background that has been blurred to direct attention toward the young lady.

Figure 7-5: You can blur unwanted details out of your photos, such as the background of this image.

Create a Zoom Blur

An interesting technique photographers often use is to mount a camera on a tripod and select a small aperture (high F-stop number) to achieve a slow shutter speed. Then they take a picture of an object with their zoom lens at its lowest magnification and quickly zoom to the highest magnification. The effect makes it look as though the object is rushing toward you. You can achieve the same effect in Photoshop Elements using the Radial Blur filter.

1. Open the image to which you want to apply the zoom blur effect.
2. Click **Filter**, click **Blur**, and click **Radial Blur**. The Radial Blur dialog box appears. Notice that this dialog box does not have a preview area.

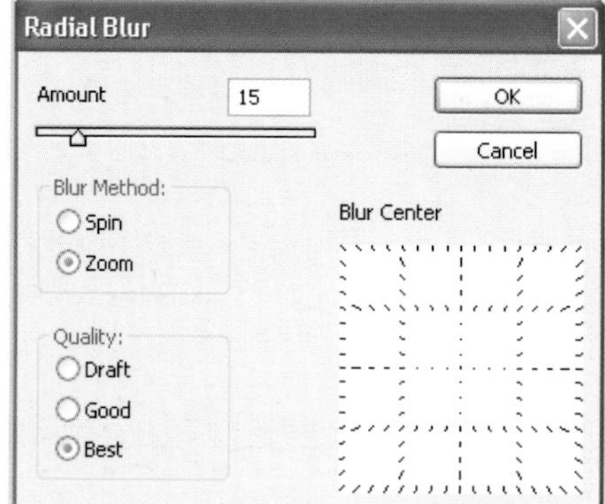

3. Drag the **Amount** slider to the desired blur amount. A value between 10 and 15 works well for this effect.
4. In the Blur Method area, click **Zoom**.
5. In the Quality area, click the desired option. Click **Best** for the highest quality image (at the expense of a longer render time; that is, the time it takes the computer to render, or create, the effect).
6. Click **OK** to apply the effect.

Distort Images

Photoshop Elements includes several filters you can use to distort images. You'll find these under the Distort menu. The following technique uses the Spherize filter in conjunction with other tools to create a fish-eye-lens effect.

1. Open the image that you want to appear as though it was photographed with a fish-eye lens.
2. Click the **Crop** tool.
3. Click at the top of the image, and, while holding down the **SHIFT** key, drag the tool to the bottom of the image. When you hold down the **SHIFT** key, you constrain the cropping box to a square, which is perfect for a fish-eye look.
4. Click the **Commit** button on the Options bar. Alternatively, you can press **ENTER**.
5. Click the **Elliptical Marquee** tool, and create a circular section that stretches from top to bottom and side to side, as shown in the upper-left illustration. To create a perfect circle, hold down the **SHIFT** key while dragging. Press **SPACEBAR** momentarily to move the selection while creating it.
6. Click **Filter**, click **Distort**, and click **Spherize**. The Spherize dialog box appears.
7. Drag the **Amount** slider to **100**.
8. Click **OK** to apply the filter.
9. Click **Select** and then click **Inverse**.
10. Click **Edit** and then click **Fill Selection**. The Fill Layer dialog box appears.
11. Click the **Use** down arrow, and click **Black**.
12. Click **OK** to fill the selection.
13. Click **Select** and then click **Deselect**.

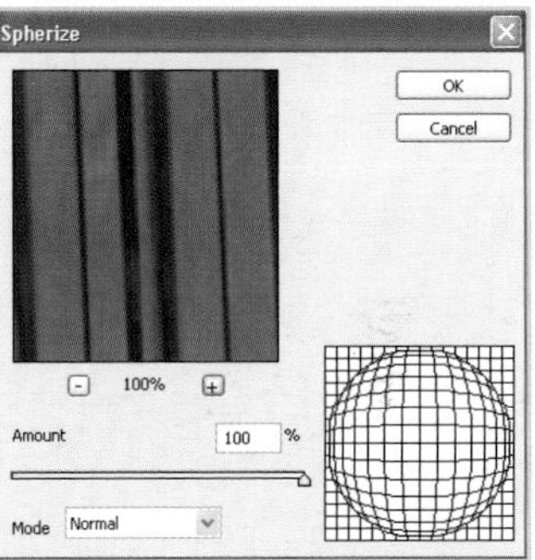

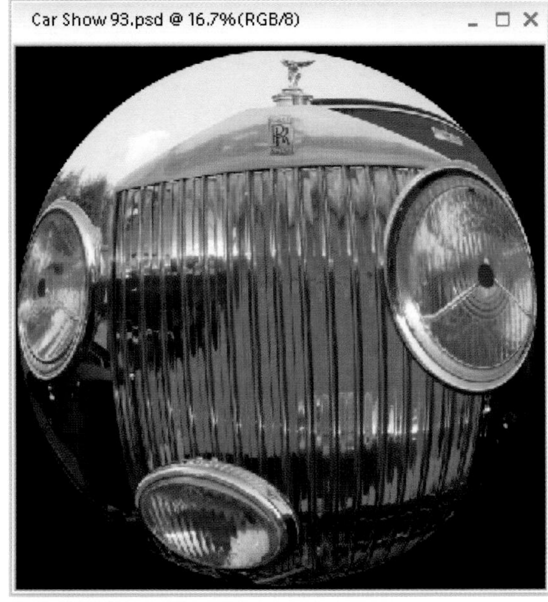

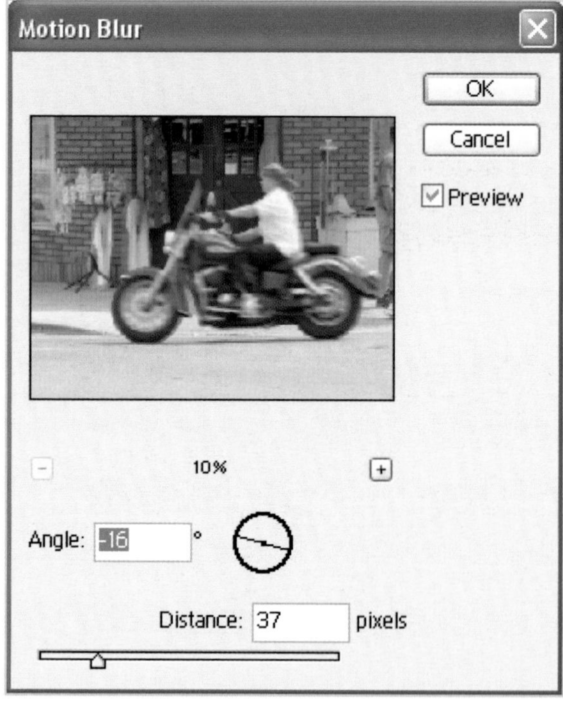

Add a Motion Blur Effect

You can make a stationary object appear to be moving by using the Motion Blur filter. You can also use the Motion Blur filter to add authenticity to an image of a moving object that appears to be standing still because you captured it at too high a shutter speed.

1. Open the image you want to enhance with the Motion Blur filter.
2. Click one of the **Lasso** tools, or click the **Selection Brush** tool, to make a selection around the object you want to blur, as shown in the illustration on the left. The selection doesn't need to be precise, as the blur will compensate for any small areas you've missed. In fact, if you select a little more than the object, the effect will appear more natural because you won't have any sharp edges after the blur is applied.
3. Click **Filter**, click **Blur**, and click **Motion Blur**. The Motion Blur dialog box appears.
4. Click the diagonal line in the circle, and drag to set the angle. Alternatively, you can type the desired angle in the Angle field. As you change the angle, you'll be able to see the effects in the preview window, as well as in your object, if you have the **Preview** check box selected.
5. Drag the **Distance** slider to set the distance in pixels that the blur extends from the object. Alternatively, you can type a value in the Distance field.
6. Click **OK** to apply the filter.
7. Click **Select** and then click **Deselect All**. Figure 7-6 shows the finished motion blur effect.

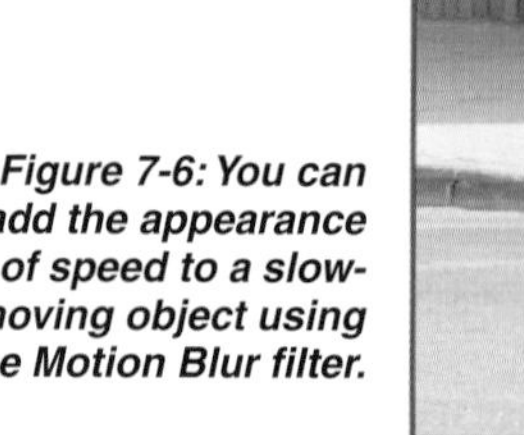

Figure 7-6: You can add the appearance of speed to a slow-moving object using the Motion Blur filter.

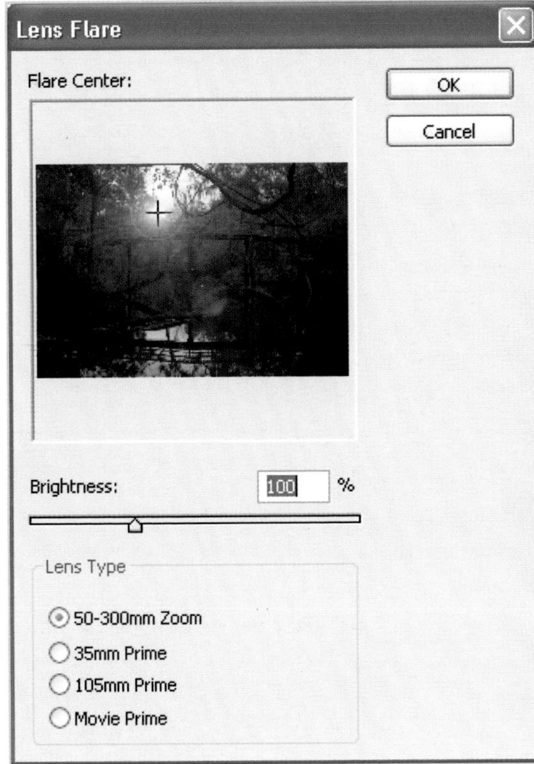

Add a Lens Flare

Photographers sometimes go out of their way to avoid shooting into the sun. Other times, however, they do so deliberately so they can include a lens flare in the image. You can add a lens flare effect to any image through the use of a filter.

1. Open the image to which you want to apply a lens flare.
2. Click **Filter**, click **Render,** and then click **Lens Flare**. The Lens Flare dialog box is displayed.
3. Drag the **crosshairs** pointer to position the lens flare.
4. Drag the **Brightness** slider to set the intensity of the lens flare. Alternatively, you can type a value between 0 and 300 in the Brightness field.
5. Click the applicable option to choose the type of lens flare. Each preset effect mimics the lens flare of a lens with a given focal length.
6. Click **OK** to apply the lens flare.

Cut Out an Image

You can cut out a portion of your image using the Cookie Cutter tool. This tool features a wide variety of shapes you can use to create interesting effects.

1. Open the image to which you want to apply the effect.
2. Click the **Cookie Cutter** tool. 
3. In the Options bar, click the down arrow to open the Custom Shape Picker menu.

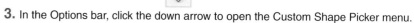

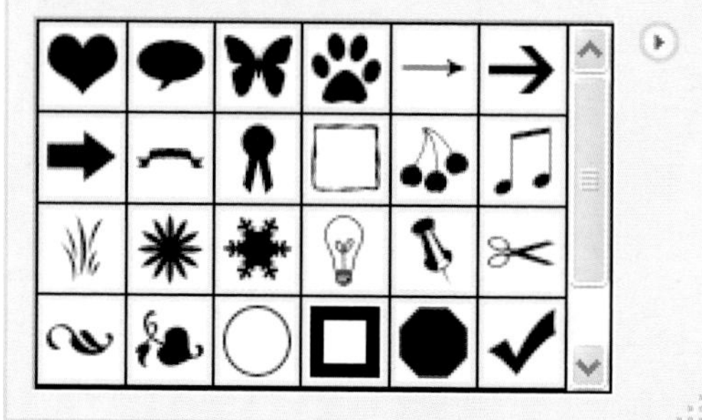

4. Click the desired shape.
5. Drag inside the image to define the shape.
6. Drag any handle to fine-tune the size of the shape.
7. Click **Commit** to cut out the image.
8. Set the foreground color to the color you want to surround the cut-out image.
9. Click the **Fill** tool.
10. Click outside the cut-out image to fill the perimeter.

Liquefy an Image

If you want to have some fun with a picture of a friend or significant other, consider using the Liquefy filter. The Liquefy filter is like virtual Silly Putty®. Click inside the image and drag to apply distortion. Figure 7-7 shows the Liquefy dialog box and an image prior to using the Liquefy tools.

1. Open the image to which you want to apply the liquefy effect.
2. Click **Filter,** click **Distort**, and then click **Liquefy**. The Liquefy dialog box appears.
3. Click the desired tool from the toolbox.

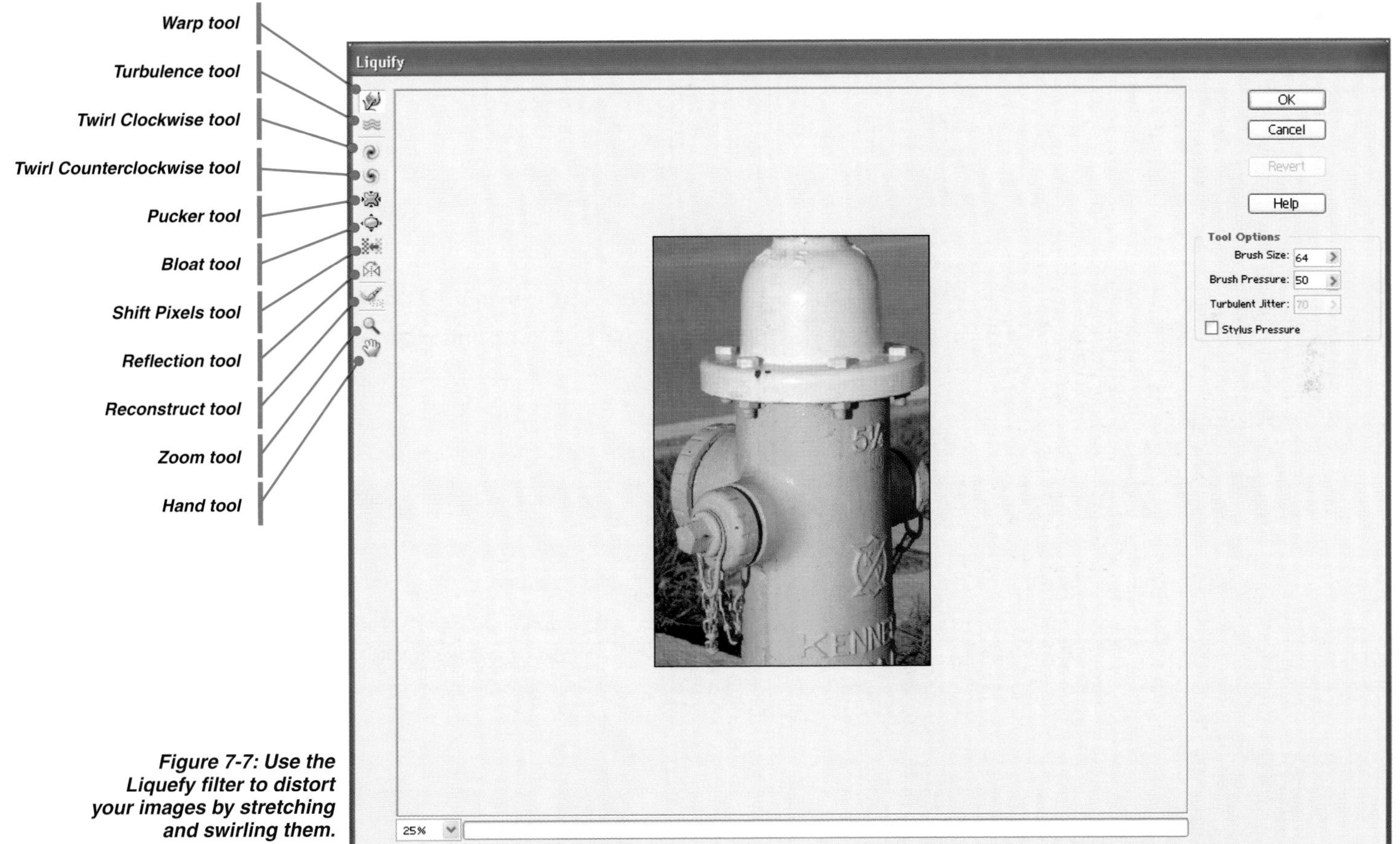

Figure 7-7: Use the Liquefy filter to distort your images by stretching and swirling them.

TIP

Click the **Reconstruct** tool and drag it across any areas of the image you wish to restore to their original states.

TIP

Click **Revert** to restore the image to its original state.

4. Click the **Brush Size** down arrow, and drag the slider to set the brush size.
5. Click the **Brush Pressure** down arrow, and drag the slider to set the brush pressure. Lower values produce subtler changes.
6. Click the **Turbulence Jitter** down arrow (it becomes available when you select the Turbulence Jitter tool), and drag the slider to set the amount of turbulence jitter. Lower values produce less jitter.
7. Click the **Stylus Pressure** check box if you're using a digital tablet to liquefy the image.
8. Drag inside the image to liquefy it.
9. Click **OK** to apply the changes.

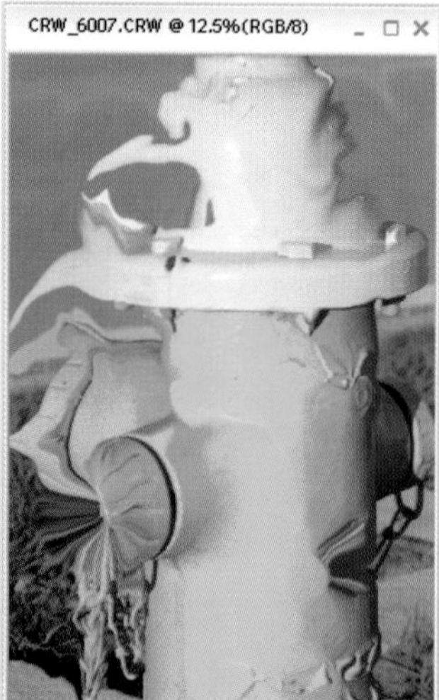

Create a Vignette

One way you can enhance a portrait of a person is by adding a vignette—an elliptical border around the subject that blends gradually into the background. You can create your own custom vignettes in Photoshop Elements through the use of layers and the Elliptical Marquee selection tool.

1. Open a head-and-shoulders portrait of a person or a close-up shot of an animal or pet.
2. Click **Windows** and click **Layers**. The Layers palette is displayed.
3. Click the background layer and drag it to the **Create New Layer** icon.
4. Double-click the default layer name, and type Vignette in the text box.
5. Click the **Elliptical Marquee** tool.
6. Create a selection around the desired section of the portrait. Remember, you can press **SPACEBAR** to move the selection as you are creating it. To fine-tune the position of the selection, click inside the selection and drag to the desired location.

7. Click **Select** and then click **Feather**. The Feather Selection dialog box appears. When you feather a selection, you create a region where the pixels inside the selection are gradually blended with the pixels outside of the selection. This prevents a hard edge when you're creating an effect like a vignette.

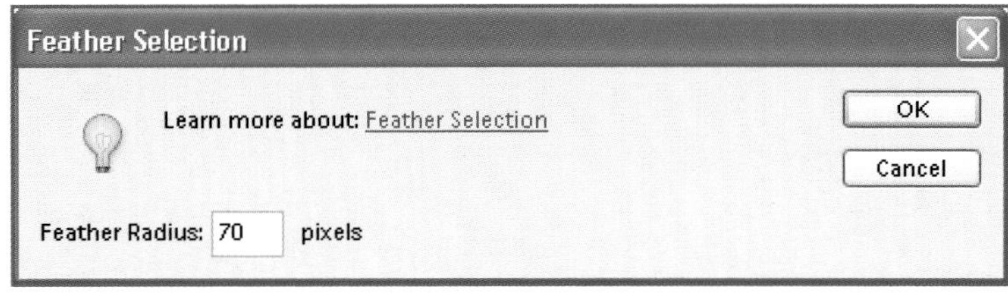

8. Type the desired value in the Feather Radius field. This value is in pixels and determines how many pixels beyond the selection will be used for the feather. The amount you type depends on the size of the image to which you're applying the effect. If you're creating a vignette around a large image, experiment with values 100 pixels or larger.
9. Click **OK** to apply the feather and close the dialog box.
10. Click **Select** and click **Inverse** to select the area where the vignette will be applied.
11. Click **Edit** and then click **Fill Selection**. The Fill Layer dialog box appears.

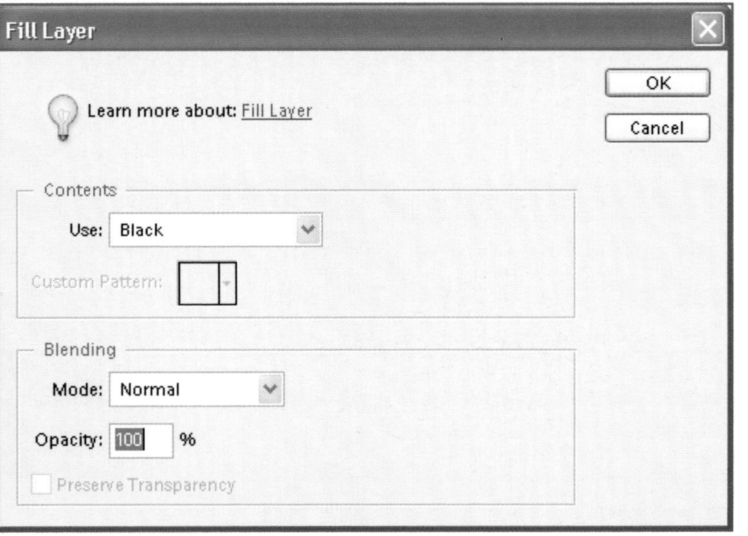

TIP

For a different effect, choose a fill color that matches a color in your image. To do this, click the **Use** down arrow, and then click **Color** to open the Color Picker. Click the color swatch in the upper-right corner of the image, and then click the desired color inside the image for a perfect match. After you close the Color Picker, the selected color apears inside the vignette.

TIP

To achieve a different vignette effect, click the **Mode** down arrow in the Blending section of the Fill Layer dialog box. Click **Multiply** to vary the opacity of the blending mode.

NOTE

When you flatten layers, you can no longer edit them. Flattening layers is the final step when you're satisfied with the image.

12. Click the **Use** down arrow, and click **Black**.
13. Click **OK** to apply the fill.
14. Click the **Vignette** layer and drag the **Opacity** slider to **85** percent. Choose a higher value to reveal less of the underlying layer; choose a smaller value to reveal more. To see the effect the opacity has, click the **eyeball** icon on the background layer to momentarily hide the layer.
15. Click **Select** and then click **Deselect** to remove the selection.
16. Click the **More** button in the Layers palette, and click **Flatten Image**. This command flattens all the layers into the background layer in the image. This step is not necessary if you're saving the file as a Photoshop (.psd) file.

How to...

- *Create Text*
- *Committing Type*
- *Edit Text*
- *Transforming Type*
- *Move Text*
- *Warp Text*
- *Create Text on a Path*
- *Finding and Using Layer Styles*
- *Edit Text on a Path*
- *Add Special Type Effects with Layer Styles*
- *Create Type Masks*

Chapter 8
Working with Type

In the course of working with Photoshop Elements, you might want to type text on an image to make it more effective and dramatic or simply to label it. In this chapter you will discover how to create and edit type on images using typical formatting. Once you have mastered these basic tasks, you will see how to play with your type using such techniques as warping, rotating, skewing, and resizing. You will find out how to use layer styles to create special effects such as drop shadows, beveling and embossing, inside and outside glows, and gradient fills. Finally, you will learn how to mask your type, enabling you to copy images as fill for type, and how to make a selection of type, which can then be manipulated just like any other selection.

Create and Edit Text

When you enter text, a type layer is created, which can be edited until you rasterize it. Initially, text is vector-based; when you rasterize it, it becomes a bitmap object. At this point, it can no longer be accessed as editable text. Some of the special tools and effects, however, such as the paint tools and filter effects, can be used once the type is rasterized.

When you select a type tool, the Options bar becomes a formatting toolbar. Figure 8-1 shows the tools available to you for creating and editing text.

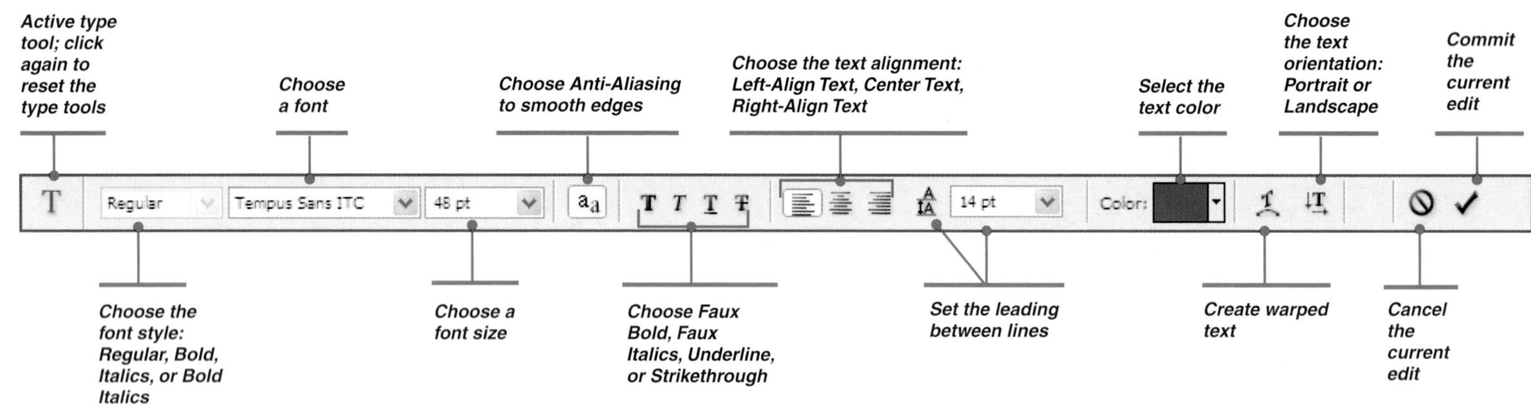

Figure 8-1: The Options bar contains various formatting tools. When you select a type tool, the formatting tools available to you change accordingly.

Create Text

You type text using one of two text tools: the Horizontal Type tool or the Vertical Type tool. As you would expect, the Horizontal Type tool allows you to type text horizontally, and the Vertical Type tool allows you to type text vertically. The two mask tools allow you to create a selection of text for special effects, as discussed in the section "Create Text Masks" later in this chapter.

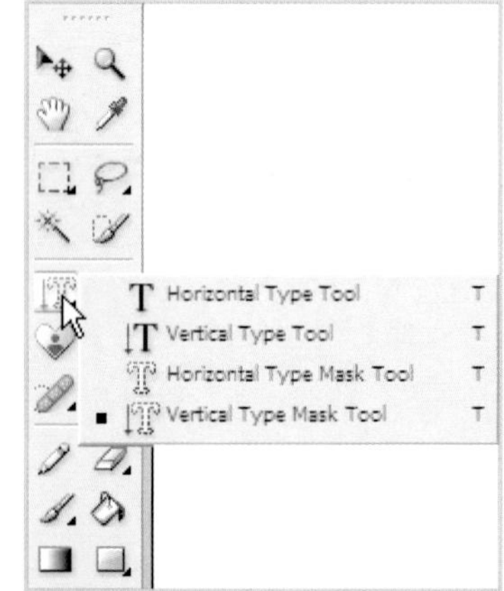

NOTE

Pressing **ENTER** when typing horizontal text begins a new line beneath the previous one. Pressing **ENTER** when typing vertical text begins a new line to the left.

QUICKSTEPS

COMMITTING TYPE

After your text has been entered and you are satisfied with the results, you commit the text to accept the changes. Perform one of the following actions to commit the changes:

- Click Commit on the Options bar.
- On the numeric keyboard, press **ENTER**.
- Click in the image.
- On the main keyboard, press **CTRL+ENTER**.
- Select another tool, or select a menu option.

ENTER TYPE

As you type text, a new type layer is created. The text doesn't wrap to the next line; rather, it continues on the same line. To move text to a new line, press ENTER.

1. Click either the **Horizontal Type** tool or the **Vertical Type** tool.
2. Set the attributes for the text. (See the section "Edit Text" later in the chapter for more information on how to set the attributes.)
3. Click in the image area, and the pointer changes to an I-beam pointer. Place it where you want the text to begin. For horizontal type, the small intersecting line indicates where the bottom of the text will appear. For vertical type, the intersecting line identifies the center of the text. Figure 8-2 shows vertical text typed onto a photo.
4. Type the text you want. Press **ENTER** to begin a new line.
5. Select any changes in formatting you want from the Options bar (see "Edit Text" later in this chapter).
6. Click **Commit** on the Options bar. (See the QuickSteps "Committing Type" for more information on how to use Commit.)

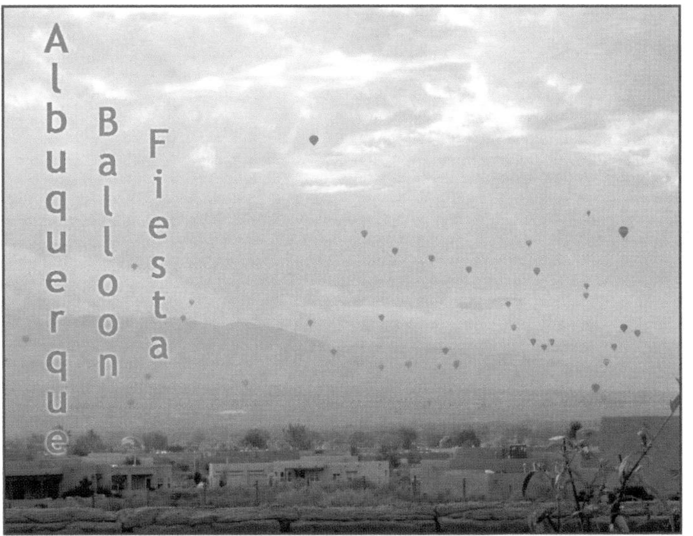

Figure 8-2: Use the Vertical Type tool to create an interesting label for a photo.

NOTE

To add characters, click the insertion point in the place where you want to add text, and type the characters. To delete characters, either place the insertion point immediately before the characters to be deleted, and press **DELETE**, or place the insertion point after the characters and press **BACKSPACE** for each character you want to delete.

Leading smaller than point size
Second line is crowded

Leading larger than point size
Second line has more space

Leading same as point size
Second line has slight separation

Figure 8-3: You can control the space between lines by varying the leading.

Edit Text

While editing text, you can change the font, text color, font size and style, and *leading* (the spacing between lines of text), as well as add and delete characters. You do this using the Options bar shown earlier in Figure 8-1.

1. In the Standard Edit window, on the Layers Palette, select the text layer to be edited if it is not already selected.
2. Select the text you want to edit by highlighting it.
3. Select from among the following options:

- **Font Style** You can choose to make your text formatted in bold, italics, bold italics, or with regular formatting.

- **Font Attributes** If the font you are choosing does not have a bold or italics typeface (in this case, the Font Style drop-down box will be unavailable or fixed in place), click the **Faux Bold**, **Faux Italics**, **Underline**, or **Strikethrough** button.
- **Font** You can change the default font used when you typed your text.
- **Font Size** You can change the point size of the characters.

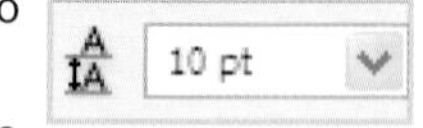

- **Leading** You can change the spacing between lines of text. Auto is the default. Usually, you want to select a leading larger than the size of the text. So if the point size is 20 points, you might use a leading of 24 or larger. You can reduce the leading and overlap lines of text to create special effects. Figure 8-3 shows examples of different leading selections.
- **Text Color** You can change the color of your text.
- **Anti-Aliasing** You can smooth the rough edges of text by blending the pixels of the edges of the text with the surrounding pixels of colors. Clicking None provides the least amount of adjustment; clicking Smooth, the most amount of adjustment.

with anti-aliasing

without anti-aliasing

TRANSFORMING TYPE

You can transform type by manipulating the *bounding boxes* (the boxes that appear when you select the text) using one or more of the following techniques.

SELECT A BOUNDING BOX

To display the bounding box with handles for rotating and resizing:

- In Standard Edit mode, click the layer containing the text you want to transform to select the text.
- Click the **Move** tool and click the text. The layer and the text are both selected.

RESIZE A BOUNDING BOX

To resize a bounding box:

1. Place your pointer over the bounding-box handles until it changes to a double-headed arrow. 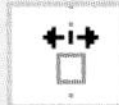
2. Drag the handles until the bounding box is the size you want.
3. To change the size proportionally (so that the height and width are changed in proportion to each other), press SHIFT while you drag.

ROTATE A BOUNDING BOX

To rotate a bounding box:

1. Place the pointer outside the bounding box until the pointer changes to a curved double-headed arrow.
2. Drag the pointer in the direction you want to rotate the box. To constrain the rotation to 15-degree increments, you need to hold down the SHIFT key.

Continued...

4. To apply the edit, click the **Commit** button.
5. To cancel the edit, click the **Cancel** button. 

Move Text

To move the text on an image:

1. Select the type layer you want to move.
2. Click the **Move** tool. A selection box surrounds the text. 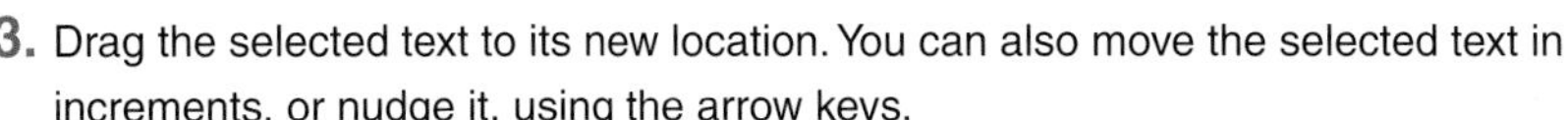
3. Drag the selected text to its new location. You can also move the selected text in increments, or nudge it, using the arrow keys.
4. Click in an area of the image away from the selected text to deselect the text.

Warp Text

Warping is used to shape or distort text. For instance, you may have a shape or path that you want the text to follow (see the section "Create Text on a Path"), or you may shape the text to create interesting effects.

1. In the Layers palette, click the layer containing the text you want to warp.
2. Click the **Layer** menu, click **Type**, and click **Warp Text**. The Warp Text dialog box appears.

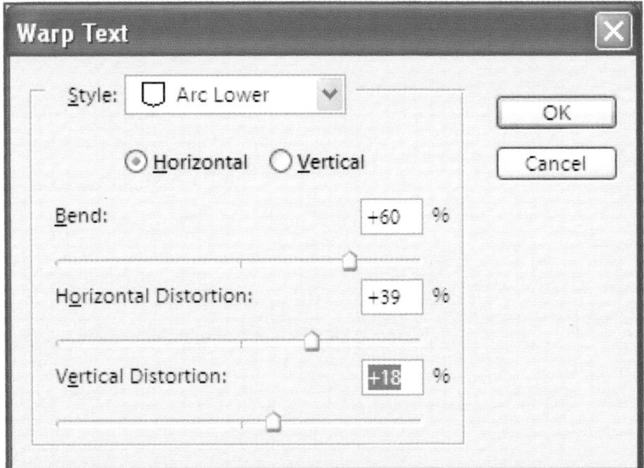

TRANSFORMING TYPE *(Continued)*

SKEW A BOUNDING BOX

To skew a bounding box, press **CTRL** while you drag a corner handle. The pointer changes to an arrow that can be used to skew the shape of the bounding box.

FLIP THE TEXT

To flip text, drag a bounding-box handle from one side to another. For example, click the right handle and drag it to the left until the text flips.

TIP

You can verify that you are in Edit mode by looking for the Commit and Cancel tools in the Option bar.

TIP

You can quickly select the text in a layer by double-clicking the **T** icon in the selected type layer in the Layers palette. You can alternate between the text editor, where you make changes to the characters, and the bounding box, where you can edit the block of text.

- Click the **Style** list down arrow, and select a warp style, such as that shown in Figure 8-4.

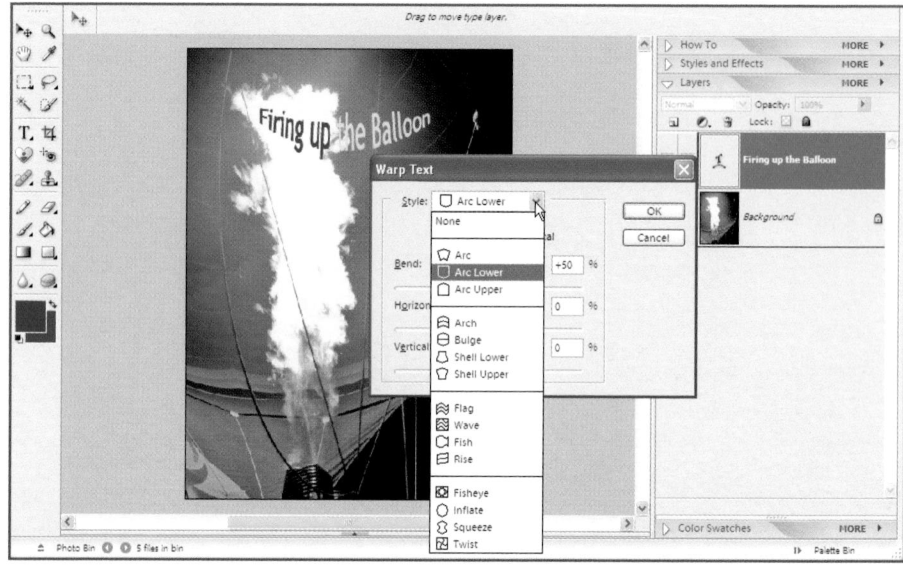

Figure 8-4: The Warp Text dialog box presents options for the style of warp you want.

- Click **Horizontal** or **Vertical** to orient the text horizontally or vertically.
- Drag the **Bend** slider to exaggerate or lessen the warp of the text. Alternatively, you can type a percentage to set the degree of warp.
- Drag the **Horizontal Distortion** slider to increase or decrease the horizontal warp, or type a percentage in the text box.
- Drag the **Vertical Distortion** slider to increase or decrease the vertical warp, or type a percentage in the text box.

3. Click **OK** when finished.

Create Text on a Path

You can align text along a path, such as that shown in Figure 8-5. To do this, you warp, rotate, and skew the text. First you type your text, and then you warp or rotate the text to fit the path as best it can. If necessary, you finish the job by

TIP

To remove the warp effects from text, select the relevant layer. Then select a type tool, and highlight the text to select it, which also reveals the Options bar for the text. Click the **Warp** button on the Options bar, click **None**, and click **OK**.

NOTE

You cannot use the Warp Text command if your text uses Faux Bold or Faux Italics. Remove these attributes before working with the Warp Text dialog box, or you will see the pictured error message.

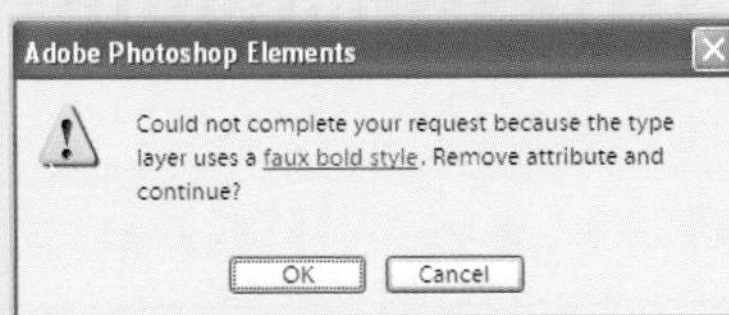

skewing the text so that it precisely follows the path. Obviously there will be some paths that do not work as well, but simple curves work fine.

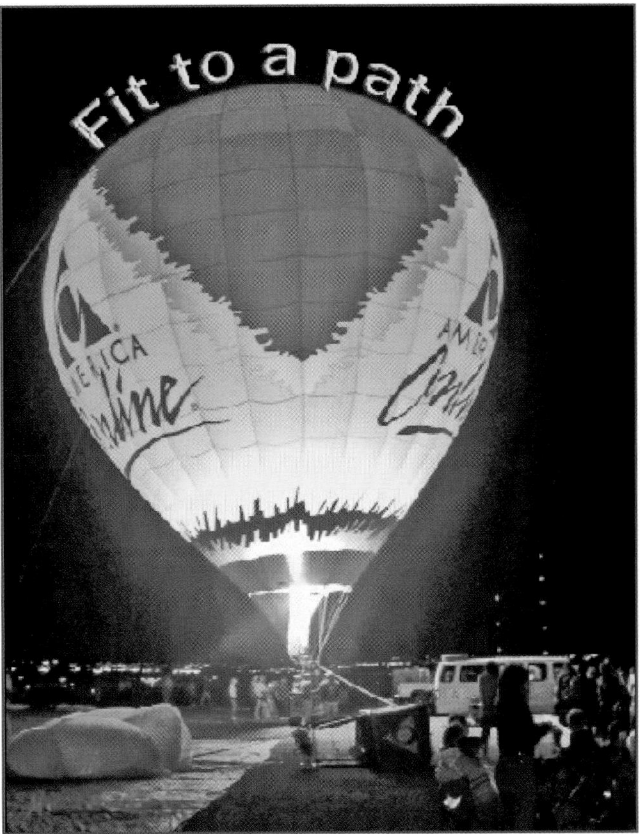

Figure 8-5: To fit the text to the shape of the balloon, the Warp Arc shape was selected.

1. Either create a layer for your text, or allow Photoshop Elements to do it for you as you type and commit your text.
2. Select the **Horizontal Type** tool for text parallel to the path, or select the **Vertical Type** tool for text perpendicular to the path. Type the text on the type layer.
3. Drag the typed text above the path on the image. For instance, in Figure 8-5, the text was dragged above the balloon that formed the path or shape along which the text would be placed.

FINDING AND USING LAYER STYLES

You can use Photoshop Element's preset layer styles to create text with special effects.

USE THE STYLES AND EFFECTS PALETTE

1. Click the **Window** menu and click **Styles And Effects**. The Styles And Effects palette is displayed.
2. Click the **Layer Styles** list down arrow, and select a layer style. Click the down arrow in the list box located to the right of the Layer Styles list box, and select a specific style option. Thumbnails showing the style effects available with a given style option are displayed beneath the list boxes.

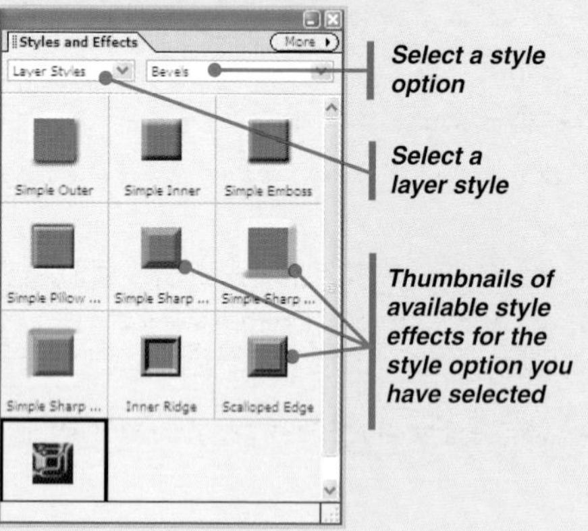

3. Click the **Move** tool and select the text layer to which the layer style will be applied.
4. Click or drag the style to apply it to the selected text.

USE THE LAYER STYLE SETTING FOR PRECISE STYLE SETTINGS

1. To refine a style setting, select the text layer containing the style.
2. Click the **Edit** icon. The Style Settings dialog box is displayed.

Continued...

4. Click the **Warp** button on the Options bar. The Warp Text dialog box appears. Select a style, which forces the text to follow the path. Click **OK**.
5. Drag the warped text to the precise location on the path.
6. Click the **Warp** button again, and use the **Bend** slider to fit the shape precisely.
7. Click the **Move** tool and click the text to select it. Drag the corners of the bounding box to skew or rotate the text to fit the path if needed.

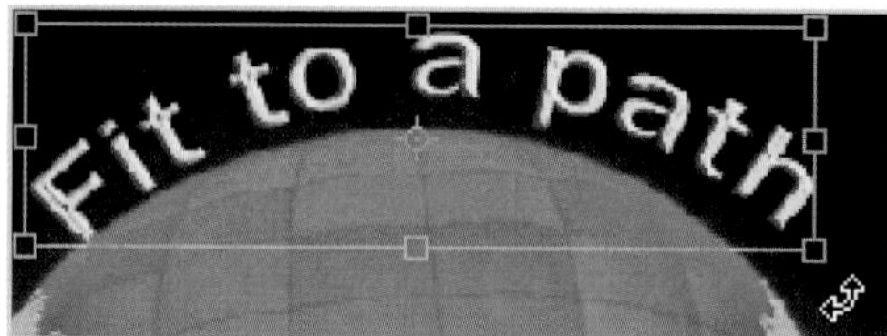

Edit Text on a Path

To edit the text on a path by inserting and deleting letters or making needed formatting changes:

1. Select the relevant text layer.
2. Click either the **Horizontal Type** tool or the **Vertical Type** tool.
3. Click in the text string where you want to place the insertion point, or highlight the text to select it.
4. Make your changes.

Add Special Type Effects with Layer Styles

You can apply special effects to your text using options from the Styles And Effects palette. Photoshop Elements has several predefined, or preset, styles that can be used to create several effects using drop shadows, embossing or beveling, inside and outside glows, and more. Figure 8-6 shows examples of a few common effects described in this section.

FINDING AND USING LAYER STYLES *(Continued)*

3. Select the relevant settings for the style option you chose. These options will vary, depending on your style selection. For example, you can vary the size or direction of the bevel. Refer to the section "Add Special Type Effects with Layer Styles" in this chapter for specifics on common styles used.
4. Click **OK** when finished.

TIP

Press **SHIFT** while you drag to add styles to text in a cumulative fashion. If you don't press **SHIFT**, the currently applied style overrides previously applied styles.

TIP

To modify the distance of the shadow, double-click the **Layers Style** icon for the relevant text layer in the Layers palette. From the Style Settings dialog box, move the **Shadow Distance** slider to pull the shadow away from the text, as shown here.

Figure 8-6: Common effects that you can create using layer styles include drop shadows, embossing, and more.

DROP SHADOWS

To create a drop shadow:

1. Click the **Move** tool and select the text to which you want to apply the drop shadow, or select the relevant text layer from the Layers palette.
2. On the Styles And Effects palette, click the **Layer Styles** list down arrow, and click **Layer Styles**.
3. Click **Drop Shadows** in the second list box. Figure 8-7 shows the Drop Shadow styles that are available. (If the Styles And Effects palette is not in the Palette Bin, click the **Window** menu and click **Styles And Effects**.)
4. Experiment with the various style options by clicking them and viewing the effects on the selected text.
5. When you are satisfied, click **OK**.

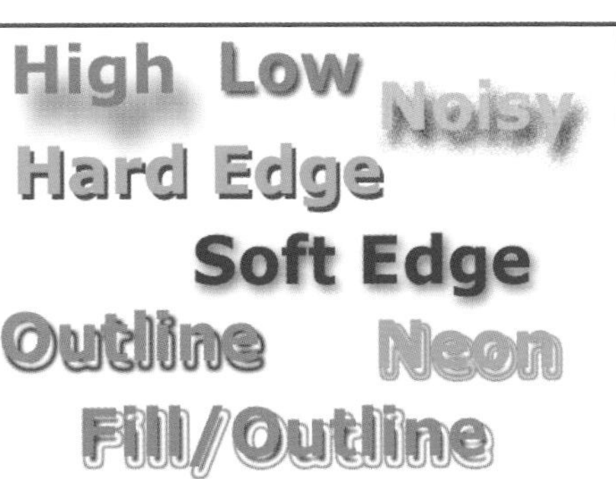

Figure 8-7: The Drop Shadow options allow you precise control over shadowing effects.

TIP

To quickly open the Style Settings dialog box, double-click the **Layer Styles** icon on the Layers palette.

TIP

To modify the degree of bevel, or distance, double-click the **Layers Style** icon for the relevant text layer in the Layers palette. From the Style Settings dialog box, move the **Bevel Size** slider to increase or decrease the degree of bevel. Click **Up** to give the characters a more rounded effect, or click **Down** to indent the character, as shown in the illustration.

Figure 8-8: You can choose among various bevel and emboss effects, examples of which are shown here.

Simple Outer
Simple Inner
Simple Emboss
Simple Pillow Emboss
Simple Sharp Pillow Emboss
Simple Sharp Inner
Inner Ridge
Scalloped Edge
Wacky Metallic

BEVEL AND EMBOSS

Use the Bevel style on the Styles And Effects palette to create both beveling and embossing effects. Figure 8-8 demonstrates the difference between the two. To create either beveling or embossing effects:

1. Click the **Move** tool and select the text to which the effect is to be applied, or select the desired text layer. 
2. Click the **Styles And Effects** palette in the Palette Bin. (If the Styles And Effects palette is not in the Palette Bin, click the **Window** menu and click **Styles And Effects**.) On the Styles And Effects palette, click the **Layer Styles** list down arrow, and select **Layer Styles**.
3. Select **Bevels** from the second list box.
4. Experiment with the options by clicking the various bevel options and viewing the effect on your selected text.
5. When you are satisfied, click **OK**.

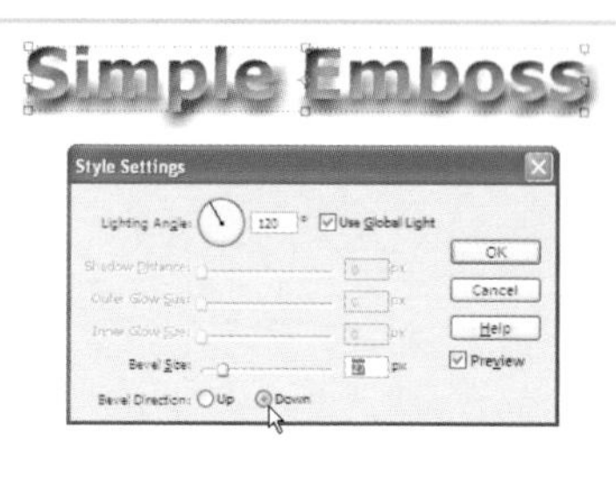

MAKE TYPE GLOW INSIDE OR OUT

The Inside Glow and Outside Glow styles make your text look as if there were a light source inside or behind the type, respectively.

1. Click the **Move** tool and select the text to which you want to apply a glow effect, or select the desired text layer from the Layers palette.
2. Click the **Styles And Effects** palette in the Palette Bin. (If the Styles And Effects palette is not in the Palette Bin, click the **Window** menu and click **Styles And Effects**.) On the Styles And Effects palette, click the **Layer Styles** list down arrow, and click **Layer Styles**.
3. Click **Inner Glows** or **Outer Glows** from the second list box.
4. Experiment with the glow options by clicking them and viewing the effect on your selected text.
5. When you are satisfied, click **OK**.

TIP

To modify the extent of the glow, double-click the **Layers Style** icon on the type layer in the Layers palette. From the Style Settings dialog box, move the **Outer Glow Size** or **Inner Glow Size** slider to extend or reduce the glow surrounding or within the type, as shown here.

Figure 8-9: The words "Balloon Glow" were first cut out of the balloon part of the picture using a type mask and then enlarged and filled with a gradient fill.

Create Type Masks

You can use a type mask either to create a selection from text or to fill text with the background from another image or layer and apply it to a current image or layer. It is like making a cutout of one image to use in another. Figure 8-9 shows an example of a text mask.

1. In the Layers palette, select the layer that contains the image you want to use. To create a new layer, click the **Layer** menu, click **New**, click **Layer**, and click **OK** to accept the default name.
2. Select the **Horizontal Mask Type** tool or the **Vertical Mask Type** tool.
3. Set your formatting the way you want, as described previously in this chapter. Click in the image where you want the masking layer to be placed. The canvas is filled with a protective red masking layer.
4. Type the words you want to mask, and then click **Commit**.

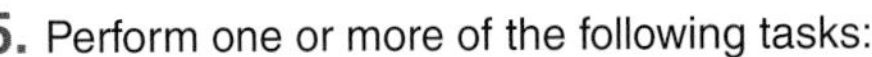

5. Perform one or more of the following tasks:
   - Create a copy of the filled text by following the previous steps to create a type selection. Then click the **Layer** menu; click **New Fill Layer**; click **Solid Color**, **Gradient**, or **Pattern**; and click **OK**. The Layers palette will show the fill layer and the text will be filled with the color (or the gradient or pattern), as shown here.

   - Move the filled type selection by clicking the **Move** tool, clicking the type selection to select it, and dragging the type selection to where you want it on the image.

CAUTION

When working with a mask selection, you can stretch the selection box and otherwise distort the text, but you cannot directly edit the text.

NOTE

When you create a mask, it will not have its own layer—it is just a selection of text on the active layer. It is advisable not to place the mask on another type layer because all the text will be selected at one time; you will not be able to edit each type selection separately.

NOTE

To make changes to a type selection on its own layer, you may have to simplify the layer first. If you don't do this and try to change the text, you will see a "Pixels not selected" error message. When you simplify an image, you convert it from a vector-based image to a bitmap image. To simplify the layer, click **Simplify Layer** from the More menu on the Layer palette, or click the **Layer** menu and click **Simplify Layer**.

- Create a cutout of the text in the image by creating a type mask (choose the appropriate mask tool, and click in the image), as described previously (the mask must be on the image, not on its own layer). Then cut the selected text by pressing **CTRL+X** or by clicking the **Edit** menu and then clicking **Cut**. A cutout of the image remains. You can also create a cutout of the selected text by moving the selection using the Move tool.
- Copy and paste the masked text in a new layer without cutting the text from the background image. While the type mask is selected, it can be moved, copied, filled, or treated like another selection.
- Tile a second image in the document window (open two images, click **Window**, click **Images**, and click **Tile** to place the images side by side), and drag it onto another image. This is a great way to transfer text masked on one type of background onto another image.
- Create a separate image of the selection by copying the selection to the Clipboard and then creating another image. To do this, click **Edit Copy** to place the copy of the selected text to the Clipboard. Then click the **File** menu, click **New**, and click **Image From Clipboard**.

CREATE GRADIENT-FILLED TYPE

You may want to fill selected text with a color gradient design.

1. Select the layer containing the text to which you want to apply the effect, or create a new layer.
2. Create a type selection by clicking the **Horizontal Type Mask** tool or the **Vertical Type Mask** tool. Click the type layer, type your text on the red-filled layer, and click **Commit**.
3. Click the **Gradient** tool.
4. On the Options bar, choose a gradient design.
5. Drag your pointer across the type selection in the direction that you want the gradient to flow.
6. Deselect the type selection by clicking the **Select** menu and clicking **Deselect**. The gradient fill is applied to the text.
7. If you want, you can now apply type effects, such as Inner Glow or Outer Glow, as shown in Figure 8-9.

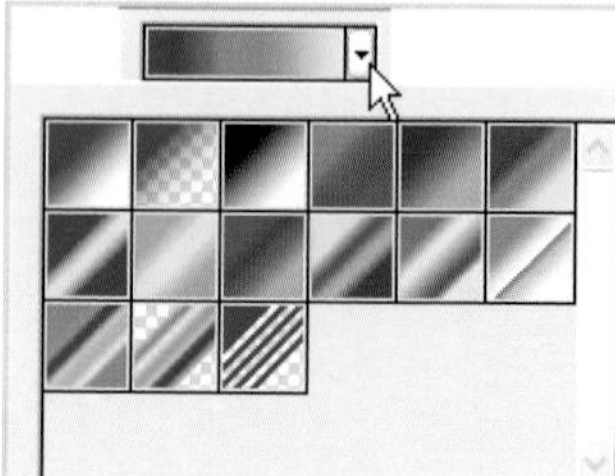

How to...

Chapter 9 Creating Images for the Web, E-Mail, and Automation

Whether you capture images from your scanner or digital camera, they come into Photoshop Elements at a size and resolution that's suitable for printing. Images of this size and resolution, however, are not suited for e-mail or for displaying on a web site. In this chapter you'll learn to optimize images for e-mail and web display, as well as create a web photo gallery, a PDF slide show, and more.

Start the File Browser

In Chapter 2 you learned to use the Photo Browser to find, organize, and catalog images. Photoshop Elements has another browser that is also used for finding images, converting images to other file formats, and much more. This marvelous organizational tool is known as the File Browser.

1. Start Photoshop Elements.
2. Click **Window** and then click **File Browser**. Figure 9-1 shows the File Browser opened within Photoshop Elements.

1

2

3

4

5

6

7

8

9

10

Figure 9-1: You can automate many image-related tasks using the File Browser.

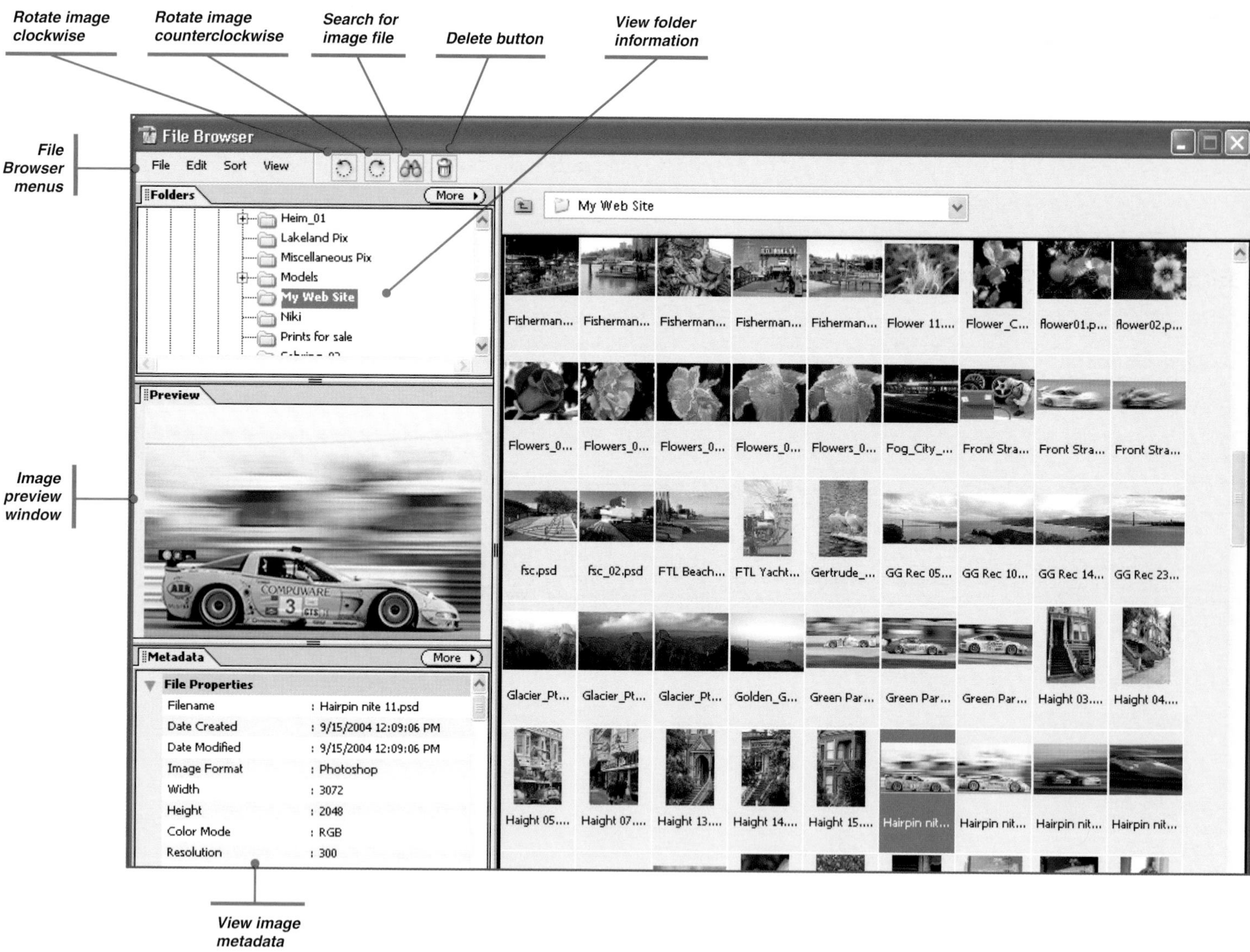

Navigate to a Folder of Images

If you use the Adobe Capture plug-in to transfer images from your digital camera to your hard drive, they are saved in folders. You may have additional folders on your computer with images in them. You can use the File Browser to navigate to these folders and choose files within them. When you start the Photoshop Elements File Browser, it displays the last folder you viewed. To navigate through the folders on your hard drive to view the desired folder:

1. Click **Window** and then click **File Browser**. The File Browser opens.
2. In the Folders window, navigate to the folder you want to open.

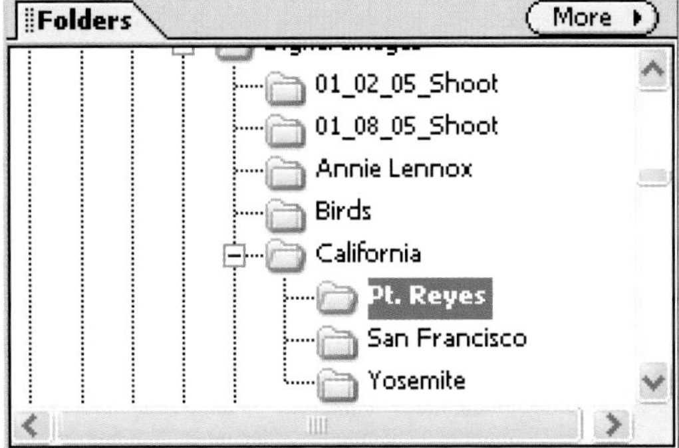

3. Double-click a folder to display thumbnail versions of the images within the folder, as shown in Figure 9-2.

TIP

When working with images from within the File Browser, hide all palettes and resize the File Browser to view more image thumbnails.

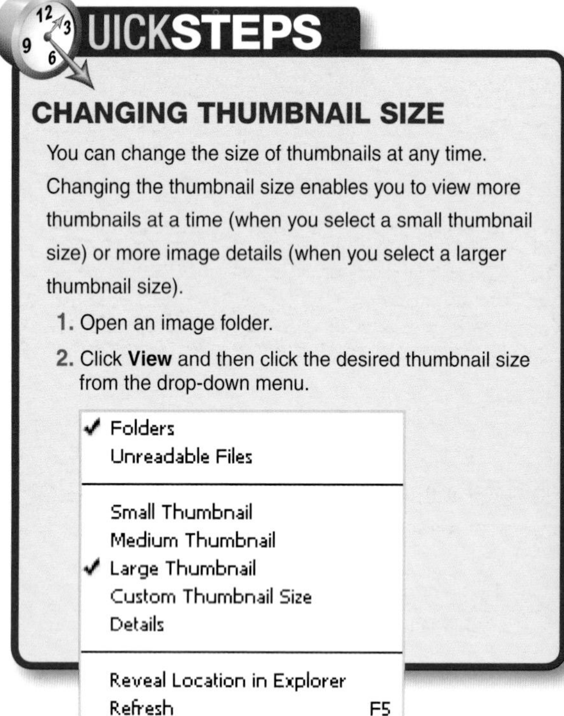

CHANGING THUMBNAIL SIZE

You can change the size of thumbnails at any time. Changing the thumbnail size enables you to view more thumbnails at a time (when you select a small thumbnail size) or more image details (when you select a larger thumbnail size).

1. Open an image folder.
2. Click **View** and then click the desired thumbnail size from the drop-down menu.

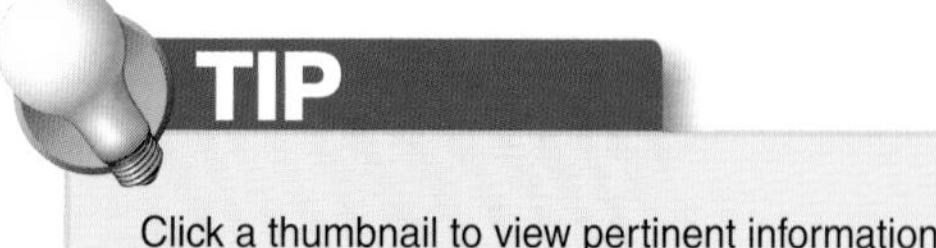

Click a thumbnail to view pertinent information about the image in the Metadata window.

Figure 9-2: You can display thumbnail images of all photos in a folder.

Work with Thumbnails

When you open the File Browser to a folder of images, they are displayed in the format used when you last opened the File Browser. You can display images as small, medium, or large thumbnails, or you can display each image file as a thumbnail followed by pertinent file details, such as the date it was created and the last date on which it was modified.

VIEW IMAGE DETAILS

If you require more information than the thumbnail image offers, you can view a smaller thumbnail of a file and more details, such as the date the image was photographed, the document size in pixels, and file size. This option is handy when you need to know information about a file before opening it.

QUICKSTEPS

CREATING CUSTOM THUMBNAILS

If you work with a desktop size larger than 1024 x 768, you may find it beneficial to view thumbnails in a size larger than the three default sizes Photoshop Elements provides. You can specify the desired custom thumbnail size, and then click a menu command to display your images at that custom size in the File Browser.

1. From within the File Browser, click **Edit**, click **Preferences**, and then click **File Browser**.

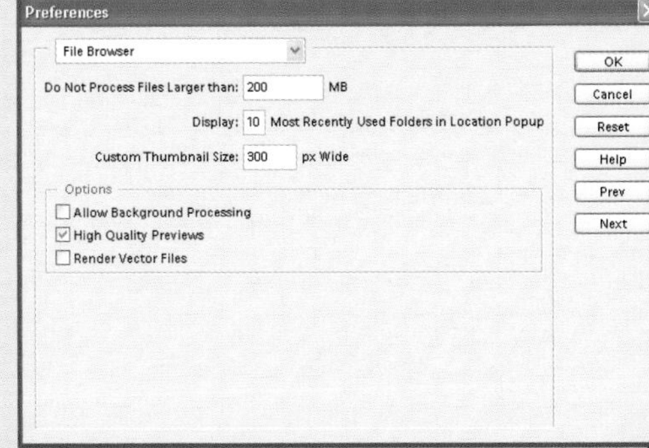

2. Type the desired thumbnail width in the Custom Thumbnail Size text box.
3. Click **OK** to exit the Preferences dialog box.
4. Click **View** and then click **Custom Thumbnail Size**.

NOTE

After rotating the thumbnails, Photoshop Elements displays a dialog box telling you that only the thumbnails are rotated and that the images will be rotated the next time the files are opened in Photoshop Elements.

1. Navigate to the desired image folder.
2. Double-click the folder to display image thumbnails.
3. Click **View** and then click **Details**. Photoshop Elements displays image details in the File Browser.

Pt_Reyes010.jpg
Date Modified: 6/13/2003 11:59:38 AM JPEG File
Date Created: 2/21/2004 8:23:22 PM RGB (sRGB IEC61966-2.1)
No Copyright Notice 2560px x 1920px (8.533 inches x 6.4 inches) @300ppi
1.61M

Pt_Reyes011.jpg
Date Modified: 6/13/2003 12:08:20 PM JPEG File
Date Created: 2/21/2004 8:23:22 PM RGB (sRGB IEC61966-2.1)
No Copyright Notice 2560px x 1920px (8.533 inches x 6.4 inches) @300ppi
1.61M

ROTATE IMAGES

If your camera does not have an option to rotate images, pictures that were photographed with a vertical composition will be displayed horizontally in the File Browser. You can rotate images as needed in the File Browser.

1. Open an image folder.
2. Click a thumbnail image to select it, and then press **CTRL** and click to select any additional images you want to rotate.
3. Click the **Rotate Clockwise** icon at the top of the File Browser to rotate selected images 90 degrees clockwise.

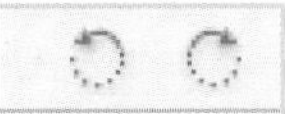

4. Click the **Rotate Counterclockwise** icon at the top of the File Browser to rotate selected images 90 degrees counterclockwise.

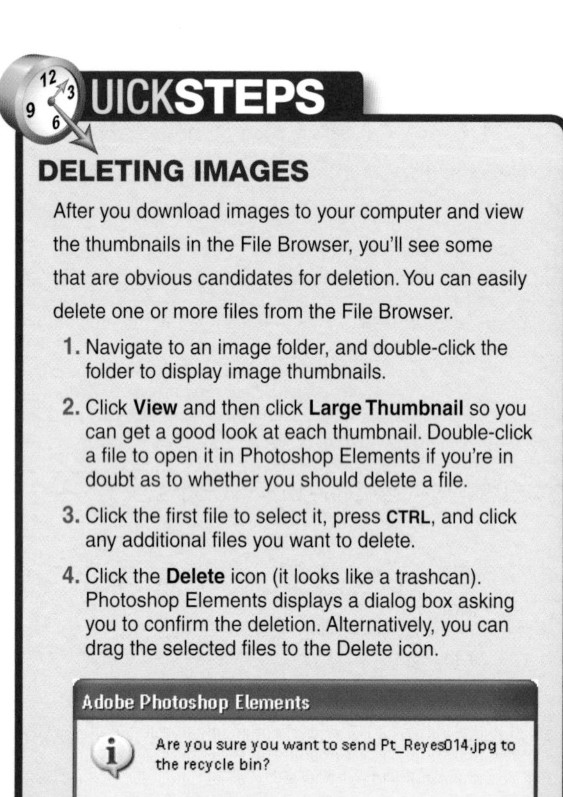

QUICKSTEPS

DELETING IMAGES

After you download images to your computer and view the thumbnails in the File Browser, you'll see some that are obvious candidates for deletion. You can easily delete one or more files from the File Browser.

1. Navigate to an image folder, and double-click the folder to display image thumbnails.
2. Click **View** and then click **Large Thumbnail** so you can get a good look at each thumbnail. Double-click a file to open it in Photoshop Elements if you're in doubt as to whether you should delete a file.
3. Click the first file to select it, press **CTRL**, and click any additional files you want to delete.
4. Click the **Delete** icon (it looks like a trashcan). Photoshop Elements displays a dialog box asking you to confirm the deletion. Alternatively, you can drag the selected files to the Delete icon.

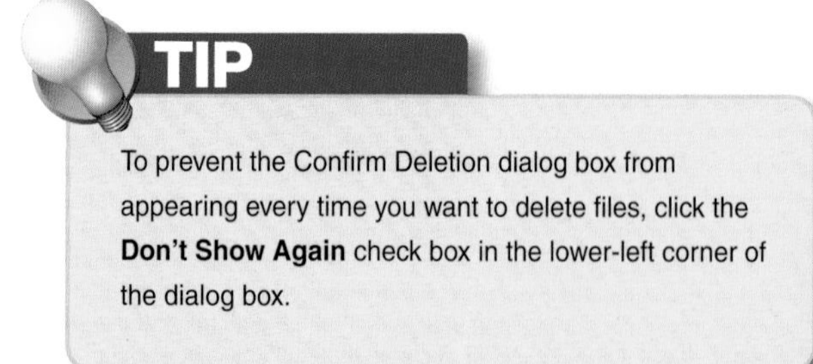

TIP

To prevent the Confirm Deletion dialog box from appearing every time you want to delete files, click the **Don't Show Again** check box in the lower-left corner of the dialog box.

Convert a Folder of Images to a Different File Type

When you capture images from a digital camera or scanner, you usually capture them in a file format and resolution that is suitable for print. You can quickly convert all images in a folder to a different file type, for example, JPEG, which is suitable for the Web.

1. Click **File** and then click **Process Multiple Files**. The Process Multiple Files dialog box is displayed.

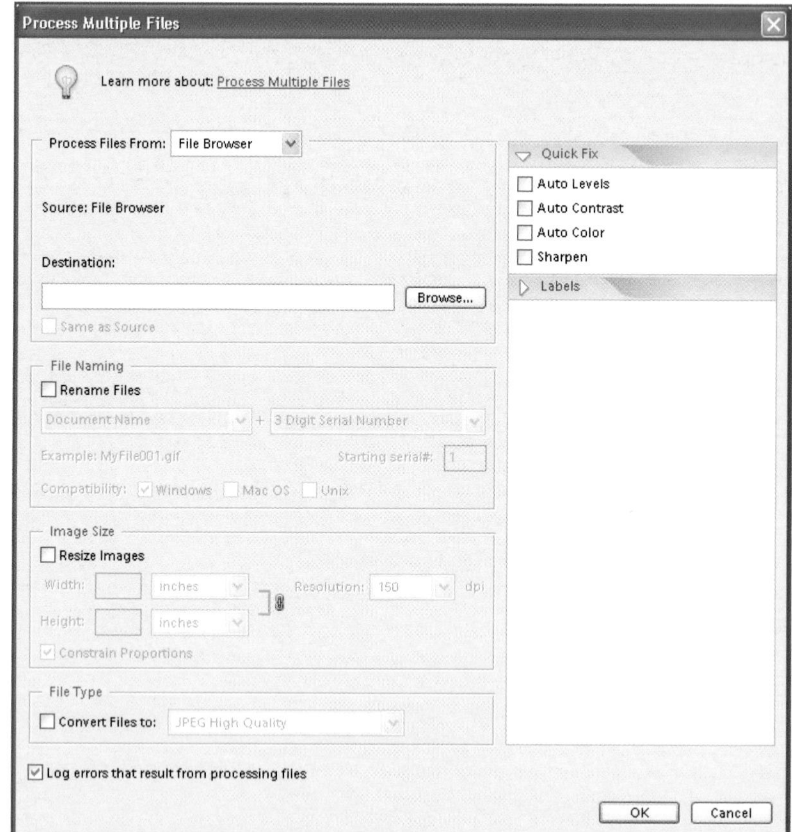

2. Click the **Process Files From** down arrow, and then click **Folder**.

CAUTION

If you save batch-processed files in the same folder and do not change the file name, the original files will be overwritten. To rename files, see the "Rename Image Files" section.

NOTE

If an error occurs during batch processing, Photoshop Elements creates an error log, which is a text file created in the destination folder.

TIP

You can also use the Quick Fix options when processing multiple files. In the Quick Fix area of the Process Multiple Files dialog box, click one or more Quick Fix options that you want performed on the images folder.

3. Click the **Browse** button and then navigate to the folder of images you want to convert.
4. Click the **Include All Subfolders** check box if you want images in subfolders converted as well.
5. Click the **Same As Source** check box to save converted files to the same folder. Alternatively, you can click the **Browse** button, and navigate to the folder in which you want to store the processed files.
6. In the File Type area, click the **Convert Files To** check box, and then click the down arrow to the right of the field, and choose the desired file type, for example, **JPEG High Quality**.
7. Click **OK** to convert the files.

PSD
BMP
EPS
GIF
JPEG Low Quality
JPEG Medium Quality
JPEG High Quality
JPEG Max Quality
PCX
PDF
PICT
Pixar
PNG
Photoshop Raw
Scitex CT
Targa
TIFF

Rename Image Files

When you capture images from your digital camera, they are given a default name—usually letters designated by the camera manufacturer followed by a number. While this is convenient, in that by using the camera's default numbering system you won't inadvertently erase any existing images in the same folder, the names are not descriptive. You can rename an entire folder of images to a single name followed by a serial number, which is useful when you've photographed images from the same location or of the same person.

1. Click **File** and then click **Process Multiple Files**. The Process Multiple Files dialog box appears.
2. Click the **Process Files From** down arrow, and click **Folder**.
3. Click the **Browse** button and navigate to the folder of images you want to convert.
4. Click the **Include All Subfolders** check box if you want images in subfolders converted as well.
5. Click the **Same As Source** check box to save converted files to the same folder. Alternatively, you can click the **Browse** button, and navigate to the folder in which you want to store the processed files.
6. Click the **Rename Files** check box.

1 2 3 4 5 6 7 8 9 10

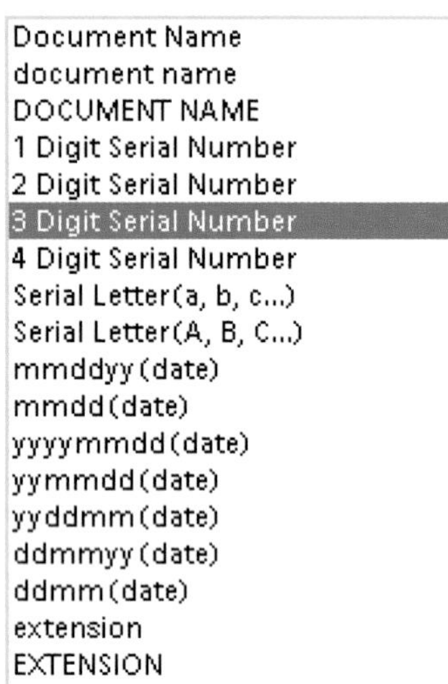

7. Type the desired file name in the first text field.
8. Click the down arrow to the right of the next field, and click **1 Digit Serial Number**, **2 Digit Serial Number**, **3 Digit Serial Number**, or **4 Digit Serial Number**, or choose a different option from the drop-down menu.
9. Type the desired starting serial number in the Starting Serial # field.
10. Click **OK** to rename the files. If, for example, you renamed a series of TIFF files of your Colorado vacation "Colorado," followed by a one-digit serial number, the files would be named "Colorado1.tiff," "Colorado2.tiff," "Colorado3.tiff," and so on.

If you click the Same As Source check box and do not rename the files as outlined previously, the original files will be overwritten.

Resize Images in a Folder

If you're processing images for a specific destination, such as a web page, you need to resize the images to a size suitable for display in a web browser. When you resize images for the Web, you can also convert them to a web-friendly file type, which, when you're working with photo-realistic images, will be the JPEG file type.

1. Click **File** and then click **Process Multiple Files**. The Process Multiple Files dialog box appears.
2. Click the **Process Files From** down arrow, and then click **Folder**.
3. Click the **Browse** button and navigate to the folder of images you want to convert.
4. Click the **Include All Subfolders** check box if you want images in subfolders of the selected folder converted as well.
5. Click the **Same As Source** check box to save converted files to the same folder. Alternatively, you can click the **Browse** button, and navigate to the folder in which you want to store the processed files.
6. Click the **Resize Images** check box.

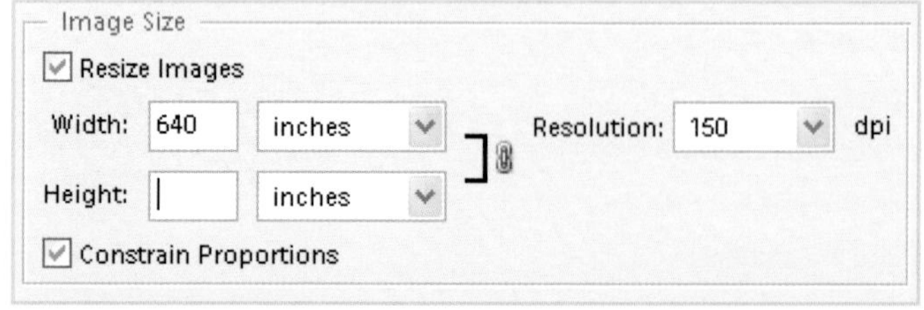

7. Type the desired value in the Width or Height fields. As long you accept the selected default option, **Constrain Proportions**, Photoshop Elements will provide the opposite dimension.
8. Click the **Convert Files To** check box, and then click the down arrow to select the image file type, if needed.
9. Click **OK** to process the images.

Optimize Images for the Web

When you create images to display on a web site or to send via e-mail, you need to convert them to a web-friendly format. Your goal is to create an image that looks good and downloads quickly. Fortunately, this is not rocket science, thanks to the Save For Web command. You can choose the desired file format and image quality and resize the images from within the same dialog box.

1. Open the image you want to optimize for the Web.
2. Click **File** and then click **Save For Web**. The Save For Web dialog box appears, as shown in Figure 9-3. Note that this figure shows the dialog box as configured when optimizing an image using the JPEG format.

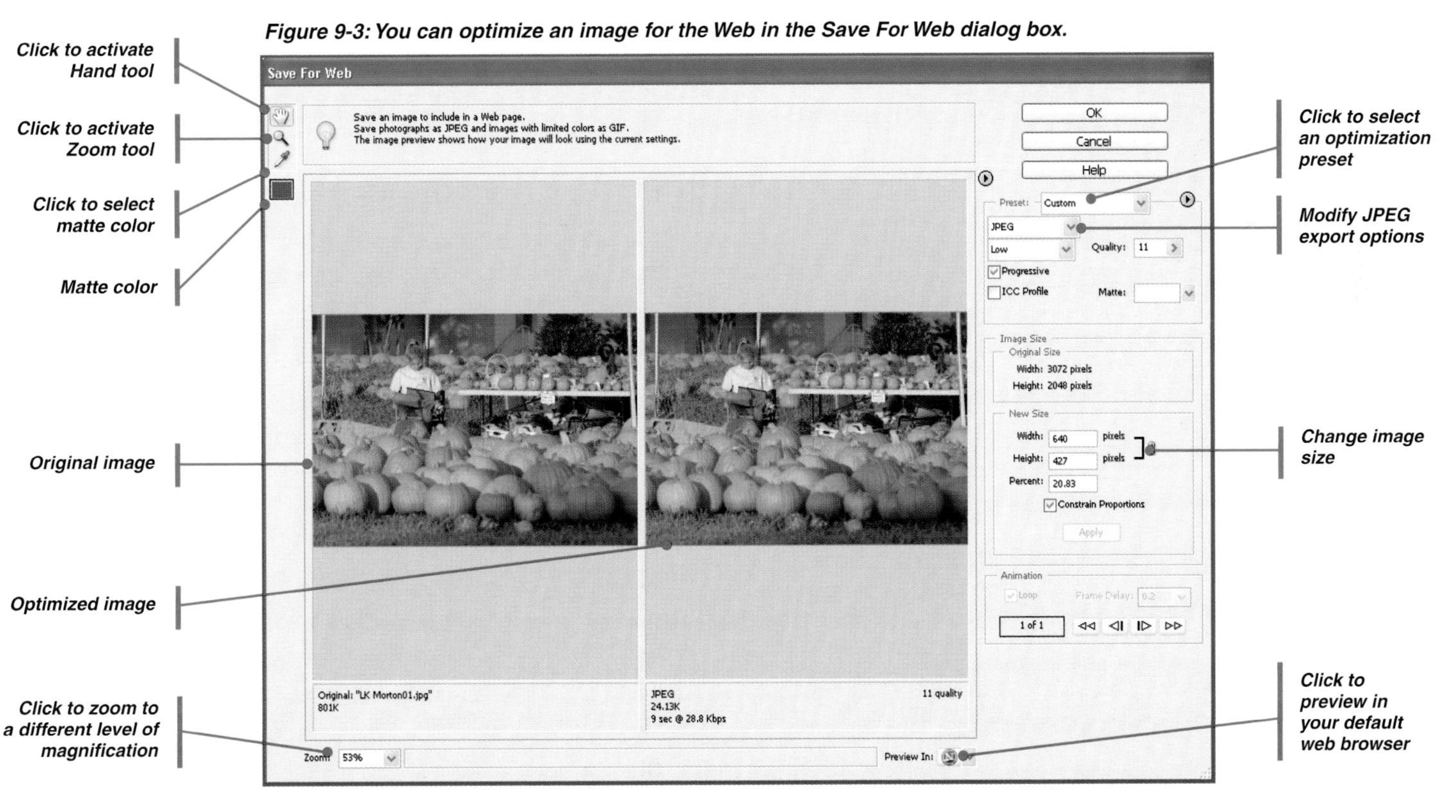

***Figure 9-3:** You can optimize an image for the Web in the Save For Web dialog box.*

NOTE

When you optimize a photo-realistic image for the Web, you'll get better results and a smaller file size using the JPEG format.

TIP

If you're optimizing an image using the JPEG format and your intended audience has a slow Internet connection, click the **Progressive** check box. This creates an image that downloads to the viewer's browser in stages. The viewer gets instant gratification with a pixilated version of the image. On the second pass, the optimized version of the image loads.

3. Click the **Preset** down arrow, and click an option. If the image is photo-realistic, click one of the **JPEG** options. If the image is a graphic, such as a logo with large areas of solid color, click one of the **PNG** or **GIF** options. After choosing the desired option, the image in the right pane of the Save For Web dialog box updates to reflect the new file format. The format type, file size, and estimated download time appear beneath the optimized image.
4. If the image quality and download times are acceptable, click **OK** to save the file in the specified format. Alternatively, you can click **Custom** in step 3, and then click the desired file-optimization format. Your options will differ, depending on the file format you choose. As you experiment with different options, the optimized image in the right pane of the dialog box updates to show how the image looks with the current optimization settings. Also displayed are the file size and estimated download time of the optimized image with a 28.8-kbps Internet connection. To view the download time at a different connection speed, click the right-pointing arrow located to the right of the image, and choose the desired connection speed.

GIF 128 Dithered
GIF 128 No Dither
GIF 32 Dithered
GIF 32 No Dither
GIF 64 Dithered
GIF 64 No Dither
JPEG High
JPEG Low
JPEG Medium
PNG-24
PNG-8 128 Dithered
Custom

5. In the Image Size area, type a value in the Width or Height fields. After typing one value, Photoshop Elements supplies the other value as long as you accept the selected default option, **Constrain Proportions**. If you deselect this option and type values that are not proportionate with the image's original size, the image will be distorted.
6. Click **Apply** to view the image at its new size.
7. Click the **Preview** In button to preview the optimized image in your default web browser.
8. Click **OK** to save the image with the current optimization settings.

Create GIF Images for the Web

If you use Photoshop Elements to create text banners for a web site or edit a lot of images with large areas of solid color, such as logos, you'll want to optimize your images using the GIF format. When you optimize using the GIF format, you can specify the number of colors in the color palette and specify dithering to simulate colors not present in the palette. You can choose from one of the presets or create a custom palette.

CHOOSING A FILE FORMAT FOR THE WEB

When you optimize an image for the Web, you need to decide which file format is best suited for the image. Your decision will be based on the type of image you are editing and on the connection speed of your intended viewing audience. The information provided in the Save For Web dialog box will aid you in making these decisions; however, a bit of knowledge concerning the available file types will speed up your workflow when optimizing images:

- **JPEG** is your best choice for photo-realistic images with millions of colors. When you choose this option, you specify the amount of compression by selecting a quality setting. High settings provide high-quality images with little or no compression, while low settings provide smaller file sizes with high compression at the expense of poorer image quality. You can also create a progressive JPEG image that downloads into the viewer's browser in stages.
- **PNG 24** is also suited for photo-realistic images with millions of colors; however, when you choose this format, you cannot compress the image, therefore, the file size is larger than with images optimized using the JPEG format. Choose PNG 24 if your image has transparency, as the JPEG format does not support transparent colors.
- **GIF** is suited for images with large areas of solid color and text. This is the type to use if you are optimizing an animated image for the Web. When you choose the GIF format, you can choose the color palette and specify the number of colors in the palette, as well as how the colors are reduced. Other options include dithering (to create a reasonable facsimile of a color in the original image but not in the web-safe palette), interlacing (to download the image to the browser in stages), and transparency.
- **PNG 8** is a less popular alternative for images with large areas of solid color and text. It's not supported by some image-editing applications, and the file sizes can be somewhat larger. In addition, the format does not support animation.

1. Open the image you want to optimize for the Web.
2. Click **File** and click **Save For Web**. The Save For Web dialog box appears. Figure 9-4 shows the dialog box after choosing one of the GIF presets.

Figure 9-4: You can optimize images for the Web using the GIF format.

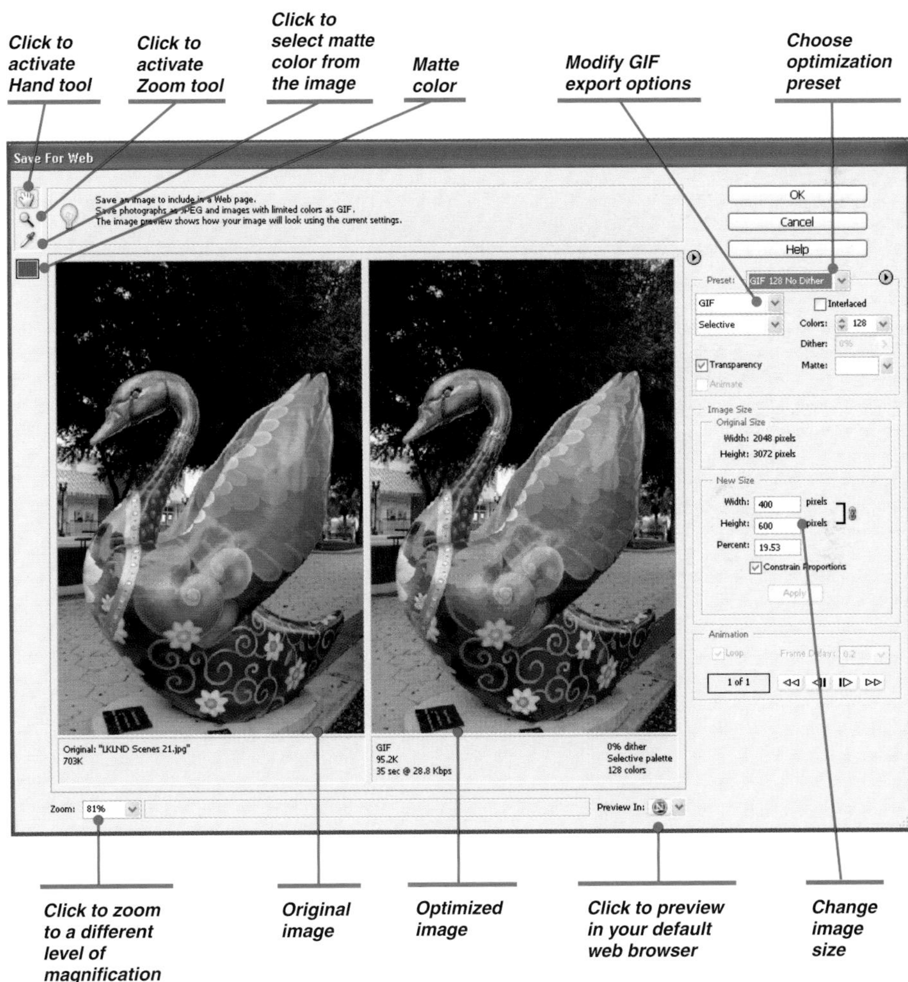

NOTE

Dithering increases the file size of the optimized image.

TIP

The Adaptive Color Reduction Algorithm is the best choice when you're optimizing an image and want to preserve as many of the original colors as possible.

3. Click the **Preset** down arrow, and click one of the following options:
   - **GIF 128 Dithered** creates an image with a 128-color palette. Colors from the original image not present in the palette are dithered to simulate the original colors.
   - **GIF 128** creates an image with a 128-color palette. Colors from the original image not present in the palette are snapped to the closest color in the palette.
   - **GIF 64 Dithered** creates an image with a 64-color palette. Colors from the original image not present in the palette are dithered to simulate the original colors.
   - **GIF 64** creates an image with a 64-color palette. Colors from the original image not present in the palette are snapped to the closest color in the palette.
   - **GIF 32 Dithered** creates an image with a 32-color palette. Colors from the original image not present in the palette are dithered to simulate the original colors.
   - **GIF 32** creates an image with a 32-color palette. Colors from the original image not present in the palette are snapped to the closest color in the palette.
4. Click the **Color Reduction Algorithm** down arrow, and choose one of the following options:
   - **Perceptual** creates a color palette that favors colors to which the human eye has greater sensitivity, such as the reds and oranges used to create flesh tones.
   - **Selective** creates a color palette similar to the Perceptual palette, using broad areas of color while preserving web-safe colors. The resulting image has better color integrity than other color-reduction algorithm options.
   - **Adaptive** creates a color palette by sampling the image and using the colors most predominant in the image. For example, if you're converting an image of a mountain scene with a large area of trees that reflects into a mountain lake, the palette will be predominantly greens and blues.
   - **Restrictive (Web)** creates a color palette using colors from the web-safe, 216-color palette. Dithering is not available with this option. Unused colors are removed from the palette. For example, if you choose an option with 128-colors, 88 unused colors are removed from the palette.
5. Click the **Transparency** check box to preserve transparent pixels from the original image. If you deselect this option, fully and partially transparent pixels are filled with the matte color.
6. Click the **Interlaced** check box to create an interlaced GIF file. Interlaced GIF images download to the viewer's browser in stages.

NOTE

Large dithering values increase file size.

TIP

Click the **Matte** down arrow, click **Eyedropper Color**, and click inside the image to sample the desired matte color.

TIP

Click the **Matte** down arrow, and click **Other** to choose a matte color from the Color Picker.

7. Click the **Colors** down arrow, and click an option. Alternatively, you can click the spinners to increase or decrease the number of colors in the palette by a value of one, or you can type a value in the Colors field. As soon as you change the number of colors from the preset you selected in step 3, the Preset field reads "Custom."
8. Click the **Dithering** right arrow, and drag to set the dithering percentage. Alternatively, you can type a value between 0 and 100 percent.
9. Accept the default color in the Matte field (white); or click the **Matte** down arrow, and click an option.
10. If the image consists of multiple frames, the Animate option becomes available. Click the **Animate** check box to create an animated GIF file.
11. In the Image Size area, type a value in the Width or Height fields. After typing the value, Photoshop Elements supplies the other value as long as you accept the selected default option, **Constrain Proportions**. If you deselect this option and type values that are not proportionate with the image's original size, the image will be distorted.
12. Click **Apply** to view the image at its new size.
13. Click the **Preview In** button to preview the optimized image in your default web browser.
14. Click **OK** to save the image with the current optimization settings.

None

Eyedropper Color
White
Black

Other...

Create a Contact Sheet

Contact sheets are useful when you have a large selection of images you want to display on a single page. You can create contact sheets for the images you archive to CD or DVD and store them in a loose-leaf binder, which provides a visual reference for the images stored on the disk.

1. In the Photo Browser or File Browser, select the images you want to print as a contact sheet.
2. Click **File** and click **Print**. The Print Selected Photos window opens.

QUICKSTEPS

ADDING WEB BROWSERS FOR PREVIEWING IMAGES

If you create web sites for a living, you probably preview your work in multiple browsers. You can add web browsers in addition to the default browser that you use to preview images while optimizing them for the Web.

1. Click **File** and click **Save For Web**. The Save For Web dialog box appears.
2. Click the **Preview In Default Browser** down arrow, and click **Edit List**. The Browsers dialog box appears.

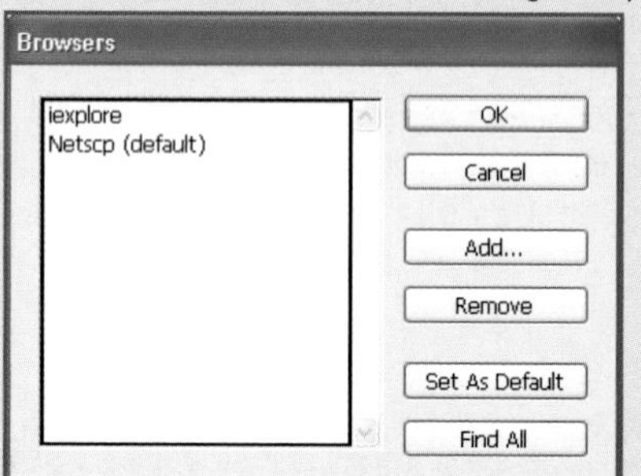

3. Click **Find All** to display all browsers installed on your system.

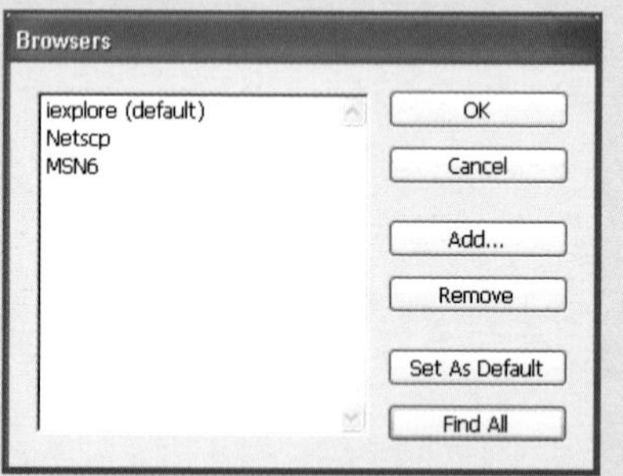

4. To delete a browser from the list, click the browser name and then click **Remove**.
5. To change the default browser for viewing, click the desired browser and then click **Set As Default**.
6. Click **OK** to finish editing the browser list.

Continued...

3. Click the **Select Type Of Print** down arrow, and then click **Contact Sheet**. The window reconfigures, as shown in Figure 9-5.

Figure 9-5: You can print selected photos as a contact sheet.

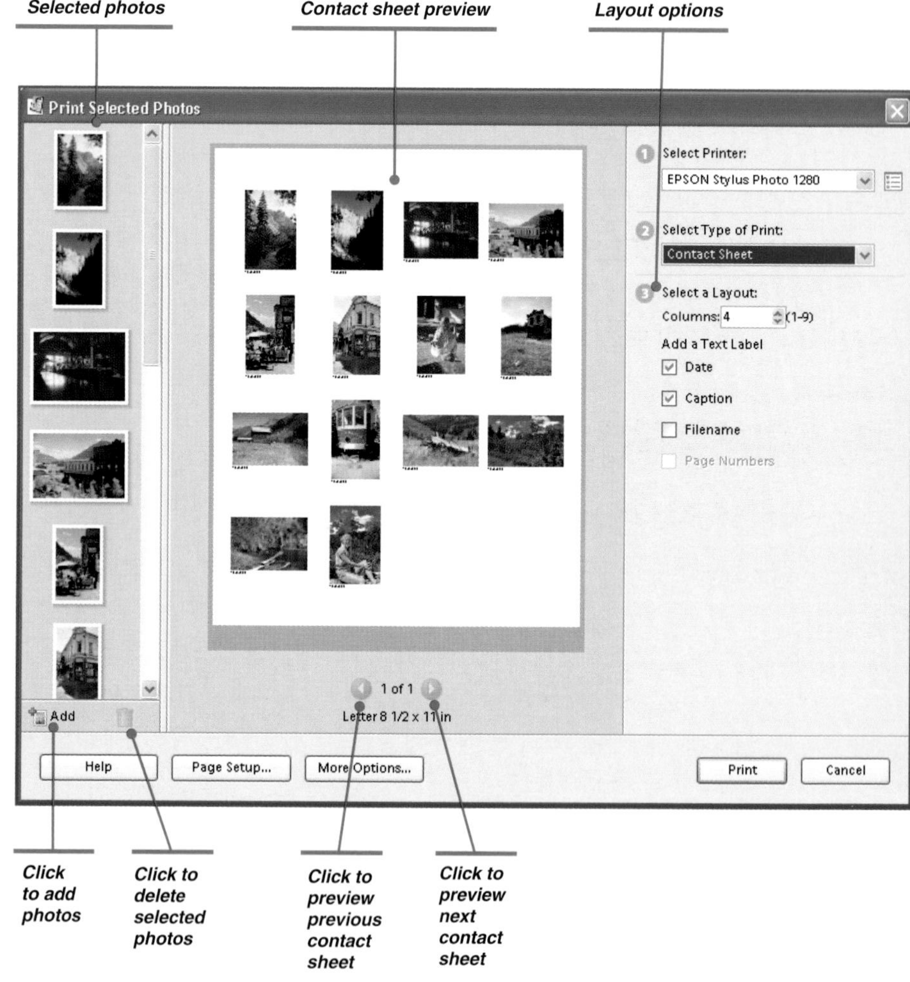

PREVIEWING IMAGES *(Continued)*

PREVIEWING AN IMAGE IN ANOTHER BROWSER

After adding additional browsers to the browser list, you can preview images in other browsers.

1. Click the **Default Browser** down arrow.
2. Click the desired browser from the drop-down list. Photoshop Elements displays the image in the selected browser (indicated by a check mark).

✔ iexplore
Netscp
Other...
Edit List...

NOTE

After editing the browser list, the icon for the default browser replaces the Photoshop Elements default browser icon.

QUICKFACTS

UNDERSTANDING WEB-SAFE COLORS

When you optimize images for the Web using the GIF format and choose Selective or Restrictive (Web) as the color-reduction algorithm, the web-safe, 216-color palette is used to create color for the optimized image. The web-safe, 216-color palette is comprised of colors that look identical regardless of the browser in which the image is viewed and regardless of the operating system on which the browser is installed.

4. Accept the default number of columns deemed optimum for your contact sheet in the Columns field, or type a value between 1 and 9. Alternatively, you can click the spinners to increase or decrease the number of columns by one.
5. In the Add A Text Label area, the **Date** and **Caption** options are selected by default. You can leave these selected or click the check boxes to deselect them. You can also click the **Filename** and/or **Page Numbers** check boxes to add these as text labels to your contact sheet.
6. To add a photo to the contact sheet, click the **Add** button (located in the lower-left corner). The Add Photos dialog box appears.
7. Click the applicable option in the Add Photos From section.
8. Select the desired photos and click **OK**.
9. If the selected photos require more than one contact sheet, click the **Next** and **Previous** buttons to preview the other contact sheet pages.
10. Click **Print** to print the contact sheet(s).

Master the Photo Browser Create Environment

If you're the creative type, you can use the options on the Photo Browser Create menu to create a web photo gallery, a calendar, a PDF slide show, and much more. Every creation is wizard-guided. In the following sections, you'll learn how to use the Create environment to create a web photo gallery and a PDF slide show. After mastering these tasks, you'll be able to create the other items in the Create environment with ease.

QUICKSTEPS

OPTIMIZING IMAGES TO A FILE SIZE

You can optimize an image to a specific file size. When you do this, you can start with a preset file type or let Photoshop Elements decide whether the GIF or JPEG format is best suited for the job.

OPTIMIZE TO A FILE SIZE BASED ON A PRESET

1. Click **File** and click **Save For Web**. The Save For Web dialog box appears.
2. Click the **Preset** down arrow, and click an option. Photoshop Elements uses the selected preset as the basis for optimizing the image to the file size you specify.
3. Click the **Optimize To File Size** right arrow to the right of the Preset field, and then click **Optimize To File Size**. The Optimize To File Size dialog box appears.

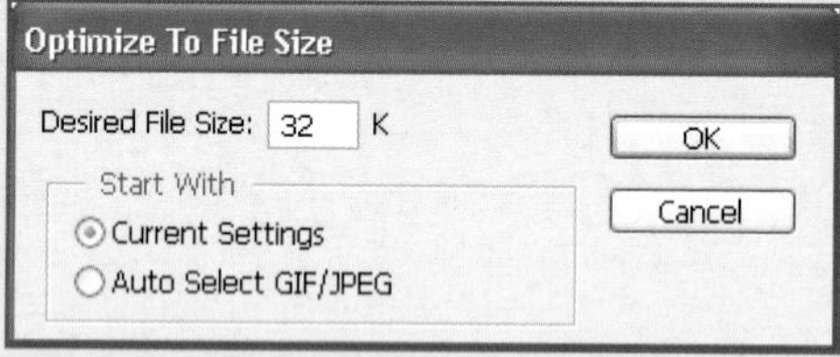

4. Click in the **Desired File Size** field, and type the value you want.
5. Click **OK**. Photoshop Elements optimizes the image to the desired file size using as many parameters from the preset as possible.

OPTIMIZE TO A FILE SIZE USING AUTO SELECT

1. Click **File** and then click **Save For Web**. The Save For Web dialog box appears.
2. Click the **Preset** down arrow, and click an option. Photoshop Elements uses the selected preset as the basis for optimizing the image to the file size you specify.

Continued...

Create a Web Photo Gallery

If your Internet service provider (ISP) gives you free web space, or you own a web site, you can share your images with the world. With Photoshop Elements, you don't need to be a web-design guru to post your images on the Web.

1. Open the Photo Browser.
2. Select the photos you want to display on a web page.
3. Click **Create** in the Organizer toolbar. The Creation Setup Wizard starts.

4. Click **Web Photo Gallery** and click **OK**. The Adobe Web Photo Gallery window opens.
5. Click the **Gallery Style** down arrow, and choose the desired layout. After you select a layout, a sample image of that layout is displayed.

OPTIMIZE TO A FILE SIZE USING AUTO SELECT

(Continued)

3. Click the **Optimize To File Size** right arrow to the right of the Preset field, and then click **Optimize To File Size**. The Optimize To File Size dialog box appears.

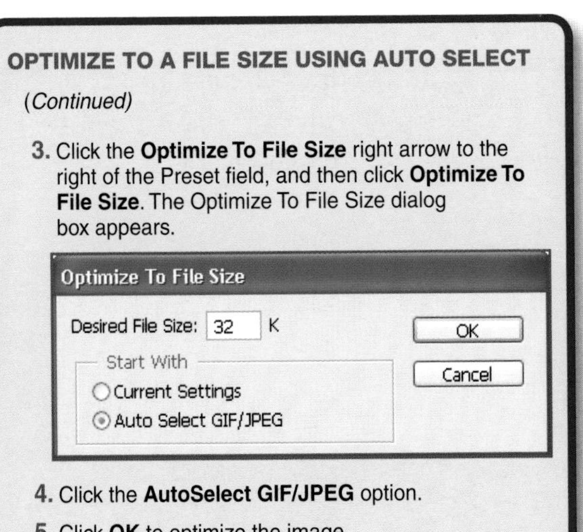

4. Click the **AutoSelect GIF/JPEG** option.
5. Click **OK** to optimize the image.

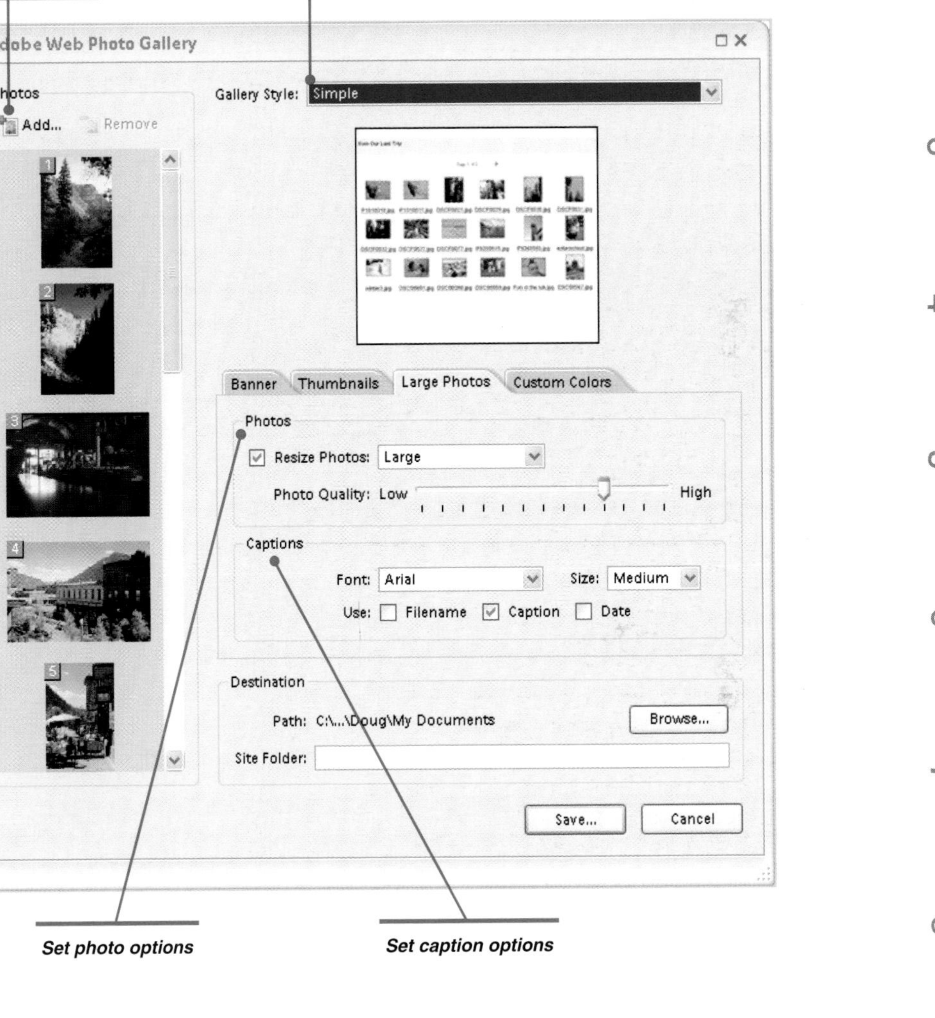

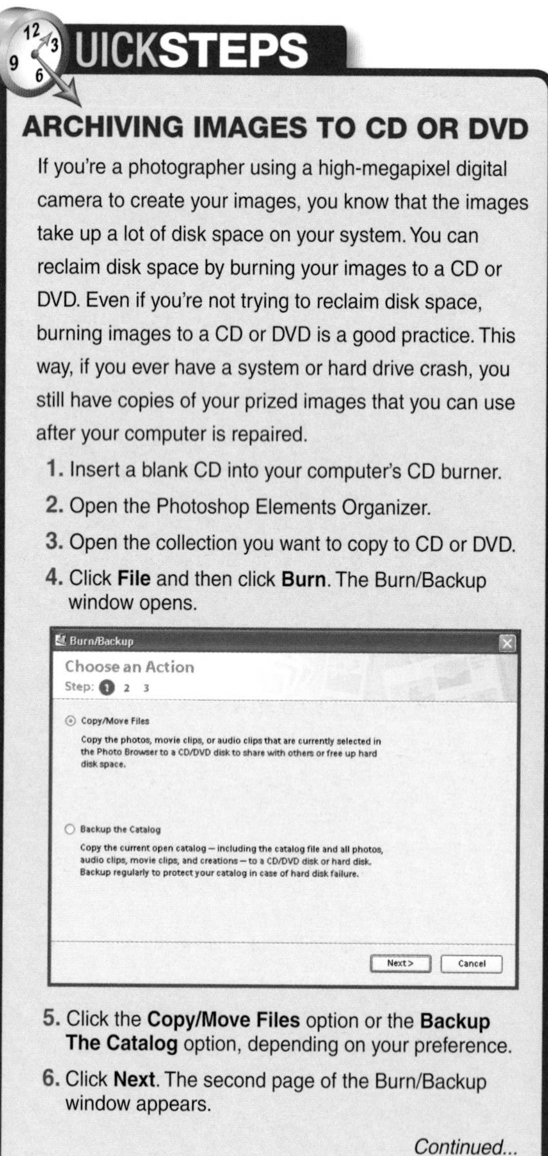

QUICKSTEPS

ARCHIVING IMAGES TO CD OR DVD

If you're a photographer using a high-megapixel digital camera to create your images, you know that the images take up a lot of disk space on your system. You can reclaim disk space by burning your images to a CD or DVD. Even if you're not trying to reclaim disk space, burning images to a CD or DVD is a good practice. This way, if you ever have a system or hard drive crash, you still have copies of your prized images that you can use after your computer is repaired.

1. Insert a blank CD into your computer's CD burner.
2. Open the Photoshop Elements Organizer.
3. Open the collection you want to copy to CD or DVD.
4. Click **File** and then click **Burn**. The Burn/Backup window opens.

5. Click the **Copy/Move Files** option or the **Backup The Catalog** option, depending on your preference.
6. Click **Next**. The second page of the Burn/Backup window appears.

Continued...

6. Click the **Banner** tab and type a name for the web page banner. From within this tab, you can also type a subtitle and e-mail address, choose a font from the drop-down menu, and set the font size.

Banner | Thumbnails | Large Photos | Custom Colors

Banner

Title: My Web Site

Subtitle:

E-mail Address:

Font: Arial Size: Medium

7. Click the **Thumbnails** tab. Click the **Thumbnail Size** down arrow, and choose a thumbnail size. You can display a caption with each thumbnail by clicking the applicable check box. You can then select the font type and size from the drop-down menus.

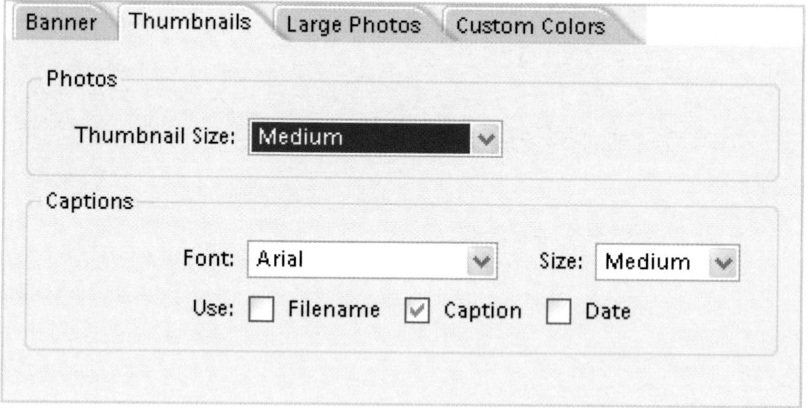

ARCHIVING IMAGES *(Continued)*

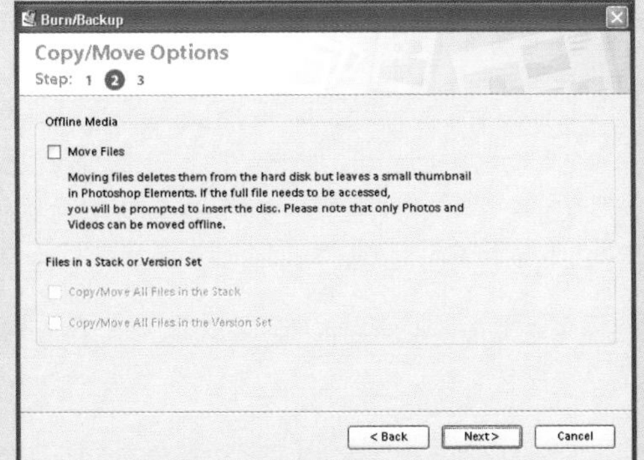

7. Click the **Move Files** check box to erase the selected files from your hard drive and archive them to CD or DVD. Alternatively, leave the check box clear, which is the default. If you have stacked files or a version set selected or in the catalog, you can click the **Copy/Move All Files In The Stack** or **Copy/Move All Files In The Version Set** check boxes to erase the stack or version set, respectively, from the hard drive and archive them to the CD.
8. Click **Next**. The third page of the Burn/Backup window appears.

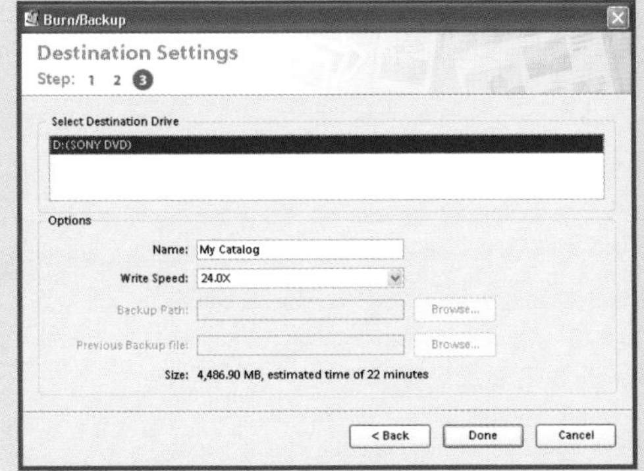

9. Click in the **Name** field, and type a name for the CD or DVD.

Continued...

8. Click the **Large Photos** tab. Choose the settings for the photo that will be displayed when a thumbnail image on the completed web page is clicked:

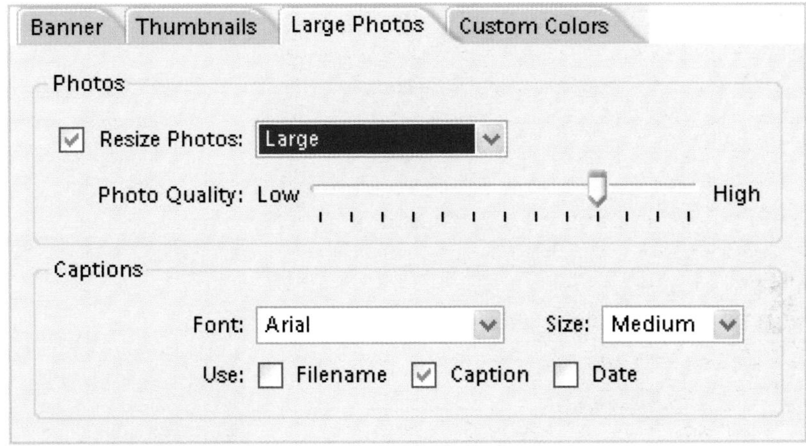

- Click the **Resize Photos** check box to resize the image. This option may be selected if your images are too large for display in a web browser.
- Click the **Resize Photos** down arrow, and click a size option.
- Drag the **Photo Quality** slider to set the quality of the images that will be displayed in your web photo gallery. High settings produce crisp and clear images, but they will take longer to download.
- In the Captions area, click the desired check boxes to add captions to your web photo gallery.
- Click the **Font** and **Size** down arrows to select the font style and size.

9. Click the **Custom Colors** tab.
10. Accept the default colors, or click a color swatch to choose a different color from the Color Picker.

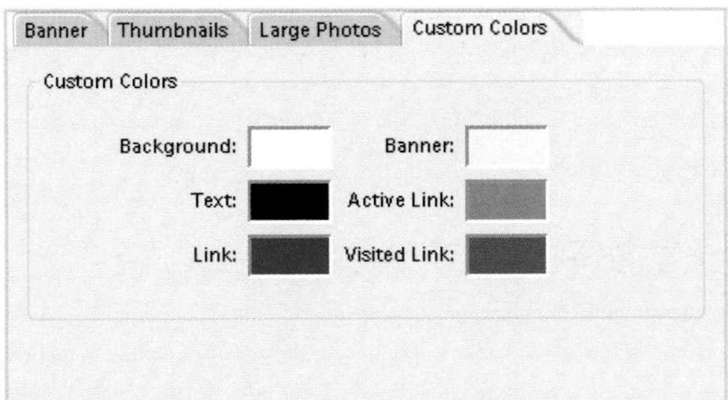

1 2 3 4 5 6 7 8 9 10

ARCHIVING IMAGES *(Continued)*

10. Click the **Speed** down arrow, and click an option. The default speed is the maximum speed of your CD burner.
11. Click **Done**. Photoshop Elements burns the selected files to the CD or DVD. After the files are burned, you can verify that the files have been correctly copied. Click **Verify** and Photoshop Elements will compare the copied files to the originals. This may take a while, depending on the number of files you have copied. Click **Don't Verify** if you don't want to take the time to verify the files.

NOTE

If you have more than one CD burner attached to your system, these are listed in the Select Destination pane of the Burn/Backup dialog box. Click the device to which you want to burn the CD.

NOTE

If the files you've selected are larger than the available space on the CD or DVD, you will be prompted to insert additional discs as needed during the burn process.

TIP

If your intended viewing audience does not have high-speed Internet access, click the **Sizes** down arrow, click **Medium**, and drag the **Quality slider** to the middle of the range.

11. In the Destination area (located near the bottom of the Adobe Web Photo Gallery window), accept the default file path for the site folder, or click the **Browse** button to open the Browse For Folder dialog box, from which you can select a different location for the site folder.
12. Click **Save**. Photoshop Elements creates the web photo gallery by creating thumbnails, creating large images, and then creating the necessary HTML (Hypertext Markup Language) to display the photo gallery as a web page. Figure 9-6 shows an example of a web photo gallery created with Photoshop Elements.

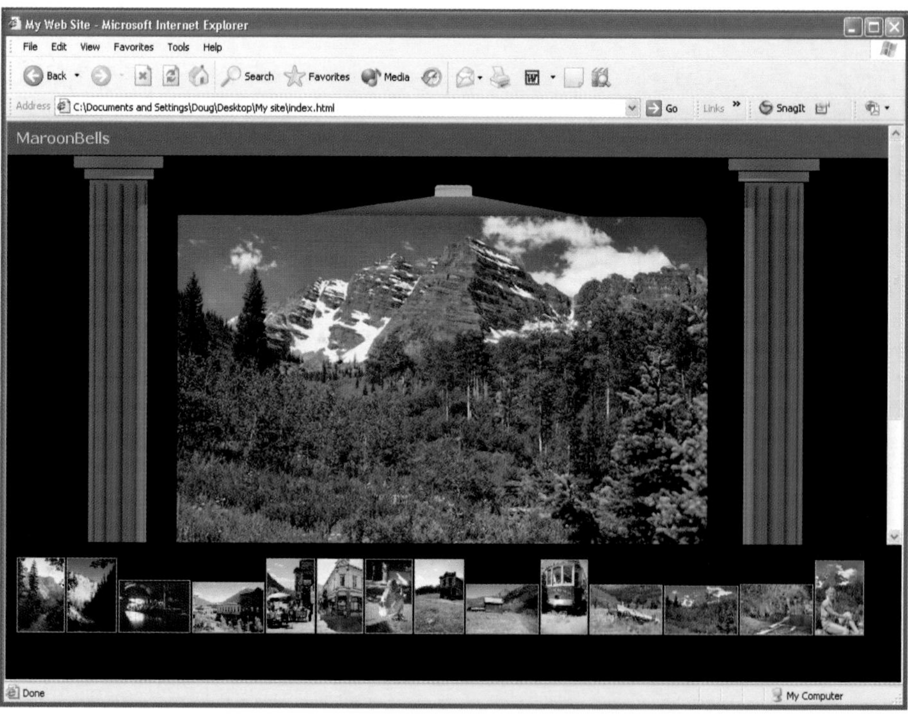

Figure 9-6: You can display your images as a web photo gallery.

TIP

Contact your ISP or web hosting service for instructions on how to upload your web photo gallery to your web site.

Make a PDF Slide Show

You can create a PDF slide show from within Photoshop Elements. Your slide show includes one-second transitions between images. You can change the type of transition between slides and modify the transition duration.

1. Open the Photo Browser.
2. Click the photos you want to include in your slide show.
3. Click the **Create** button on the Photo Browser toolbar. The Creation Setup dialog box appears.

4. Click **Slide Show** and then click **OK**. The Select A Slide Show Format page of the Creation Setup dialog box appears.
5. Click **Create A Custom Slide Show**, and click **OK**. The Photoshop Elements Slide Show Editor window opens, as shown in Figure 9-7.

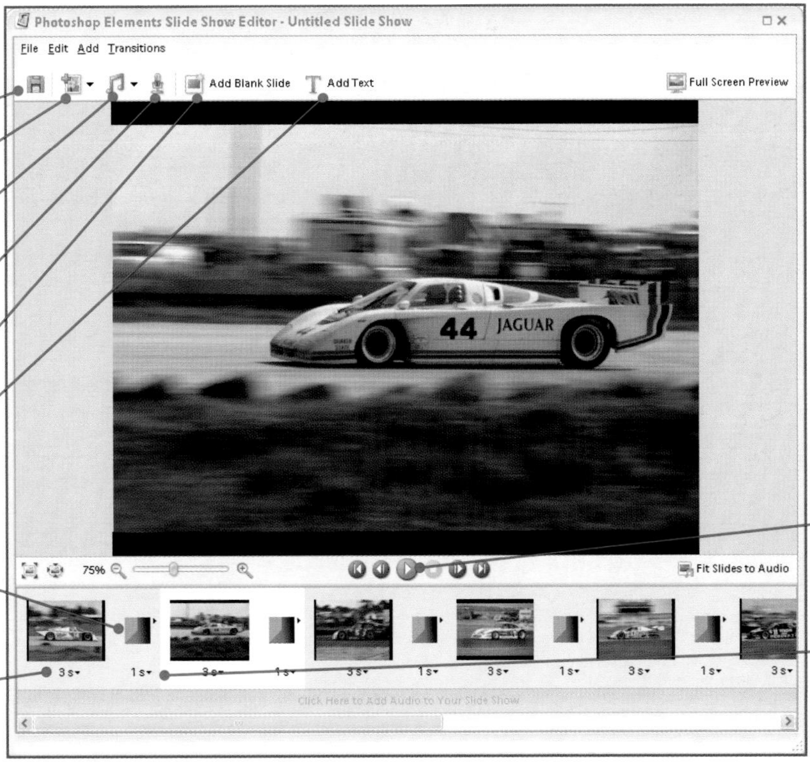

Click to save slide show

Click to add photos

Click to add audio file to slide show

Click to add narration to slide

Click to add a blank slide

Click to add text to slide

Click to edit transitions

Click to change transition duration

Click to preview the slide show

Click to change slide duration

Figure 9-7: You can create custom slide shows from your photos.

TIP

Click a slide and drag it to another position on the storyboard to change the order in which the slides are displayed.

TIP

After changing the duration of one slide, it appears as the new default on the top of the drop-down list. Click the modified slide duration, and then click **Set All Slides To *the new duration***.

TIP

Click **Add Photo**s and then click **Add Photos From Organizer** or **Add Photos From Folder** to add photos from the Organizer or to select a folder of photos, respectively. You can then click the photos you want to add to your slide show.

TIP

To add narration to a slide, click the desired slide and click **Add Narration For The Current Slide**. The Edit Narration dialog box appears. Choose an audio file already on your computer, or click **Edit Narration** to open the Edit Audio File dialog box. Click the **Record** button and then record the narration using the microphone attached to your computer.

6. To add a soundtrack to the slide show, click **Add Audio From Organizer Or Folder**, and then click the desired menu command. The following step shows how to add an audio file from the Organizer. If you choose to add an audio file from a folder, the Choose Your Audio Files dialog box appears, which enables you to navigate to the desired folder and click the audio file you want to play as background music.

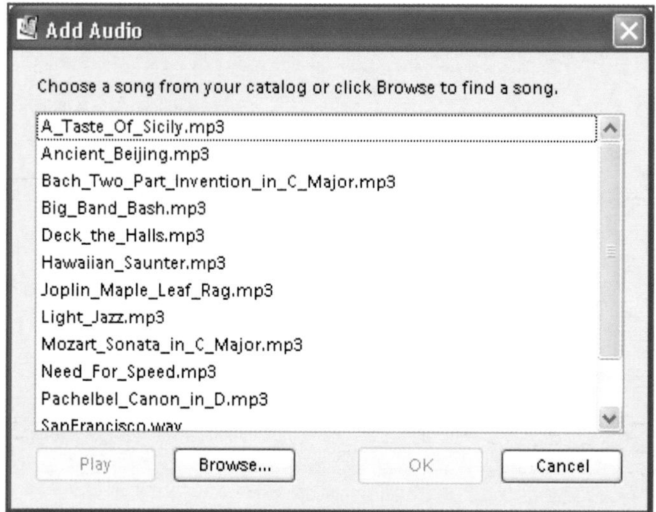

7. Click the desired file. You can then click **Play** to preview the audio file. **Click Stop** to end it.

8. Click **OK** when you've found the audio file you want. The audio file is added to the storyboard.

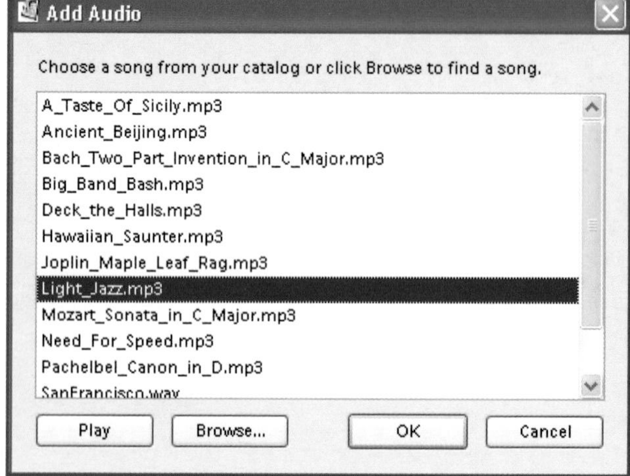

TIP

You can apply a different transition to each slide transition by selecting each transition in turn and repeating steps 6 and 7. To apply a transition to the entire slide show, click any photo transition right arrow, click the desired transition from the drop-down list, and then click **Apply To All**.

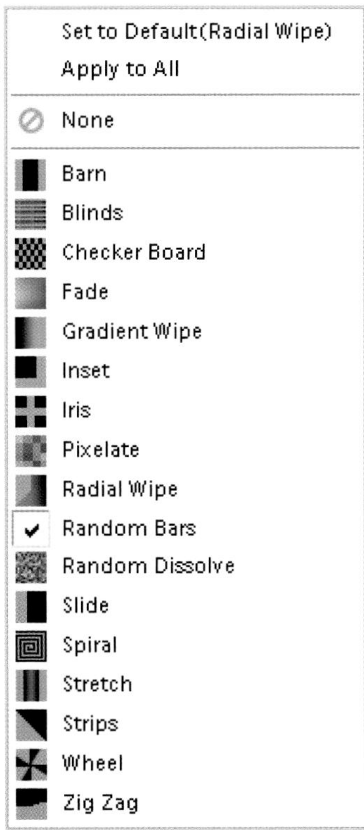

9. Click **Fit Slides To Audio** (located in the lower-right corner) to alter the duration of each slide so that the screen does not turn black if the audio is longer than the duration of the slide show.

10. To change slide duration, click the current slide duration, and click an option from the drop-down list.

Set all Slides to 3 s
1 s
2 s
3 s
4 s
5 s
Custom...
3 s

11. Click the **Transition** right arrow. The Transition drop-down menu is displayed.

12. Click the desired transition.

13. To change the transition duration, click a transition duration and then click the desired option from the drop-down list.

14. To add text to any slide, click the slide and then click **Add Text**. The Edit Text Properties dialog box appears.

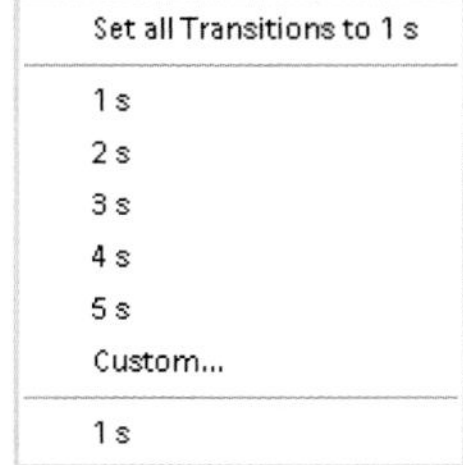

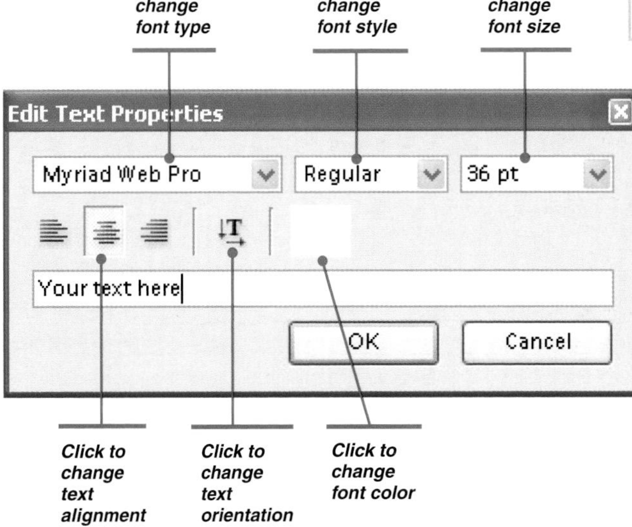

TIP

After creating the text, you can drag it to a different position on the slide.

TIP

Double-click slide text to open the Edit Text Properties dialog box and apply edits to the text.

15. Click the **Font** down arrow, and click the desired font from the drop-down list. This list includes all fonts installed on your computer in addition to Adobe Pro fonts.
16. Click the **Font Style** down arrow, and then click the desired style.
17. Click the **Font Size** down arrow, and then click the desired size.
18. Click the desired text alignment icon to left-align, center, or right-align the text.
19. Click the **Text Orientation** button to change the text from horizontal to vertical or vice versa.
20. Click the text color swatch to open the Color Picker, and then select the desired text color.
21. Drag to select the words "Your Text Here," and then type the desired text.
22. Click **OK**.
23. Click the **Play** button to preview the slide show. Click the other VCR-like controls to navigate to the next, previous, first, or last slide.
24. Click **Save**. The Adobe Photoshop Elements dialog box appears.
25. Type a name for your slide show, and then click **Save**. The slide show is saved to the current collection.

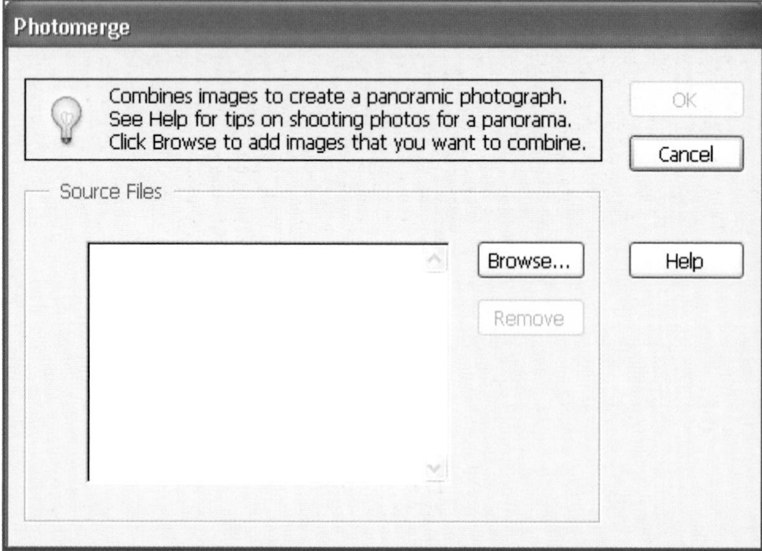

Create Panoramic Images

If you own a tripod, you can create the raw elements of your panorama by taking a picture, rotating the tripod, and then taking additional pictures while continuing to rotate the tripod. As long as you have elements in each picture that overlap, you can stitch them together as a panorama in Photoshop Elements.

1. In the Editor, click **File**, click **New,** and then click **Photomerge™ Panorama**. The Photomerge dialog box appears.

CREATING PHOTOS FOR A PANORAMA

When you're creating images for a panorama, keep a few things in mind:

- Keep the camera level and mounted on a tripod.
- Stay in the same position for each shot. Rotate your tripod head to frame each photo.
- Make sure there's a sufficient overlap between images so that Photoshop Elements can find features to align. Adobe recommends an overlap of between 15 and 40 percent for optimum stitching.
- Maintain the same exposure for each image.
- Use the same focal length for each image. Do not zoom in or out.
- When photographing from a high position, keep the tripod level. Do not attempt to level the horizon in the viewfinder, as this will lead to distortion when the image is stitched together.

TIP

Some tripods have degree marks on the head, which you can use to create your overlaps. If yours is not equipped with degree marks, you can paint marks every 15 degrees on the head of your tripod.

2. Click the **Browse** button. The Open dialog box appears.
3. Navigate to the folder in which your panorama images are stored.
4. Click the images to select them, and then click **Open**. The selected images are listed in the Photomerge dialog box.
5. Click **OK**. Photoshop Elements opens the images and stitches them together in the Photomerge dialog box, as shown in Figure 9-8.

Figure 9-8: You can create dazzling panoramas using the Photomerge™ Panorama command.

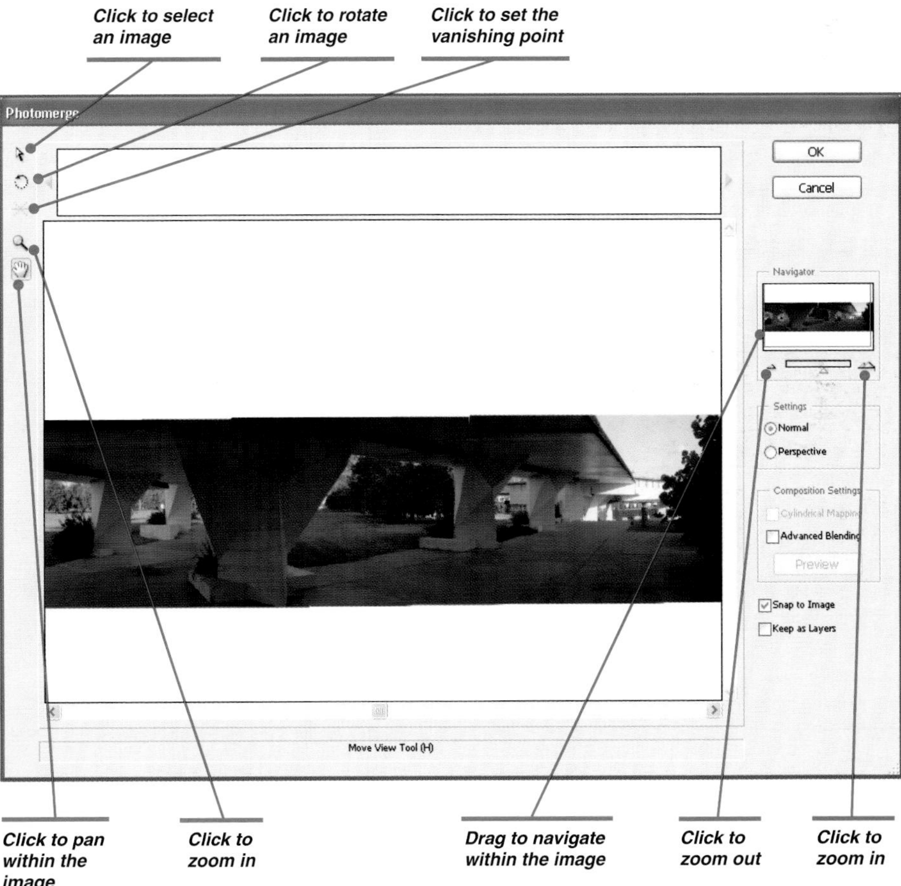

TIP

Use the Zoom tool to zoom in on an individual image you are aligning. Press **ALT** while using the Zoom tool to zoom out. Alternatively, you can drag the slider in the Navigator to navigate within the image, or click the **Navigator Zoom In** or **Zoom Out** buttons.

6. In the Settings area, **Normal** is selected by default. You can leave this or click **Perspective** to create a perspective panorama.
7. Examine the image. If you see any blurring, that's an indication that you need to manually realign the images by doing one of the following:
   - Click the image that needs to be realigned with the **Select** tool, and then move the image until it blends perfectly with the neighboring images.
   - Click the image the needs to be realigned with the **Rotate** tool, and then drag to rotate the image until it blends perfectly with the neighboring images.
8. After the images are aligned, click **OK**. Photoshop Elements combines the images into a panorama.
9. Click the **Crop** tool and crop away any unwanted areas. Figure 9-9 shows a completed panorama.

Figure 9-9: The completed panorama appears as though it was photographed with a single click of the shutter.

E-Mail an Image

You can e-mail an image as an attachment from within Photoshop Elements. You can select a photo from the Photo Browser or e-mail the document currently open in the Editor.

1. If you're working in the Photo Browser, click the image you want to send as an e-mail attachment. Alternatively, in the Editor, click **File** and then click **Open** to select the image you want to send as an e-mail attachment.
2. Click **File** and then click **Attach To E-Mail**. The command sequence is the same whether you're working in the Editor or Photo Browser. The Attach Selected Items To E-Mail dialog box appears.
3. The **E-Mail Client** option is selected by default (your system's default e-mail application), or you can click the down arrow to select a different e-mail application from the drop-down list.
4. Click **OK**. A dialog box appears, asking you to confirm the e-mail client.
5. Click **OK**. The Attach Selected Items To E-Mail dialog box appears.

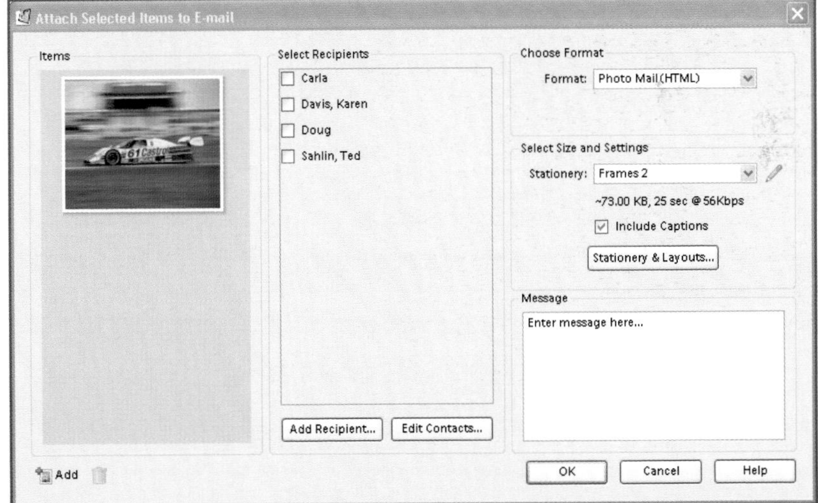

6. Click a recipient from the Select Recipients list. Alternatively, you can click the **Add Recipient** button to open the Add A Recipient dialog box. Type the recipient's first and last name and e-mail address, and then click **OK**.

NOTE

Depending on the number of e-mail clients you have installed on your system, you may or may not be asked to confirm your e-mail client the first time you send a photo by e-mail. In the future, you can change to another e-mail application by clicking **File** and then clicking **Preferences**. Click **E-Mail** to open the e-mail section of the Preferences dialog box, and click a different e-mail application from the drop-down list.

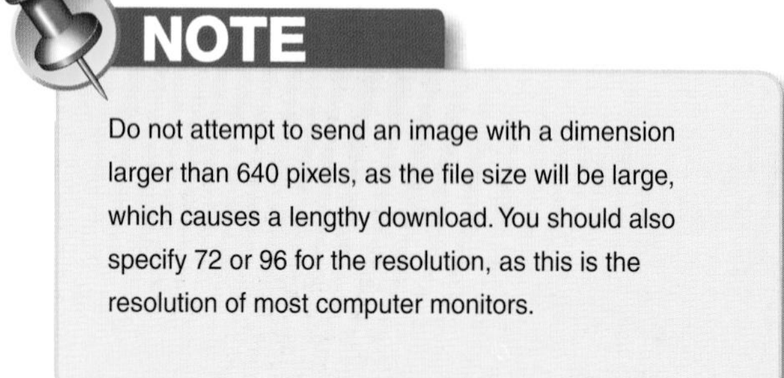

NOTE

Do not attempt to send an image with a dimension larger than 640 pixels, as the file size will be large, which causes a lengthy download. You should also specify 72 or 96 for the resolution, as this is the resolution of most computer monitors.

7. Click the **Format** down arrow, and click the desired option.

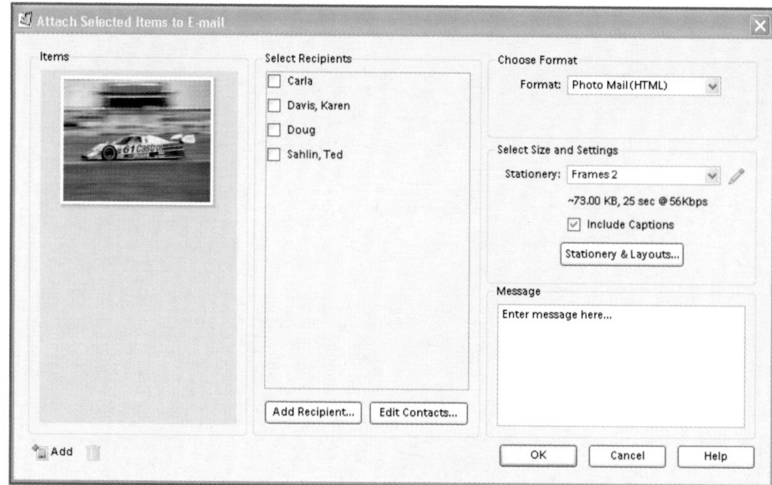

8. Click the **Stationery And Layouts** button to start the Stationery And Layouts Wizard.

9. Click the desired stationery group, and then click a preset to preview it in the wizard, as shown in Figure 9-10.

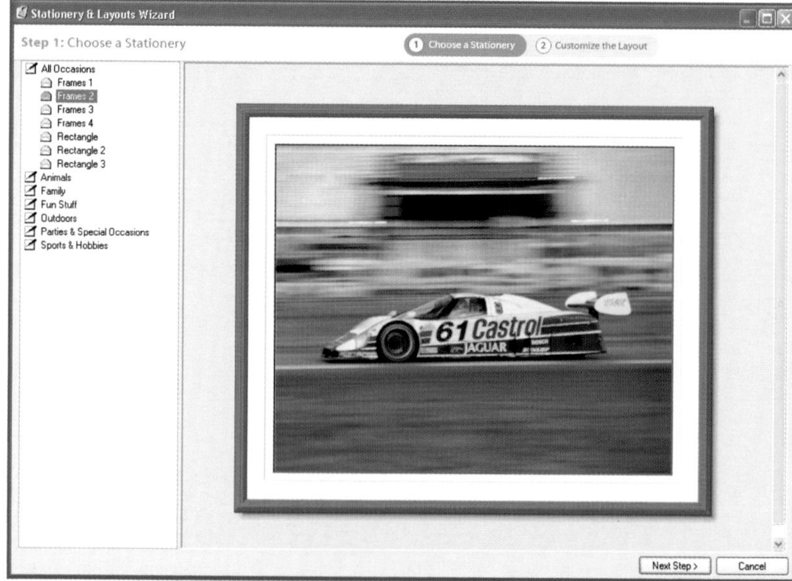

Figure 9-10: You can choose which type of stationery is displayed with your image.

10. Click **Next Step**. The Customize The Layout Page of the wizard appears, as shown in Figure 9-11.

Figure 9-11: You can customize the stationery to suit your preferences.

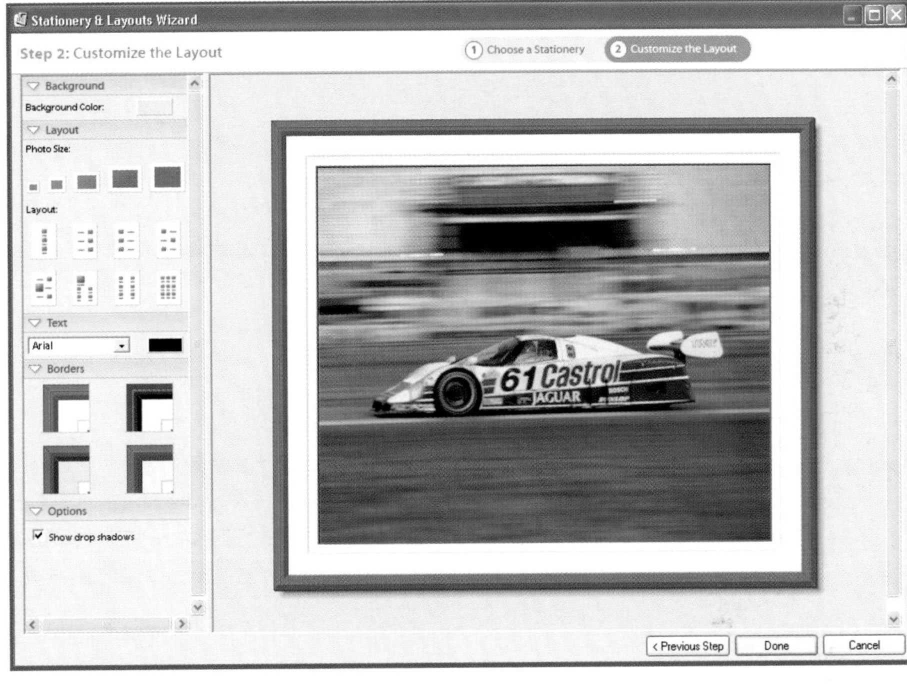

11. Accept the default options, or perform any of the following actions:
   - In the Photo Size area, click the desired icon to change the photo display size.
   - In the Layout area, click the desired icon to determine how multiple images are displayed in the e-mail.
   - In the Text area, click the **Font** down arrow, and click the desired font from the drop-down list.
   - In the Text area, click the color swatch and then click the desired color from the Color Picker.
   - In the Borders area, click the desired border.
   - Click the **Show Drop Shadows** check box to deselect this option.
12. Click **Done**. The Stationery And Layout Wizard closes.
13. Type your message in the body of the e-mail.

NOTE

The Borders area only appears with the All Occasions stationery. Other stationery options offer different border options or no border options at all.

14. Click **OK**. The image appears in your default e-mail application, as shown in Figure 9-12.

Figure 9-12: You can send an image in an e-mail message.

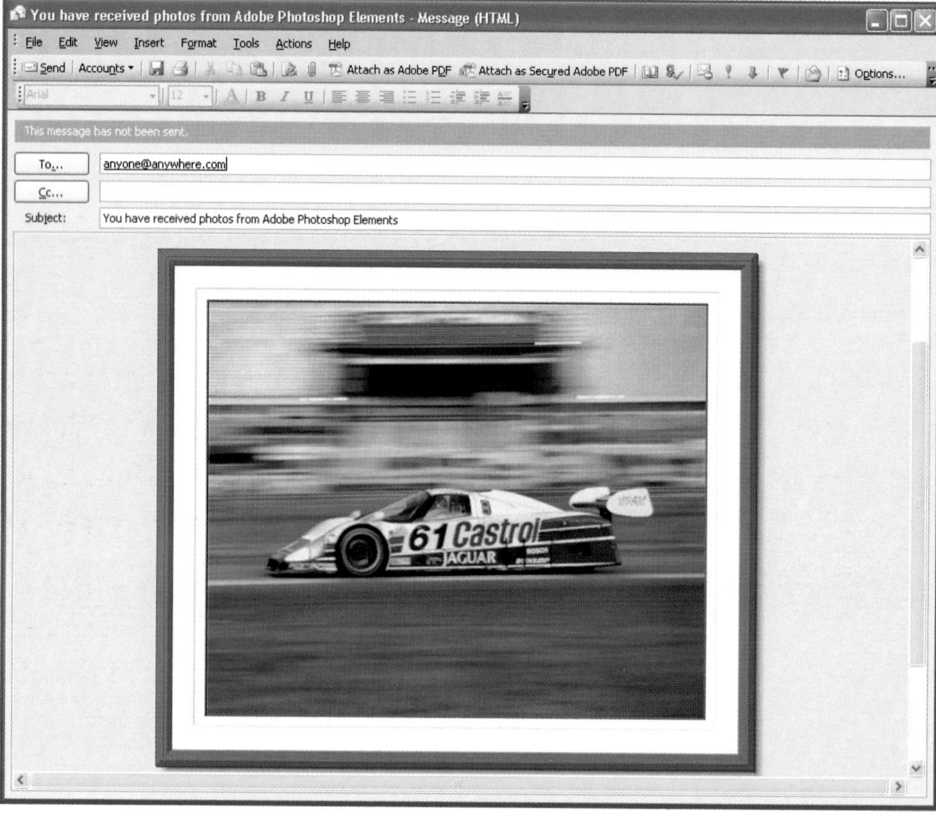

15. Type a new subject, if necessary, and edit the message text.
16. Click **Send**.

How to...

Chapter 10
Printing and Saving Images

After you use Photoshop Elements to edit your images to perfection, it's time to save them for future use. If you're going to be working on an image in the future, you can save it with any layers you may have used during your editing session. You can save multiple versions of the image that are intended for different purposes, such as e-mailing to friends and relatives, creating high-resolution prints on your inkjet printer, or displaying the image on a web site.

Save Images to a File

After you finish editing your images, you can save them for future use. The Save command does not become available until you edit an image. When you use the Save command, you can save the image with the same file name and file format. You can also specify the folder in which the image is saved.

1. Click **File** and then click **Save**. The Save As dialog box appears.

UNDERSTANDING FILE FORMATS

Photoshop Elements offers a wide variety of formats in which you can save your work. The file format you choose depends on the destination of the image. The following list explores the most popular Photoshop Elements file formats and provides a description of their uses:

- **BMP** This popular, Windows-only format enables you to save images in the Windows or OS/2 format and specify a bit depth. You can apply RLE (Run Length Encoding) compression for 4-bit or 8-bit images you save in the Windows format.
- **CompuServe GIF** This format enables you to save 8-bit (256-color) images and is commonly used for images displayed on web sites. This format is best suited for images with large areas of solid color, such as graphics or logos.
- **JPEG** This format enables you to save images with lossy compression, which means data is lost when the file is compressed. The amount of image data lost when the file is saved is determined by the amount of compression you apply. You'll get high-quality images with large file sizes when you choose a high image quality (quality value between 8 and 12), low-quality images with small file sizes when you choose a low image quality (quality value between 0 and 4), and medium-quality images with intermediate file sizes when you choose a medium image quality (quality value between 5 and 8). This file format is best suited for photo-realistic images for display on a web site or e-mailed to friends and relatives.
- **JPEG 2000** This file format ensures better image quality with better compression, resulting in smaller file sizes than JPEG. The format also supports color management and offers more metadata options than JPEG.
- **Photoshop PSD** Photoshop's native file format enables you to save files complete with layers and other image data. Save images in this format if you're going to apply further edits.

Continued...

2. Click the **Save In** down arrow, and select the folder in which you want to save the file. Alternatively, you can accept the default folder.

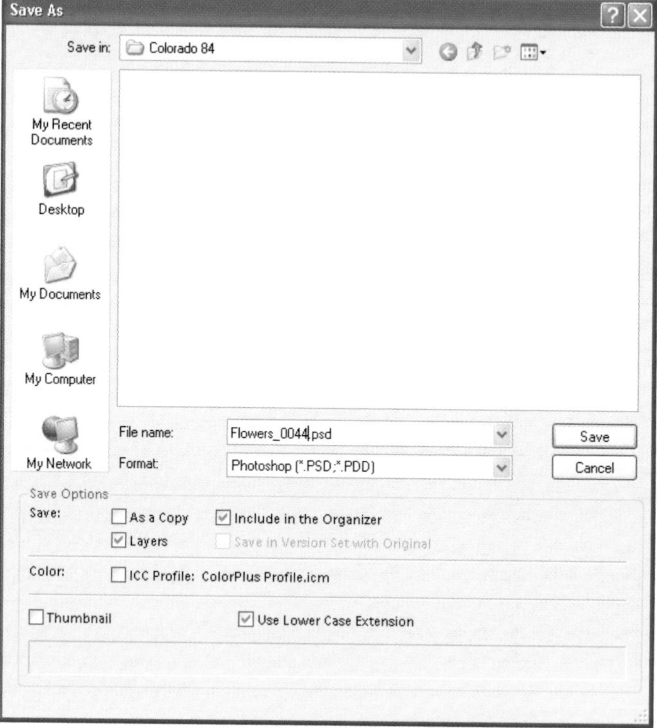

3. Accept the original file name, or type a different file name.
4. Accept the original file format, or click the **Format** down arrow, and click a different file format.
5. In the Save Options area, you have the following options:
   - Click the **As A Copy** check box to save the image as a copy of the original. This option appends the original file name with "(Copy)" if you save it in the same folder as the original. This option is useful, as it does not overwrite the original file.
   - Click the **Include In The Organizer** check box to deselect the default option, in which case Photoshop Elements will not include the file in the Organizer.
   - Click the **Layers** check box to preserve any layers you've created while editing the image. Saving layers increases file size.

UNDERSTANDING FILE FORMATS

(Continued)

- **PCX** This file format enables you to save images in a bitmap format that is supported by many image-editing applications and by a wide variety of platforms.
- **Photoshop PDF** This file format enables you to save image files as Acrobat PDF documents. If you're going to be sharing the file with others or extracting images within Acrobat for use in other applications, you should convert files to 8-bit before saving.
- **PNG** This file format enables you to save 8-, 16-, or 24-bit files with lossless compression. This format supports background transparency without introducing jagged edges and is often used for displaying images on web sites.
- **TGA** This file format enables you to save an RGB image with a pixel depth of 16, 14, or 32 bits with RLE compression. It was originally designed for systems using the Truevision video board.
- **TIFF** This file format enables you to save a high-quality image with or without compression. This format is an excellent choice if you're going to print the image or use it in another application. It is also the default file format for many scanners.

NOTE

If you don't save layers, you won't be able to apply further edits to the image. If you intend to apply further edits to an image, save it in Photoshop Elements' native PSD format with layers. You can then use the Save As command to save a version of the file with no layers in a different file format, such as TIFF or JPEG.

- Click the **Save In Version Set With Original** check box to save the edited file as a version of the original. If you click this check box, the file name is appended with "edited-" followed by the version number of the original. For example, the first version set of a JPEG file named "myimage" would be "myimage edited-1.jpeg." This option enables you to save multiple versions of the original on which you've applied different techniques or filters.

6. In the Color area, click the **ICC Profile** check box to save the current ICC (International Color Consortium) profile assigned to your monitor.
7. Click the **Thumbnail** check box to save a thumbnail preview image with the file.
8. Click the **Use Lower Case Extension** check box (which is selected by default unless you clicked Use Upper Case; see the QuickSteps "Setting Save Preferences").
9. Click **Save**. Photoshop Elements saves the file.

Compress Files

Sometimes, you need to compress a file in order to achieve a smaller file size. You can compress files when saving in the JPEG, JPEG 2000, or TIFF formats.

Compress a File Using the JPEG Format

When you compress an image using the JPEG format, image data is lost when the file is compressed. As you apply more compression, more data is lost, which results in a lower-quality image and a smaller file size. The optimum compression produces a high-quality image that downloads quickly to the viewer's browser.

1. Click **Image**, click **Resize**, and then click **Image Size**. The Image Size dialog box appears.
2. Type the values for the file's intended destination.
3. Click **OK** to resize the image.
4. Click **File** and then click **Save As**. The Save As dialog box appears.
5. Click the **Format** down arrow, and click **JPEG**.

QUICKSTEPS

SETTING SAVE PREFERENCES

You can set preferences for the way Photoshop Elements saves your files. For example, you can save files with a preview image or not, specify maximum PSD file compatibility, and more.

1. In the Editor, click **Edit**, click **Preferences**, and then click **Saving Files**. The Preferences dialog box appears with the Saving Files section displayed.

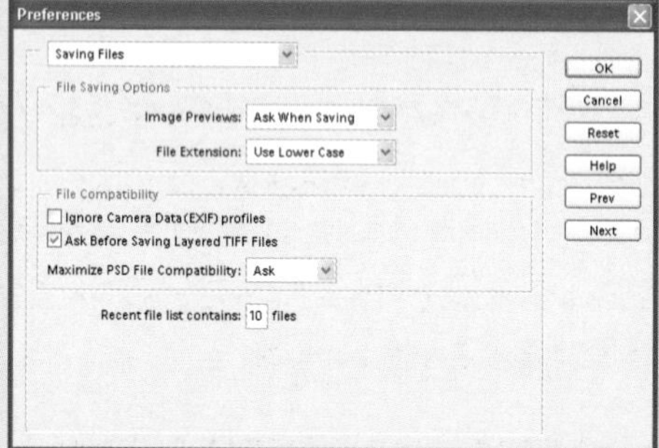

2. Click the **Image Previews** down arrow, and click one of the following:
   - **Never Save** does not save a preview with the image.
   - **Save Preview** saves a preview with the image.
   - **Ask When Saving** prompts you whether to save a preview with each file you save.
3. Click the **File Extensions** down arrow, and choose one of the following:
   - Click **Use Upper Case** to list the file extension in uppercase letters.
   - Click **Use Lower Case** to list the file extension in lowercase letters.
4. In the File Compatibility section, you have the following options:
   - Click the **Ignore Camera Data (EXIF) Profiles** check box, and the EXIF (Exchangeable Image File) data generated by your camera will not be saved with the file.

Continued...

6. Click the other options as outlined previously in the QuickFacts "Using the Save As Command to Change File Formats."

Photoshop (*.PSD;*.PDD)
BMP (*.BMP;*.RLE;*.DIB)
CompuServe GIF (*.GIF)
Photoshop EPS (*.EPS)
JPEG (*.JPG;*.JPEG;*.JPE)
JPEG 2000 (*.JPF;*.JPX;*.JP2;*.J2C;*.J2K;*.JPC)
PCX (*.PCX)
Photoshop PDF (*.PDF;*.PDP)
Photoshop Raw (*.RAW)
PICT File (*.PCT;*.PICT)
Pixar (*.PXR)
PNG (*.PNG)
Scitex CT (*.SCT)
Targa (*.TGA;*.VDA;*.ICB;*.VST)
TIFF (*.TIF;*.TIFF)

7. Click **Save**. The JPEG Options dialog box is displayed.
8. Drag the **Quality** slider to determine how much compression is applied to the image. Alternatively, you can type a value between 0 and 4 (low image quality; small file size), between 5 and 7 (better image quality; larger file size), between 8 and 11, (better image quality; larger file size), or 12 (best image quality; largest file size).

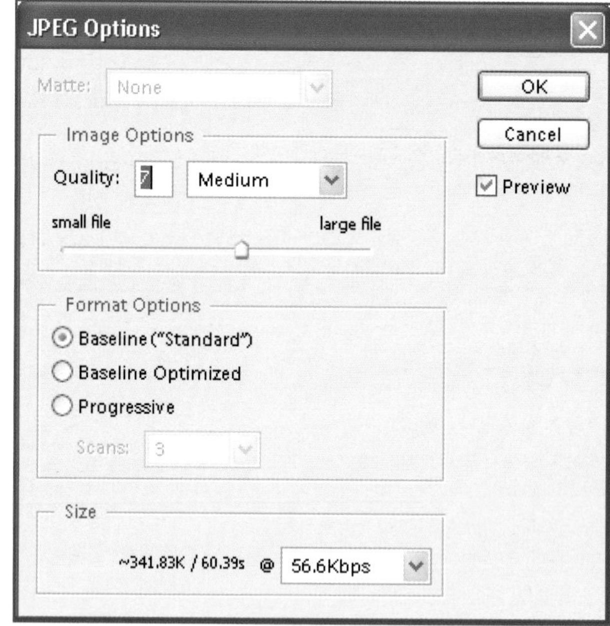

9. In the Format Options area, choose from among the following options:
   - Click **Baseline ("Standard")** to make the image appear line by line on the computer monitor.

SETTING SAVE PREFERENCES
(Continued)

- Click the **Ask Before Saving Layered TIFF Files** check box (which deselects it since the option is selected by default), and when you save a file that contains layers in the TIFF format, Photoshop Elements will not display a dialog box warning you that layers increase file size.

5. Click the **Maximize PSD File Compatibility** down arrow; and click **Never, Always**, or **Ask**. When Photoshop Elements maximizes PSD compatibility, you can use the file in other applications that support the PSD file format.
6. Click in the **Recent Files List Contains** text field, and type the number of files displayed on the list of recently opened files. The default value is 10.
7. Click **OK** to exit the Preferences dialog box and apply the changes.

USING THE SAVE AS COMMAND TO CHANGE FILE FORMATS

You can choose a different file format when using the Save command; however, you often need to save a file in multiple formats. For example, you might need to save one version of an image for printing and another version for the Web. When this is the case, the Save As command lets you save the document in a different file format than the original. This is a handy option when you want to save one version of the file in Photoshop Elements' native PSD format and another version in a different format.

- Click **Baseline Optimized** to apply optimized Huffman encoding to the Standard formatting option. Huffman encoding is designed to give better image quality through a form of lossless compression.
- Click **Progressive** to make the image appear in multiple scans. When you click this option, the Scans field becomes available. This option determines how many scans occur before the full image quality is revealed. Accept the default number of scans (3), or type a different number.

10. Click **OK** to save the file.

Compress a File Using the JPEG 2000 Format

When you choose the JPEG 2000 format, the resulting image has a higher quality than those compressed with the JPEG format. When you use this format to compress an image, you can specify the desired file size or image quality to determine the amount of compression applied to the image.

1. Click **Image**, click **Resize**, and then click **Image Size**. The Image Size dialog box appears.
2. Type the values for the file's intended destination. Click **OK**.
3. Click **File** and then click **Save As**. The Save As dialog box appears.
4. Click the **Format** down arrow, and click **JPEG 2000**.
5. Click the other options as outlined previously in the QuickFacts "Using the Save As Command to Change File Formats."
6. Click **Save**. The JPEG 2000 dialog box shown in Figure 10-1 appears, presenting the following options:

Photoshop (*.PSD;*.PDD)
BMP (*.BMP;*.RLE;*.DIB)
CompuServe GIF (*.GIF)
Photoshop EPS (*.EPS)
JPEG (*.JPG;*.JPEG;*.JPE)
JPEG 2000 (*.JPF;*.JPX;*.JP2;*.J2C;*.J2K;*.JPC)
PCX (*.PCX)
Photoshop PDF (*.PDF;*.PDP)
Photoshop Raw (*.RAW)
PICT File (*.PCT;*.PICT)
Pixar (*.PXR)
PNG (*.PNG)
Scitex CT (*.SCT)
Targa (*.TGA;*.VDA;*.ICB;*.VST)
TIFF (*.TIF;*.TIFF)

NOTE

Not all formats support layers.

NOTE

Some file formats, such as JPEG and TIFF, have formatting options that cause an Options dialog box to appear after you click Save.

TIP

When you save an image for the Web, type a resolution of 72, and don't type a value larger than 600 pixels for the width or height.

Figure 10-1: You can achieve higher image quality using the JPEG 2000 format.

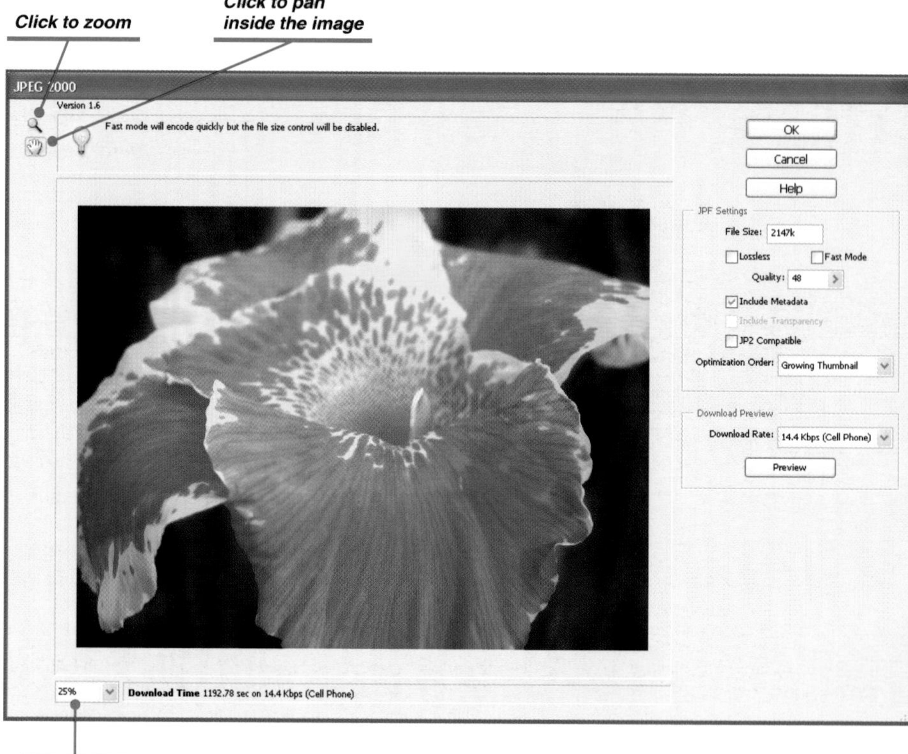

Click to set preview magnification

- Click in the **File Size** field, and type the file size. This option is not available with the Lossless or Fast Mode check boxes selected.
- Click the **Lossless** check box, and Photoshop Elements applies no compression to the file. This results in the highest image quality with the largest file size.
- Click the **Fast Mode** check box to save the file faster with fewer options, which may result in a larger file size.

TIP

The Size area in the JPEG Options dialog box displays the file size with the current compression applied and the download time with an Internet connection of 56 Kbps. Click the down arrow to right of the field, and select an option from the drop-down menu to see the download time with a faster or slower connection.

- Click the **Quality** arrow and drag the slider to set compression. Alternatively, you can type a value between 0 (heavy compression; poorer image quality; small file size) and 100 (light compression; better image quality; larger file size). This option is not available if you click the Lossless check box.
- Click the **Include Metadata** check box to save information, such as copyright information, with the file.
- Click the **Include Transparency** check box to preserve transparency from the original image. This option is unavailable if the image does not support transparency.
- Click the **JP2 Compatible** check box if the image will be displayed in browsers that do not support the extended JPEG 2000 format (JPX).

7. Click the **Optimization Order** down arrow, and choose one of the following options:

Growing Thumbnail
Progressive
Color

   - **Growing Thumbnail** creates an image that first appears in the browser as a small thumbnail, gradually growing larger until the image is displayed at full size.
   - **Progressive** creates an image file that loads into the viewer's browser in stages until it is displayed at full quality.
   - **Color** creates an image file that is first displayed in a web browser as a grayscale image and then in full color.

8. Click the **Download Rate** down arrow, and click a download speed.

14.4 Kbps (Cell Phone)
28.8 Kbps (Modem)
56.6 Kbps
128 Kbps
512 Kbps (DSL)
1.5Mbps (Broadband)

9. Click the **Preview** button to preview the download at the rate you selected in step 8.
10. Click **OK** to save the image.

Compress a File Using the TIFF Format

When you save a file using the TIFF format, you can choose to apply no compression, LWZ (Lempel Ziv Welch) compression, ZIP compression, or JPEG compression. You can only apply ZIP and JPEG compression if Ask Before Saving Layered TIFF Files is selected (see the QuickSteps "Setting Save Preferences"). Use the TIFF format when you need a high-quality image for use in another application that supports the format.

QUICKSTEPS

ADDING FILE DESCRIPTIONS AND INFORMATION

When you shoot a photo with your digital camera, metadata—such as the camera model, lens focal length, shutter speed, date created, and so on—is added to the image file. You can view metadata information in the File Browser Metadata window or in the Organizer Properties window. You can also add additional information to any image file, such as the title of the document, the author, copyright notice, copyright status, and so on.

1. Open the desired image file.
2. Click **File** and click **File Info**. A dialog box appears, as shown in Figure 10-2.
3. In the Description area, type the relevant information in each field.
4. Click the **Copyright Status** down arrow, and click the desired option.

   Unknown
   Copyrighted
   Public Domain

5. Click in the **Copyright Notice** field, and type the relevant information.
6. Click in the **Copyright Info URL** field, and type the URL to your web site, if you have one.
7. Click **OK** to exit the dialog box and add the metadata to the image.

---

1. Click **File** and then click **Save As**. The Save As dialog box appears.
2. Click the **Format** down arrow, and click **TIFF**.

   Photoshop (*.PSD;*.PDD)
   BMP (*.BMP;*.RLE;*.DIB)
   CompuServe GIF (*.GIF)
   Photoshop EPS (*.EPS)
   JPEG (*.JPG;*.JPEG;*.JPE)
   JPEG 2000 (*.JPF;*.JPX;*.JP2;*.J2C;*.J2K;*.JPC)
   PCX (*.PCX)
   Photoshop PDF (*.PDF;*.PDP)
   Photoshop Raw (*.RAW)
   PICT File (*.PCT;*.PICT)
   Pixar (*.PXR)
   PNG (*.PNG)
   Scitex CT (*.SCT)
   Targa (*.TGA;*.VDA;*.ICB;*.VST)
   TIFF (*.TIF;*.TIFF)

3. Click the other options as outlined previously in the QuickFacts "Using the Save As Command to Change File Formats."
4. Click **Save**. The TIFF Options dialog box appears.

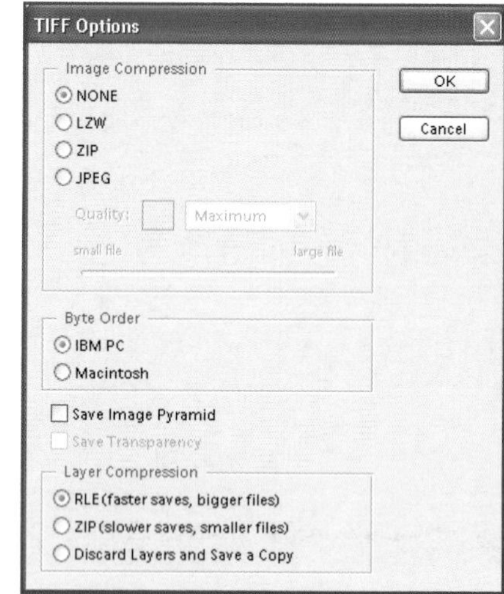

5. In the Image Compression area, click one of the following options:
   - **None** applies no compression to the image.
   - **LZW** applies the LZW method of lossless compression to the image. Use this method when your image has large areas of solid color.
   - **ZIP** applies the ZIP method of lossless compression to the image. This option would be the second choice for an image with large areas of solid color.
   - **JPEG** applies lossy compression to the image. When you click this option, the Quality slider becomes available. Drag the slider to determine the amount of compression applied to the image. Alternatively, you can type a value between 0 (small file size; heavy compression; poor image quality) and 12 (larger file size; small amount of compression; high image quality). This is your best choice if your image is photo-realistic with millions of colors.

NOTE

Multi-resolution information is used by programs such as Adobe InDesign. Photoshop Elements has no options for opening multi-resolution files and uses the highest resolution present in the image.

NOTE

You can only add keywords using tags in the Organizer.

TIP

You can create your copyright status with the copyright symbol in a word-processing application that has the capability of inserting symbols into a document. Insert the copyright symbol (©) followed by the year and then your name. Select the copyright notice and copy it to the Clipboard. In Photoshop Elements, place your cursor in the Copyright Information field, and press **CTRL+V** to paste the information into the field.

6. In the Byte Order area, click the **IBM PC** option if the image will be opened on computers running Windows, or click **Macintosh** if the image will be opened on Macintosh computers.
7. Click the **Save Image Pyramid** check box to preserve multi-resolution information.
8. Click the **Save Transparency** check box to preserve image transparency as an alpha channel.
9. In the Layer Compression area, click one of the following options:
   - **RLE** compresses layers faster and results in a larger file size.
   - **ZIP** takes longer to save and results in a smaller file size.
   - **None** flattens all layers and saves the image as a copy.
10. Click **OK** to save the file.

Figure 10-2: You can add information to image metadata in the file information dialog box.

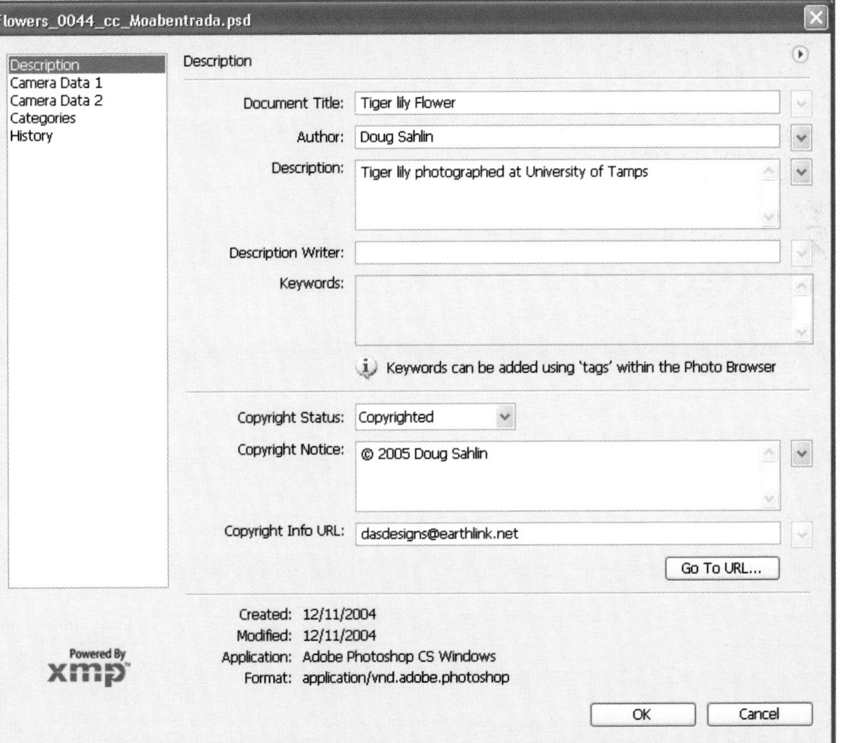

NOTE

Photoshop and Photoshop Elements users can view the file information dialog box when they open your file in either application. If they click the Go To URL button, their default web browser starts and opens the web site listed in the Copyright Info URL field.

NOTE

Copyright laws vary depending on the country in which you live. In the United States, the photographer retains copyright status unless the rights to the image are transferred when the image is sold. In other countries, the owner of the image retains copyright status (who may not be the same person as the photographer). This Note is by no means definitive when it comes to copyright laws. If you are in doubt about whether you own the copyright to an image or if you need permission to display an image publicly or on a web site, contact an attorney who specializes in intellectual property law.

TIP

To print a portion of the image, create a selection with the **Rectangular Marquee** tool. When you open the Print Preview dialog box, the Print Selection check box becomes available. Click the **Print Selection** check box to print only the selection.

Print Images

In addition to editing images for viewing on monitors, you can also create high-resolution versions of your images for print. Most digital cameras have a default resolution of 180 dpi (dots per inch) or greater, and most scanners have a default resolution of 200 dpi or better. When you edit an image with a resolution of 180 dpi or larger, you can create a high-quality print of the image using photo-quality paper on a photo-quality (four or more colors) inkjet printer.

Scale and Position Images for Printing

After setting your print options, you can scale the image to fit the media. You can choose a preset size or manually resize and position the image within the boundary of the selected media.

1. Click **File** and click **Print**. The Print Preview dialog box appears.
2. Click the **Print Size** down arrow, and click the size from the drop-down list. Alternatively, if you want to create a custom size not on the list, you can resize the image to different dimensions, as outlined in step 3.

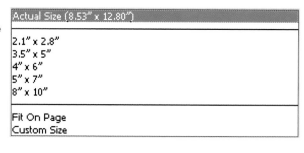

3. In the Scale Size area, click in the **Scale** field, and type a value. This value represents the percentage the image will be scaled down from the document size in inches. Alternatively, you can type a value in the Width or Height fields, and Photoshop Elements will resize the image proportionately.

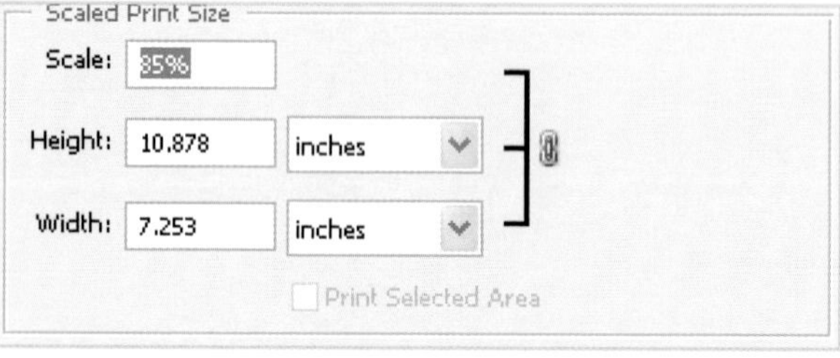

OPENING THE PRINT PREVIEW WINDOW

When you print an image in Photoshop Elements, you have complete control over the placement of the image within the page, the size of the image relative to the page, where the image is placed on the page, and so on. In addition, you can select an ICC profile that matches the paper on which you are printing the image.

1. Open the image you want to print.
2. Click **File** and click **Print**. The Print Preview dialog box appears, as shown in Figure 10-3.

When you deselect the **Center Image** check box and the image is scaled to less than 100 percent, four handles appear on the image perimeter. Drag a handle to manually resize the image.

***Figure 10-3:** You have precise control over image printing through the Print Preview dialog box.*

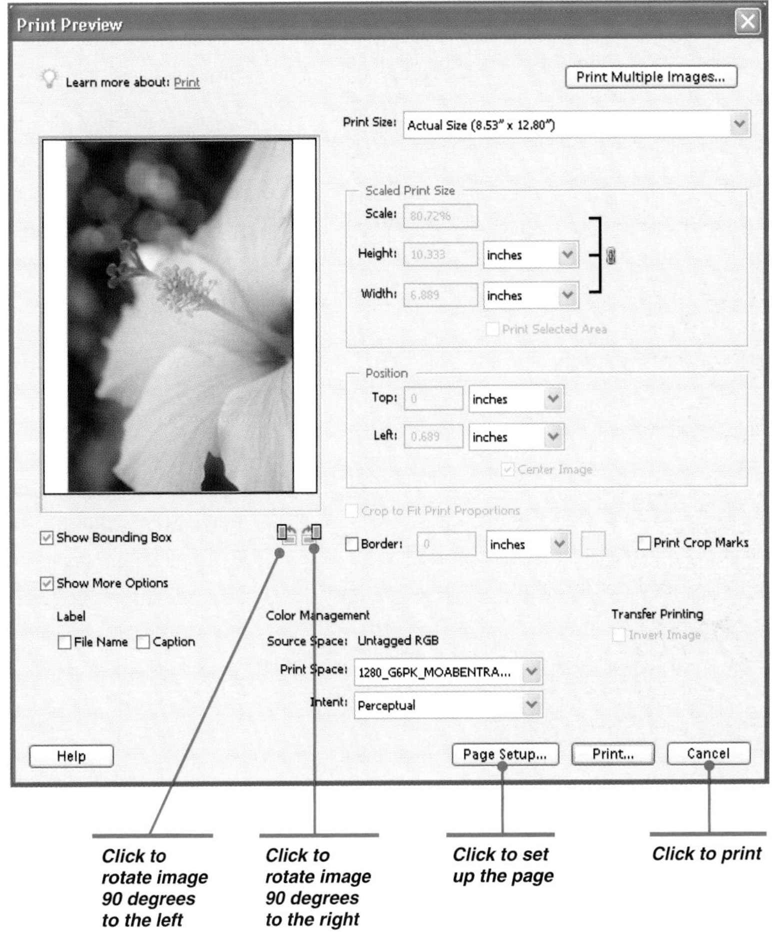

4. In the Position area, click the **Center Image** check box (selected by default) to deselect it, which enables you to manually reposition the image within the boundary of the media. Drag the image to the desired position. Alternatively, you can type values in the Top and Left fields to position the image.
5. Click **Print** to send the image to your printer, or set other options prior to printing (see the QuickSteps "Setting Print Output Options" later in the chapter).

QUICKSTEPS

SETTING PRINT OUTPUT OPTIONS

You have additional output options that enable you to add crop marks, a border, or more to the printed image.

1. Open the **Print Preview** window (see the QuickSteps "Opening the Print Preview Window").
2. Click the **Rotate 90 Degrees Left** button or the **Rotate 90 Degrees Right** button to reorient the image.

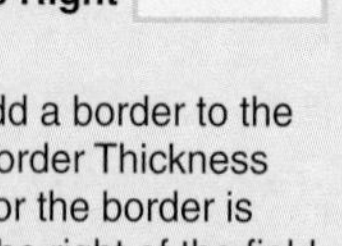

3. Click the **Border** check box to add a border to the image, and type a value in the Border Thickness field. The default measurement for the border is inches. Click the down arrow to the right of the field, and click either **MM** or **Points** if your measurement isn't in inches. Click the **color swatch** icon (located to the right of the Border Thickness field) to choose a border color from the Color Picker.
4. Click the **Show More Options** check box to reveal additional options.

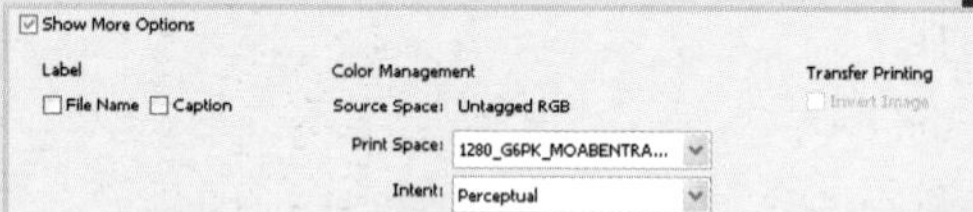

5. In the Label area, click the **File Name** check box to display the file name on the printed image.
6. Click the **Caption** check box to display on the printed image any caption you added to the image in the Organizer.
7. Click the **Print** button to print the image, or add color management to the image as outlined in the section, "Use Color Management when Printing."

Use Color Management when Printing

When you print an image, you can let the printer control color management or use any ICC profile currently installed on your computer. If you use an ICC profile, you must remove your printer's ability to control color management. This is done in the Properties dialog box for your printer. Refer to your printer manual for further instructions.

1. Open the Print Preview window (see the QuickSteps "Opening the Print Preview Window").
2. Scale and position the image (see "Scale and Position Images for Printing").
3. Click the **Show More Options** check box, and set output options as outlined in the previous section.
4. In the Color Management area, click the **Print Space** down arrow, and click an option from the drop-down menu, which is a list of all color profiles present on your computer.

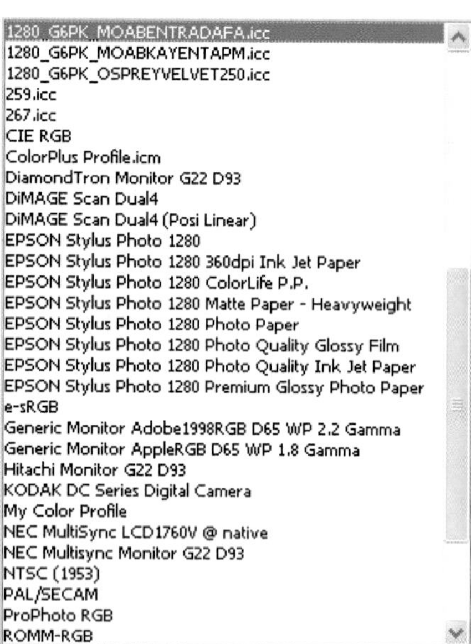

5. Click the **Intent** down arrow, and click one of the following options:
   - **Perceptual** is the default option and works well in most cases. It preserves the visual relationship of image colors, although colors may be shifted to suit the selected ICC profile. This option will shift out-of-gamut colors to printable colors.
   - **Saturation** preserves color saturation—ensuring rich, vivid images—at the expense of accurate color rendition. This option is best suited for graphics such as business logos in which rich, saturated color is important.
   - **Relative Colorimetric** preserves colors in both the source and destination color spaces. Out-of-gamut colors are shifted to the closest possible match in the printer's color space. Colors are shifted so that the overall appearance of the image is preserved.

USING THIRD-PARTY PAPER

Each printer manufacturer has presets in the printer's settings for the papers they sell. You can purchase a wide variety of third-party papers for printing fine art images that look like they were printed on watercolor paper, canvas, and so on. When you purchase a third-party paper, the printer manufacturer's settings may not give you the desired results. Most third-party paper manufacturers create ICC profiles for popular printers, which you can use to ensure that the final print matches what you see on the monitor. Check with your paper supplier to see if ICC profiles for their third-party papers are available for your printer. When you use an ICC color profile for third-party paper, follow the paper manufacturer's instructions for setting up your printer. In most cases, this means using advanced settings for your printer. Refer to your printer manual for detailed instructions. The following illustration shows the advanced settings for an Epson 1280 printer when using Moab Entrada Fine Art paper.

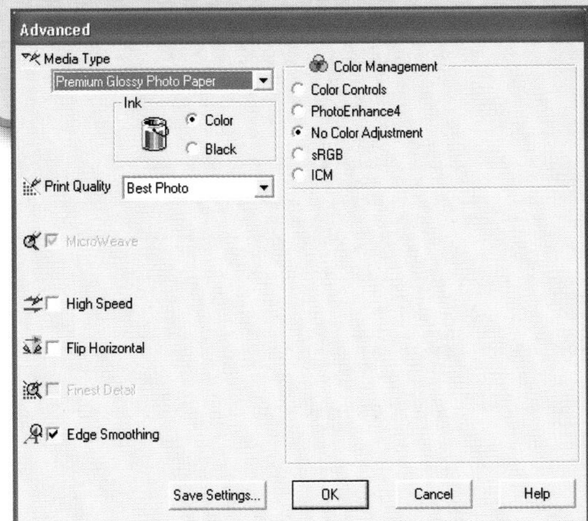

- **Absolute Colorimetric** is best used for proofing when you want to simulate another printer or paper.

6. Click the **Print** button to print the image, or modify any other print options as needed.

Set Print Options

You can set various options when printing, such as the paper size and orientation, and choose the printer if you have more than one printer on your system. You can also specify printer options.

1. After opening the Print Preview window, scale and position the image as outlined previously (see "Scale and Position Images for Printing"). If needed, apply additional output options as outlined previously (see "Setting Print Output Options").
2. Click **Page Setup**. The Page Setup dialog box appears.
3. Click the **Size** down arrow, and click a paper size from the drop-down list.
4. Click the **Source** down arrow, and click an option from the drop-down list. The list shows the available sources of paper for your printer.
5. In the Orientation area, click the **Portrait** option if your image is taller than it is wide, or click the **Landscape** option if your image is wider than it is tall.
6. Click the **Printer** button. A different Page Setup dialog box appears.
7. Click the **Name** down arrow, and choose a printer from the drop-down list.

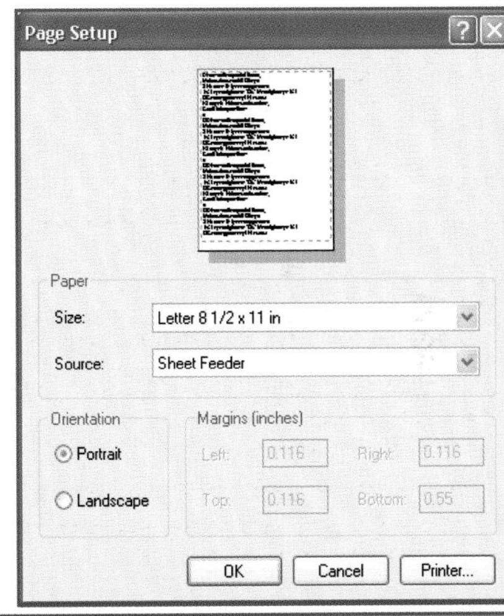

> **NOTE**
>
> You can also open the Page Setup dialog box by clicking **File** and then clicking **Page Setup**.

> **NOTE**
>
> If your printer is connected to a different computer that's networked to your computer, click the **Network** button to open the Connect To Printer dialog box.

8. Click the **Properties** button to open the Properties dialog box for the selected printer. The options differ depending on the type of printer you're using. The following illustration shows the Properties dialog box for an Epson 1280.

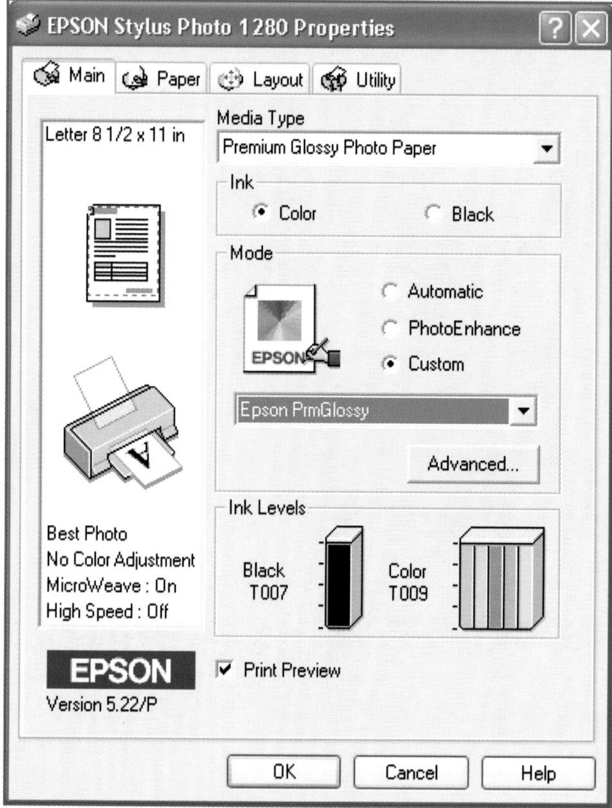

9. Click **OK** to exit the Properties dialog box.
10. Click **OK** to exit the second Page Setup dialog box.
11. Click **OK** to exit the first Page Setup dialog box.
12. Click **Print** to send the image to your printer.

TIP

You can add images to the layout by clicking the **Add** button, and then clicking the images you want to add to the picture package. You can then click the **One Photo Per Page** check box to create separate pages for each image, or leave the check box clear, in which case each image will be printed on the same page.

Create a Picture Package

If you need to print the same image in different sizes, you'll love the Picture Package option. For example, if you need to print two 4 x 5-inch images and eight 2.5 x 3.5-inch images or a file on a single sheet of 8½ x 11-inch paper, you can easily do so.

1. To open the Print Photos dialog box (shown in Figure 10-4), do one of the following:

Figure 10-4: You can print a picture package from the Print Photos dialog box.

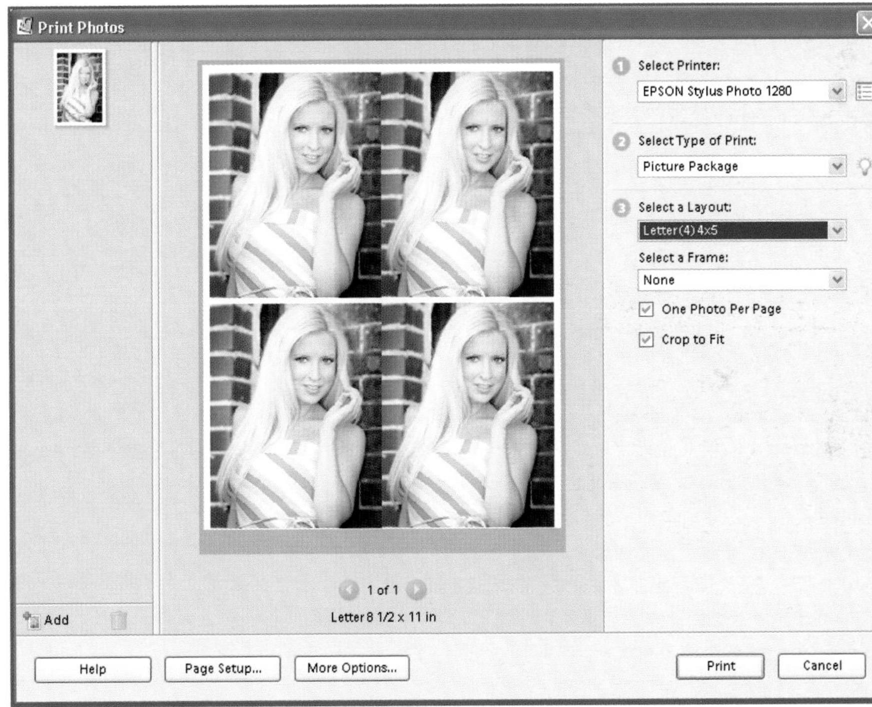

- Open an image in Standard Edit mode, click **File**, and click **Print Multiple Photos**.
- Click an image in the Organizer, click **File**, and click **Print**.
- Click an image in the File Browser, click **File**, and click **Print**.

2. Click the **Select Printer** down arrow, and then click the desired printer from the drop-down list.

USING ONLINE SERVICES

If you don't own a photo-quality printer, you can order prints online. As of this writing, you can order prints from Adobe Photoshop Services by Ofoto. To access this service, with your image open, click **File** and then click **Order Prints**. When you click **Use This Service For The First Time**, you're prompted to enter some basic information and a password. Then you are led through a multistep process in which you customize your order, enter the recipients of the photos, review a summary, provide your billing information, and then confirm the transaction. Follow the prompts to place your order, as shown in Figure 10-5.

Figure 10-5: You can order prints online.

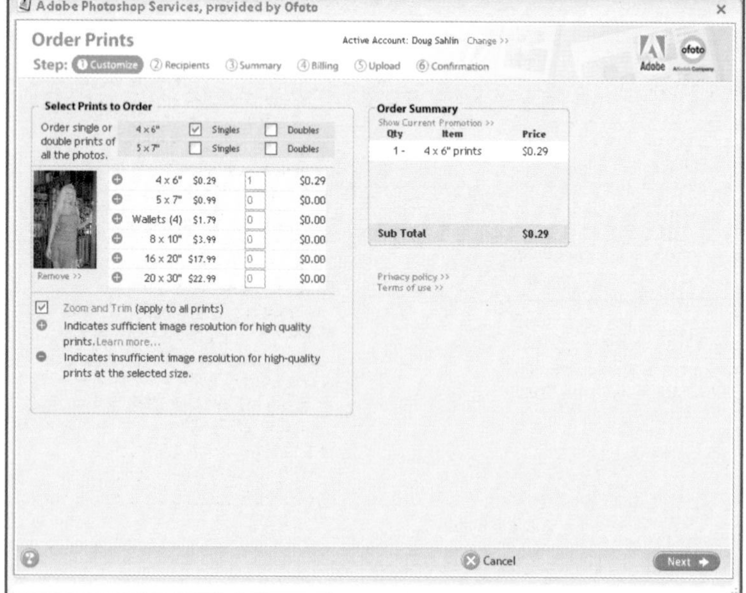

3. Click the **Select Type Of Print** down arrow, and then click **Picture Package**.
4. Click the **Select A Layout** down arrow, and then click the layout from the drop-down list.
5. Click the **Select A Frame** down arrow, and then click a frame type from the drop-down list.
6. Click the **One Photo Per Page** check box.
7. Click the **Crop To Fit** check box (selected by default), and Photoshop Elements will not crop the image to fit the layout. It is recommended that you leave this check box selected; otherwise, the image may not fit the layout.
8. Click the **Page Setup** button to select the media type and orientation as outlined in the "Set Print Options" section of this chapter.
9. Click the **More Options** button. The More Options dialog box appears. This step is optional if you want to print the image using a different profile than the profile associated with the image.
10. Click the **Print Space** down arrow, and click the desired profile from the drop-down list.
11. Click **OK** to exit the More Options dialog box.
12. Click **Print** to print your picture package.

Letter(4) 4x5
Letter(2) 4x5 (2) 2.5x3.5 (4) 2x2.5
Letter(2) 4x5 (8) 2x2.5
Letter(2) 4x5 (4) 2.5x3.5
Letter(3) 4x6
Letter(4) 3.5x5
Letter(20) 2x2
Letter(16) 2x2.5
Letter(8) 2.5x3.5
Letter(4) 2.5x3.5 (8) 2x2.5

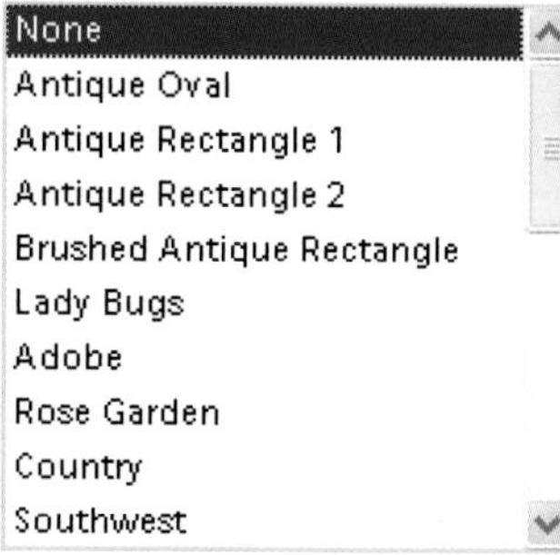

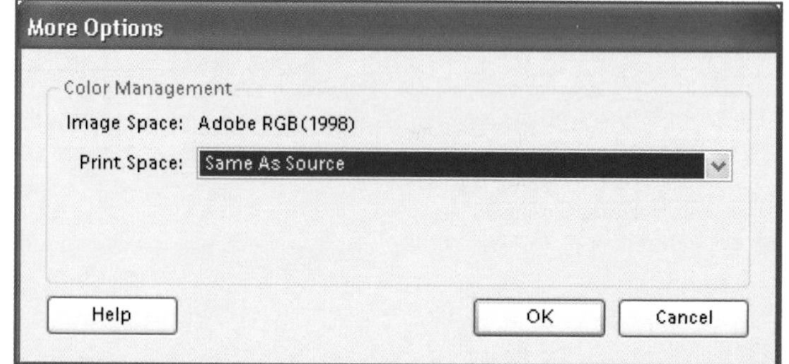

Index

Note: Italicized page numbers indicate definitions of terms.

A

B

C

D

E

F

G

H

I

J

K

L

M

N

O

P

Q

R

S

International Contact Information

AUSTRALIA
McGraw-Hill Book Company Australia Pty. Ltd.
TEL +61-2-9900-1800
FAX +61-2-9878-8881
http://www.mcgraw-hill.com.au
books-it_sydney@mcgraw-hill.com

CANADA
McGraw-Hill Ryerson Ltd.
TEL +905-430-5000
FAX +905-430-5020
http://www.mcgraw-hill.ca

GREECE, MIDDLE EAST, & AFRICA
(Excluding South Africa)
McGraw-Hill Hellas
TEL +30-210-6560-990
TEL +30-210-6560-993
TEL +30-210-6560-994
FAX +30-210-6545-525

MEXICO (Also serving Latin America)
McGraw-Hill Interamericana Editores S.A. de C.V.
TEL +525-1500-5108
FAX +525-117-1589
http://www.mcgraw-hill.com.mx
carlos_ruiz@mcgraw-hill.com

SINGAPORE (Serving Asia)
McGraw-Hill Book Company
TEL +65-6863-1580
FAX +65-6862-3354
http://www.mcgraw-hill.com.sg
mghasia@mcgraw-hill.com

SOUTH AFRICA
McGraw-Hill South Africa
TEL +27-11-622-7512
FAX +27-11-622-9045
robyn_swanepoel@mcgraw-hill.com

SPAIN
McGraw-Hill/Interamericana de España, S.A.U.
TEL +34-91-180-3000
FAX +34-91-372-8513
http://www.mcgraw-hill.es
professional@mcgraw-hill.es

UNITED KINGDOM, NORTHERN, EASTERN, & CENTRAL EUROPE
McGraw-Hill Education Europe
TEL +44-1-628-502500
FAX +44-1-628-770224
http://www.mcgraw-hill.co.uk
emea_queries@mcgraw-hill.com

ALL OTHER INQUIRIES Contact:
McGraw-Hill/Osborne
TEL +1-510-420-7700
FAX +1-510-420-7703
http://www.osborne.com
omg_international@mcgraw-hill.com